Enterprise Big Data Engineering, Analytics, and Management

Martin Atzmueller
University of Kassel, Germany

Samia Oussena
University of West London, UK

Thomas Roth-Berghofer
University of West London, UK

A volume in the Advances in Business Information
Systems and Analytics (ABISA) Book Series

An Imprint of IGI Global

Published in the United States of America by
Business Science Reference (an imprint of IGI Global)
701 E. Chocolate Avenue
Hershey PA, USA 17033
Tel: 717-533-8845
Fax: 717-533-8661
E-mail: cust@igi-global.com
Web site: http://www.igi-global.com

Library of Congress Cataloging-in-Publication Data

Names: Atzmueller, Martin, editor. | Oussena, Samia, 1962- editor. |
  Roth-Berghofer, Thomas R., editor.
Title: Enterprise big data engineering, analytics, and management / Martin
  Atzmueller, Samia Oussena and Thomas Roth-Berghofer, editors.
Description: Hershey : Business Science Reference, 2016. | Includes
  bibliographical references and index.
Identifiers: LCCN 2016006898| ISBN 9781522502937 (hardcover) | ISBN
  9781522502944 (ebook)
Subjects: LCSH: Big data. | Database management. | Data mining.
Classification: LCC QA76.9.B45 E58 2016 | DDC 005.7--dc23 LC record available at https://lccn.loc.gov/2016006898

This book is published in the IGI Global book series Advances in Business Information Systems and Analytics (ABISA) (ISSN: 2327-3275; eISSN: 2327-3283)

British Cataloguing in Publication Data
A Cataloguing in Publication record for this book is available from the British Library.

Advances in Business Information Systems and Analytics (ABISA) Book Series

Madjid Tavana
La Salle University, USA

ISSN: 2327-3275
EISSN: 2327-3283

MISSION

The successful development and management of information systems and business analytics is crucial to the success of an organization. New technological developments and methods for data analysis have allowed organizations to not only improve their processes and allow for greater productivity, but have also provided businesses with a venue through which to cut costs, plan for the future, and maintain competitive advantage in the information age.

The **Advances in Business Information Systems and Analytics (ABISA) Book Series** aims to present diverse and timely research in the development, deployment, and management of business information systems and business analytics for continued organizational development and improved business value.

COVERAGE

- Data Management
- Geo-BIS
- Performance Metrics
- Big Data
- Business Systems Engineering
- Management information systems
- Decision Support Systems
- Business Models
- Data Strategy
- Strategic Information Systems

IGI Global is currently accepting manuscripts for publication within this series. To submit a proposal for a volume in this series, please contact our Acquisition Editors at Acquisitions@igi-global.com or visit: http://www.igi-global.com/publish/.

Titles in this Series

For a list of additional titles in this series, please visit: www.igi-global.com

Automated Enterprise Systems for Maximizing Business Performance
Petraq Papajorgji (Canadian Institute of Technology, Albania) François Pinet (National Research Institute of Science and Technology for Environment and Agriculture, France) Alaine Margarete Guimarães (State University of Ponta Grossa, Brazil) and Jason Papathanasiou (University of Macedonia, Greece)
Business Science Reference • copyright 2016 • 312pp • H/C (ISBN: 9781466688414) • US $200.00 (our price)

Improving Organizational Effectiveness with Enterprise Information Systems
João Eduardo Varajão (University of Minho, Portugal) Maria Manuela Cruz-Cunha (Polytechnic Institute of Cávado and Ave, Portugal) and Ricardo Martinho (Polytechnic Institute of Leiria, Portugal & CINTESIS - Center for Research in Health Technologies and Information Systems, Portugal)
Business Science Reference • copyright 2015 • 318pp • H/C (ISBN: 9781466683686) • US $195.00 (our price)

Strategic Utilization of Information Systems in Small Business
M. Gordon Hunter (The University of Lethbridge, Canada)
Business Science Reference • copyright 2015 • 418pp • H/C (ISBN: 9781466687080) • US $195.00 (our price)

Enterprise Management Strategies in the Era of Cloud Computing
N. Raghavendra Rao (FINAIT Consultancy Services, India)
Business Science Reference • copyright 2015 • 359pp • H/C (ISBN: 9781466683396) • US $210.00 (our price)

Handbook of Research on Organizational Transformations through Big Data Analytics
Madjid Tavana (La Salle University, USA) and Kartikeya Puranam (La Salle University, USA)
Business Science Reference • copyright 2015 • 529pp • H/C (ISBN: 9781466672727) • US $245.00 (our price)

Business Technologies in Contemporary Organizations Adoption, Assimilation, and Institutionalization
Abrar Haider (University of South Australia, Australia)
Business Science Reference • copyright 2015 • 388pp • H/C (ISBN: 9781466666238) • US $205.00 (our price)

Business Transformation and Sustainability through Cloud System Implementation
Fawzy Soliman (University of Technology, Sydney, Australia)
Business Science Reference • copyright 2015 • 367pp • H/C (ISBN: 9781466664456) • US $200.00 (our price)

Effects of IT on Enterprise Architecture, Governance, and Growth
José Carlos Cavalcanti (Federal University of Pernambuco, Brazil)
Business Science Reference • copyright 2015 • 335pp • H/C (ISBN: 9781466664692) • US $195.00 (our price)

www.igi-global.com

701 E. Chocolate Ave., Hershey, PA 17033
Order online at www.igi-global.com or call 717-533-8845 x100
To place a standing order for titles released in this series, contact: cust@igi-global.com
Mon-Fri 8:00 am - 5:00 pm (est) or fax 24 hours a day 717-533-8661

Editorial Advisory Board

Table of Contents

Section 2
Tools and Methods

Section 3
Case Studies and Application Areas

Detailed Table of Contents

**Section 1
Foundational Issues**

Martin Stange, Leuphana University, Germany
Burkhardt Funk, Leuphana University, Germany

Collecting and storing of as many data as possible is common practice in many companies these days. To reduce costs of collecting and storing data that is not relevant, it is important to define which analytical questions are to be answered and how much data is needed to answer these questions. In this chapter, a process to define an optimal sampling size is proposed. Based on benefit/cost considerations, the authors show how to find the sample size that maximizes the utility of predictive analytics. By applying the proposed process to a case study is shown that only a very small fraction of the available data set is needed to make accurate predictions.

Stephen Andrew Roberts, University of West London, UK
Bruce Laurie, University of West London, UK

Public, organizational and personal data has never been so much in the forefront of discussion and attention as at the present time. The term 'Big Data' (BD) has become part of public discourse, in the press, broadcast media and on the web. Most people in the wider public have very little idea of what it is and what it means but anyone who gives it a thought will see it as contemporary and relevant to life as much as to business. This paper is directed towards the perspectives of people working in, managing and developing organizations which are dedicated to fulfilling their respective purposes. All organizations need to understand their strategic purpose and to develop strategies and tactical responses accordingly. The organizations' purpose and the frameworks and resources adopted are part of its quest for achievement which creates value and worth. BD is a potential and actual source of value.

Complex Event Processing has been a growing field for the last ten years. It has seen the development of a number of methods and tools to aid in the processing of event streams and clouds though it has also been troubled by the lack of a cohesive definition. This paper aims to layout the technologies surrounding CEP and to distinguish it from the closely related field of Event Stream Processing. It also aims to explore the work done to apply Data Mining Techniques to both of these fields. An outline of stream processing technologies is laid out including the Data Stream Mining techniques that have been adapted for CEP.

The term Big Data refers to large-scale information management and analysis technologies that exceed the capability of traditional data processing technologies. Big Data is differentiated from traditional technologies in three ways: volume, velocity and variety of data. Big data analytics is the process of analyzing large data sets which contains a variety of data types to uncover hidden patterns, unknown correlations, market trends, customer preferences and other useful business information. Since Big Data is new emerging field, there is a need for development of new technologies and algorithms for handling big data. The main objective of this paper is to provide knowledge about various research challenges of Big Data analytics. A brief overview of various types of Big Data analytics is discussed in this paper. For each analytics, the paper describes process steps and tools. A banking application is given for each analytics. Some of research challenges and possible solutions for those challenges of big data analytics are also discussed.

Section 2
Tools and Methods

Data analytics and modeling are powerful analytical tools for knowledge discovery through examining and capturing the complex and hidden relationships and patterns among the quantitative variables in the existing massive structured Big Data in efforts to predict future enterprise performance. The main purpose of this chapter is to present a conceptual and practical overview of some of the basic and advanced analytical tools for analyzing structured Big Data. The chapter covers descriptive and predictive analytical methods. Descriptive analytical tools such as mean, median, mode, variance, standard deviation, and data visualization methods (e.g., histograms, line charts) are covered. Predictive analytical tools for analyzing Big Data such as correlation, simple- and multiple- linear regression are also covered in the chapter.

Janine Viol Hacker, University of Erlangen – Nuremberg, Germany
Freimut Bodendorf, University of Erlangen – Nuremberg, Germany
Pascal Lorenz, University of Haute Alsace, France

Enterprise Social Networks have a similar set of functionalities as social networking sites but are run as closed applications within a company's intranet. Interacting and communicating on the Enterprise Social Networks, the users, i.e. a company's employees, leave digital traces. The resulting digital record stored in the platform's back end bears great potential for enterprise big data engineering, analytics, and management. This book chapter provides an overview of research in the area of Enterprise Social Networks and categorizes Enterprise Social Network data based on typical functionalities of these platforms. It introduces exemplary metrics as well as a process for the analysis of ESN data. The resulting framework for the analysis of Enterprise Social Network data can serve as a guideline for researchers in the area of Enterprise Social Network analytics and companies interested in analyzing the data stored in the application's back end.

Martin Atzmueller, University of Kassel, Germany
Dennis Mollenhauer, University of Kassel, Germany
Andreas Schmidt, University of Kassel, Germany

Large-scale data processing is one of the key challenges concerning many application domains, especially considering ubiquitous and big data. In these contexts, subgroup discovery provides both a flexible data analysis and knowledge discovery method. Subgroup discovery and pattern mining are important descriptive data mining tasks. They can be applied, for example, in order to obtain an overview on the relations in the data, for automatic hypotheses generation, and for a number of knowledge discovery applications. This chapter presents the novel SD-MapR algorithmic framework for large-scale local exceptionality detection implemented using subgroup discovery on the Map/Reduce framework. We describe the basic algorithm in detail and provide an experimental evaluation using several real-world datasets. We tackle two algorithmic variants focusing on simple and more complex target concepts, i.e., presenting an implementation of exceptional model mining on large attributed graphs. The results of our evaluation show the scalability of the presented approach for large data sets.

Yogesh Kumar Meena, MNIT Jaipur, India
Dinesh Gopalani, MNIT Jaipur, India

Automatic Text Summarization (ATS) enables users to save their precious time to retrieve their relevant information need while searching voluminous big data. Text summaries are sensitive to scoring methods, as most of the methods requires to weight features for sentence scoring. In this chapter, various statistical features proposed by researchers for extractive automatic text summarization are explored. Features that perform well are termed as best features using ROUGE evaluation measures and used for creating feature combinations. After that, best performing feature combinations are identified. Performance evaluation of best performing feature combinations on short, medium and large size documents is also conducted using same ROUGE performance measures.

Section 3
Case Studies and Application Areas

Chapter 9

Benjamin Klöpper, ABB Corporate Research Center, Germany
Marcel Dix, ABB Corporate Research Center, Germany
David Arnu, RapidMiner GmbH, Germany
Dikshith Siddapura, ABB Corporate Research Center, Germany

Dispersed data sources, incompatible data formats and a lack of non-ambiguous and machine readable meta-data is a major obstacle in data analytics and data mining projects in process industries. Often, meta-information is only available in unstructured format optimized for human consumption. This contribution outlines a feasible methodology for organizing historical datasets extracted from process plants in a big data platform for the purpose of analytics and machine learning model building in an industrial big data analytics project.

Chapter 10

Andreas Schmidt, University of Kassel, Germany
Martin Atzmueller, University of Kassel, Germany
Martin Hollender, ABB Corporate Research Center, Germany

This chapter provides an overview of methods for preprocessing structured and unstructured data in the scope of Big Data. Specifically, this chapter summarizes according methods in the context of a real-world dataset in a petro-chemical production setting. The chapter describes state-of-the-art methods for data preparation for Big Data Analytics. Furthermore, the chapter discusses experiences and first insights in a specific project setting with respect to a real-world case study. Furthermore, interesting directions for future research are outlined.

Chapter 11

Sebastian Furth, denkbares GmbH, Germany
Joachim Baumeister, denkbares GmbH, Germany & University of Würzburg, Germany

The complexity of machines has grown dramatically in the past years. Today, they are built as a complex functional network of mechanics, electronics, and hydraulics. Thus, the technical documentation became a fundamental source for service technicians in their daily work. The technicians need fast and focused access methods to handle the massive volumes of documentation. For this reason, semantic search emerged as the new system paradigm for the presentation of technical documentation. However, the existent large corpora of legacy documentation are usually not semantically prepared. This fact creates an invincible gap between new technological opportunities and the actual data quality at companies. This chapter presents a novel and comprehensive approach for the semantification of large volumes of legacy technical documents. The approach especially tackles the veracity and variety existent in technical documentation and makes explicit use of their typical characteristics. The experiences with the implementation and the learned benefits are discussed in industrial case studies.

Chapter 12

Healthcare is a growth area for event processing applications. Computers and information systems have been used for collecting patient data in health care for over fifty years. However, progress towards a unified health care delivery system in the UK has been slow. Big Data, the Internet of Things (IoT) and Complex Event Processing (CEP) have the potential not only to deal with treatment areas of healthcare domain but also to redefine healthcare services. This study is intended to provide a broad overview of where in the health sector, the application of CEP is most used, the data sources that contribute to it and the types of event processing languages and techniques implemented. By systematic review of existing literature on the application of CEP techniques in Healthcare, a number of use cases have been identified to provide a detailed analysis of the most common used case(s), common data sources in use and highlight CEP query language types and techniques that have been considered.

Chapter 13

Big data emerged as a dominant trend for predictive analytics in many areas of industry and commerce. The study aimed to explore whether similar trends and benefits have been observed in the area of collaborative learning. The study looked at the domains in which the collaborative learning was undertaken. The results of the review found that the majority of the studies were undertaken in the Computing and Engineering or Social Science domains, primarily at undergraduate level. The results indicate that the data collection focus is on interaction data to describe the process of the collaboration itself, rather than on the end product of the collaboration. The student interaction data came from various sources, but with a notable concentration on data obtained from discussion forums and virtual learning environment logs. The review highlighted some challenges; the noisy nature of this data and the need for manual pre-processing of textual data currently renders much of it unsuitable for automated 'big data' analytical approaches.

Foreword

In the early years of my PhD research, we were excited to use a little more than 1.000 medical records for data analysis and knowledge discovery. The records were "hand-crafted" and "valuable-as-gold". Those days, some of the advanced research methods needed an overnight run, but we had no issue in storing and accessing the data in the standard file system. This changed a lot in recent years. Today, machines and users generate data volumes of an unimagined scale. Typical examples are user-generated content in the (social) web, sensor data or operating data from machines. This development is massively supported by the increasing digitalization of our environment. Thereby, data is produced not only by digitalized processes but also by capturing many of our other daily private- and work-life situations. These different kinds of data sources determine that big data typically comes rich in variety and sometimes high velocity. In contrast to machine-generated data, the user-generated data typically lacks in quality and transparency. For industrial use cases, the collected data represents the "new oil" of our times since many value-added uses are promised from the utilization of the data. However, new challenges need to be tackled to reveal the data's business potential.

Big data methods are already installed in end-user environments: Search engines and online shops, for example, use the collected mass data of users to predict the interestingness of links or shopping goods. In contrast, the digitalization of the industrial enterprise and the application of big data technologies are just in their beginnings. Current state-of-the-art machinery produces data streams continuously for monitoring systems. The collected data streams can be used to predict maintenance opportunities and to diagnose possible trouble spots. The effective use of this data demands for novel methods that are capable to handle large volumes of data possibly streamed, in different structures, and in different qualities.

The editors of the book, Martin Atzmueller, Samia Oussena, and Thomas Roth-Berghofer, uncover the relevant topics in big data for the engineering, analytics and the management of big data with a special focus on the enterprise. The book offers a selection of current research trends and methods.

Two chapters address the task of preprocessing big data: Stange and Funk discuss the question of the appropriate sample size in the chapter "How big does Big Data need to be" and Schmidt et al. present use cases and experiences with preprocessing industrial big data in their chapter "Data Preparation for Big Data Analytics". A perspective on strategic and organizational issues in the context of Big Data is discussed by Roberts and Laurie in the chapter "Strategic management of data and challenges for organizations, strategy development and business value".

The velocity of big data is determined by data streams. The related area of complex event processing is discussed by two contributions: A review of complex event processing methods is given by Mohamedali and Oussena in their chapter "Application of Complex Event Processing Techniques to Big Data Related to Healthcare. A Systematic Literature Review of Case Studies". Wrench et al. discuss the relations of complex event processing and the closely related field of event stream processing in their chapter "Data Stream Mining of Event and Complex Event Streams".

How to get the promised value from big data? Appropriate analytical methods help to uncover interesting patterns and correlations from the data. Kalaian et al. introduce analytics in their chapter "Descriptive and Predictive Analytical Methods for Big Data" by describing descriptive and predictive analytical methods. Chokkalingam and Vijayarani motivate research directions for analytics in their chapter "Research Challenges in Big Data Analytics". The topics are motivated by practical examples. A dedicated analytics method is presented by Atzmueller et al. in their chapter "Big Data Analytics Using Local Exceptionality Detection".

From the beginning of the research, the term "big data" was motivated by practical challenges and experiences. The book showcases a number of interesting use cases. The authors Sokolowski and Oussena review the applicability of big data methods in collaborative learning environments in their chapter "Using Big Data in collaborative learning". The use of big data in an industrial application is reported by Klöpper et al. in "Data Modeling and Knowledge Discovery in Process Industries". The application of big data methods on large technical text corpora is discussed by Furth and Baumeister in "Semantification of Large Corpora of Technical Documentation". Interesting patterns can be extracted from large text corpora by summarization techniques, as shown by Meena and Gopalani in their chapter "Statistical Features for Extractive Automatic Text Summarization". The analysis of big data collected from social networks is systematically introduced by Viol et al. in their chapter "A Framework to Analyze Enterprise Social Network Data".

In summary, the book provides an interesting and current compilation of theoretical research questions, practical recommendations as well as industrial use cases in the emerging field of big data, and researchers and practitioners will benefit from the included contributions.

Joachim Baumeister
denkbares GmbH, Germany

Preface

With every passing day, the data deluge becomes deeper, making it challenging to analyze, comprehend, and make use of the collected data. As the author John Naisbitt once said: "We are drowning in information, but starved for knowledge."

Millions of networked sensors are being embedded in devices such as mobile phones, smart energy meters, automobiles, and industrial machines that sense, create, and communicate data. Social media sites, smart phones, and other consumer devices including PCs and laptops have also contributed to the deluge of data. This has been coined as the "Big Data" problem. Furthermore, Big Data also involves the integration of heterogeneous complex data sources, ranging from structured to unstructured data which first must be processed to extract the relevant information that needs to be integrated and aligned with the other data sets. With the variety of possible data sets, typical Big Data solutions need to cope with the volume, velocity, and variety of data. The significance of Big Data can be observed in the process of any decision-making, because Big Data can be used for forecasting and predictive analytics. Secondly, Big Data can be used to build a holistic view of an enterprise by collecting large amounts of data, and then analyzing them retrospectively.

The majority of foundational concepts in "big data" such as data mining, artificial intelligence, and information extraction have been well-researched in academia. The objective of the book is to provide a platform for retargeting research within these areas.

This book presents novel methodological as well as practical contributions. The former is provided by different methods and approaches for engineering, managing and analyzing big data. The latter is tackled by a set of case studies and application areas for big data in the enterprise. With Big data as an emerging highly relevant topic, especially the focus on the enterprise and the tight coupling of engineering, management and analytics are two of the unique selling points of the book. With many of the foundational concepts in "big data" such as data mining, artificial intelligence and information extraction that have been well-researched in academia, the objective of this book is also to provide a platform for retargeting the research within these areas.

The book comprises three sections. The first section broadly covers foundational issues of big data. Section 2 describes data analytical tools and methods for handling big data. The third section then presents various case studies and application areas.

SECTION 1: FOUNDATIONAL ISSUES

Collecting and storing as many data as possible has become common practice in many companies. To reduce costs of collecting and storing data that is not relevant, it is important to define which analytical questions are to be answered and how big Big Data needs to be to make useful predictions. Chapter 1 presents a process to define an optimal sampling size. Based on benefit/cost considerations, the authors show how to find the sample size that maximizes the utility of predictive analytics. By applying the proposed process in a case study shows that only a very small fraction of the available data set is needed to make accurate predictions.

All organizations need to understand their strategic purpose and to develop strategies and tactical responses accordingly. Chapter 2 is directed towards the perspectives of people working in, managing and developing organizations that are dedicated to fulfilling their respective purposes. The organizations' purpose and the frameworks and resources adopted are part of its quest for achievement which creates value and worth. Big Data is a potential and actual source of value.

Complex Event Processing (CEP) has been a growing field for the last ten years. It has seen the development of a number of methods and tools to aid in the processing of event streams and clouds though it has also been troubled by the lack of a cohesive definition. Chapter 3 aims to layout the technologies surrounding CEP and to distinguish it from the closely related field of Event Stream Processing. It also aims to explore the work done to apply Data Mining Techniques to both of these fields. An outline of stream processing technologies is laid out including the Data Stream Mining techniques that have been adapted for CEP.

Since Big Data is a new emerging field, there is a need for developing new technologies and algorithms for handling big data. The main objective of Chapter 4 is to provide knowledge about various research challenges of Big Data analytics. A brief overview of various types of Big Data analytics is discussed in this paper. For each analytics, the authors describe process steps and tools. A banking application is given for each analytics. Some of research challenges and possible solutions for those challenges of big data analytics are also discussed.

SECTION 2: TOOLS AND METHODS

Data analytics and modelling are powerful analytical tools for knowledge discovery through examining and capturing the complex and hidden relationships and patterns among the quantitative variables in the existing massive structured Big Data in efforts to predict future enterprise performance. Chapter 5 presents a conceptual and practical overview of some of the basic and advanced analytical tools for analyzing structured Big Data. The chapter covers descriptive and predictive analytical methods. Descriptive analytical tools such as mean, median, mode, variance, standard deviation, and data visualization methods (e.g., histograms, line charts) are covered. Predictive analytical tools for analyzing Big Data such as correlation, simple- and multiple- linear regression are also covered in the chapter.

Enterprise Social Networks have a similar set of functionalities as social networking sites but are run as closed applications within a company's intranet. Interacting and communicating on the Enterprise Social Networks, the users, i.e. a company's employees, leave digital traces. The resulting digital record stored in the platform's back end bears great potential for enterprise big data engineering, analytics, and management. Chapter 6 provides an overview of research in the area of Enterprise Social Networks and categorizes Enterprise Social Network data based on typical functionalities of these platforms. It introduces exemplary metrics as well as a process for the analysis of ESN data. The resulting framework for the analysis of Enterprise Social Network data can serve as a guideline for researchers in the area of Enterprise Social Network analytics and companies interested in analyzing the data stored in the application's back end.

Large-scale data processing is one of the key challenges concerning many application domains, especially considering ubiquitous and big data. In these contexts, local exceptionality detection provides both a flexible data analysis and knowledge discovery method. The basic idea is to identify subgroups covering instances of the dataset, which show some interesting, i.e., unexpected, deviating or exceptional behavior, concerning a given target concept. This notion can be flexibly formalized using a quality function that, for example, measures the deviation of the mean of a numeric target concept in the subgroup compared to the whole dataset. Exceptional model mining provides for more complex quality functions, e.g., also covering heterogeneous data like attributed graphs. Chapter 7 provides an overview on approaches based on subgroup discovery and exceptional model mining methods on big data, and presents algorithms for scalable processing of large datasets.

Automatic Text Summarization (ATS) enables users to save their precious time to retrieve their relevant information need while searching voluminous Big Data. Text summaries are sensitive to scoring methods, as most of the methods requires to weight features for sentence scoring. In Chapter 8, various statistical features proposed by researchers for extractive automatic text summarization are explored. Features that perform well are termed as best features using ROUGE evaluation measures and used for creating feature combinations. After that, best performing feature combinations are identified. Performance evaluation of best performing feature combinations on short, medium and large size documents is also conducted using same ROUGE performance measures.

SECTION 3: CASE STUDIES AND APPLICATION AREAS

Dispersed data sources, incompatible data formats and a lack of non-ambiguous and machine readable meta-data is a major obstacle in data analytics and data mining projects in process industries. Often, meta-information is only available in unstructured format optimized for human consumption. Chapter 9 outlines a feasible methodology for organizing historical datasets extracted from process plants in a big data platform for the purpose of analytics and machine learning model building in an industrial big data analytics project.

Chapter 10 provides an overview of methods for preprocessing structured and unstructured data in the scope of Big Data. Specifically, this chapter summarizes methods in the context of a real-world dataset in a petro-chemical production setting. The chapter describes state-of-the-art methods for data preparation for Big Data Analytics and discusses experiences and first insights. Furthermore, interesting directions for future research are outlined.

The complexity of machines has grown dramatically in the past years. Today, they are built as a complex functional network of mechanics, electronics, and hydraulics. Thus, the technical documentation became a fundamental source for service technicians in their daily work. The technicians need fast and focused access methods to handle the massive volumes of documentation. For this reason, semantic search emerged as the new system paradigm for the presentation of technical documentation. However, the existent large corpora of legacy documentation are usually not semantically prepared. This fact creates a gap between new technological opportunities and the actual data quality at companies. Chapter 11 presents a novel and comprehensive approach for the semantification of large volumes of legacy technical documents. The approach especially tackles the veracity and variety existent in technical documentation and makes explicit use of their typical characteristics. The experiences with the implementation and the learned benefits are discussed in industrial case studies.

Healthcare is a growth area for event processing applications. Computers and information systems have been used for collecting patient data in health care for over fifty years. However, progress towards a unified health care delivery system in the UK has been slow. Big Data, the Internet of Things (IoT) and Complex Event Processing have the potential not only to deal with treatment areas of healthcare domain but also to redefine healthcare services. Chapter 12 provides a broad overview of where in the health sector, the application of CEP is most used, the data sources that contribute to it and the types of event processing languages and techniques implemented. By systematic review of existing literature on the application of CEP techniques in Healthcare, a number of use cases have been identified to provide a detailed analysis of the most common used case(s), common data sources in use and highlight CEP query language types and techniques that have been considered.

Chapter 13 explores whether similar trends and benefits have been observed in the area of collaborative learning. The study looked at the domains in which the collaborative learning was undertaken. The results of the review found that the majority of the studies were undertaken in the Computing and Engineering or Social Science domains, primarily at undergraduate level. The results indicate that the data collection focus is on interaction data to describe the process of the collaboration itself, rather than on the end product of the collaboration. The student interaction data came from various sources, but with a notable concentration on data obtained from discussion forums and virtual learning environment logs. The review highlights some challenges; the noisy nature of this data and the need for manual pre-processing of textual data currently renders much of it unsuitable for automated 'big data' analytical approaches

CONCLUSION

We believe this book will serve a broad audience including academics, researchers, students and practitioners in the fields of data mining, data science, social computing, health, environmental services, government, manufacturing and networking industries. The book captures foundational issues in big data from a research perspective. It also outlines and identifies areas that potential PhD students should concentrate on. We hope that you find the ideas and experiences helpful.

Martin Atzmueller
University of Kassel, Germany

Samia Oussena
University of West London, UK

Thomas Roth-Berghofer
University of West London, UK

Section 1
Foundational Issues

Chapter 1
How Big Does Big Data Need to Be?

Martin Stange
Leuphana University, Germany

Burkhardt Funk
Leuphana University, Germany

ABSTRACT

Collecting and storing of as many data as possible is common practice in many companies these days. To reduce costs of collecting and storing data that is not relevant, it is important to define which analytical questions are to be answered and how much data is needed to answer these questions. In this chapter, a process to define an optimal sampling size is proposed. Based on benefit/cost considerations, the authors show how to find the sample size that maximizes the utility of predictive analytics. By applying the proposed process to a case study is shown that only a very small fraction of the available data set is needed to make accurate predictions.

INTRODUCTION

Today, collecting and storing of as many data as possible is common practice in many companies (Beath et al. 2012, Auschitzky et al. 2014). One of the purposes is the generation reports, which may contain descriptive statistics about customer acquisition, sales or the supply chain. Although such reports enable managers to make decisions based on past performance data, their ability to predict future company needs is limited. In contrast, predictive analytics use historical data and apply methods from machine learning and data mining to derive predictions about the future (Waller & Fawcett 2013). For instance, predictive analytics can be used to prevent potential malfunctions in production or to predict future sales to determine the needed number of products in stock. Due to the potential benefits of predictive analytics, the collection of as many data as possible is supposed to be very beneficial for many companies. However, on the other hand, storage of these mass data is combined with significant costs (Stange & Funk 2014). These may be infrastructure costs or monthly fees for the use of cloud services, such as Amazon S3. A question that arises from this discrepancy is: "How much data do the authors actually need to make the best predictions about the future?"

DOI: 10.4018/978-1-5225-0293-7.ch001

To reduce costs of collecting and storing data that is not relevant, it is crucial to first define which predictions are required, i.e., to determine, which analytical questions are to be answered. Afterwards—to prevent storing irrelevant data—the amount of data that is needed to obtain useful predictive results can be determined. In this chapter, the authors extend a generally applicable framework (Stange & Funk 2015) to determine this amount, i.e., to find the minimum amount of data that is needed to obtain optimal predictive results. The process can be used to maximize the benefits of predictive analytics with respect to the costs for data collection and storage. Due to the scalability of cloud services, companies that use such services can benefit from the proposed process in particular. The authors apply the process to a data set from the online marketing field and observe convergence of the predictive accuracy when the sample size is increased. Thereby, the authors show that—compared to the available amount of data—only a very small sample is needed to achieve a desired predictive accuracy.

BACKGROUND

Sample size determination is a topic that has often been examined in medical or sociological science (e.g., Brutti et al. 2009, Sahu & Smith 2006, Santis 2007), since, in these fields, samples are often expensive in comparison to big data environments. Additionally, the available methods to determine the needed sample size often focus on a specific task, such as to find the needed number of participants of a survey. Therefore, these methods do not seem appropriate for a generally applicable framework in predictive analytics with its variety of machine learning and data mining techniques.

In contrast to the available methods that calculate the needed sample size a priori, the proposed process is based on the evaluation of the predictive accuracy and the calculation of the economic value of the classifier.

The predictive accuracy of classifiers with dichotomous outcomes can be calculated by integrating the receiver operator characteristic (ROC) curve. The obtained value is called the area under the curve (AUC; Bradley 1997), which represents the probability that a data record with unknown class is classified correctly. In the case study, the authors employ two logistic regression models with elastic net regularization (Friedman et al. 2010) to estimate the model parameters that the authors use to predict the dependent variable on the holdout sample. Based on these predictions, the authors show that increasing the sample size results in convergence the AUC. Other types of dependent variables, such as multinomial outcomes, require other measures, such as the misclassification error.

The so-called learning curve sampling method (Meek et al. 2002) is an approach for obtaining the relation between sample size and predictive accuracy. This generally applicable sampling approach is based on the observation that an increase in the sample size reduces the uncertainty in the parameter estimates of the learned model (Stange & Funk 2015, Gu et al. 2001, Meek et al. 2002). This observation has been formalized by Meek et al. (2002) who find the optimal sample size by continuously increasing the sample size while observing the predictive accuracy. The optimal sample size is found when additional samples do not further increase the predictive accuracy by a predefined value of $\epsilon > 0$.

However, the predictive performance of a classifier does not provide information about its economic value. How the economic value can be obtained has been shown by Nottorf & Funk (2013). Based on a clickstream data set from a German retailer for electronic devices, they build a user journey model in order to predict future user behavior. In particular, they predict the users' conversion probability based on their user journey. To measure the economic value of the applied model, they multiply the number of true and false predictions by the benefits and costs that can be assigned to these forecasts. Thus, they show that it is beneficial for an advertiser to apply the proposed model in real-time advertising, where a bidding agent decides whether a given user should be exposed to a display ad or not. Based on this approach and the finding of Meek et al. (2002), Stange & Funk (2015) develop a framework to determine the optimal sample size for a data analysis and apply it to two case studies. The idea behind this framework is to train a model with increasing sample sizes and to monitor the resulting predictive accuracy. As soon as a critical sample size is reached, the predictive accuracy of the model does not further increase. Since additional data records are related to additional computational costs, increasing the sample size to train the model is not recommended when the critical sample size is reached. Based on their approach, this chapter provides a business process model and an algorithm for a more structured view of this framework. In addition, the authors calculate the costs for additional data records and thereby show that the benefits of an analysis decrease when the sample size is further increased.

Although the authors focus on dichotomous classification in this chapter, the presented process is not limited to this kind of classification. The economic value of classifiers with multinomial outcomes can be obtained by applying the same methods as for the binomial case.

THE OPTIMAL SAMPLE SIZE

Before the proposed process can be applied, it is crucial to thoroughly define the questions that ought to be answered by the analysis. It is clear that these questions highly influence the actually needed amount of data. In this chapter, however, the authors suppose that the purpose of the analysis has already been defined and do not further discuss this issue.

Figure 1 provides the business process model of the proposed framework, which is explained step by step in this section. The process is split up into data collection and data analysis, which are both represented by a single lane in the process diagram. The data collection step can be an arbitrary automatic mechanism that systematically collects data. The succeeding filtering and storing step persists the generated data.

How much data is required depends on the following: First, the model updating frequency determines how often the analysis needs to be repeated based on new data to obtain "fresh" results. Second, the sampling strategy influences the filter settings in the data collection step. For instance, if stratified sampling is chosen, only "interesting" data is stored. Third, the model complexity influences which types of data need to be stored and which can be omitted.

These three steps result in a set of requirements for the filtering mechanism, which are indicated by the dashed arrows that end in the filter object in Figure 1.

The sub-process beginning with the increase of the sample size and ending with the determination of the economic value can be transferred into an algorithm (Algorithm 1) to find the optimal sample size. This optimal sample size N_{opt} is obtained when the additional benefits B related to the increase of the sample size by m samples do not outweigh the additional costs C for the related data storage and analysis.

In Algorithm 1, the function getSample(N, m) returns a sample S of size $N + m$, estimateAndPredict(S, H) estimates the parameters based on the training sample S and returns the predictions P based on the holdout sample H with sample size N_H, calculateCosts(S) returns the costs C that are related with storing, preparing and analyzing the sample S, and calculateBenefits(P, H) returns the benefits B that are related to the application of the classifier. N_0 is the initial sample size. Although Algorithm 1 is rather intuitive, its containing functions can be very complex. The authors focus on the individual functions in greater detail.

Figure 1. Finding the optimal sample size

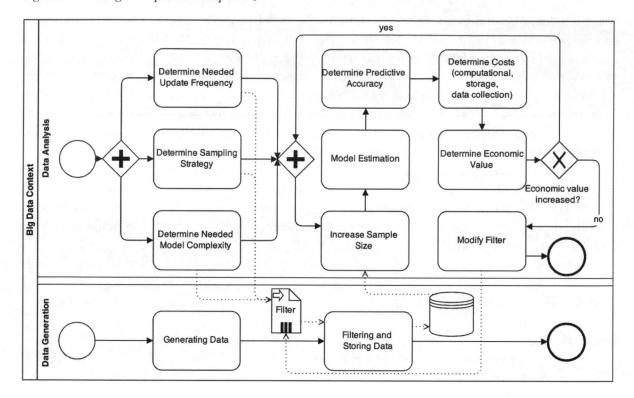

Algorithm 1. Determination of optimal sample size N_{opt}

```
C, B, ΔC, ΔB, C_old ← 0
N ← N_0
H ← getSample(N_H)
while ΔB ≥ΔC do
     S ← getSample(N, m)
     C_old ← C
     P ← estimateAndPredict(S, H)
     C ← calculateCosts(S)
     ΔC ← C - C_old
     B_old ← B
     B ← calculateBenefits(P, H)
     ΔB ← B - B_old
     N ← length(S)
end while
Nopt ← length(S)
```

- **getSample(*N[,m]*):** The selection of the new sample is depending on the sample size increment and the sampling strategy. In addition, it should be decided whether the complete data is re-sampled or a sample of size m is added to the previous sample. In addition, the number of additional samples m may vary between two succeeding iterations. In our case study, for instance, the authors exponentially increase the number m of the additional data records in each iteration.
- **estimateAndPredict(*S, H*):** The parameters of the given model are estimated based on the sample S. Various machine learning methods are available that enable classifying new data. Cross-validation can be used to avoid over-fitting. The holdout sample H is used to evaluate the classifier, i.e., predictions are made for each data record from the holdout sample H. For each data record from the holdout sample the function returns the probability that the data record belongs to a certain class.
- **calculateCosts(*S, P*):** The costs of the analysis are given by the costs for data collection, storage and computational efforts. These costs grow with the amount of data, because faster CPUs and larger storages are needed. In general, it might be difficult to determine these costs exactly.
- **calculateBenefits(*P, H*):** The benefits that result from data analyses grow with the amount of available data, because the applied algorithm has more data to learn from. The benefits that result from a data analysis can be calculated as follows: First, the costs for false predictions have to be determined (e.g., an undetected downtime in production, a competitor who is about to leave the company). Second, the benefits (or saved costs) for true predictions have to be determined (e.g., the detection of a malfunction of a tablet press in advance, the prevention of churn). Third, these values have to be multiplied by the number of true positive, true negative, false positive, and false negative predictions (based on the probabilities P) of the classifier to obtain the benefits from the prediction.

The while-loop in Algorithm 1 stops, when the additional benefits B are smaller than the additional costs C. After the model has been deployed to predict new data, N_{opt} can be used to modify the filter settings of the data collection step. This results in a smaller amount of collected data and thus in reduced costs.

Once the model has been deployed into the productive environment, monitoring the predictive accuracy is required to quickly address changes in the data generation process, such as changed user behavior or the go-live of a new production line. If significant changes are observed, the complete process should be re-executed. Consequently, the data collection mechanism needs to be adjusted so that enough data is available to re-execute the process.

CASE STUDY

The case study selected for this paper belongs to the real-time advertising field. In this field of online advertising, every second thousands of records are generated that can be used to analyze and predict user behavior.

The authors use two different models to predict the users' purchasing behavior based on web tracking data and show the convergence of the predictive accuracy with increasing sample size.

The section is structured as follows: First, the authors provide a brief overview over the real-time advertising field. Second, the authors describe the tracking data as the basis for the proposed models. Third, the authors describe the modeling approach before the authors present the results from the analysis.

Real-Time Advertising

In real-time advertising (RTA) free advertising spaces on publisher websites are sold through auctions. In the moment a user visits a website using this form of advertising an auction is issued and so-called bid requests are broadcast to all potential bidders (the advertisers). Storing these messages from multiple ad exchanges quickly results in Tbytes or Pbytes of data, which can be associated with significant costs (Stange & Funk 2014).

On the other hand, RTA enables advertisers to optimize their campaigns, by only targeting users who show a particular tendency to click on an ad (Perlich et al. 2012). As a prerequisite, these companies need to know the individual click and/or conversion probabilities. Our case study demonstrates how these individual conversion probabilities can be determined. This information can be used to optimize marketing campaigns and to increase economic benefit (Nottorf & Funk 2013). However, considering the costs for collection and storage, advertisers should carefully assess payoffs from related analyses (Stange & Funk 2014).

Data Description

The authors use the data set from a German online retailer as it has been used by Stange & Funk (2015). The data set contains user tracking data (approx. 60 million records) from one month (December 2013) and, thus, includes seasonal effects, which results in shorter user journeys due to spontaneous gift purchases. Approximately 90% of the overall data is related to user behavior on the retailer's website. The remaining 10% contain information about the advertising channels used to access the website. The authors only focus on user journeys with more than four interactions to reduce noise in our signal. Thereby, the authors remove 651.991 user journeys and finally obtain 280.459 user journeys that the authors split into a training set of 180.459 journeys and a holdout set of 100.000 user journeys. The average user journey length is 7.45.

The data set contains every interaction with the retailer's website for every user. An interaction is meant to be the contact of a user with a certain advertising channel, such as a search engine advertising (SEA) or a newsletter. Each data record also contains the type of the interaction which can be a click (e.g. on a newsletter or a banner ad) or a conversion, i.e., the purchase of a product.

In addition to the online tracking data, the data set contains TV advertising data. This enables us to model the spillover effects from online advertising to the online purchasing behavior.

Model Description

The set of touch points for each user is converted into their user journey according to Stange & Funk (2015). Each entry in the user journey contains information about the type of the current interaction and the number of previous touch points for each advertising channel within the current web session and across previous sessions (Chatterjee et al. 2003).

The classifiers presented in this section are based on the logistic regression model. The authors compare two models $M1$ and $M2$: Model $M1$ is only based on online tracking data, model $M2$ additionally involves TV advertising data. In the following, the authors explain the independent variables. The dependent variable for each touch point is a binary variable which is 1 if the user purchases a product, and 0 otherwise.

The authors adopt the modeling approach from previous studies (Nottorf & Funk 2013, Stange & Funk 2015). The conversion probability is depending on the advertising channel through which the current touch point has been established as well as short term advertising effects from the current session (last 60 minutes) and from previous sessions. In our model the design matrix D consists of three parts First, the intercept terms I can be interpreted as a measure for the baseline probability for a conversion after using a certain channel to interact with the retailer's website. Second, the authors include the number of previous interactions with the online shop within one session, denoted as X, the number of interactions in previous sessions, denoted as Y. Third, the authors introduce additional control variables, i.e., the number of the current session SN, the number of purchases in previous sessions CPS and the time between two sessions IST (Stange & Funk 2015). The second model $M2$ additionally contains variables that are set to 1 if a certain TV spot Sp has been broadcast on a certain TV station St within the last 30 minutes before the touch point, and 0 otherwise. This modeling approach can be used to measure the spillover effect of TV advertising on the online customer journey.

Equation 1 and 2 show the jth interaction of the ith user, which is represented as one row $(D_i)_j$ of the users design matrix D_i. Refer to the left hand side of Table 1 for possible values for C, i.e., the subscripts for I, X and Y. The additional covariates used in the design matrix are listed on the right hand side of Table 1.

$$M1: (D_i)_j = \{I_C, X_C, Y_C, SN, IST, CPS\}_{ij}$$

$$M2: (D_i)_j = \{I_C, X_C, Y_C, SN, IST, CPS, TV_{St}^{Sp}\}_{ij}$$

The authors use the elastic net regularized logistic regression of the R package glmnet (Friedman et al. 2010) as classification method with $\alpha = 0.5$. This method is feasible, because it automatically selects important parameters by shrinking unimportant parameters towards 0. Hence, in the context of finding the optimal sample size, this method also determines which types of data can be deleted while maintaining high predictive accuracy (Table 1).

Table 1. Advertising channels and additional control variables used to model the design matrix as stated in Equation 1 and 2

Advertising Channels (C)	Index	Additional Control Variables
• Search engine advertisement • Organic search • Referral from another website • Affiliate marketing • Display advertisement • Direct type-in • Cooperation link • Price search engine • Email advertisement	SN	Session Number
	IST	Time between two sessions
	CPS	Number of conversions in previous session
	TV_{St}^{Sp}	Spot Sp was aired on Station St

Stange & Funk 2015.

Results

To determine the optimal sample size, the authors execute 9 analyses including $N =500, 1,000, 2,000,$ $4,000, 8,000, 16,000, 32,000, 64,000, 128,000$ user journeys for both models.

The elastic net model selects different numbers of features for both models. The authors report the number of features selected for each sample size in Table 2. The model *M2* contains more variables due to the inclusion of TV advertising effects. Therefore, the number of selected features is higher compared to model *M1*.

Using the results from the elastic net regression, the authors run five out-of-sample tests ($N^{1,...,5} =$ 10,000) for each sample size and model. For each observation from the holdout sample the authors predict the conversion probabilities *P*. Based on the actual values of the target variables from the hold-out sample and the probabilities *P*, the authors are able to measure the AUC for each sample size and model, which are presented in Figure 2. The variance in the predictive accuracy is indicated by the error bars in the plot. The simpler model M1 outperforms the model including online advertising data *M2* at lower sample $N < 8,000$. For greater sample sizes, model *M2* shows higher predictive accuracies. This indicates that model complexity and required sample sizes are positively correlated.

Although the AUC can be used to as a measure for the predictive performance of the classifier, it cannot be used to estimate the economic value of the classifier. The predictions have to be weighted with the costs for true and false predictions. The authors assume the economic values of the models *M1* and *M2* by applying the two different cost matrices given in Table 3.

Table 2. Different sample sizes and number of selected features for M1 and M2; the index min denotes the number of features that results in the highest AUC value. The index sd represents the lowest number of features that result in an AUC that lies within the standard error of the maximum AUC value.

Sample Size	$M1_{min}$	$M2_{min}$	$M1_{sd}$	$M2_{sd}$
500	13	7	10	6
1000	21	42	10	13
2000	27	23	12	11
4000	22	21	14	11
8000	23	24	14	12
16000	21	32	14	13
32000	19	26	15	14
64000	22	34	15	17
128000	21	49	15	18

Table 3. Two different cost matrices (CM$_1$ and CM$_2$) for true positive predictions (TP), true negative predictions (TN), false positive predictions (FP) and false negative predictions (FN)

Type	Description	CM_1 (EUR)	CM_2 (EUR)
TP	Ad impression costs minus contribution margin	-0.14	-0.19
TN	No loss	0.00	0.00
FP	Ad impression costs	0.01	0.01
FN	Lost contribution margin	0.15	0.20

Figure 2. Area under the curve for both models and different sample sizes; the predictive accuracy converges with increasing sample sizes.

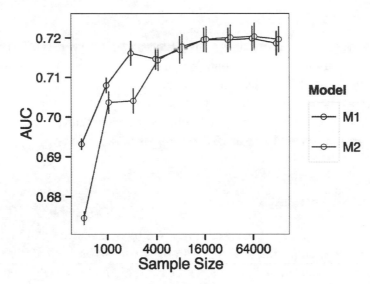

By multiplying the costs for true and false predictions with the number of true and false predictions, the authors obtain the overall costs of the classifiers. To calculate the benefits of the classifier, its costs C_{min} have to be compared to the costs (C_{max}) of a trivial classifier that would always predict a conversion. The benefit of the advanced classifier is given by the costs of a trivial classifier minus the costs of an advanced classifier ($C_{max} - C_{min}$).

To include infrastructure costs the authors assume 0.0001 EUR for collecting and storing a single user journey. The difference between the benefit of the advanced classifier and the infrastructure costs C_I for collection and storage of the training sample divided by the number of data records N_H in the holdout sample results in the effective benefits per decision:

Figure 3. Mean benefits per decision for both models and different sample sizes and different benefit costs ratios (in EUR): left hand side ratio: 15/1; right hand side ratio: 20/1

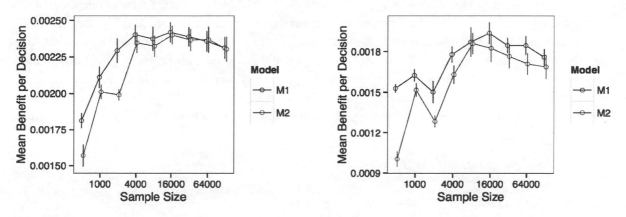

$$B = \frac{C_{\max} - C_{\min} - C_I}{N_H}$$

Figure 3 shows the benefits per decision for both models and cost matrices. The difference in the two diagrams results from the different ratios of contribution margin and costs for an impression in CM_1 and CM_2. This shows that the benefits of a classifier are highly dependent on this ratio. Figure 3 also shows that the maximum benefit is obtained at $N = 16000$ user journeys for both ratios. If the sample size is further increased, the costs ΔC for additional samples become greater than the related benefits ΔB. Thus, the while-loop in Algorithm 1 would stop at 16,000 samples in this scenario.

CONCLUSION

In this chapter, the authors extend the framework proposed by Stange & Funk (2015) to determine the optimal sample size in a predictive analytics application, which can be applied in a broad range of scenarios. The authors apply the developed process to a case study and show that a maximum benefit is obtained with a sample size of 16,000 user journeys, which is far less than typically available user journeys in the online marketing field. Thus, companies in this field should consider to reduce the amount of data in order to save costs from collecting and storing unnecessary data. For instance, the proposed process can be very beneficial in the area of real-time advertising where thousands of bid requests per second are sent to advertisers. Only a very small fraction of this data would be required to predict user behavior accurately. Due to the users' growing privacy concerns, applying the proposed process could also have a positive effect on the companies' image. Although the authors only apply our process to data from the online marketing field, it can be used by other companies generating and collecting big data for predictive analytics, for instance for demand planning, replenishment or predictive maintenance.

Although the authors show that the application of the process can be beneficial, our study includes some limitations: First, the authors neither investigate the need for model updates nor discuss the sampling strategy. Frequent model updates require collecting and storing new data, which leads to additional costs, especially when third party data is used. The authors use random sampling for our analyses. However, even fewer data might be required, if the authors decided to use stratified sampling. Second, the costs for true and false predictions as well as the costs per user journey are set by the authors according to typical costs from the industry. However, as Figure 3 shows, the benefit of a classifier is highly dependent on these values. In general, these values might not be constant over time and might also vary between different users. Hence, the results from the case study can only be seen as an approximation and a starting point for more advanced analyses. Third, user journey creation requires the complete set of touch points of a user. Hence, to predict the outcome (conversion or no conversion) for future touch points, historical data is needed—data that has to be collected and stored. Consequently, in addition to the needed amount of data for the training sample, data for the prediction of future user behavior has to be stored as well, which is combined with additional costs.

In summary, the proposed process can be beneficial for companies collecting and storing data in an unsystematic manner and often do not even use a small fraction of the overall available data (Stange & Funk 2015). The process can be a starting point for further investigations in this field and for discussions among researchers and practitioners who face a dramatically growing amount of data without knowing exactly how much data they have to keep to obtain appropriate results from analyses.

REFERENCES

Auschitzky, E., Hammer, M., & Rajagopaul, A. (2014). *How big data can improve manufacturing*. McKinsey.

Beath, C., Becerra-Fernandez, I., Ross, J., & Short, J. (2012). Finding value in the information explosion. *MIT Sloan Management Review, 53*(4).

Bradley, A. (1997). The use of the area under the ROC curve in the evaluation of machine learning algorithms. *Pattern Recognition, 30*(7), 1145–1159. doi:10.1016/S0031-3203(96)00142-2

Brutti, P., Santis, F. D., & Gubbiotti, S. (2009). Mixtures of prior distributions for predictive Bayesian sample size calculations in clinical trials. *Statistics in Medicine, 28*(17), 2185–2201. doi:10.1002/sim.3609 PMID:19462415

Chatterjee, P., Hoffman, D. L., & Novak, T. P. (2003). Modeling the clickstream: Implications for web-based advertising e⌐Jorts. *Marketing Science, 22*(4), 520–541. doi:10.1287/mksc.22.4.520.24906

Friedman, J., Hastie, T., & Tibshirani, R. (2010). Regularization Paths for Generalized Linear Models via Coordinate Descent. *Journal of Statistical Software, 33*(1), 1–22. doi:10.18637/jss.v033.i01 PMID:20808728

Gu, B., Hu, F., & Liu, H. (2001). 'Modelling Classification Performance for Large Data Sets', Advances in The authorsb-Age. *Information & Management*, 317–328.

Meek, C., Thiesson, B., & Heckerman, D. (2002). The Learning-Curve Sampling Method Applied to Model-Based Clustering. *Journal of Machine Learning Research, 2*, 397–418.

Nottorf, F., & Funk, B. (2013). A cross-industry analysis of the spillover effect in paid search advertising. *Electronic Markets, 23*(3), 205–216. doi:10.1007/s12525-012-0117-z

Perlich, C., Dalessandro, B., & Hook, R. (2012). Bid optimizing and inventory scoring in targeted online advertising. *Proceedings of the 18th ACM SIGKDD international conference on Knowledge discovery and data mining* (pp. 804–812). doi:10.1145/2339530.2339655

Sahu, S., & Smith, T. (2006). A Bayesian method of sample size determination with practical applications. *Journal of the Royal Statistical Society. Series A, (Statistics in Society), 169*(2), 235–253. doi:10.1111/j.1467-985X.2006.00408.x

Santis, F. (2007). Alternative Bayes factors: Sample size determination and discriminatory power assessment. *Test*, *16*(3), 504–522. doi:10.1007/s11749-006-0017-7

Stange, M., & Funk, B. (2014). Real-Time-Advertising. *Business & Information Systems Engineering*, *56*(5), 305–308. doi:10.1007/s12599-014-0346-0

Stange, M., & Funk, B. (2015). How Much Tracking Is Necessary - The Learning Curve in Bayesian User Journey Analysis. *23rd European Conference of Information Systems*.

Waller, M., & Fawcett, S. E. (2013). Data Science, Predictive Analytics, and Big Data: A Revolution That Will Transform Supply Chain Design and Management. *Journal of Business Logistics*, *34*(2), 77–84. doi:10.1111/jbl.12010

Chapter 2
Strategic Management of Data and Challenges for Organizations:
Strategy Development and Business Value

Stephen Andrew Roberts
University of West London, UK

Bruce Laurie
University of West London, UK

ABSTRACT

Public, organizational and personal data has never been so much in the forefront of discussion and attention as at the present time. The term 'Big Data' (BD) has become part of public discourse, in the press, broadcast media and on the web. Most people in the wider public have very little idea of what it is and what it means but anyone who gives it a thought will see it as contemporary and relevant to life as much as to business. This paper is directed towards the perspectives of people working in, managing and developing organizations which are dedicated to fulfilling their respective purposes. All organizations need to understand their strategic purpose and to develop strategies and tactical responses accordingly. The organizations' purpose and the frameworks and resources adopted are part of its quest for achievement which creates value and worth. BD is a potential and actual source of value.

BIG DATA: A NEW PUBLIC DISCOURSE

The young child's incessant question on a journey "are we nearly there yet?" is apposite when it comes to the usefulness of Big data for business. Big Data is certainly with us but how useful is it for the normal business practitioner and how does the hype live up to the reality? Have we the skills in IT and in the business to fully exploit it? Have the legal and privacy issues been fully addressed? Does it give strategic advantage or does it provide better management information? This paper will try to shed some light on these questions relevant to business. But there are two other significant dimensions: one is that of the

DOI: 10.4018/978-1-5225-0293-7.ch002

public and citizen at large, and the other of governments and public bodies who interpret the multitude of factors which impact the domain and who have to establish both a legal framework and manage the reality of social, personal, economic and organizational / business life.

Public, organizational and personal data has never been so much in the forefront of discussion and attention as at the present time: Chen, Mao and Liu (2104) provide a conspectus. The term 'Big Data' (BD) has become part of public discourse, in the press, broadcast media and on the web. Most people in the wider public have very little idea of what it is and what it means but anyone who gives it a thought will see it as contemporary and relevant to life as much as to business. This may be a basis for further understanding or even misunderstanding!

Other contributors to this volume are providing routes to greater understanding and have addressed matters of definition and of the development of the concept. This paper, as its title suggests, is directed towards the perspectives of people working in, managing and developing organizations which are dedicated to fulfilling their respective purposes. All organizations need to understand their strategic purpose and to develop strategies and tactical responses accordingly. The organizations' purpose and the frameworks and resources adopted are part of its quest for achievement which creates value and worth. In this paper we will assume that BD is a potential and actual source of value. If data is, as we believe it can be, a strategic asset, we will argue that it is also strategic. From this follows the need to address its strategic management and to explore and affirm how it can link together organizational work, strategy and process to create measureable value.

DATA: A NEW INFORMING RESOURCE

At the root of typical definitions of data are the ideas of the power to define and inform as well as to represent reality in terms of identity and state. Additionally, data carries the idea of unity, definition and lack of ambiguity. Numerical data maximises these unitary properties with added advantage that they can be manipulated mathematically: we often call this 'hard data' / quantitative data. The concept and realization of data can also be used to represent levels of ambiguity and endowed with structure and durability through the use of tools such as coding, categorization, compression and abstraction. The term 'soft data/qualitative data is used to describe this data. Both types of data can be regarded as valid from a user perspective, but soft data often requires human intervention for its capture and this modifies or even potentially degrades it quality. This becomes more significant when sources of data are created and processed, and similarly may affect its interpretation and integrity.

Big data could easily be called 'wide data', or 'deep data'. One view is essentially that BD is a convenient way of naming the concept of linking one data set of one kind to one or more others of different kinds. It is a metaphor: the core quality is not its 'bigness' but its origin, informing quality and the properties required to manipulate and process it. And it is not only a matter of linkage, but also of ambition and concept. What can be linked to what? And, what needs to be linked to what? As a concept it can be regarded as a 'state of mind'. You have constructed the techniques to identify and link data sets, which then leads to the 'state of mind' as processing articulates the informing qualities revealed in the embedded content. The term Big Data then describes the end results of the process as it is revealed through the evidence it provides and comprehended. This definition subsumes the data itself and the processes that have created it: data is a gathered, stored (warehoused, processed, analysed (with specific analytics and tools), accessed and displayed, evaluated and then the results are applied cognitively (an interpretation and decision process) to underpin an action.

The more potential and actual value is revealed by the process and the more relevant it is to the social and organizational context of realization, the more we can proclaim the reality of 'Big Data'. It is the way that large scale data processing contributes to the revelation of meaning that justifies the attraction of the concept to users. This can then extend to better known and recognized techniques and resources for decision making. In the end the reality and value of BD is set by its power to contribute to decisions, and thereby to useful and strategic knowledge. In this way we arrive at the proposition that informs the argument of this paper. This is that approaching data with a sense of strategic purpose identifies the need for developmental strategy which when absorbed into action contributes to strategic value and worth. This maps out the fact that there is an underlying relationship between data, and information, intelligence, knowledge and wise action. This is the core of both information management (IM) and knowledge management (KM). Data management (DM) is now coming into being as a third component in a generative sequence, which at the knowledge end of the spectrum is developing as experience management (EM).

Clearly, the parameters of BD as added value and worth will be set by technology, by communications, and by software as well as by the availability and accessibility of data sets. On the one hand data exploration can be done in a bounded environment: this approximates to a localized form of data warehousing, data management and data mining. For this you simply make a plan, define a strategy and then use the methods to hand, so that there is a boundary and the structures can be explored within this framework. This can be called 'closed access'. On the other hand there is an unbounded possibility. This is driven by the motivation to explore data resources wherever they can be found and accessed and then from there to explore where the possibilities lie. The analogy here is 'open access' and the notion of the world wide web (of data). The capacity of the technology is one driver. But the others and are more likely to be constraints: law, ethics, privacy and intellectual property rights. The idea of a public responsibility to free up and make available public data sets has become an established notion in governance and government, but still requires regulation and legal framework. The cases of Julian Assange and Edward Snowden have challenged the scope to act and tested the boundaries, whilst exposing the constraints which may and can be applied. The nature of public and private domains in BD are fields yet to be fully resolved.

A strategic view of data highlights some distinctive properties. If we suggest that data can play a critical and vital role as a source of value and worth the reverse is also true. It implies that a lack of data can have a range of negative consequences for any purpose. A strategic view of data must incorporate both breadth (range and variety) and depth (detail and substance). That strategy is the route to success is a received truth in business and organizational life and demonstrates a combination of vision, purpose and structure accomplished through a process of rationales, analysis, rigour and development. Fulfilment of strategy, requires not only the demonstration of outcomes and performance but also the conversion and management of resources to produce the required ends. So, the task is to show (and it can be shown) that data is resourceful, that it can play its part in contributing and demonstrating outcomes, and thus is a source of value and worth.

So, in context, if strategy fails, then so do tactics. As information and knowledge are resources so must data also be able to play that role. Data thus has a strategic context and its management provides a combination of strategic tools and tactical techniques. The business and organizational context has become increasingly sure and accepted. The recognition of the strategic role of data is now being realised as the tools and techniques for its management have grown in sophistication and accomplishment. What is driving this process is the new power provided by the ICTs, both hardware and software and a succession of generations of evolution is now at work to make this a realty for strategic data management. But, in reality the road to progress is neither complete nor clear. This becomes visible if four perspectives on data are introduced: the public, the private, the digital and the personal.

Four Domains of Data

- **Public Data:** Originated from public organizations in central government and local government, but increasingly from international bodies and from pan-regional entities. Scientific data may also be regarded as public data, not only because it may be derived from publically funded science, but also because the cultural basis of science considers its knowledge products as public knowledge (Ziman, 1968). Historically public agencies have had a limited view of their responsibilities to the public at large to make data public. The parliamentary and democratic process provides the foundation for accountability, regulation, monitoring and ultimately for discharging a duty towards the public domain. National census data, and public financial and budgetary data have been the main competences where data has been made public but usually in summary form. The public sector has always been slower to innovate and modernize processes and the history of business computing demonstrates the lags in progress. Whilst business computing made great strides in the 1960s, public sector applications took at least another decade to materialise. It was as late as 1982 before the UK government launched IT82 as the year of formally promoting the value and potential of IT at large. Data protection legislation in the UK began about the same period although other countries like the US, Canada and Australia had established a head start.

A period of change began in the 1960s with a growing demand for 'Freedom of Information' (FOI) legislation. This could be viewed as the start of the process which has become a significant aspect of the social dimension of BD. This engendered a combination of issues to do with the balances of power, the right to know, freedom of media and the press, accountability, responsibility and transparency. In the 1970s there was the emergence of a new concept of trans-border data flow (TBDF) as the business world started to use databases and telecommunications to develop transactional computing. The public sector was never going to be able to separate itself from these issues. Gradually, frontiers and barriers were becoming ever more permeable. The growth of the internet and the WWW was to complete the conditions to make data and information traffic highly mobile and connected. Twenty years before the expression BD became popular all the ground steps were being laid down.

In due course the emergence and preliminary completion of the digital mesh of the WWW was to coincide with a growing appetite for accountability, transparency and public participation in access not only to information but also to data. The Guardian newspaper in the UK has campaigned for many years to stimulate a debate about freeing access to public data. The new technologies were to provide the capacity and the public access to convert aspiration into reality. Whether pure data or processed information the public has slowly enforced a culture of access and openness and it appetite is undiminished in the era of Julian Assange and Edward Snowden.

There can be no doubt that public data constitutes a massive resource for which the arguments about allowing its exploitation are rational and justified. Thus it can be put at the disposal of the public at large and the private sector which is a significant contributor to the public purse through taxation. The necessity for regulatory instruments to provide security and safeguarding in the public interest is an issue to be managed without compromising the general public right. The sources of data need to be known and accessible and exploitation through technologies and software need to be expedited: this could be embedded into public service and access as a service to underpin the national economic welfare of the state. This is the example of unbounded open access.

- **Private Organizational Data:** The same strategic, administrative and managerial forces have been at work in the sector of private and corporate organizations. But the private nature of the domain makes the prevailing environment one of bounded and closed access. Each private entity can develop its own regulations and practices to manage its data assets and property. This will be consistent with maximizing their competitive advantages according to classic business and market theory. But they can also consider the case for sharing and forms of altruistic behaviour, when they address whether this can also be to their competitive advantage. Furthermore, they may see this as a way to enhance their relationships with their markets and customers. The rise of social media and its significance is generating a much more open interface between private organizations and their publics and will inevitably provide data and information resources for strategic advantage.
- **The Digital Environment as a Data Resource:** The operation of the WWW and the internet has progressively enlarged the scope for data management simply as an artefact of its own identity. As a technology it can generate data and reports of its transactions. The analysis of web logs and the emergence of web metrics has generated its own data world from which multiple forms of analysis are developed. These can be both bounded and unbounded and provide opportunities for BD operations of all kinds. Web-based transactions in both public and private data environments can operate in both bounded and unbounded environments so are cases of the digital environment as a data resource.
- **Personal Data:** Data is a feature of our personal lives. The natural life cycle from birth to death is the foundation for a personal data cycle, which we are all linked to consciously or not from the beginning to the end. In the pre-digital age our lives and activities generated a data trace, which at certain points was freely accepted. A birth record, a health record and then a record at each stage of our lives was recognised and rarely challenged: it is a consequence of citizenship. Whilst this data was conserved physically and mechanically it use was legitimised and the limited power to transmit, transmute and share it engender a certain level of trust and responsibility. Simply, the computing and digital revolutions have broken that simple confidence and security (which in any case was always relative rather than absolute). From the 1960s to the 1980s we see a transition in which computing power grew formidably and which concluded with a new era of legal concepts and legislation. The idea of data protection became a reality and emerged from the shadows to protect the citizen and fundamentally to engender trust. Concerns over national, international and personal security have become matters of public debate and even anxiety. The degree of understanding about what the concept means is not always evident and transparent. It has rapidly acquired a pejorative status in some quarters, a sense of menace, threat and intrusion.

The citizen has one view which is significantly influenced by media and political perception. Big Data becomes associated with intrusion, surveillance and feelings about the power of others (government and corporate) exploiting real or imagined citizen fears and encouraging myths or realities of a 'Big Brother'. Whatever it is 'Big Data' has major links to many prevailing concerns of the information society, the knowledge economy and the digital world in which immersion is almost inevitable and the line of least resistance is a lure.

A LITTLE HISTORY: THE EVOLUTION OF TECHNOLOGY

Rather than a step change Big Data is best perceived as the continuation of a trend in the evolution of technology and its use.

The 1970's and early 1980's was the era of the mainframe with central processing highly constrained data storage, very limited enquiry facility and highly tuned hierarchical databases. The business use was basic transactional systems usually on a business functional basis with little or no data sharing. Management information such as it was came in large standard print-outs. By the end of this period the PC was making an entrance but as with Big Data today we had barely figured out how to use it beyond simple word processing information. Middle managers were needed to process and mediate between different functional systems with different data structures. Concurrent data sharing between systems incurred impossibly high processor overheads.

The dawning of relational databases in the mid 1980's such as IBM's DB2 and Oracle were heralded with as much fanfare and hype. At last there was a way to give ad-hoc enquiry facilities but again, performance issues meant that for all except the smallest systems such facilities would usually be on a copy of the data. We had the technology but not in a mature enough state to fully exploit it. Further, the vendors had little understanding of just how business could make effective use of it. Their examples lacked business understanding and business managers likewise did not understand how best to use it to real advantage. This seems remarkably to the situation with Big Data today.

The 1990's saw the full exploitation of the microchip, the phenomenal growth in processor performance. By now it was possible fully exploit relational databases for transactional systems and enquiry. The technology, the utilities and the technical and business understanding were all mature enough. This period saw the emergence of the web and HTML and search capability but we had to get beyond the 2000 "dot com boom" before we understood how best to exploit these new capabilities. Mobile phones were becoming the norm but almost exclusively for voice calls and text.

The year 2000 saw the publication of Donald Marchand's important work Competing with information (Marchand, 2000). In this work he distinguishes between:

1. The traditional transactional systems that we were integrating using ERP which he describes as "necessary to operate".
2. The information derived from those increasingly integrated systems which he describes as "necessary to compete".
3. Those systems which are differentiated and give "strategic advantage". In particular those applications include knowledge management which requires the synthesis of internal structured data, internal unstructured data and external data.

The authors have previously written about the convergence computing and information science (Laurie and Roberts, 2008), and this convergence is at the heart of effective knowledge management. Big data gives the potential to manipulate both traditional structured data and less structured information (often from multiple sources). Thus Big Data can be seen as an important enabler of Marchand's third category (3) above.

The early 2000's also saw the in the capability to handle increasingly large amounts of data, including image and voice. Data overtook voice as the largest user of telecommunications capacity. Traditional databases were adapted to address structured elements of this wider data. Computing was truly becoming information management. The use of data warehouses was becoming common, largely a large scale information resource for internal data.

By 2010, emerging technologies to support very large disparate data enquiry engines such as Hadoop became popular but as in earlier examples it was largely "hype". The utilities to enable these enquiry engines to be loaded from existing datasets were not available for the normal IT practitioner. It required the skills of an open systems system programmer, a database specialist and a business analyst combined-tasks which had become separate sub-specialties over the previous two decades. Further, the effective manipulation and analysis of the resultant data to solve business problems required mathematical skills which Gartner (Gartner Group, 2014) have estimated are possessed by less than 6 per cent of the business community. Except in specific spheres of professional activity such as merchant banking, advertising- particularly internet advertising, public health and specialist policing agencies these mathematical analysis skills are rare in business managers. This therefore poses a specific challenge to higher education. Clearly search businesses such as Google have set up their business model to support targeted advertising supported by Big Data. To this list must be added the security services and this together with the possibility of non-government or hostile organizations and this creates public policy issues about the privacy of the individual and state security which are currently being actively discussed on either side of the Atlantic, which will be discussed in more detail below.

By 2014 utilities to support these processes were emerging and Gartner have reported that it is "getting beyond the hype". In a BBC Radio "Global Business" interview with Peter Day, Martin Sorrell head of the global advertising agency WPP stated that "mathematicians have become as important as creative people in advertising". Thus we again have the use of new data storage and manipulation capability used first for information analysis. It is important here to recognise that.

FACING THE FUTURE AND DEVELOPING PRACTICE

Reflecting back to the title of this chapter 'Strategic management of data: challenges for organizations, strategy development and business value' the following relationship suggests the core matters that need to be addressed as a consequence of Big Data. Strategic management and strategy development = Data + technology + organizational requirements + stakeholder interest + regulatory compliance = business value

This is all the more so now that the application of the digital technologies has raised the overall value and worth of data in the management of information and knowledge. Organizations and businesses can rapidly discover how they can proceed to enhance performance and value in pretty well every sphere of their activities. But the much more challenging area is how stakeholder and regulatory interests have to be acknowledged and managed as vast areas of the data landscape are 'third party issues' where the nature of property, privacy, security, identity and confidentiality are issues where care, right and mutual respect have to be observed.

This relationship plants a paradigm involving the alignment of information strategies with the range of organizational processes and outcomes. There is an existing model and range of practice which aligns business / organizational processes with information resources and information systems and technologies. The so called Information Strategy triangle requires an alignment of these three factors. Given the data/ information, intelligence and knowledge relationship we argue that it also offers a consistent pattern for data management. Managing data has its own culture, academic credentials and practitioner experience. There is a case for reviewing both the business strategy / information strategy alignment in the light of the potential of such an approach for the data communities. The result of this review could be used to establish a new model or fusion of models and to consider the practical consequences of them.

Towards a Strategic View of Data Management

We strongly believe that data management and Big Data need to have a high and higher profile in information and business strategy. Given the richness of the data environment this short paper cannot provide too much detailed exemplification, and anyway, our primary concern is the bigger picture. So we provide an illustration from a widely used application in business and marketing. Getting to the customer in whatever shape or context is fundamental to organizational strategy: this underpins any value chain and the business value of Big Data (to quote our equation).

Whether Big Data will enable "mass customisation" which as a concept embodies the holy grail of "customer choice" is a discussion as well as property of "satisfaction", most customers do not want choice, they want what they want, and usually have a decided view about that often tempered by what they can afford. Usually, they know what they want when they encounter it in the real or on the Web. This is at the heart of where Big Data is at present. Targeted advertising using Big Data increases the chances of a sale; but how many times have you bought something as a result of the internet advertisement at the side of a search or other transaction. Traditionally direct mail has had a 1-5 per cent success rate depending on the degree of targeting of the market. Using Big Data to target customers can increase the average success rate to around 6 per cent i.e. an approximate doubling of the success rate and at a lower publication and delivery cost via the internet. This is important for the efficiency of the sales process it is hardly revolutionary. Even in the security services their analysis just increases their chances of identifying possible and maybe probable suspects. We know from the Iraq War intelligence debacle that the summation of many pieces of poor quality data is likely to be a poor quality result.

Thus data quality issues and the correct interpretation of results are perhaps more important now than previously as we deal with less structured data from many sources. The chair of the UK National Health Service Information Centre in a recent interview with the author summed up his view "that Big Data is very good at solving small questions". There are examples which are more encouraging: in public health effective policy making can requires population level information; in complex legal cases such as large scale fraud- a typical large fraud would involve between one and five million documents each containing of large amounts of information. The effective scrutiny of these documents by prosecution and defence has until recently been near impossible and there have been a number of both fraud and terrorist cases which have been overturned because subsequently (in the old ways often years later) critical evidence has been uncovered which would have changed the result in court.

Chris Yapp a fellow of the Chartered Institute of IT in the UK has blogged on the BCS website:

... big data has both elements of challenge and opportunity.

In retrospect, after 9/11/2001, the fact that a group of individuals were interested in flying lessons but didn't want to take off or land turned out to be crucial. That information was known to the security services but its significance was not understood. Hindsight is a wonderful thing. Even when we have the data turning it into useful information is often more difficult than the protagonists would have you believe

The use of Big Data by insurance companies has the potential to more accurately assess risk, an important goal for the companies in managing risk, but especially when combined with genetic information may make some people virtually uninsurable.

It is clear that current use of Big Data can be seen as a continuum from the use of data warehouses but that it, like previous examples of new technology has started with improved management information. However as with those previous examples over a period of up to 10 years both business began to fully understand the potential and the vendors to understand the effective use. In the twentieth century the main use of IT was in automating clerical and manufacturing processes. The business processes were essentially simple and the IT solutions based on Taylorist work study principles. The period from the mid 1990's saw the increasing integration of those process manifested in Enterprise Resource Planning and Customer Relationship Management systems. The work of first line supervisors has changed as automated work allocation has become the norm. The work of middle management has been decimated as their jobs of reconciling and collating information has been automated from more integrated systems. The work of professionals has been largely untouched except for basic spreadsheet and word processing.

Big Data is currently where relational databases were in the mid 1980's: early adopters with the right skills can make use of vastly larger information sources and useful piloting learning from use of data warehouses is taking place. This view is held both by Gartner in their report (Gartner Group, 2014) and by a blog on the British Chartered Institute of Computing, both of which will be summarised in more detail below. What is yet speculative is whether, like previous technologies, in due course we will move beyond mere large scale information processing to developing business solutions which use all the capabilities of scale and the ability to deal with a much wider range of information types. The authors postulate that in due course Big Data(bases) supported by end user tools and utilities will be the basis of "professional workbenches" where the aim is to enhance and support the professional rather than to reduce everything to a process flow diagram. In this way the doctor would have a wide range of sources to assist with diagnosis and prescribing and eventually to individualized prescriptions; the construction engineer would have to ability to access a wide range of internal and external resources and work collaboratively with strategic partners.

For this to happen, the quantitative analytical skills of a critical mass of professionals will need to be enhanced, the utilities and end user tools will have to be developed in the same way that products like "Crystal Reports" has enabled managers to manipulate existing databases, and approaches to application development which go beyond prototyping to involve professionals in the design task.

So what did Gartner recommend in September 2014?:

Information management leaders must:

- Build a big data strategy tied to use cases, business goals and outcomes, and adapt IM strategies accordingly.
- Cut through the hype and confusion by basing big data experiments on identified use cases that reveal the real challenges and benefits.
- Evaluate the gaps in current information infrastructures and plan to evolve the organization's architecture, skills and practice accordingly.
- Accept the need to develop a new approach, as very few best practices exist.

Where do Gartner put big data in the process of technology maturity:

Traditionally IT handled data from within its own organization but Big Data often uses data from multiple sources: we trusted our own information; much of the data that organizations use in a big data context comes from outside the enterprise, or is of unknown structure and origin. This means that the likelihood of data quality issues is even higher than before. So data quality is actually more important in the world of big data.

It is still the case that rubbish in = rubbish out.

Thus the governance arrangements, the appropriate data quality and timeliness and the correct interpretation of big data are as important and it ever was. However the governance needs special consideration because of the amount of personal data that can be collected and collated without the individual's knowledge. The individual could apply the following logic: 'when I do a Google search for instance, there is an implicit trade: I sort of recognise that I get better results if Google keeps track of my search patterns. However I am less happy if Google accesses all my emails and other personal information'.

REFLECTIONS ON THE CONTEMPORARY SITUATION

This paper has isolated and explored a number of core issues in the two of the three headline themes of the collection: Big Data and Management. Fellow contributors have provided the insight into both the technology aspects and the analytic techniques. From our Big Data and Management viewpoint we have covered only a few aspects of the blueprint, but these could all be taken forward in due course.

If there is one statement which could serve as a contribution and as a basis for further debate it is our assertion that Big Data then describes the end results of the process [of managing data] as it is revealed through the evidence it provides and comprehended. Much of the debate about BD especially in the media has given it a reputation that it does not entirely deserve. However, the processing of data with technology is only as legitimate as the safeguards it needs and these must be fulfilled through legal, social and cultural obligations which regulators of whatever proper kind can and do strive to provide. Rather than tarring Big Data with every brush available, each step in the process of managing and using data needs its own tools and 'brushes' to ensure it is of quality and for purpose. With our finalist view of what big data really is we raise not only a terminological issue but also make a plea for care in the use of language and the construction of proper definition. Acts of 'Big Data' came about through each step and precursor in an often lengthy series of processes and consequences.

The development of ICT platforms, the creativity of software engineers, the shift to online and virtual presence in all walks of life in the developed economies (and increasingly in the developing one's) have all contributed to the ability to engage with all aspects of the data cycle and to increasingly realize great potentials for exploiting data as a manageable resource and as a means to release value into activities, processes, businesses, organizations and in many forms of exchange and transaction.

The Gartner Group report conclusions noted above draw attention to the central role of one key group of people in the data, information and knowledge complex. These are the business managers themselves as well as the managers of all the varied information resources. Whether information professional and / or a business practitioner and leader they have an entirely justified belief in the power of modern technologies and a true belief that information and knowledge are power, and at the very least a rational resource of potential and value. There has to be a dual awareness of both potential (and legitimacy) and danger (and harm) in every action concerning data. It is the conscience of both professionals and users together that will really underpin the use of Big Data.

As information academics and business professionals writing on this topic we tend to prefer the rational view to the emotional and sensational one. But enthusiasm and respect for the creative power of the technology has to be tested by a social critique to make us aware of the balance between pitfall and potential. Our review has developed a discussion around these often opposing perspectives might be resolved around the headline theme: Strategic management of data: challenges for organizations, strategy development and business value.

REFERENCES

Chen, M., Mao, S., & Liu, Y. (2014). Big data: A survey. *Mobile Networks and Applications*, *19*(2), 171–209. doi:10.1007/s11036-013-0489-0

Gartner Group. (2014). *Major myths about Big Data's impact on information infrastructure*. Retrieved from https://www.gartner.com/doc/2846217/major-myths-big-datas-impact

Laurie, B., & Roberts, S. A. (2008). The convergence of information systems and information management: Environmental changes and pedagogical challenges. *Aslib Proceedings*, *60*(6), 661–671. doi:10.1108/00012530810924320

Marchand, D. (2000). *Competing with information: a manager's guide to creating business value with information content*. Academic Press.

Ziman, J. M. (1968). *Public knowledge: the social dimension of science*. Cambridge, UK: Cambridge University Press.

Chapter 3

Data Stream Mining of Event and Complex Event Streams:
A Survey of Existing and Future Technologies and Applications in Big Data

Chris Wrench
University of Reading, UK

Giuseppe Di Fatta
University of Reading, UK

Frederic Stahl
University of Reading, UK

Vidhyalakshmi Karthikeyan
BT, UK

Detlef D. Nauck
BT, UK

ABSTRACT

Complex Event Processing has been a growing field for the last ten years. It has seen the development of a number of methods and tools to aid in the processing of event streams and clouds though it has also been troubled by the lack of a cohesive definition. This paper aims to layout the technologies surrounding CEP and to distinguish it from the closely related field of Event Stream Processing. It also aims to explore the work done to apply Data Mining Techniques to both of these fields. An outline of stream processing technologies is laid out including the Data Stream Mining techniques that have been adapted for CEP.

INTRODUCTION

Event Stream Processing (ESP) and *Complex Event Processing* (CEP) are increasingly wide and valued fields of study in Big Data Analytics. As the Internet of Things becomes more prominent so do events and the need for new and interesting ways of interpreting them. The purpose of this chapter is to clarify the positions of ESP and CEP within the field of Big Data Analytics and outline the range of Data Mining opportunities within ESP and CEP. This is done by identifying the challenges in the field and describing a range complementary and contrasting approaches to overcome them. Though there are numerous papers on the subject, a collection of this specific application was needed.

On this subject there is a useful body of knowledge spread across a wide area rife with different aliases and synonyms and it is difficult to see how the landscape is laid out. Both ESP and CEP evolved

DOI: 10.4018/978-1-5225-0293-7.ch003

out of necessity and independently from multiple problem domains with their own bespoke vocabulary creating a lack of consensus as to the proper title of the field and its components, a phenomenon labelled "Tower of Babel Syndrome" (Cugola & Margara, 2012).

Events and Event Streams are the focus of much of this chapter. An event can be defined in many different ways but at this point it is simplistic to say an event is a thing that *happens*. An Event Stream is an unbounded series of ordered events which, like all Data Streams, is potentially unbounded (Owens, 2007; Yu, Li, Gu, & Hong, 2011). They are a frequent part of our daily lives and, if monitored and processed intuitively, can be an extremely valuable commodity (Eckert, Oriented, Soa, & Eda, 2009). An Event Stream is effectively a specialised Data Stream and as Big Data teaches us, where there is data there is often information and knowledge to be found (Bramer, 2013).

CEP is the means by which meaningful repeated patterns can be discovered amongst a dynamic collection of low level events. Event Stream Processing is the range of technologies used to process the stream and perform Big Data Analytics. It can be argued that ESP is a specialised form of CEP or the two are different approaches to a similar problem, here again is a debate present throughout the literature.

Event Streams are generated and used in many applications. Those generated by the Stock Market are popular subjects for predictive analytics, the transaction history of users on a website and can be used to optimise said website and predict user behaviour, presenting opportunities for profit from advertisement. *Radio Frequency IDentification* (RFID) tags have become cheaper, smaller and common place in high street shops. Sensors positioned around a shop register these tags and the Event Stream can be used to prevent shop lifting (Li, 2010). A further example is that of intrusion detection in which a system administrator employs CEP to identify an intrusion on a network amongst legitimate traffic in the stream (Axelsson, 2000). There are many more examples to be found from the briefest of research into the topic.

Event Stream Processing is a subtopic of Data Stream Mining which has very similar goals but is a far more clearly understood and well defined field. Data Streams present their own unique challenges (i.e. those associated with the **V**elocity, **V**olume and **V**ariety; Ebbers, Abdel-Gayed, Budhi, & Dolot, 2013) which have been the subject of a great deal of research. These same problems apply to Event Streams so it makes sense to first look at the techniques used in Data Stream Mining.

Studying a stream in real-time enables a system or user to react to events in real-time which is of paramount importance for some applications. It also places special requirements on any stream processing technology. The standard database systems used in the majority of Big Data Analytics are not able to meet these requirements. To address this, the database has been adapted or superseded by the Active Database or the Data Stream Management System (DSMS) along with bespoke stream processing query languages and finally CEP systems. Many of these technologies will be looked at later in this chapter. The chapter will then detail several applications of Big Data Analytics and Machine Learning to ESP and CEP.

DATA STREAMS

What Are Data Streams?

Big Data Analytics is a major field of research due to the explosion of data brought about by large corporations and the Internet. Data appears in many different forms and Data Mining applications are developed to match. Initially data was primarily static. It may have been enormous but it was centralised and non-volatile. Data Streams, however, are quite different. The volume is still large (arguably larger) but the data is generated at such a rate that it takes on new properties which cause issues with traditional Data Mining techniques used for relatively static data (Golab & Özsu, 2010).

Data Streams are useful as they can describe the state of a real world application, action or thing in real-time. Two different types, distinguished by their purpose and source, have emerged: the Measurement stream (where the property or state of an object is monitored) and the Transactional stream (often where the transactions between two objects or users are monitored) (Chaudhry, Shaw, & Abdelguerfi, 2006). The former may be a reading from a machine used in manufacturing to keep actions within a given tolerance or the temperature from a fusion reactor. The latter may be the mouse clicks (known as *Clickstreams*; Bucklin & Sismeiro, 2015) on a webpage allowing a web administrator to track a user through a website and determine user behavioural patterns and identify the more popular areas (Adi, Botzer, Nechushtai, & Sharon, 2006; Hinze, Sachs, & Buchmann, 2009) . A popular application is tracking financial data such as the stock market whose analysis can prove to be quite lucrative. Analysing these Data Streams or simply tracking one stream against the other allows financial professionals to make predictions as to how a stock will rise or fall (Cugola & Margara, 2012). There are many sources of Data Streams and many good reasons to monitor them and apply Big Data Analytics. Transaction streams are synonymous with Event Streams and in this chapter they will be referred to as such.

Data Streams are a specialised type of data set with a few unique properties. Most notably the Data Stream can potentially be infinite in size making it impractical to store. It can be continuous or it can be sparsely populated as data points or events can enter a system at any rate, this may take the form of 'bursty' data. There are four properties of Data Streams that need to be accounted for in Big Data Analytics: Volume, Velocity, Veracity and Variety (Ebbers et al., 2013)(though other literature may include Variability or even Verbosity and Viscosity; Desouza & Smith, 2014) .

- **Velocity:** Data is generated at such a rate that an algorithm can only pass the stream once. The Stream is potentially infinite so if an algorithm requires more than one pass it will never be current.
- **Volume:** Closely related to velocity, the total volume of a stream is unknown and potentially too large to process completely. Load shedding and sampling techniques have been developed to combat this.
- **Veracity:** The reliability of streaming data is often poor and in need of scrutinising. A strong Data Mining technique must take this into account.
- **Variety:** Data Streams are typically heterogeneous but are often accompanied by one or more other Data Streams of different types. To get a complete picture of the problem domain all streams may need to be accounted. Data may need to be fused on the fly.

These characteristics make special demands upon the algorithms applied to them. Traditional data mining algorithms are designed to expose a trend or concept concealed within the data. This information is hopefully an informative observation about the data that holds for the whole data set. When dealing with data that changes over time the issue of concept drift arises. Concept drift occurs when this observation is only true for a finite period of time before changing or becoming entirely invalid (Widmer & Kubat, 1996). Data Stream Mining algorithms must be able to adapt to any concept drift in the data.

Issues of Real-Time Data Processing

We have mentioned above that Data Streams arrive and need to be processed in real-time. This is a very general statement that requires examining. How one defines real-time can have a substantial impact on the requirements of a system. Applications will have varying requirements as to what kind of delay is tolerable and whether a system must update in real-time.

There are some applications where a quick reaction is paramount, for instance, too large a delay between one of the hundreds of sensors in a modern car triggering an alert and the appropriate response being taken may result in a loss of life. A long delay between when a pattern is recognised as an item being shoplifted and the item being taken out the door renders the system pointless; the theft has already occurred. However, there must be sufficient time allowed to recognise the pattern before raising an alarm. Both of these examples require a quick response but the order of magnitude of time is very different, from nanoseconds to seconds, though both seem instantaneous relative to human reactions.

In terms of a Data Stream raising an alert it may be that the alert is raised as soon as the anomalous data point is produced, but what if the production time of that data point is dissimilar to the processing time due to delays? Fülöp et al. (2012) identify that their algorithm, though in an early and simplified stage, cannot be real-time as measurements are taken every 30 minutes. If this time is arbitrary and can be reduced to a second or below it is still unclear if it is real-time or just approaching real-time. Processing a stream as each point arrives, where each point has no delay between being produced and being read may be unfeasible, especially for large systems. These systems are often referred to as near real-time (Demers et al., 2007; Elmagarmid, 2005).

Various systems have to contend with a delay between the creating and processing of events and there has been some work done to counter this (Mansouri-Samani & Sloman, 1999; Wei et al., 2009). Particularly with ESP which relies on the strict ordering of events to identify causal patterns, delays in the stream can lead to erroneous patterns being detected or interesting patterns being distorted. This can be mitigated by introducing a delay whilst order is checked which further hampers the timeliness of the algorithm, this will be examined later in this chapter.

As well as mitigating out of order data, Stonebraker, Çetintemel, & Zdonik (2005) propose seven additional requirements for real-time Stream Processing. They are listed below with some additional examples from the literature:

- The ability to keep data *moving,* that is to minimize delays by not storing the data, a large number of data stream systems retain only a current history or a model representation of the stream to process.
- Support for queries using a high level (SQL-like) languages such as CQL (Arasu, Babu, & Widom, 2006) enabling a user to query the stream with reference to its relative properties (such as specifying a window).
- To supply "deterministic and repeatable" results which is dependent upon ordering of events by production time rather than processing time using methods such as punctuation to determine when it is safe to process an entry (Tucker, Maier, Sheard, & Fegaras, 2003).
- Have a readily accessible history of the stream or at least a determined base state or signature that can be used as a status-quo from which anomalies can be compared against. This must be tempered against the first requirement.

- Employ a system to ensure availability and mitigate failures such as those detailed by (Hwang et al., 2005).
- Be scalable to handle increased volume by supporting parallel processing.
- Have minimum overhead and real-time response.

The above are presented as rules to consider to "excel at a variety of real-time processing" though all eight features need to be present for an effective, if bespoke, system. Some are business orientated (supporting high level, SQL-like query languages may be good for ease of use but there are other options explored below), but others, such as the ability to keep data moving, are clearly paramount. Later in this chapter we look at the problems with traditional databases that require polling, where the overhead created makes real-time response difficult, and some technologies developed to combat this. Next we outline some approaches used in Data Stream Mining to enable real-time processing.

Real-Time Processing of Data Streams

Mentioned above are some of the problems with data stream mining that make up the four V's. Velocity and Volume can be addressed using techniques such as sampling and load shedding (Maletic & Marcus, 2010). Sampling is a technique familiar to 'static data miners' and statisticians; it entails the creation of a subset of data points that accurately reflect the set as a whole when the set is too large to process in good time. It is a commonly used form of pre-processing in Big Data Analytics that enables a Data Mining Algorithm to produce results in an effective time frame, however it must be used cautiously to avoid misrepresenting the data set and the risk of losing key data points is ever present. Methods used in stationary data mining include linear sampling and basic random sampling methods. In data stream mining the set is assumed to be infinite which creates problems for processing and storing data points, sampling is a useful tool to help address this (Babcock, Babu, Datar, Motwani, & Widom, 2002). Traditional methods have the advantage of knowing the total size of the set and can use this to create a reliable sample. This is not afforded to Data Stream Mining where the size will constantly be increasing. Below are some of the methods of sampling that have been developed to combat this problem.

- **Sliding Window:** Windowing is a method of keeping a snapshot of the stream. There have been many varieties developed, including the landmark window, the damped window and the titled-time window (Hutchison & Mitchell, 2011). Perhaps the most widely used of these is the sliding window. The sliding window (Figure 1) technique is used to keep a current history of the data stream that moves over time. As new data enters from the *right* of the window, old data is excluded from the *left* as the window moves on. In this way the sample is able to adapt to any concept drift in the data (Tsymbal, Pechenizkiy, Cunningham, & Puuronen, 2008; Widmer & Kubat, 1996). The window may progress with every new item or a given unit of time. Ricardo Vilalta, Ma, & Hellerstein (2001) had success with a time window of 20 minutes. Within the window is a snapshot of the stream that can be used for data mining. This does have the disadvantage of losing the history of the stream as data points are forgotten once the window has moved on, but it is computationally efficient.
- **Reservoir Sampling:** Reservoir sampling (Figure 2) has been directly adapted to streams from static techniques where the total number of points are known in advance (Vitter, 1985). Sampling entails the probabilistic insertion of points from the data stream into a *reservoir* of points. Unlike

the Sliding Window technique, the reservoir contains a history of the stream that grows wider as the stream continues. The initial sample of the reservoir is gradually replaced with newer data points to maintain relevancy and the bias towards newer points can be adjusted according to application. Reservoir sampling opens up the sample to batch processing techniques as well as tailored ESP.

- **Hoeffding Bound:** As mentioned above, sampling any data stream may result in an imperfect representation of the set and may lead to the extraction of misleading information, especially in the case of an undetected concept drift. Sampling from a reservoir or a window still carries this risk. The Hoeffding bound can be used to further mitigate this. It states that the true mean of a random variable within a known range will not differ from the estimated mean after n independent observations (Hoeffding, 1963). The n in this definition refers to the minimum sample size needed to establish a good estimate of the true mean of the sample and this can be used to great effect when sampling a stream. It is also used in other Data Mining algorithms looked at later in this chapter. Johnson, Muthukrishnan, & Rozenbaum (2005) provide further examples of Data Stream Sampling techniques. After sampling has taken place a number of Data Stream Mining Techniques can be applied to the stream.

Figure 1. Sliding window: data enters the window from the right and leaves from the left maintaining an up-to-date sample within the window. Data that leaves from the left is forgotten.

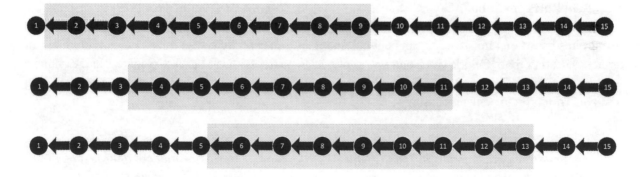

Figure 2. Reservoir sampling: data is selected from stream and replaced over time maintaining a sample representative of the stream history. A bias can be set to replace older points with more recent points to keep the sample more current.

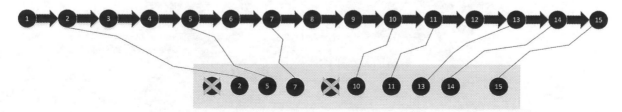

DATA STREAM MINING TECHNIQUES

Once a stream is known to be of a manageable size it can be further processed in order to extract information. Data Mining can be categorised into two different groups known as Predictive and Descriptive techniques. Descriptive techniques aim to describe and classify the data by finding similarities between groups of data points. Predictive techniques use patterns in the data to predict the class labels or values. Following are examples of these algorithms found in Data Stream Mining from both categories.

Predictive Techniques

A common predictive method is to form a decision tree to classify data points as they arrive. In batch data there exist algorithms such as C4.5 and ID3 (Quinlan, 1993) which use metrics such as frequency, entropy or the GINI index to determine which attribute to test at each node of the tree (Bramer, 2013). From the root node down, the data set is split until each base node contains members of only one class. To increase the speed of classification and to make the tree more general a phase of pruning can optionally be included to remove the more specific base nodes. To make decision trees viable to Data Streams the Hoeffding Tree was developed in the system *Very Fast Decision Trees* (VFDT) (Domingos & Hulten, 2000). These trees incorporate the Hoeffding bound, mentioned above, and are able to produce a Decision Tree similar in structure to one produced in a batch method from a stream.

There have recently been a number of algorithms developed based on the PRISM algorithm (Cendrowska, 1987), a rule based algorithm for classification. This has been modified and improved upon since its conception into different forms, notably eRules (Stahl, Gaber, & Salvador, 2012) and the very recent G-eRules (Le, Stahl, Gomes, Gaber, & Di Fatta, 2008). PRISM was developed in response to a problem with decision trees known as the subclass tree problem. The way trees divide the data into two groups based on one attribute can be problematic as it may replicate the same decision on different branches. Rather than 'Divide and Conquer', as per decision trees, PRISM uses a 'Separate and Conquer' approach, where rules are developed to fit a portion of the data points resulting in these points being removed from any further processing (Figure 3).

Figure 3. Separate and conquer (left) and divide and conquer (right): divide and conquer results in two or more groups which may require duplicated rules to divide further. PRISM produces rules to cover a subset of points and removes those points from the main data set.

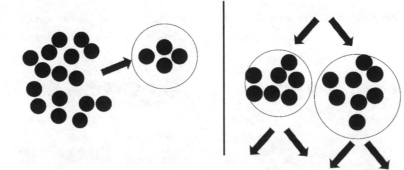

eRules is an adaption of PRISM for data streams and directly tackles the issues of concept drift, where the stream fundamentally changes in composition over time. The algorithm consists of three phases: the first learns a classification problem in batch mode; the second phase is triggered when the number of data points not covered by the established rules reaches a threshold, these points are then used to create additional rules; the third reviews all current rules and prunes those rules with a low classification accuracy. If the classification accuracy is altogether too low then the classifier is retrained in batch mode as per the first phase (Figure 4).

Descriptive Techniques

One of the most widely used descriptive techniques for static data are clustering algorithms. CluStream (Aggarwal, Han, Wang, & Yu, 2003), see Figure 5, is a form of k-means that has been adapted for streams through the use of micro-clusters. Data points are first grouped into many micro-clusters before being further grouped into k clusters. Both types of cluster are represented by cluster feature vectors holding statistical information on the cluster which allows the stream data to be reduced to a manageable size. Micro-clusters are a temporal extension of the cluster feature vector. They store key statistics of a cluster at a particular point in time, namely the sum and sum of squares for each attribute as well as

Figure 4. eRules: the three phases: to produce rules in batch mode to cover all data points, to remove and add rules as the number of unclassified data points increases and to return to batch mode if the total accuracy falls below a threshold

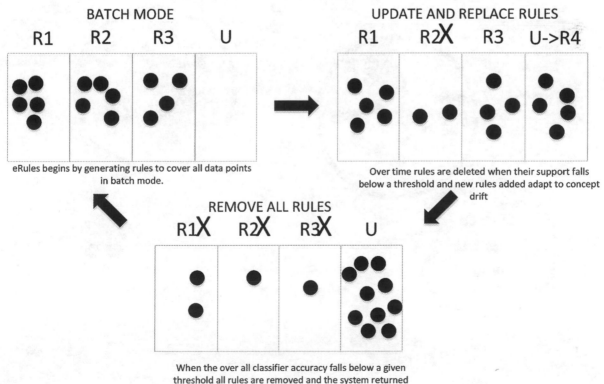

the sum and sum of squares of the current timestamp. A number of snapshots are stored along with the current micro-cluster (Aggarwal, 2014). If it is necessary to view a micro-cluster from a past snapshot it is trivial to work back using the vectors to the timestamp required. k-means is run on an initial batch of points to produce the initial micro-clusters. New points are added to the clusters as they arrive if they are within a set threshold distance; otherwise a new cluster is formed. Memory constraints dictate the maximum number of micro-cluster available, if the maximum is reached then a new cluster is formed at the expense of merging two clusters into one. Similar to CluStream, DenStream (Cao, Ester, Qian, & Zhou, 2006) is a stream clustering algorithm based DBSCAN (Ester, Kriegel, Sander, & Xiaowei, 1996). Micro-clusters have also been adapted for classification on Data Streams as in the MC-NN algorithm (Tennant, Stahl, & Gomes, 2015).

EVENTS

Events have been defined in a multitude of different ways and there seems to be no consensus as to which definition is wholly correct. Definitions include the overly broad "Anything that happens" or "a significant change in the state of the universe"(Hinze et al., 2009). A more detailed description can be

Figure 5. Groups of data points (black dots) are absorbed into micro-clusters (dotted lines) which are then in turn used to create K many global clusters (3 in this example).

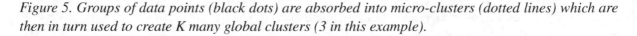
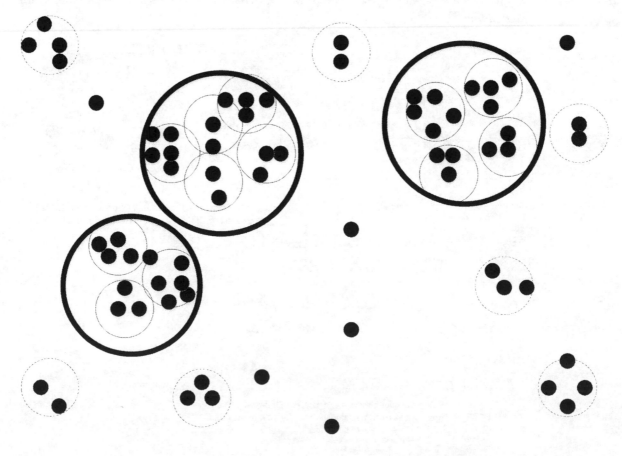

found in (Etzion & Niblett, 2010): "An Event is an occurrence within a particular system or domain; it is something that has happened, or is considered as having happened in that domain." Wang, Liu, Liu, & Bai (2006) proposes "an occurrence of interest in time, which could be either a primitive event or a complex event." These definitions vary in levels of specificity but are often a question of semantics. The reader has likely a valid notion of what an event is before reading any of the above definitions and no attempt is made here to add to any of the definitions.

Event Streams are a subset of Data Streams where attributes are both quantative and qualitative. Event Mining is a very similar discipline to Data Stream Mining and many of the same considerations have to be taken into consideration, i.e. the four V's still apply to event streams. There are no guarantees as to how quickly events will be generated, and events by nature come in a large variety of types and instances. The Event Stream must also be assumed, for storage and processing purposes, to be infinite. An Event Stream is a Data Stream that focuses on discrete and/or quantative forms of data often in a more complicated data structure. Events are simply encapsulated packets of data arranged in tuples, often containing one or more timestamps and descriptions of the event. These tuples can be in XML, JSON (below) or various other formats.

```
<13.02.201518:12, TEMPERATURE_ALERT, SENSOR1, 75c>
```

Where a Data Stream describes the state of a particular entity, an event usually describes a particular action. For example a Data Stream may indicate the temperature of a component is gradually increasing, an event may be an alert triggered by an unusual temperature. By this example it is easy to see that a Data Stream may be converted to or may generate events and at least some Event Streams can be converted back into a Data Stream with a dimensionality equal to the number of values in the tuple. There are established techniques of making this conversion for example the simplistic method of (Paton & Díaz, 1999):

```
IF temp > X: CREATE_ALERT_EVENT() ;
```

The above example might be the input to a fire alarm system that triggers an alert when the temperature goes above a given threshold and effectively converts the data stream points to an event.

Early on in the evolution of Event Processing was the Publish/Subscribe Architecture. Devices were either Event Producers (RFID tags or website notifications) or event consumers (a phone app or a fire alarm console). Either the producer or the consumer can be an active part in the process by pushing or pulling events respectively. In most incarnations today it is usually a combination through middleware such as an Event Service (Etzion & Niblett, 2010; Eugster, Felber, Guerraoui, & Kermarrec, 2003) which may also filter events according to the subscribers specified preference. This concept has been built upon to bring about the two technologies discussed here.

Event Processing Tools

Big Data Analytics has traditionally been done on large databases or data warehouses as these have been one of the most efficient methods to retrieve and store data for long periods on a large scale. These systems have been adequate for the majority of Big Data for many years however they are not designed to tackle the additional challenges posed by Data Streams. The traditional relational database has undergone several revisions with several types now in existence, one of the latest being the NoSQL movement that is very popular at the time of writing (Leavitt, 2010). Two types of databases have been developed to deal with an event rich or streaming environment. These are the *Active Database*, a more dynamic version of the traditional database, and the *Data Stream Management System* (DSMS) designed to work purely with streams. The latter introduces concepts used by CEP.

The Active Database system distinguishes itself from the classic Passive Database system by incorporating additional features into the standard application i.e. actions that are possible in a classical SQL application (specifically triggers and constraints) and that require additional overhead and explicit invocation are brought inside the database model and performed as default. Standard queries such as Update and Insert are invoked only at user request (Widom & Ceri, 1996). Triggers are a powerful tool in classical databases. They allow the user to set rules that will fire given a certain event, mostly an update of a row or value. Constraints are additional rules or parameters that can be incorporated into a field to enforce a realistic value, i.e. a rule may prevent a field representing temperature going below absolute zero. Both of these functions are available to classical databases but are added extras on top of the main application. In the active database they are a fundamental part of the database. This is advantageous when dealing with Event Streams and Event Processing as the overhead of each polling of the database is much reduced when compared to passive databases (Widom & Ceri, 1996). When the polling is as much as several times per second (or faster in many data streams) this can significantly impact the database and results in an intolerable amount of time spent locking the database and delaying further transactions (Dittrich, Gatziu, & Geppert, 1995).

Active Databases use the *Event – Condition – Action* (ECA) format of rules (Chakravarthy, Krishnaprasad, Anwar, & Kim, 1994). These are very simplistic and intelligible to produce. The event is the subject of change or simply a thing that changes (see the difficulty in defining this term as detailed earlier). The event can be any of the basic SQL commands or in addition something external to the database or a given unit of time elapsing. The Condition is the boundary or threshold that an attribute must pass to trigger the Action. This can be seen in the fire alarm example above. When the *temperature* surpasses *X Celsius* then an *alarm is triggered*. Some active databases forgo the full ECA rules and omit one of the first two components. Removing the event creates a production rule where the condition is checked at every possible event, removing the condition creates an Event Action Rule where the rule is triggered in response to a specified event regardless of whether or not a condition is met (Etzion, 1995; Paton & Díaz, 1999).

Data Stream Management Systems also utilize a recurring polling mechanism to process a data stream. Streams flow into the management system where they are buffered and queries run either on each stream or many streams using joint functionality. Rather than employing ECA rules the DSMS uses queries written in a bespoke language such as Continuous Query Language (CQL) (Arasu et al., 2004) or *Cayuga* (Demers et al., 2007). The focus of DSMS is on not storing the data from the stream, but rather on saving only the metadata produced by the queries. They are also more suited to dealing with unbounded streams. Unlike the Active Database the history of the stream is not stored (Cugola & Margara, 2012; Golab & Özsu, 2010).

This area of research is populated with numerous different kinds of languages, each with their own distinct implementations. Already mentioned are the widely used SQL in passive databases and the adapted SQL for streams such as CQL (Arasu et al., 2006). Another example is examined here – Event Processing Language (EPL) (Fülöp et al., 2010; Luckham & Schulte, 2011). DSMS systems often come with their own bespoke EPL though the majority incorporate the same features as outlined in (Owens, 2007). These are: the ability to retrieve event data, the ability to specify a time criteria in the query and the ability to extract patterns from the events. The latter feature is used heavily when looking at CEP and further languages are specialised towards this aim. Surveys of these languages are available from both (Eckert, Bry, Brodt, Poppe, & Hausmann, 2011) and (Owens, 2007).

Complex Event Processing entails the amalgamation of events into more abstract and meaningful events (Schultz-Moller, 2008). The process consists of many smaller events that are recognisable when they are combined (Owens, 2007). There is a further comparison to be made in linguistics where each event represents a phoneme of language, when these individual utterances are combined they create meaning in the form of words and sentences. Earlier we mentioned the use of RFID tags in preventing shop lifting, this could be represented as a complex event and go on to be processed further, for instance the stream could be fed centrally for purposes of crime statistics.

CEP is not specifically targeted at Event Streams, its origins lie in methods of processing events across large business systems with a great many heterogeneous and parallel event producers. This setting is labelled an event cloud and may contain a great many event streams. The cloud is often so diverse that ordering of events is not so lightly assumed as in Event Streams, see Figure 6, instead the Cloud is defined as a *Partially Ordered SET* of events (POSET). Event Streams can be viewed as a specialised and simplified form of event clouds (Luckham, 2006).

The CEP algorithms are applied in a central CEP module. The input will be a series of events (primitive, complex etc.) and the output a combination of primitive and complex events ideally as a single ordered event stream. These events are then fed either forward for further processing or potentially back into the CEP module where they can be further aggregated. In this way CEP is as much a form of pre-processing as it is pattern detection. The higher level events go on to be used by other parts of the system as in Figure 7.

Already mentioned are two different kinds of events, the simple event and the complex event. Further distinctions between events are available in (Luckham & Schulte, 2011). Fülöp et al. (2012) define different types of *Event Processing Agents* (EPA) along with their corresponding events adding Mediated Event Processing in which events are enriched, transformed, and validated and Simple Event Processing

Figure 6. An event stream (left) and event cloud (right): the cloud has no guarantee of ordering due to the varying latencies on different streams.

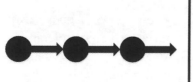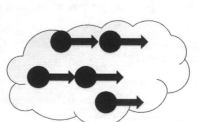

Figure 7. Complex event processing: one or more streams of heterogeneous events can be aggregated and/or sorted. Further processing, in the form of event stream processing, can take place on the output of the CEP engine.

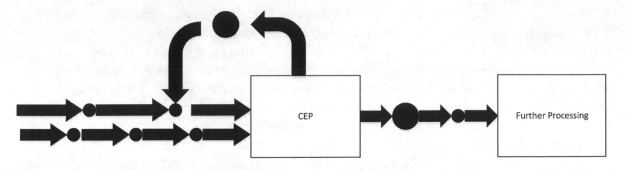

in which events are filtered and routed. The three types (Simple, Mediated and Complex) can be combined together to form an event processing network – equating to three fundamental data mining steps: sourcing data, pre-processing and mining.

Simple or Primitive events are summed together often using event algebra or Event Language. Like the Event Processing Languages above there have been many new types of these languages proposed across the literature that focus on specific use cases or more general functionality. Repeated queries are run on the event stream with operators such as AND, OR and NOT to construct complex events. More advanced temporal languages have been created with further operators dealing with the streams temporal characteristics, operators such as *Sequences* (event *A* occurs after *B*) and *Time Sequence* (event *A* occurs within time *t* of event *B*). These vary from the ECA languages discussed above in that they operate at an event instance level, distinguishing between instances of events and event types (event types here meaning database transactions). The event component of an ECA rule can be defined using Event Processing Language granting the ECA rule greater fidelity. ECA rules are also markedly more human interpretable. Fülöp et al. (2010) provide a survey of these languages. Detection using EPL is commonly depicted graphically in a tree structure as in Figure 8.

```
(A AND B) occur WITHOUT C.
```

A Complex Event is constructed here if *A AND B occur WITHOUT C* within a given time interval. This complex event can then be used as an argument for further construction if placed on the node of another tree.

To mitigate potential errors from the weak ordering within a POSET one of two approaches may be used - *aggressive* or *conservative*. In an aggressive approach, errors are tolerable and the output must be maximised so little ordering mitigation takes place. An example of this would be any system where a quick response is necessary, such as in the use of an insulin pump where delays can be fatal (Wei et al., 2009). In a conservative approach it is critical to keep errors to a minimum and so ordering must be conserved at the cost of system throughput. This usually involves events being buffered before release. An example of this would be the RFID anti-shoplifting system. Clearly there is a trade-off to be made, the RFID system does not want to trigger false alarms, nor can it wait until the theft has successfully taken place to react. Systems have been developed that offer a *Quality of Service* (QoS) feature by offering a sliding scale of order guarantee (Liu, Li, Golovnya, Rundensteiner, & Claypool, 2009; Wei et al., 2009).

Figure 8. Complex event composition tree: read from bottom up

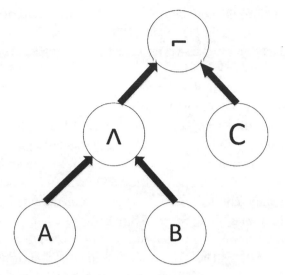

K-Slack is a conservative method of ensuring ordering (Li, Liu, Ding, Rundensteiner, & Mani, 2007). It buffers each event for k units of time using the timestamp values to determine when to release an event. The value of k can be set to match a meaningful value such as the maximum latency of a network, however, it is still a static value and likely not optimal for the duration of the stream. Punctuation is a second conservative method whereby events are buffered until a punctuation packet declares that no more of a certain timestamp will be seen on that particular stream. Following this, the events in the buffer can be released (Babu, Srivastava, & Widom, 2004; Wang, Zhou, & Nie, 2013).

BIG DATA ANALYTICS ON EVENT STREAMS

There has been some work done on developing data mining methods of extracting information from event streams, less so from CEP though this is possibly because CEP can be looked at as preparing streams for data mining to take place. As mentioned earlier CEP suffers from a confusion of terms throughout the literature and this may be the case in some of the following examples. The following are listed under the categories of ESP or CEP depending on the definitions given earlier.

Event Stream Processing

Twitter is a short broadcast micro-blogging application with an estimated 232 million *active* users (as recorded at the end of 2013; Edwards, 2013) producing in the region of 50 million discrete events, called *Tweets*, every day (Mathioudakis & Koudas, 2010). These are essentially strings (limited to 140 characters) with an attached label (*hashtag*) to declare the messages subject. Hashtags form hyperlinks and allow users to browse other connected tweets. These Tweet Events form a dense Event Stream made available through the Twitter API, *Firehose* (Twitter, 2015).

Adedoyin-Olowe et al.(2013), Bifet & Frank (2010) and Cameron et al. (2012) treat these broadcasts as text strings and process them to extract events. Social Media is fast to react and publish explicit news and is monitored closely by News publishers. It is also recognised that through proper analysis it may implicitly broadcast events before the community themselves are aware of it, for example monitoring search queries to predict epidemics (Ginsberg et al., 2009).

Each Tweet can be treated as an event however further processing needs to be done to determine the event type. The strict language of events (*valve = open or temperature > 50*) does not apply here, instead there is a textual description of an event that must first be formalised. This task is commonly fulfilled by text mining. Marcus et al. (2011) developed an API to monitor manually set events via Twitter using a string matching technique, i.e. the user specifies the string to filter the tweets by and the API returns a graph depicting tweets over time with peaks representing particularly poignant moments. This method is one of the simplest and is an extension to the early filtering of Publish/Subscribe architecture mentioned above. Bifet & Frank (2010) in their approach to Sentiment Analysis (determining whether a tweet was positively or negatively inclined to an event or object) applied three different Data Stream Mining methods. These were a Multinomial Naïve Bayes, a Stochastic Gradient Descent and a Hoeffding Tree.

Adedoyin-Olowe et al. (2013) use only the hashtags from tweets, treating each hashtag as an event for *Association Rule Mining* (ARM). The Apriori algorithm (Agrawal, Imieliński, & Swami, 1993) is applied on the data set to uncover Association rules between subsets of hashtags. Apriori was developed as a means to lower the search space of all possible combinations of events to those whose subset surpass a threshold value for support. The strength of each rule is measured using Support and Confidence, support is defined as the probability that a randomly selected item set will be in all the items in a rule whilst confidence is the conditional probability that all the items will appear given the presence of one of the items. Ranking the rules by these two values will produce a list of reliable rules such as:

```
#KNN => #Datamining (Adedoyin-Olowe et al., 2013)
```

The above suggests that the presence of the hashtag #KNN is likely to coincide with the hashtag #Datamining, a very real possibility but not an interesting discovery. The support and confidence of the rules are subject to change over time as Twitter users react and broadcast to the world around them. This appears in the stream as a concept drift and is addressed here using *Tweet Change Discovery* (TCD) and *Transaction Based Rule Change Mining* (TRCM). In TCD the different rule sets generated from each Tweet are compared in a rule matching process and the degree of change is evaluated. This is used to place each rule into one of five categories: *Unexpected Consequent Change in Tweet, Unexpected Conditional Change in Tweet, Emerging Change in Tweet, New Rules,* and *'Dead' Rules.* TRCM uses this to monitor rule changes in real world events with a goal for these rules to be used as a decision support tool.

Complex Event Processing

The effectiveness of CEP to identify patterns and create meaningful complex events depends largely on the quality and relevance of the rules in place. These can be specified a priori or they can be formed with predictive analytics, i.e. mining the event stream or cloud.

Bayesian networks are an established method of machine learning where Bayes theorem is used to calculate probabilities based on the input. Each node is the likelihood of a state connected to the affecting probabilities above and influencing the probabilities below. The representative probabilities in the network are updated with each new data point it processes keeping the network current. A strength of a Bayesian Network is that it performs well over uncertain data. Naïve Bayesian networks are a specialised form in which the network is simplified by the assumption that all input attributes are independent of each other (which in most cases is a large assumption). Wasserkrug, Gal, Etzion, & Turchin (2008) propose an algorithm to construct a Bayesian network from a set of events in order to predict subsequent events with some accuracy. This network is created anew with each set of events making it computationally inefficient however, it is noted that this can be improved by an approach which updates the existing network.

The authors of Debar, Becker, & Siboni (1992) use an *Artificial Neural Network* (ANN) in conjunction with two Expert Systems to identifying network incursions and issuing an alert to the system administrator. In this instance the data is stored in logs but is fed into the system as an Event Stream. The ANN is limited to numerical inputs and outputs and is unable to correctly interpret the network and raise alarms. This function is fulfilled by the accompanying Expert Systems that take as an input the ANN output as well as parts of the Network Stream unavailable to the ANN. The system has quite a few components to adapt around the ANN however it does perform well. Widder, von Ammon, Schaeffer, & Wolff (2008) similarly use an ANN in conjunction with Discriminant Analysis of Clusters to provide the ANN with an interpretable input. Discriminant Analysis determines the key variables that differentiate two groups or functions. A discriminant function is derived for each group and compared against the *Critical Discriminant Function* (CDF) to determine if this group is much altered from the norm. Widder, von Ammon, Schaeffer, & Wolff (2007) also use this technique to identify unusual (suspicious) transactions (those whose discriminant function is greater than the CDF) and record these patterns to be implemented as future rules.

When looking at a POSET of events (with aggressive or no ordering guarantee) the Event Cloud takes on quantifiable properties differing from a stream that can be exploited by statistical means. These include the altering size of the cloud (the total population of events within) and the change in breakdown of this population. The ordering, or near ordering, of events need not be a defining characteristic. For example, studying the dimensions of a histogram of event types can be used to trace the concept drift on an event cloud and derive patterns based on the makeup of the cloud at different times of the day. ARM can be applied to a POSET (Olmezogullari & Ari, 2013) as it can be to a data stream as in (R. Vilalta & Ma, 2002) in an effort to predict target events. Here it is assumed that the data is out of order and equates different combinations of the data set to each other. The rules developed from these patterns are then used to predict future target events, these events are specified a priori and patterns that do not precede an instance of the target event are filtered out.

A problem faced when dealing with Complex Events is the variety of events that may be available. Data Streams and Event Streams will contain specific primitive events or tuples of known size, a complex event can contain additional or modified characteristics, for example where a simple event has an occurrence time a complex event may have a duration which is problematic for the windowing techniques discussed earlier. Where clustering is readily applied to Data or Event Streams it is less readily applied to a cloud or stream of both primitive and complex events. A technique that can be adapted is MC-STREAM (Kwon, Lee, Balazinska, & Xu, 2008), an adaptation itself of CluStream. MC-Stream creates micro clusters of what are labelled contexts, a complex event made of groups of primitive events. The nature of these events make centroids very difficult to ascertain, where CluStream maintains a vector of statistics based off each cluster's centroids MC-STREAM uses the clusters medoid along with a distance metric based on the distances between each attribute, tuple and *aspect* (the collection of homogenous event types calculated using Earth Movers Distance; Rubner, Tomasi, & Guibas, 2000). Clusters are drawn up initially with events in batch mode and updated with each new context.

(Lee, You, Hong, & Jung, 2015) propose a clustering method to create complex events from primitives using k-means applied to a series of events leading to an *expert* (human) taking an action. The process involves a number of clustering steps to overcome the difficulty in comparing primitive and complex events mentioned above. Individual primitive events and actions (reactions to a complex event) are clustered and used as a basis for comparing event sequences and complex events. Using this similarity the event sequences are then clustered and refined using Markov Probabilities to identify and remove low impact primitive events. These new event sequences are used to create ECA rules for business use. Both methods of clustering complex events have to create a new characteristic with which to compare complex events to perform clustering and as such are more computationally expensive than the corresponding approaches on Data or Event Streams.

A final example of the application of machine learning to CEP is not to produce and refine events but rather speed up the application of event detection. (Schultz-Møller, Migliavacca, & Pietzuch, 2009) propose a method of improving the response time of individual queries by the application of operator specific algorithms, termed *Query Rewriting*. The cost of each operator is defined according the operators function but is always based upon CPU consumption. The Union operator is commutative and as such can be freely rearranged into its lowest cost form. This is found through an algorithm which arranges the queries into prefix trees in a manner similar to Huffman Coding(Huffman, 1952) . Union queries containing the same subsets of events are rearranged from bottom up with a pair of events with the combined lowest CPU cost forming the base much in the same way as a Huffman tree, the result is the optimal event pattern. The Next operator is optimised using genetic programming to find the lowest costing sub-pattern of the query. Optimising each query in this way is shown to significantly increase throughput and increase the total number of operators that can be applied to a stream.

DISCUSSION AND CONCLUSION

In this chapter we have given an outline of the three data stream processing techniques, Data Stream Mining, Event Stream Mining and Complex Event Processing. All three have to approach the issues of Velocity, Variety, Volume and Veracity though some of these prove larger problems than others. Veracity and Variety are more difficult to approach when dealing with CEP, the increased complexity of the data structures used increases Variety, making it harder to deal directly with an event's attributes whilst the expansiveness of the system and the Veracity this entails reduces a set of ordered event streams to an event cloud.

Veracity is addressed through a range of strategies that introduces some level of ordering guarantee however there is a large trade-off between performance and ordering. Aggressive ordering strategies make too much of an assumption of the cloud and will hinder any further processing. A basic range of statistical techniques are available for treating the POSET as an event cloud without any ordering concerns, however, the information available from this is limited. There is a lack of Data Mining Techniques that are targeted at event clouds, instead there are several adaptations of established Data Mining techniques for measurement streams and adaptations of ARM for streams. MC-STREAM is a promising approach that with further work may develop into a fully-fledged complex event clustering algorithm. The majority of other work has been undertaken with Bayesian networks and ANN, often with an accompanying system to interpret the results.

Active Databases and DSMS have been contrasted and a use case established for either one. They were developed to address the same problem but go about it in different ways. It is recognised that the majority of stream processing is best done with a DSMS though for smaller systems or systems where a history of the stream is essential an Active Database should be considered. CEP engines have been developed that can serve as a pre-processor to either of these.

There is very little work done on detecting and adapting to concept drift in CEP. Algorithms presented in Debar et al. (1992) and Widder et al. (2007) are designed to automate the production of rules from the data but these algorithms are not designed to adapt to a concept drift. These algorithms exist in ESP and Data Stream Mining (Adedoyin-Olowe et al., 2013) but none were found for CEP. The incorporation of Hoeffding bound in Data Stream algorithms (as in VFDT) has been accompanied by notable increases in performance, its inclusion into ESP and CEP is an area worth investigating.

Throughout the research for this chapter it has become very apparent that ESP and CEP are used interchangeably. This harkens back to the Tower of Babel issues mentioned in the introduction but also there is a misunderstanding as to what CEP entails. Whilst some refer to CEP as the processing of many loosely ordered events within a cloud other focus on the aggregation of primitive events into a complex one. It may well be both as described earlier, a kind pre-processing in preparation for further analyses that incorporates ordering of clouds and higher level events. The field is evolving alongside event processing and, as put by Luckham, (2006) may well become further synonymous with each other.

REFERENCES

Adedoyin-Olowe, M., Gaber, M. M., & Stahl, F. (2013). TRCM: A methodology for temporal analysis of evolving concepts in Twitter. In Artificial Intelligence and Soft Computing (LNAI), (Vol. 7895, pp. 135–145). Springer. doi:10.1007/978-3-642-38610-7_13

Adi, A., Botzer, D., Nechushtai, G., & Sharon, G. (2006). Complex Event Processing for Financial Services. In 2006 IEEE Services Computing Workshops (pp. 7–12). IEEE. doi:10.1109/SCW.2006.7

Aggarwal, C. C. (2014). A Survey of Stream Clustering Algorithms. In Data Clustering: Algorithms and Applications (pp. 231–255). CRC Press.

Aggarwal, C. C., Han, J., Wang, J., & Yu, P. S. (2003). A Framework for Clustering Evolving Data Streams. *Proceedings of the 29th International Conference on Very Large Data Bases, 29*, 81–92. doi:10.1016/B978-012722442-8/50016-1

Agrawal, R., Imieliński, T., & Swami, A. (1993). Mining association rules between sets of items in large databases. *SIGMOD Record, 22*(2), 207–216. doi:10.1145/170036.170072

Arasu, A., Babcock, B., Babu, S., Cieslewicz, J., Mayur, D., Ito, K., … Widom, J. (2004). *STREAM: The Stanford Data Stream Management System*. Academic Press.

Arasu, A., Babu, S., & Widom, J. (2006). The CQL continuous query language: Semantic foundations and query execution. *The VLDB Journal, 15*(2), 121–142. doi:10.1007/s00778-004-0147-z

Axelsson, S. (2000). Intrusion Detection Systems: A Survey and Taxonomy. *Computer Engineering*, 1–27.

Babcock, B., Babu, S., Datar, M., Motwani, R., & Widom, J. (2002). Models and Issues in Data Stream Systems. In *Proceedings of the twenty-first ACM SIGMOD-SIGACT-SIGART symposium on Principles of database systems* (pp. 1–16). ACM. doi:10.1145/543613.543615

Babu, S., Srivastava, U., & Widom, J. (2004). Exploiting K-Constraints To Reduce Memory Overhead in Continuous Queries Over Data Streams. *ACM Transactions on Database Systems*, *29*(3), 545–580. doi:10.1145/1016028.1016032

Bifet, A., & Frank, E. (2010). *Sentiment Knowledge Discovery in Twitter Streaming Data. Discovery Science*. Berlin: Springer.

Bramer, M. A. (2013). *Principles of Data Mining* (2nd ed.). London: Springer. doi:10.1007/978-1-4471-4884-5

Bucklin, R. E., & Sismeiro, C. (2015). A Model of Web Site Browsing Behavior Estimated on Clickstream Data. *JMR, Journal of Marketing Research*, *40*(3), 249–267. doi:10.1509/jmkr.40.3.249.19241

Cameron, M. a., Power, R., Robinson, B., & Yin, J. (2012). Emergency situation awareness from twitter for crisis management.*Proceedings of the 21st International Conference Companion on World Wide Web - WWW '12 Companion*, 695. doi:10.1145/2187980.2188183

Cao, F., Ester, M., Qian, W., & Zhou, A. (2006). Density-based Clustering over an Evolving Data Stream with Noise. *SDM*, *6*, 328–339.

Cendrowska, J. (1987). PRISM: An algorithm for inducing modular rules. *International Journal of Man-Machine Studies*, *27*(4), 349–370. doi:10.1016/S0020-7373(87)80003-2

Chakravarthy, S., Krishnaprasad, V., Anwar, E., & Kim, S.-K. (1994). Composite Events for Active Databases: Semantics, Contexts and Detection. In VLDB (pp. 606–617).

Chaudhry, N., Shaw, K., & Abdelguerfi, M. (2006). *Stream Data Management*. Springer.

Cugola, G., & Margara, A. (2012). Processing Flows of Information: From Data Stream to Complex Event Processing. *ACM Comput. Surv.*, *44*(1), 15:1–15:62.

Debar, H., Becker, M., & Siboni, D. (1992). A neural network component for an intrusion detection system. In *Proceedings 1992 IEEE Computer Society Symposium on Research in Security and Privacy* (pp. 240–250). IEEE. doi:10.1109/RISP.1992.213257

Demers, A., Gehrke, J., Hong, M., Panda, B., Riedewald, M., Sharma, V., & White, W. (2007). Cayuga: A General Purpose Event Monitoring System. *CIDR 2007*, *Third Biennial Conference on Innovative Data Systems Research*.

Desouza, K. C., & Smith, K. L. (2014). *Big Data for Social Innovation | Stanford Social Innovation Review*. Retrieved February 9, 2015, from http://www.ssireview.org/articles/entry/big_data_for_social_innovation

Dittrich, K. R., Gatziu, S., & Geppert, A. (1995). The Active Database Management System Manifesto: A Rulebase of ADBMS Features.*2nd Workshop on Rules in Databases*. doi:10.1007/3-540-60365-4_116

Domingos, P., & Hulten, G. (2000). Mining high-speed data streams.*Proceedings of the Sixth ACM SIGKDD International Conference on Knowledge Discovery and Data Mining - KDD '00*. doi:10.1145/347090.347107

Ebbers, M., Abdel Gayed, A., Budhi, V., & Dolot, F. (2013). *Addressing Data Volume, Velocity, and Variety with IBM InfoSphere Streams V3.0*. Academic Press.

Eckert, M., Bry, F., Brodt, S., Poppe, O., & Hausmann, S. (2011). A CEP babelfish: Languages for complex event processing and querying surveyed. *Studies in Computational Intelligence, 347*(242438), 47–70. doi:10.1007/978-3-642-19724-6_3

Eckert, M., Oriented, S., Soa, A., & Eda, E. A. (2009). Complex Event Processing (CEP) Types of Complex Event Processing Event Queries. *Informatik-Spektrum, 32*(2), 1–8. doi:10.1007/s00287-009-0329-6

Edwards, J. (2013). *Twitter's "Dark Pool": IPO doesn't mention 651 million users who abandoned twitter*. Retrieved April 20, 2015, from http://www.businessinsider.com/twitter-total-registered-users-v-monthly-active-users-2013-11

Elmagarmid, A. K. (2005). Stream Data Management. New York: Springer.

Ester, M., Kriegel, H.-P., Sander, J., & Xiaowei, X. (1996). A Density-Based Algorithm for Discovering Clusters in Large Spatial Databases with Noise. *KDD, 96*(34), 226–231.

Etzion, O. (1995). *Reasoning about the behavior of active databases applications. Rules in Database Systems*. Springer.

Etzion, O., & Niblett, P. (2010). *Event Processing in Action. Online*. Stamford, CT: Manning Publications Co.

Eugster, P. T., Felber, P., Guerraoui, R., & Kermarrec, A.-M. (2003). The many faces of publish/subscribe. *ACM Computing Surveys, 35*(2), 114–131. doi:10.1145/857076.857078

Fülöp, L. J., Beszédes, Á., Tóth, G., Demeter, H., Vidács, L., & Farkas, L. (2012). Predictive Complex Event Processing : A Conceptual Framework for Combining Complex Event Processing and Predictive Analytics.*Proceedings of the Fifth Balkan Conference in Informatics, September*, (pp. 26–31). doi:10.1145/2371316.2371323

Fülöp, L. J., Tóth, G., Rácz, R., Pánczél, J., Gergely, T., Beszédes, Á., & Farkas, L. (2010). Survey on Complex Event Processing and Predictive Analytics. In *Proceedings of the Fifth Balkan Conference in Informatics* (pp. 26–31). Citeseer.

Ginsberg, J., Mohebbi, M. H., Patel, R. S., Brammer, L., Smolinski, M. S., & Brilliant, L. (2009). Detecting influenza epidemics using search engine query data. *Nature, 457*(7232), 1012–1014. doi:10.1038/nature07634 PMID:19020500

Golab, L., & Özsu, M. T. (2010). *Data Stream Management. Synthesis Lectures on Data Management* (Vol. 2). Morgan & Claypool Publishers.

Hinze, A., Sachs, K., & Buchmann, A. (2009). Event-based Applications and Enabling Technologies. In *Proceedings of the Third ACM International Conference on Distributed Event-Based Systems* (pp. 1:1–1:15). New York: ACM Press. doi:10.1145/1619258.1619260

Hoeffding, W. (1963). Probability inequalities for sums of bounded random variables. *Journal of the American Statistical Association*, *58*(301), 13–30. doi:10.1080/01621459.1963.10500830

Huffman, D. A. (1952). A Method for the Construction of Minimum-Redundancy Codes.*Proc. IRE*, *40*, 1098–1101. doi:10.1109/JRPROC.1952.273898

Hutchison, D., & Mitchell, J. C. (2011). *Transactions on Large-Scale Data- and Knowledge-Centered Systems III* (A. Hameurlain, J. Küng, & R. Wagner, Eds.). Heidelberg, Germany: Springer-Verlag Berlin Heidelberg.

Hwang, J. H., Balazinska, M., Rasin, A., Çetintemel, U., Stonebraker, M., & Zdonik, S. (2005). High-availability algorithms for distributed stream processing. *Proceedings - International Conference on Data Engineering*, (pp. 779–790).

Johnson, T., Muthukrishnan, S., & Rozenbaum, I. (2005). Sampling Algorithms in a Stream Operator. *SIGMOD '05: Proceedings of the 2005 ACM SIGMOD International Conference on Management of Data*, (pp. 1–12). doi:10.1145/1066157.1066159

Kwon, Y., Lee, W. Y., Balazinska, M., & Xu, G. (2008). Clustering events on streams using complex context information. In *Proceedings - IEEE International Conference on Data Mining Workshops, ICDM Workshops 2008* (pp. 238–247). Washington, DC: IEEE. doi:10.1109/ICDMW.2008.138

Le, T., Stahl, F., Gomes, J. B., Gaber, M. M., & Di Fatta, G. (2008). Computationally Efficient Rule-Based Classification for Continuous Streaming Data. In *Research and Development in Intelligent Systems XXIV* (p. 2014). Springer International Publishing.

Leavitt, N. (2010). Will NoSql live to Their Promise? *Computer*, *43*(2), 12–14. doi:10.1109/MC.2010.58

Lee, O., You, E., Hong, M., & Jung, J. J. (2015). Adaptive Complex Event Processing Based on Collaborative Rule Mining Engine. In Intelligent Information and Database Systems (Vol. 9011, pp. 430–439). Springer International Publishing. doi:10.1007/978-3-319-15702-3_42

Li, M. (2010). Robust Complex Event Pattern Detection over Streams. *Evaluation*, 176.

Li, M., Liu, M., Ding, L., Rundensteiner, E. A., & Mani, M. (2007). Event Stream Processing with Out-of-Order Data Arrival. In *27th International Conference on Distributed Computing Systems Workshops*. IEEE. doi:10.1109/ICDCSW.2007.35

Liu, M., Li, M., Golovnya, D., Rundensteiner, E. A., & Claypool, K. (2009). Sequence pattern query processing over out-of-order event streams. In *IEEE 25th International Conference on Data Engineering* (pp. 784–795). IEEE. doi:10.1109/ICDE.2009.95

Luckham, D. (2006). *What's the difference between ESP and CEP?* Retrieved April 20, 2015, from http://www.complexevents.com/2006/08/01/what's-the-difference-between-esp-and-cep/

Luckham, D., & Schulte, R. (2011). *Event Processing Technical Society - Event Processing Glossary - Version 2*. Retrieved April 15, 2015, from http://www.complexevents.com/wp-content/uploads/2011/08/EPTS_Event_Processing_Glossary_v2.pdf

Maletic, J. J., & Marcus, A. (2010). Data Cleansing Data Mining and Knowledge Discovery Handbook. In O. Mainmon & L. Rokach (Eds.), Data Mining and Knowledge Discovery Handbook (pp. 19–32). New York: Springer.

Mansouri-Samani, M., & Sloman, M. (1999). GEM: A generalized event monitoring language for distributed systems. *Distributed Systems Engineering*, *4*(2), 96–108. doi:10.1088/0967-1846/4/2/004

Marcus, A., Bernstein, M. S., Badar, O., Karger, D. R., Madden, S., & Miller, R. C. (2011). Tweets as data: Demonstration of TweeQL and Twitinfo. In *Proceedings of the 2011 international conference on Management of data - SIGMOD '11* (p. 1259). New York: ACM. doi:10.1145/1989323.1989470

Mathioudakis, M., & Koudas, N. (2010). Twittermonitor: trend detection over the twitter stream.*Proceedings of the 2010 ACM SIGMOD International Conference on Management of Data*, (pp. 1155–1158). doi:10.1145/1807167.1807306

Olmezogullari, E., & Ari, I. (2013). Online Association Rule Mining over Fast Data. In *IEEE International Congress on Big Data* (pp. 110–117). IEEE. doi:10.1109/BigData.Congress.2013.77

Owens, T. J. (2007). *Survey of Event Processing*. New York.

Paton, N. W., & Díaz, O. (1999). Active database systems. *ACM Computing Surveys*, *31*(1), 63–103. doi:10.1145/311531.311623

Quinlan, J. R. (1993). *C4.5: Programs for Machine Learning*. San Francisco: Morgan Kaufmann.

Rubner, Y., Tomasi, C., & Guibas, L. J. (2000). The Earth Mover's Distance as a Metric for Image Retrieval. *International Journal of Computer Vision*, *40*(2), 99–121. doi:10.1023/A:1026543900054

Schultz-Møller, N. P., Migliavacca, M., & Pietzuch, P. (2009). Distributed complex event processing with query rewriting.*Proceedings of the Third ACM International Conference on Distributed EventBased Systems DEBS 09*, 1. doi:10.1145/1619258.1619264

Schultz-Moller, P. N. (2008). *Distributed Detection of Event Patterns*. Imperial College of Science, Technology and Medicine.

Stahl, F., Gaber, M. M., & Salvador, M. M. (2012). eRules: A modular adaptive classification rule learning algorithm for data streams. *Res. and Dev. in Intelligent Syst. XXIX: Incorporating Applications and Innovations in Intel. Sys. XX - AI 2012, 32nd SGAI Int. Conf. on Innovative Techniques and Applications of Artificial Intel.*, (pp. 65–78).

Stonebraker, M., Çetintemel, U., & Zdonik, S. (2005). The 8 requirements of real-time stream processing. *SIGMOD Record*, *34*(4), 42–47. doi:10.1145/1107499.1107504

Tennant, M., Stahl, F., & Gomes, J. B. (2015). Fast Adaptive Real-Time Classification for Data Streams with Concept Drift. In *Internet and Distributed Computing Systems* (pp. 265–272). Springer. doi:10.1007/978-3-319-23237-9_23

Tsymbal, A., Pechenizkiy, M., Cunningham, P., & Puuronen, S. (2008). Dynamic integration of classifiers for handling concept drift. *Information Fusion*, *9*(1), 56–68. doi:10.1016/j.inffus.2006.11.002

Tucker, P., Maier, D., Sheard, T., & Fegaras, L. (2003). Exploiting punctuation semantics in continuous data streams. *IEEE Transactions on Knowledge and Data Engineering*, *15*(3), 555–568. doi:10.1109/TKDE.2003.1198390

Twitter. (2015). *The Twitter Firehose API*. Retrieved March 24, 2015, from https://dev.twitter.com/streaming/firehose

Vilalta, R., Ma, S., & Hellerstein, J. (2001). *Rule Induction of Computer Events*. Academic Press.

Vilalta, R., & Ma, S. M. S. (2002). Predicting rare events in temporal domains. In *IEEE International Conference on Data Mining* (pp. 474–481). IEEE.

Vitter, J. S. (1985). Random Sampling with a Reservoir. *ACM Transactions on Mathematical Software*, *11*(1), 37–57. doi:10.1145/3147.3165

Wang, F., Liu, S., Liu, P., & Bai, Y. (2006). Bridging physical and virtual worlds: Complex event processing for RFID data streams. *Advances in Database Technology-EDBT*, *2006*, 588–607.

Wang, F., Zhou, C., & Nie, Y. (2013). Event Processing in Sensor Streams. In C. C. Aggarwal (Ed.), *Managing and Mining Sensor Data* (pp. 77–102). Springer Science & Business Media. doi:10.1007/978-1-4614-6309-2_4

Wasserkrug, S., Gal, A., Etzion, O., & Turchin, Y. (2008). Complex event processing over uncertain data. In *Proceedings of the second international conference on Distributed event-based systems* (Vol. 332, pp. 253–264). ACM. doi:10.1145/1385989.1386022

Wei, M., Liu, M., Li, M., Golovnya, D., Rundensteiner, E. A., & Claypool, K. T. (2009). Supporting a spectrum of out-of-order event processing technologies: from aggressive to conservative methodologies. *Proc. ACM SIGMOD Int. Conf. on Management of Data*, (pp. 1031–1034). doi:10.1145/1559845.1559973

Widder, A., von Ammon, R., Schaeffer, P., & Wolff, C. (2007). Identification of suspicious, unknown event patterns in an event cloud. In *Proceedings of the inaugural international conference on Distributed eventbased systems* (pp. 164–170). Toronto: ACM. doi:10.1145/1266894.1266926

Widder, A., von Ammon, R., Schaeffer, P., & Wolff, C. (2008). Combining Discriminant Analysis and Neural Networks for Fraud Detection on the Base of Complex Event Processing. In *Proceedings of the 2nd international conference on Distributed event-based systems*. ACM.

Widmer, G., & Kubat, M. (1996). Learning in the presence of concept drift and hidden contexts. *Machine Learning*, *23*(3), 69–101. doi:10.1007/BF00116900

Widom, J., & Ceri, S. (1996). *Active database systems: Triggers and rules for advanced database processing*. Morgan Kaufmann.

Yu, G., Li, C. W., Gu, Y., & Hong, B. (2011). Aggressive complex event processing with confidence over out-of-order streams. *Journal of Computer Science and Technology*, *26*(July), 685–696.

KEY TERMS AND DEFINITIONS

ANN: Artificial Neural Network.
ARM: Association Rule Mining.
CDF: Critical Discriminant Function.
CEP: Complex Event Processing.
DSMS: Data Stream Management Systems.
ECA: Event-Condition-Action rules.
EPA: Event Processing Agents.
ESP: Event Stream Processing.
POSET: Partially Ordered Set (of Events).
RFID: Radio Frequency Identification.
TCRM: Transaction Rule Change Mining.
VFDT: Very Fast Decision Trees.

Chapter 4
Research Challenges in Big Data Analytics

Sivamathi Chokkalingam
Bharathiar University, India

Vijayarani S.
Bharathiar University, India

ABSTRACT

The term Big Data refers to large-scale information management and analysis technologies that exceed the capability of traditional data processing technologies. Big Data is differentiated from traditional technologies in three ways: volume, velocity and variety of data. Big data analytics is the process of analyzing large data sets which contains a variety of data types to uncover hidden patterns, unknown correlations, market trends, customer preferences and other useful business information. Since Big Data is new emerging field, there is a need for development of new technologies and algorithms for handling big data. The main objective of this paper is to provide knowledge about various research challenges of Big Data analytics. A brief overview of various types of Big Data analytics is discussed in this paper. For each analytics, the paper describes process steps and tools. A banking application is given for each analytics. Some of research challenges and possible solutions for those challenges of big data analytics are also discussed.

INTRODUCTION

The term Big Data refers to large-scale information management and analysis technologies that exceed the capability of traditional data processing technologies (Cloud Security Alliance 2013; Duggal & Paul, 2013). Big data sizes are increasing, ranging from a few dozen terabytes in 2012 to today many petabytes of data in a single data set. Big data applications are a great benefit to organizations, business, companies and many large scale and small scale industries. Some of the real time examples of Big Data are Credit card transactions made all over the world with respect to a particular Bank, Walmart customer transactions, Facebook users generating social interaction data, The New York stock exchange, Ancestry.com (the genealogy site), and The Internet Archive. Consider the following review. Today in every minute about (Skinner, 2015)

DOI: 10.4018/978-1-5225-0293-7.ch004

- More than 204 million email messages are passed.
- Over 2 million Google search queries are requested.
- 48 hours of new YouTube videos are downloaded.
- 684,000 bits of content shared on Facebook.
- More than 100,000 tweets are created.
- $272,000 spent on e-commerce.
- 3,600 new photos shared on Instagram.
- Nearly 350 new WordPress blog posts are created.

Advantages of Big Data

There are several advantages of big data. Some of the significant advantages of big data are:

- It can handle huge volume of data with high velocity and more variety.
- Easy integration of structured and unstructured data
- Ability to process semi-structured and unstructured data
- Easy to perform data analysis.
- Decreased cost of storage.
- Improved processing speed.
- Able to map the entire data landscape across a company with Big Data tools, thus allow analyzing the threats.
- Allows ever-narrower segmentation of customers and therefore possible to attain much more precisely tailored products or services.
- Sophisticated analytics can substantially improve decision-making, reduces risks and discovers valuable insights.

Need for New Technology

Some of the traditional data mining technologies fail to provide the tools to support big data. The reasons are

- Storing a very large quantity of data was not economically feasible.
- Cannot handle a very huge dynamic data.
- Unable to handle variety of data simultaneously.
- Performing analytics and complex queries on large, structured data sets was inefficient.
- Unable to analyze and manage unstructured data.
- Unable to integrate structured and unstructured data.
- Unable to discover information from unstructured data.

LITERATURE REVIEW

For literature review, see Table 1.

Table 1. Literature review

S. No.	Title of Publication and Year	Author	Topics Discussed
1	Big Data: A Review, 2013	Sagiroglu, S, Sinanc, D	The authors described content, scope, methods, samples, advantages and challenges of big data (Sagiroglu, S & Sinanc, D. 2013).
2	A Big Data implementation based on Grid Computing, 2013	Garlasu, D Sandulescu, V. Halcu, I. Neculoiu, G.	The authors used Grid Computing to implement Hadoop technology (Garlasu, D Sandulescu,V, Halcu, I, Neculoiu, G, 2013).
3	Addressing Big Data Problem Using Hadoop and Map Reduce, 2012	Patel, A. B. Birla, M. Nair, U.	In this paper authors conducted experiment on Big data problems. The paper described the optimal solutions using Hadoop cluster, Hadoop Distributed File System (HDFS) for storage and Map Reduce programming framework (Patel, A. B., Birla, M., Nair, U. 2012) .
4	Big Data Analysis: Challenges and Solutions, 2013	Puneet Singh Duggal, Sanchita Paul	This paper presented various methods for handling the problems of big data analysis through Map Reduce framework over Hadoop Distributed File System (Duggal, P.S., Paul, S. 2013).
5	Mining Big Data: Current Status, and Forecast to the Future,	Fan, W., Bifet, A.	The paper presented a broad overview of big data mining, its current status, controversy, and forecast to the future (Fan, W. & Bifet, A. 2013).
6	Securing Big Data Hadoop: A Review of Security Issues, Threats and solution	Sharma, P. P. & Navdeti, C. P.	This paper discussed about the big data security at the environment level along with the probing of built in protections. It also presented some security issues (Sharma, P. P., Navdeti, C. P. 2014).
7	Big Data and Cloud Computing: Current State and Future Opportunities, 2011.	Agrawal, D., Sudipto, D. & El Abbadi, A.	The authors presented an organized picture of the challenges faced by application developers, DBMS designers during the development and deployment of internet scale applications (Agrawal, D., Sudipto, D. & El Abbadi, A. 2011).

BIG DATA ARCHITECTURE

Generally big data consist of 7 layers i.e. 5 horizontal layers and 2 vertical layers (Larg 2014). The topmost layer is application layer, where all applications reside. Next is the data analytics layer, where various analytics process like data visualization, audio, video etc. takes place. This layer is also responsible for models like predictive models, statistical models management. The third layer is the data layer where different a source of big data lies. The fourth is the Hadoop layer where the entire big data operation resides. Last is the physical layer. The vertical layers are responsible for security and management of big data. The following figure shows the architecture of big data (Figure 1).

BIG DATA CORE TECHNOLOGIES

The following are some of the core technologies of big data.

1. **Apache Hadoop and MapReduce Framework:** The Apache Hadoop is open-source software for reliable, scalable, distributed computing (Zikopoulos et.al, 2012) and is developed by the Apache Foundation. Hadoop was designed mainly to meet up the requirements and challenges of big data.

Figure 1. Big data architecture
Source: Cloudera Big data architecture.

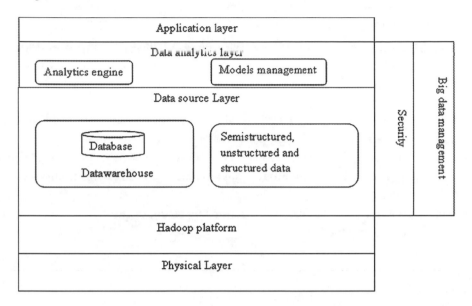

Apache Hive, Apache Pig, Apache Hcatlog, Apache HBase, Apache Sqoop, Apache Flume are some of Hadoop data services (Hadoop, 2015). These Hadoop data services tools are used to easily manipulate and process data. The two main components of Hadoop are HDFS (Hadoop Distributed File System) and MapReduce.

a. **Hadoop Distributed File System (HDFS):** HDFS is a distributed file system, provides high-throughput access to data (Hadoop, 2015). HDFS provides an interface to manage file system. HDFS creates more replicas for each data block and distributes them on computers throughout a cluster. This helps in reliable and rapid access of data. HDFS also stores individual large file across multiple machines. Hence each block is accessed in parallel, without placing the entire large file in a single memory. Once data has been loaded into HDFS, it can be processed using MapReduce.

b. **MapReduce Framework:** MapReduce is the programming model that allows Hadoop to efficiently process huge amounts of data (Hadoop, 2015). In traditional relational database environments, query language process only the structured information. In contrast, MapReduce can process unstructured data. MapReduce has two parts, called mappers and reducers. Mappers read the data from HDFS, process the data and generates the intermediate results. Then, these results are handed over to the reducers. Reducers then aggregate these intermediate results and generate the final output which is again sent to HDFS (Bakshi, K. 2013).

2. **NoSQL (Not Only SQL) Data Stores:** NoSQL is a database environment for big data. NoSQL is a distributed database, in which unstructured data is stored across multiple processing nodes. Google, Amazon, IBM INFORMIX are some of NoSQL database (Fowler 2015). NoSQL is not same as SQL. SQL is mainly dedicated for structured data and to handle transactions, whereas NoSQL can handle big data (Oussous, 2015). NoSQL does not depend on schema and hence they are capable of managing changes over time (Oussous, 2015:Harrison, 2010). To manage data and

transaction, NoSQL databases uses clusters of less expensive commodity servers, whereas RDBMS use expensive servers and storage systems. Hence the cost per gigabyte or transaction per second for NoSQL is much less than the cost for RDBMS (Harrison, 2010; Bifet 2013).

3. **Lambda Architecture:** Nathan Marz says "The lambda architecture solves the problem of computing arbitrary functions on arbitrary data in real time by decomposing the problem into three layers: the batch layer, the serving layer and the speed layer" (Marz and Warren 2015).

The batch layer is a cost-efficient active archive of big data (raw and transformed) based on parallel processing frameworks. It focused on storage of large quantities of data and its calculation.

The speed layer is a flexible, fault tolerant topology of servers for stream computing. It sits on the top of batch layer and serving layer. It sent stream raw data to batch Layer, process it into views and deploy those views on the serving Layer.

The serving layer prepares access to the views defined by business questions. It focused on the query and retrieval of views loaded by the batch layer.

BIG DATA ANALYTICS

Big data analytics is the process of analyzing large data sets containing a variety of data types to discover hidden patterns, unknown correlations, market trends, customer preferences and other useful business information (Sagiroglu & Sinanc 2013; Singh & Reddy,2014.). It leads to effective marketing, better understand of customer needs, improved operational efficiency, competitive advantages over rival organizations and other business benefits. Data Analysis is a process in which the analyst gains some knowledge by scanning the entire data set. Data analytics is a process of applying an algorithmic process to derive knowledge by scanning through various data sets and extracting meaningful correlations between data. A brief overview of the following Big Data analytics is discussed in this paper.

1. Data visualization analytics,
2. Text analytics,
3. In-memory analytics,
4. Predictive analytics,
5. SaaS-based business analytics,
6. Graph Analytics,
7. Mobile Business Analytics,
8. Video Analytics,
9. Audio analytics.

Data Visualization Analytics

Data analytics and visualization are not new. Businesses have collected data, analyzed it using BI tools and generated reports (Intel IT center, 2013). A data visualization analytics provides usability, flexibility and control over how to model and build data. It allows business user to mash up disparate data sources and create custom analytical view. It focuses on the front end of big data (Wang et al. 2015). Data visualization is representing data in any systematic and standard form that includes attributes and variables.

Advantages of data visualization tools are Improved decision-making, Better ad-hoc data analysis, Improved collaboration/information sharing, Provide self-service capabilities to end users, Increased return on investment (ROI), Time savings Reduced burden on IT etc (Wang et al. 2015). Some of the traditional data visualization methods are histogram, scatter plot, charts, time line, data flow diagram, parallel coordinates, treemap, cone tree, and semantic network, etc. (Khan & Khan 2011). Traditional data visualization tools are inadequate to visualize big data. Some of the big data visualization analytics tools (Machlis, 2011) are DataWrangler, OpenRefine (formerly Google Refine), R Project (Gohil, 2015), Google Fusion Tables, Many Eyes(Creighton M.P, 2015), Tableau Public, VIDI, Zoho Reports, Google Chart Tools. The techniques in data visualization are: Pixel oriented visualization, Aggregation and level of details (LOD), Distortion, Clutter reduction, Query base visualization (Wang et al. 2015).

According to Ben Fry (Fry 2007), there are seven stages in data visualization. During first step data are acquired from different data sources. Then the data are organized for visualization. Third stage is the filtering stage in which irrelevant information are removed. Then mining methods are applied to discover patterns. During fifth stage data are represented using basic visual model. Then data are refined for better representation and finally the model is given to the user for interaction.

Data Visualization Analytics in Banking Industry

A bank has to analyze its customer data for good banking. This customer analytics is not new. To increase customer loyalty, transaction data alone is not enough. There is also a need customer interaction data, location data, preference data, social media comments, customer interest on web, investments of customer, mortage balance etc. However the growth of big data raises serious challenges to the visualization analytics. Hence a bank needs big data visualization analytics to handle unprecedented volume, variety and velocity of data. A big data visualization analytics enables a bank to collect and organize data from different sources. Once all the data are collected, a suitable data visualizing tool to visual the data in required format are selected. Consider a bank distributed 60,816 auto loans in the quarter between April – June 2012. Here around 2.5% of overall is bad rate loans. Now the bank has to identify customer segment with distinct bad rates. It uses data visualization technique in R and relationship between loans and age of the customer.

Text Analytics

Text analytics is the process of deriving information from text sources. Text analytics allows business to convert huge amount of human generated text from various sources(like Social networks, online forums, call center logs, emails, blogs, survey responses, news) into meaningful summaries that support decision-making. The text analytics technology includes linguistics, machine learning, statistical models coupled with linguistic theories (Heger 2014). Text analytics methods are discussed below (Gandomi & Haider, 2015).

- **Information Extraction (IE):** Extracted structured data from unstructured data. Two sub-tasks in IE are Entity Recognition (ER) and Relation Extraction (RE)
- **Text Summarization:** Produced a brief summary of a single or multiple documents.
- **Question Answering (QA):** Provides answers to questions posed in natural language. Apple's Siri and IBM's Watson are examples of commercial QA systems.

- **Sentiment Analysis (Opinion Mining):** Analyze opinion text, which includes people's opinions about products, organizations, individuals etc.

The steps in text analytics are: First text is gathered from data sources and then transformation is performed which makes the text suitable for analytics. Third step is analytics where a suitable attribute and pattern is selected for analytics. Finally, results are given to the user. Some of the text analytics tools are SAS text analytics (Chakraborthy, Pagolu & Garla, 2013) IBM text analytics, SAP text analytics, Lexalytics text analytics, Smartlogic, ai-one, Provalis research, OpenText, Pingar and AlchemyAPI.

Text Analytics in Banking Industry

Banks have huge volume of unstructured data like customer blog, email, chat history, employee work logs, voice of customer from call centers, news, magazines etc. Text analytics helps banks to process such huge variety of unstructured data and extract meaningful information. Sentiment analysis and opinion mining are important process in text analytics, because they process customer feedback. This helps bank to make decision, know about their product or service etc. Baader Bank is one of the leading investment banks in the Germany. Its traders have to read 500 news per day (Heger 2014). This information overflow has often caused relevant news to be overseen. The bank implemented Clueda, a text analytics software. Clueda detects market-moving events with a processing speed of 50 milliseconds per news. Hence it reduces the burden.

In-Memory Analytics

In-memory analytics is an analytics where entire data even up to terabyte size is loaded directly into the system memory (RAM) rather than on disk (Heger, 2014). In traditional analytics platform, metadata has to be created before the actual analytics process takes place. The difficulty with this metadata is, it has to be modeled depending on the requirements. Moreover a good level of technical knowledge is also required. But in-memory analytics removes the need of metadata. Most in-memory solutions are based on a combination of DRAM and NAND flash memory arrays. Disks are only used for backup or logging purposes. It helps in taking faster business decisions. Performance is also improved as storage and operations are performed in the memory. Microsoft PowerPivot, QlikTech, and TIBCO Spotfire, are some of in-memory analytics tools (Hota, 2013).

In-Memory Analytics in Banking Industry

There is an increasing amount of data is available in banks. The bank has to enter the capital markets as early as possible and hence it has to conduct real-time analytics to a huge volume of data as quick as possible. In-memory analytics can improve the speed of data analytics by a factor of 14,000. Hence a request that previously took 5 hours can now be accomplished in just one second. This speed is due to the data analytics is done 'in memory'. Despite of the advantages of in -memory analytics, many banks and other financial institutions has not ready to adopt this technology because of lack of internal skills, lack of mature technology, lack of budget. However this may change in the near future as many of respondents believes that in-memory analytics will become the predominant architecture within the next three years. On average, it is believed that this predominance will be achieved in 2.4 years. Significantly, 90% of respondents believe that in-memory analytics will come to be the predominant architecture, indicating that, for most, in-memory analytics is seen as the future.

Predictive Analytics

Predictive analytics is a set of statistical and analytical techniques (Intel IT center, 2013) to extract information from existing data sets in order to determine patterns and predict future outcomes and trends. It will not tell us what will happen in the future but it focus what may happen in the future with an acceptable level of reliability (Mitchell 2014). It includes what-if scenarios and risk assessment. In business predictive models are used to analyze current data and historical facts in order to better understand customers, products and partners and to identify potential risks. It uses a number of techniques, including data mining, statistical modeling and machine learning to help analysts make future business forecasts.

Predictive analytics applies methods like machine learning, neural networks, robotics, computational mathematics or artificial intelligence to explore all the data and discover interrelationships and patterns. These inductive methods use algorithms to perform complex calculations specifically designed to run against highly varied or large volumes of data. The result is a predictive model (Intel IT center 2013 a).

A predictive analytics process involves the following 5 steps. During first step data are collected from sources. Then the data are analyzed and then it is transformed into suitable form for predictive analytics. During third step a statistical model is developed and then methods to create predictive models are applied. Finally analytical results to decision making are deployed. Some of predictive analytics tools are SalesPRISM, Terracotta In-Genius, Medalogix, The Lorenzi Group, Medio Platform, SAS Text Miner(Chakraborthy, Pagolu & Garla, 2013).

Predictive Analytics in Banking Industry

Predictive analytics help banks to device a more effective ways to manage their relationships with customers including developing better advertising and marketing campaigns, determining customer buying habits, creating long-term customer loyalty, retention, customer screening, rewards programs etc.,. It is also used in risk and complaint management, fraud detection. Predictive analytics must be able to handle a wide variety of data including:

- **Interactions:** Email and chat transcripts, call center notes, web click-streams, and in-person dialogues.
- **Attitudes:** Opinions, preferences, needs, and desires gathered through survey results and social media.
- **Descriptions:** Attributes, characteristics, self-declared information, and demographics.
- **Behaviors:** Orders, transactions, payment history, and usage history.

It helps decision makers to spend less time in searching for information and taking action based on best guesses.

SaaS-Based analytics

Software-as-a-Service (SaaS) is software which is owned, delivered and managed remotely by one or more providers. A single set of common code is provided in an application and it can be used by many customers at any one time. SaaS-based business analytics enables customers to quickly deploy one or more of the prime components of business analytics without significant IT involvement. SaaS lets companies to use tools without having to install, operate and maintain them on-premise, freeing customers to concentrate on creating reports and analytic queries. SaaS-based business analytics may be useful for mid and small enterprises that have yet to invest in any form of on-premise business analytics solutions. Exoprise Systems, Cloud9Analytics, Gageln, Agile Analytics are some of SaaS based analytics tools.

Graph Analytics

Graph analytics is the analysis of data that can be represented in a graph consisting of nodes and links. Graph analytics is good for solving problems which does not require the processing of all available data within a data set (Intel IT, 2013). Graph analytics can be used in many areas: In the finance sector, graph analytics is useful for understanding the money transfer pathways. A money transfer between bank accounts may require several intermediate bank accounts and graph analytics can be applied to determine the different relationships between different account holders. Optimal path analysis is the form of graph analytics that can be used in logistics distribution and shipment environments. In social media graph analytics can be used not just to identify relationships in the social network, but to understand them. So that businesses can then spend more effort in engaging this specific group of people in their marketing campaigns or customer relationship management efforts.

Some common graph analytic techniques are (Schmarzo 2014):

1. **Centrality Analysis:** To identify the most central entities in a network.
2. **Path Analysis:** To identify all the connections between a pair of entities, useful in understanding risks and exposure.
3. **Community Detection:** To identify clusters or communities.
4. **Sub-Graph Isomorphism:** To search for a pattern of relationships, searching for abnormal situations.

Steps in graph analytics:

Step 1: Gather data.
Step 2: Represent as Graph.
Step 3: Identify communities.
Step 4: Identify unusual patterns.

Graph Analytics in Banking Industry

Banks and insurance companies lose billions of dollars every year to fraud. Graph analytics provide new methods for identifying fraud rings and other sophisticated scams with a high-level of accuracy and are capable of stopping advanced fraud scenarios in real time. Unlike most other ways of displaying data, graphs are designed to express relatedness. Graph databases can uncover patterns that are difficult to detect when using traditional representations such as tables. An increasing number of companies are using graph databases to solve a multitude of connected data problems, including fraud detection. IBM G Graph analytics, Pregel, MTGL, GraphCT(Ediger et.al 2012), iGraph(Csardi & Nepusz, 2006), GRAPH VIS(Nesreen &Ryan,2015) are some of graph analytics tools. Graph analysis is a growing challenge of fraud and financial crime. By applying Data analytics to this approach, it is able to provide deep insights to detect and prevent complex cases of fraud.

Mobile Business Analytics

Mobile business analytics represents an emerging trend that is driven by the vastly growing attractiveness of mobile computing (Schmarzo 2014).It access latest analytics from back end data source using mobile workforce's perspective. In mobile analytics there is a need either to create software for specific mobile operating systems such as iOS or Android or to develop browser-based versions of their business analytics applications. Developing a browser-based version of the business analytics application is a one-time development effort and it can be made across various devices. Mobile business analytics facilitates off-site decision making. Here decision makers only need to access a few key analytics metrics churned out by the back-end data store. Having access to these metrics through mobile device can reduce decision bottlenecks, increase business process efficiency and enable broader input into the decision at hand. Some of mobile business analytics tools are(Gaikwad, 2014) Apsalar, Localytics, Flurry, Mixpanel, PercentMobile, Applicasa, AppAnnie, Google MobileAppAnalyticsss

Mobile Business Analytics in Banking Industry

Mobile is mission-critical to financial services. Customers prefer mobile banking because of instant and secure access to information anytime, Automation of processes, personalization and Ease of use, information delivered at fingertips, Choice of personalized services, Alerts, SMS, ads etc. Beyond this, power of analytics on mobile can analyze the usage of the various transactions and navigation hence getting an insight to customers' banking or finance needs. This analysis serves as input to the innovation strategy of the banks/ finance firms. Mobile Analytics gives the customers the advantage of a great visual experience. Tablet devices with wider screens make it convenient to use the information shown with the enhanced visualization. Information is showed in pictorial format rendered with great visual experience that even smaller figures/ facts get to be seen a lot easier using Mobile Analytics. Mobile Analytics renders banks with a greater user experience, ease of use and instant access to information.

Video Analytics

Video analytics is the automatic analysis of digital video images to extract meaningful and relevant information. Video analytics use computer vision algorithms to analyze video pixels. It not only identifies objects in the scene, but also tracks the movements and behavior. With a good video analytics patterns of movement of hundreds of objects in the scene, as well as their size, shape, speed, and direction of movement can be tracked efficiently. The two key concepts of video analytics are (Hammond 2013):

- **Motion Detection:** By examining each pixel in the frame, the video analytics detect even the slightest movement.
- **Pattern Recognition:** Objects are identified and distinguished within a frame.

After analyzing the system identifies these changes in each frame, correlates qualified changes over multiple frames, and finally, interprets these correlated changes.

Video Analytics in Banking Industry

Banks are already using CCTV cameras to monitor branches and ATM centers. Video analytics work with existing CCTV systems to provide both business intelligence and real-time surveillance for the safety and security of customers, employees and bank assets. It identifies entry of a person to secure areas, counting people for bank vault, Object left behind or taken etc. CCTV is used to conduct investigations after an incident. But video analytics can provide real-time alerting of activities of interest before an incident occurs. For example it can create alert when People approaching bank/building at night, Vandalism, People waiting in or near bank branch, Camera tampering etc. Ooyala, Vidyard, Youtube Analytics, Google Analytics, Vimeo Analytics, IBM® Intelligent Video Analytics are some of video analytics tools.

Union Savings Bank ($2.5 billion in assets) in USA is uses facial recognition technology, video analytics and customer data analytics to instantly identify robbers (Crosman 2010). "Our video surveillance system used to work like a VCR," recalls Bill McNamara, Union Savings Bank's SVP, technology and security. "If you wanted to find something, you had to toggle your way around." The bank's new surveillance and facial recognition technology from San Francisco-based 3VR Security will detect movement and creates short, searchable video clips. The system counts the number of pixels between the eyes and different facial points to find a match. Once a face is identified, it can be searched for across all locations, and the system will produce all relevant video. The facial recognition has been surprisingly accurate. For instance, a branch manager had long blonde hair one day and short black hair the next; the system identified her with no problem. Moreover just by typing an account number, all video clips of all transactions that took place on that account can be viewed. "That's helpful when we are doing a fraud case," McNamara says. "If we identify an account that's being defrauded, we search that account, we see who's been transacting on it, then we can search those faces to see if they are transacting on any other accounts. It takes guesswork out of an investigation and reduces the amount of time needed. This estimates that incidents can be researched in about 10 percent of the time required previously. Although video can be storage-intensive, the 3VR system uses strong compression, minimize the bandwidth and the storage needed to archive it. In addition, the surveillance system can alert staff every time somebody walks toward a vault or other high-security area.

Audio Analytics

Audio analytics uses a technique commonly referred to as audio mining where large volumes of audio data are searched for specific audio characteristics. In speech recognition audio analytics identifies spoken words in the audio and puts them in a search file. Audio analytics used in a call centre to obtain market intelligence. The call records of a call centre represents thousands of hours of the "voice of the customer". Such voice of customer represents customer view or suggestion and it can be used for business intelligence. Government agencies and regulated organizations have to handle large amounts of recorded conversations for security and intelligence purposes. Audio analytics can be applied for real-time audio streams and users can move straight to the specific point in the conversation recording where the word or phrase of interest is used.

Audio Analytics in Banking Industry

A customer communication with bank is not only with text data, but also through his voice. Every bank has its own call centers and is always ready to serve customer through interaction. Customer can express his thoughts more efficiently and effectively only through his speech. They can quickly express their thoughts. Bank has to store the voice of customer for further decisions and analysis. So a bank has massive, rapidly growing stores of audio files. It could take the archivists even few days to find the needed audio files. So an audio analytics can solve this problem. Vamp, Marsyas, SoundRuler, WaveSurfer, CLAM are some of audio analytics tools(Misra 2009). Consider a customer service centre of a bank. All calls are recorded for analytics. If a bank wants to know feedback about its new service say credit card, then it hast to retrieve all audio files. From this list, the analytics will filter out with keyword 'credit card'. Based on the keyword, it will decide the expectation of customers.

RESEARCH CHALLENGES IN BIG DATA

Big data has exponential growth of data every year and every data scientist has to manage and analyze a huge volume of data every year. The data is more diverse, larger and faster and traditional techniques cannot handle it. This leads to many research challenges (Duggal & Paul 2013; Savas et al. 2013 ; Wu et al. 2014; Wang, 2014; Sebastian et al. 2015).

In this section research challenges of big data analytics and security issues are discussed. The major challenge in big data is its three V's – Volume, Velocity and Variety.

1. **Data Integration:** Traditional data mining techniques deals only with structured data. Big data includes structured data, semi structure data and unstructured data. To analyze big data, a proper integration of these varieties of data from different sources at reasonable cost is important issue in big data analytics.
2. **Data Filtering:** Before analyzing entire data, irrelevant data should be removed (Sebastian et al. 2015). Traditional techniques use RDBMS, where data filtering is done easily. But data in big data are not well defined when it is generated (Stuempflen 2015). To define a filtering technique for such datasets is a key challenge, so that it should not discard any relevant or useful information for analytics.
3. **Data Quality:** Data to be analyzed should be clean without any noise. Context analysis may leads to wrong decision if text contains spelling mistakes or grammatical errors. Text data may contain icons, characters, symbols etc. which may or may not contextual. Text from blogs, forms and Social media may be irrelevant to the discussion. Determining data quality for unstructured data is an issue.
4. **Data Discovery:** Data discovery is a process of discovering high-quality data from huge collections of data. Moreover in big data are unstructured, heterogeneous and dynamic in nature.

5. **Information Loss:** Most of the objects in dataset are too relative to each other. Users cannot divide them as separate objects. Separation of such individual object may highly depend on other object. Removal of any object may lead to information loss (Wang et al. 2015).

6. **Data Visualization Analytics:** Scalability and dynamic nature of big data are major challenges in big data. Since the size of big data is huge, visualization needs to implement massive parallelization algorithms. These algorithms decompose a problem into independent task and executes concurrently. Decomposing a very large problem into independent task is not easy. It needs complex dimensionality reduction methods. However all such methods are always not applicable in all cases (Wang et al. 2015). It may further leads to challenges like loss of information, large image perception, noise in visualization, difficult to detect outliers.

7. **In-Memory Usage:** In-Memory usage of big data is highly expensive. Although the average price per gigabyte of RAM has been going down, it is still much higher than the average price per gigabyte of disk storage (Mitchell 2014).

8. **In-Memory Computing:** A spreadsheet-type calculation on big data is difficult because each row is independent from every other row. For simple inter-row calculations, the entire database has to be placed in memory. In such cases data has to be compressed. Systems with 1TB of RAM are widely available today. Assume that a data compression ratio of 10 to 1 systems is capable of managing 10TB of raw data. But it would be a challenge to the majority (55%) of organizations, which have more than 10TB of raw data (Pezzini 2011).

9. **Mobile Analytics:** Sensitive corporate data can be lost if device is lost. Also there is a need to integrate analytics techniques in mobile phones.

10. **Video Analytics:** The analytics may still be overwhelmed by accuracy and reliability issues, including problems caused by shadows or foliage and areas of high contrast in light. The hardware requirement for each camera, with complex video analytics algorithms is also high. Video analytics in central server requires high bandwidth. Dealing with compressed video data suffers from a number of legacy limitations.

11. **Audio Analytics:** It is difficult to have 100% accuracy in the identification of audio streams. In the case of audio analytics, the system may not be able to handle accented words. Sometimes understanding the contextual meaning of the words would still be a challenge.

12. **Data in Distributed Framework:** MapReduce framework allows parallelism and distribution of data. In MapReduce framework, mappers read data from multiple sources and perform some calculations on it. Finally it was returned to reducers. Untrusted mappers may generate wrong results and hence results in wrong aggregation results. This may leads to serious affect especially in financial and scientific organization.

13. **Data Storage and Transaction Logs:** Since big data is very huge and dynamic in nature; Automated Storage Tiering (AST) management is used. Automated storage tiering (AST) is a storage software management feature which dynamically moves data between various disks. Moreover AST does not concern about security of system, where data is places. Hence it raises another security challenge for data storage.

POTENTIAL SOLUTIONS TO BIG DATA CHALLENGES

1. Security challenges of big data can be solved by using proper techniques of authentication, authorization, encryption, audit trails, access control, logging and secure communication (Jaseena & David, 2014).
2. Other issues can be handled by proper use of hardware. Increased memory and efficient parallel processing can be implemented.
3. Place data in-memory analytics or use grid computing approach.
4. Keep an efficient domain expertise in organization.
5. Use cloud computing to address data storage issues.
6. Regarding unstructured data, organizations has to identify which information is of value. Capture of all the information available may be wasting time. Moreover resources processing those data that will add very little or even no value.

CONCLUSION

Today data in industries are growing exponentially. Traditional data mining technologies cannot handle these big data due its huge volume, heterogeneous and faster in nature. So there is a need new technology. Big data analytics is the process of analyzing big data to discover hidden patterns, unknown correlations, market trends, customer preferences and other useful business information. In this paper we list some of big data analytics and discussed about various research challenges in those analytics. For each analytics, the process steps, research challenges and tools are explained. Some of the possible solutions to address those solutions are also discussed. An application of each analytics in banking industry is given. The work is limited to present detailed discussion about various types of big data analytics in theoretical format. Also list some of its research challenges and core technologies of big data are illustrated. In future the authors planned to incorporate practical implementation of each analytics.

REFERENCES

Agrawal, D., Das, S., & El Abbadi, A. (2011). *Big Data and Cloud Computing: Current State and Future Opportunities in*. EDBT. doi:10.1145/1951365.1951432

Bakshi, K. (2013). Technologies for Big Data. In *Big Data Management, Technologies, and Applications*. IGI Global.

Bifet, A. (2013). Mining Big Data in Real Time. *Informatica, (37)*, 15–20.

Chakraborthy, G., Pagolu, M., & Garla, S. (2013). *Text mining and analysis Practical methods, Examples and case studies using SAS*. SAS Publishing.

Cloud Security Alliance. (2013). *Big Data Analytics for Security Intelligence*. Retrieved from www.cloudsecurityalliance.org/research/big-data

Creighton, M. P. (2015). *School Library infographics - How To Create Them Why To Use Them*. Libraries Unlimited Publishers.

Crosman. (2010). 3 of Banking's Most Unusual Analytics Deployments. *InformationWeek*. Retrieved 19 November 2010 from http://www.banktech.com/data-and-analytics/3-of-bankings-most-unusual-analytics-deployments/d/d-id/1294335?

Csardi, G., & Nepusz, T. (2006). The igraph software package for complex network research, InterJournal. *Complex Systems*, 1695.

Duggal, P. S., & Paul, S. (2013), Big Data Analysis:Challenges and Solutions. *Proceedings of International conference on cloud, Big data and trust*.

Ediger, D., Jiang, K., Jason, E., & Bader, D. (2012). GraphCT: Multithreaded Algorithms for Massive Graph Analysis. In Proceedings of IEEE Transactions On Parallel And Distributed Systems.

Fan, W., & Bifet, A. (2013). Mining Big Data: Current Status and Forecast to the Future. *SIGKDD Explorations*, *14*(2), 1–5. doi:10.1145/2481244.2481246

Fowler, A. (2015). *10 Advantages of NoSQL over RDBMS. NoSQL For Dummies*. Wiley.

Fry, B. (2007). *Visualizing data: exploring and explaining data with the Processing environment*. O'Reilly Media, Inc.

Gaikwad, P. (2014). *List of 23 Mobile Analytics Tools useful for your Inbound Marketing*, Retrieved on January 7, 2014 from http://www.inboundio.com/blog/list-of-23-mobile-analytics-tools-useful-for-your-inbound-marketing/

Gandomi, A., & Haider, M. (2015). Beyond the hype: Big data concepts, methods, and analytics. *International Journal of Information Management*, *35*(2), 137–144.

Garlasu, D., Sandulescu, V., Halcu, I., & Neculoiu, G. (2013). A Big Data implementation based on Grid Computing. In *Proceeding ofRoedunet International Conference (RoEduNet)*.

Gohil, A. (2015). *R data Visualization cookbook*. Mumbai: PACKT publishers.

Hadoop. (2015). *Apache Software Foundation (ASF)*. Retrieved on 18 December 2015 from http://hadoop.apache.org

Hammond, M. (2013). Video Analytics: How it Works, It's Benefits and it's Limitations. *Socialnomics*. Retrieved on October 1 2013 from http://www.socialnomics.net/2013/10/01/video-analytics-how-it-works-it%E2%80%99s-benefits-and-it%E2%80%99s-limitations/

Harrison, G. (2010). 10 things you should know about NoSQL databases. *Data Management*. Retrieved on August 2010, from http://www.techrepublic.com/resource-library/downloads/10-things-you-should-know-about-nosql-databases/?docid=2006531

Heger, D. A. (2014). Big Data Analytics - Where to go from Here. *International Journal of Developments in Big Data and Analytics,* (1), 42 - 58.

Hota, J. (2013). Adoption of in-memory analytics. *CSI Communications*, 20-22.

Intel IT Center. (2013a). *Big Data Visualization: Turning Big Data Into Big Insights.* Retrieved on 1 March 2013 from http://www.intel.com/content/dam/www/public/us/en/documents/white-papers/big-data-visualization-turning-big-data-into-big-insights.pdf

Intel IT center. (2013b). Predictive Analytics 101: Next-Generation Big Data Intelligence. *Intel IT center.* Retrieved on 1 March 2013 from http://www.intel.in/content/dam/www/public/us/en/documents/best-practices/big-data-predictive-analytics-overview.pdf

Jaseena, K. U., & David, J. M. (2014). *Issues, Challenges, And Solutions: Big Data Mining* (pp. 131–140). CS & IT-CSCP.

Khan, M., & Khan, S. S. (2011). Data and Information Visualization Methods and Interactive Mechanisms: A Survey. *International Journal of Computers and Applications, 34*(1), 1–14.

Larg George. (2014). *Getting Started with Big Data Architecture.* Retrieved on 10 September 2014 from http://blog.cloudera.com/blog/2014/09/getting-started-with-big-data-architecture/

Machlis, S. (2011). 22 free tools for data visualization and analysis. *Computer World.* Retrieved on 20 April 2011 from http://www.computerworld.com/article/2507728/enterprise-applications/enterprise-applications-22-free-tools-for-data-visualization-and-analysis.html

Marz, N., & Warren, J. (2015). Big Data Principles and best practices of scalable realtime data systems. Manning Publications.

Misr, A. (2009). *Tapestrea: Techniques And Paradigms For Expressive Synthesis, Transformation, And Re-Composition Of Environmental Audio.* (Thesis). Princeton University.

Mitchell, R. L. (2014). 8 big trends in big data analytics. *Computerworld.* Retrieved on 23 October 2014 from http://www.computerworld.com/article/2690856/8-big-trends-in-big-data-analytics.html

Nesreen, K. A., & Ryan, A. R. (2015). Interactive visual graphics analytics on web. In *Proceedings of the Ninth International AAAI Conference on Web and Social Media* (pp 566- 569). Association for the Advancement of Artificial Intelligence

Oussous, A., Benjelloun, F. Z., Lahcen, A. A., & Belfkih, S. (2015). Comparison and Classification of NoSQL Databases for Big Data. In *Proceedings of International conference on Big Data, Cloud and Applications.*

Patel, A. B., Birla, M., & Nair, U. (2012). Addressing Big Data Problem Using Hadoop and Map Reduce. In *Proceedings of NUiCONE -Nirma University International Conference on Engineering.*

Pezzini, M. (2011). *In - Memory Computing, Thinking the Unthinkable Applications.* Retrieved on 9 July 2012 from: http://agendabuilder.gartner.com/ESC23/webpages/SessionDetail.aspx?EventSessionId=1066

Sagiroglu, S., & Sinanc, D. (2013). Big data: A review. Institute of Electrical and Electronics Engineers, 42 -47.

Savas, O., Sagduyu, Y., Deng, J., & Tactical, L. J. (2013). *Big Data Analytics: Challenges, Use Cases and Solutions.* Big Data Analytics Workshop in Conjunction with ACM Sigmetrics.

Schmarzo, B. (2014). How Can Graph Analytics Uncover Valuable Insights About Data? *EMC² Infocus.* Retrieved from https://infocus.emc.com/william_schmarzo/how-can-graph-analytics-uncover-valuable-insights-about-data/

Sebastian, L. R., Babu, S., & Kizhakkethottam, J. K. (2015). Challenges with big Data Mining – A Review.*International Conference on Soft computing and Network Security.*

Sharma, P. P., & Navdeti, C. P. (2014). Securing Big Data Hadoop: A Review of Security Issues, Threats and Solution. *International Journal of Computer Science and Information Technologies, 5*(2), 2126–2131.

Singh, D., & Reddy, C. K. (2014). A survey on platforms for big data analytics. *Journal of Big Data, 1*(8). PMID:26191487

Skinner, M. (2015). *The big deal about big data.* Retrieved from http://www.lba.org/files/MikeSkinner%20-%20Big%20Data.pdf

Stuempflen, V. (2015). CEO, Clueda AG. *Real-Time Text Analytics for Event Detection in the Financial World.* Retrieved on 1 April 2015 from http://www.textanalyticsworld.com/pdf/SF/2015/Day1_1015_Stuempflen.pdf

Wang, L., Wang, G., & Alexander, C. A. (2015). Big Data and Visualization: Methods, Challenges and Technology Progress. *Digital Technologies, 1*(1), 33–38.

Wang, W. (2014). Big Data, Big Challenges In *Proceedings of IEEE International conference on Semantic computing.*

Wu, X., Zhu, X., Wu, G. Q., & Ding, W. (2014). Data Mining with Big Data. *IEEE Transactions on Knowledge and Data Engineering, 26*(1).

Zikopoulos, C., Eaton, C., deRoos, D., Deutsch, T., & Lapis, G. (2012). *Understanding Big data Analytics for Enterprise class Hadoop and Streaming data.* New York: McGraw Hill.

Section 2
Tools and Methods

Chapter 5
Descriptive and Predictive Analytical Methods for Big Data

Sema A. Kalaian
Eastern Michigan University, USA

Rafa M. Kasim
Indiana Tech University, USA

Nabeel R. Kasim
University of Michigan, USA

ABSTRACT

Data analytics and modeling are powerful analytical tools for knowledge discovery through examining and capturing the complex and hidden relationships and patterns among the quantitative variables in the existing massive structured Big Data in efforts to predict future enterprise performance. The main purpose of this chapter is to present a conceptual and practical overview of some of the basic and advanced analytical tools for analyzing structured Big Data. The chapter covers descriptive and predictive analytical methods. Descriptive analytical tools such as mean, median, mode, variance, standard deviation, and data visualization methods (e.g., histograms, line charts) are covered. Predictive analytical tools for analyzing Big Data such as correlation, simple- and multiple- linear regression are also covered in the chapter.

INTRODUCTION

Data analytics tools are used in variety of disciplines and fields of study such as business, engineering, information technology, environmental studies, information systems, health informatics, and other disciplines and fields of study. The demand for effective and sophisticated knowledge discovery using data analytical tools (descriptive, predictive, and perspective analytics) have been grown exponentially over the years as a result of the rise of using the web and mobile communication devices (e.g., mobile phones, iPads, GPS) to collect massive amount of data as well as technological advances in computer processing power including data storage, data warehouses, and integrated systems capabilities. Such

DOI: 10.4018/978-1-5225-0293-7.ch005

data is most often referred to as "Big Data" and characterized with the following four main features: Volume; Variety; Velocity; and Value.

Discovering knowledge using data analytics tools help business executives and leaders of for-profit and nonprofit organizations make informed data-based decisions to solve complex organizational and enterprise problems. For example, the survival of businesses and organizations in a knowledge-and-data driven economy is derived from the ability to transform large quantities of data and information to knowledge (Kalaian & Kasim, 2015). However, a decade ago, most such data was either not collected or entirely overlooked as a key resource for enterprise success because lack of knowledge and understanding of the value of such information and knowledge (Hair, 2007) and lack of computer storage, processing, and computing capabilities to handle such massive amount of data. However, the ability to design, develop, analyze, and implement a Big Data analytical application is directly dependent on the technical knowledge about of the architecture of the storage, processing, networking, and computing platforms from both of a hardware and software perspectives (Loshin, 2013).

However, most enterprises and businesses need to transform the massive amount of the collected data into intelligent information (knowledge) and insights about the characteristics and the underlying structure of the data such as trends, patterns, and relationships. Consequently, the intelligent information can be used to create a holistic and comprehensive view of an enterprise to make smart and informed data-based competitive enterprise decisions and strategic planning, strategic enterprise performance improvements, data-based and analytics-based competitive actions in delivering performance gains, and predictions of future organizational performance to gain competitive and global advantage.

However, conducting Big Data analytics depends on many factors and one of these key factors is the data scientist's ability to analyze the massive collected data using the most appropriate Big Data analytical tools to make valid future enterprise performance decisions and predictions. The collected Big Data could be structured (e.g., numerical data such as total sales, transaction amount, transaction time of the day, etc.) or unstructured (e.g., texts, videos, images, photos, audio recordings, etc.). In other words, a data scientist or analyst must choose the proper descriptive and predictive analytical tools to analyze the data at hand to draw valid conclusions about the characteristics of the "Big Data" and then make valid future predictions of, for example, enterprise performance. The focus of this chapter is on descriptive and predictive analytical methods for analyzing structured data. Accordingly, the chapter will be organized into two major sections. In section I, descriptive analytical tools are covered. In section II, predictive analytical tools are covered.

DESCRIPTIVE ANALYTICS

Descriptive analytics are statistical methods in the data analytics including Big Data analytics toolbox for describing, summarizing, and visualizing massive amount of data that can be used for data discovery purposes. Any collected data is usually overwhelming and uninformative and it needs to be cleaned, organized, and summarized. In situations when we have massive amount of data, it is necessary to use descriptive analytics to summarize the data to gain insights about the characteristics of the data. The descriptive analytical methods help the data analyst to describe a data set by organizing, summarizing, and visualizing the information in the quantitative data using simple descriptive summary measures and visualization methods.

Using descriptive analytics for analyzing quantitative data is the first and the most significant step in the data analytics efforts. For example, besides its aim to organize and summarize the data, it also helps the data analyst to be familiar with the data to be able to discover and detect in advance any anomalies and problems in the data set. The following are descriptions of some of the descriptive analytics tools that often used for analyzing data including Big Data.

Descriptive Analytics Using Data Visualization

Charts (graphs) are important and useful visual representations of a quantitative data set. Graphical presentations of a data set provide powerful, informative, and interesting message to wide variety of audiences. Visual representations translate a massive data into a visible form to provide meaningful insights and help data analysts to visually:

- Summarize, describe, and examine the shape of the distribution of a large amount of quantitative data in graphical formats;
- Examine the required assumptions (e.g., normality assumption) of the different descriptive and analytical tools;
- Detect one or more outliers (unusual extreme values) in a data set; and
- Explore and describe the hidden structures or patterns in the data (e.g., relationships between the quantitative variables).

Therefore, the visual representations of a data make it easy for data scientists and analysts as well as technical and nontechnical audiences such as executives and leaders to quickly perceive the salient aspects and patterns in the data. EMC Education Services (2015) stated that the best data visualization is to use the simplest, clearest visual to illustrate the key points and context. Although there are many visual representations for quantitative data such as histograms, line graphs, box plots, stem-and-leaf plots, and scatter plots, but in this chapter the histograms, line graphs, and scatter plots are the only three visualization tools that are described and illustrated.

1. **Histograms:** *Histograms* are one the most commonly used visualization tools that visually illustrates the overall pattern and shape of a frequency distributions of variables in a Big Data sets. One of the advantages of using histograms as visual analytical tools is that it provides insights about:
    a. The shape of the distribution of each of the variables in the data set, and
    b. The outliers (extreme values).
       Examining the shape of a distribution and knowing the existence of outliers are two impor- tant steps in a data analytics process for enterprise Big Data. For example, most of the descriptive and predictive analytical tools require that the quantitative variables in the data set to possess normal distributions in order to have valid, accurate, and trusted data analytical results. For example, the histogram shown in Figure 1 depicts a distribution of numerical values of a variable in an enterprise Big Data set. This histogram shows that the distribution of the numerical values is normal. A normal distribution is bell shaped and symmetrical around the mean of the numerical values of the variable.
2. **Line Charts:** *Line charts (line graphs)* represent a set of continuous straight lines that connect between the midpoints at the top of each of the bars (columns) of a histogram, which represent the

Figure 1. A histogram of a distribution of numerical data of a variable in a Big Data set

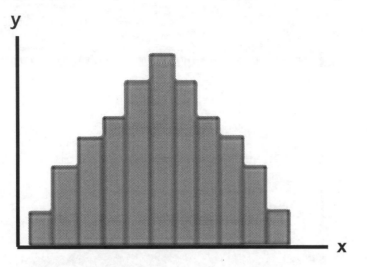

frequencies of the numerical values of a quantitative variable in a data set. Similar to histograms, line charts provide insights, especially when there is large volume of numerical data such as enterprise Big Data. It is also a valuable tool when comparing the distributions of a particular variable (e.g., employee satisfaction) for two or more groups (e.g., managers and executives) or comparing the organizational performances of two or more enterprises (e.g., enterprise A and B) in a single graph. For example, the line graph shown in Figure 2 depicts a distribution of numerical values of a variable in an enterprise Big Data set, which has a normal distribution because it is bell shaped and symmetrical around the mean (average) of the numerical values of the variable.

Descriptive Analytics Using Measures of Central Tendency

Central tendency measures are descriptive summary measures that represent the central location of the distribution of a quantitative variable in a data set. Although histograms and line graphs of variables in a data set are important basic visual analytical procedures that provide visual representations of data, basic descriptive summary measures such as means (averages), medians, variances, and standard deviations provide additional valuable descriptive and representative measures of the distribution of each of the variables in the Big Data set. The most commonly used measures of central tendency that can be used for analyzing enterprise Big Data are presented below:

1. **Mode:** *Mode* is the numerical value with the highest frequency in a set of numerical values in a distribution of a variable. For example, for the following numerical values that represent the ages of employees in a company (46, 25, 57, 68, 27, 35, 42, 29, and 35), the mode is 35 because it has the highest occurrence frequency (it occurred twice in this data set).

   Although the mode is the easiest and simplest measure of all central tendency measures to find in a set of numerical values, it also has some limitations. One of the key limitations, especially when we have a Big Data set is that the mode focuses only on the most frequently occurring numerical

Figure 2. A line graph of a distribution of numerical data of a variable in a Big Data set

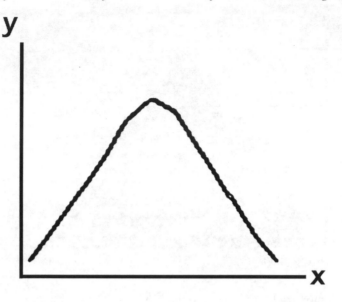

value and ignores all the other numerical values in a distribution of massive amount of data. In other words, much information in a data might be lost by using the mode, especially when we are dealing with Big Data. The other limitation is that the mode is not a reliable measure because any change or error in one numerical value in the data can have a dramatic effect on the value of the mode.

It is important to note that it is possible that a set of numerical values of a variable in a data set to have more than one mode (i.e., two or more modes). For example, if a distribution of a set of numerical values of a variable has two modes, which is a common phenomenon with massive amount of data (Big Data), then the distribution is characterized to be "*bimodal.*"

2. **Median:** *Median* is the middle point in a distribution of numerical values, where 50% of the numerical values are above the value of the median of a variable in a data set and the other 50% are below the median value. It is important to note that since the median is only the middle value of the set of numerical values of a quantitative variable and ignores the other numerical values (numerical values below and above the median) of the variable, it is usually not influenced by the extreme numerical values (outliers, which have either extremely high or low numerical values). Therefore, in such cases, the median would be the most representative central tendency measure for describing the distribution of a quantitative variable in a Big Data set. Similar to the mode, one of the key limitations of the median, especially when we have a Big Data set, is that the median focuses only on the middle numerical value in the Big Data set and ignores all the other numerical values in a distribution of massive amount of data.

3. **Mean:** M*ean is* commonly referred to as average and represents the central value of a quantitative data set. Computationally, it is the total sum of all the numerical values of a variable in a data set, including a Big Data set, divided by the number of the numerical values of the variable in the data set. The mean is the most commonly used measure of the central tendency measures for analyzing quantitative data because it takes into account all the numerical values in the quantitative data set. Therefore, it is considered a representative descriptive measure for summarizing a set of numerical values in a data set. The formula for the computation of the mean ($\bar{X}$) is as follows:

$$\bar{X} = \sum \frac{X}{n}$$

where, $\sum X$ is the sum of the numerical values of each of the quantitative variables in a Big Data set; and n is the number of individuals with numerical values (measurements) for each of the variables in the Big Data set.

It is important to note that since the mean takes into account all the numerical values for each of the variables in a data set, it is usually influenced by the extreme numerical values (outliers, which have extremely either high or low numerical values). Therefore, in a Big Data set with extreme numerical values (few large or small numerical values), the mean can be deflated (lower) or inflated (higher) depending on the numerical values of the extreme values. In such cases, the mean, as a summary descriptive measure, would misrepresent the central tendency of the distribution of the numerical values in a quantitative data set including Big Data set.

Descriptive Analytics Using Measures of Variability

Analytical tools for measuring *variability* (spread or dispersion) are very useful tools in descriptive analytics, especially when they are used side-by-side with measures of central tendency to provide a comprehensive outlook of the distribution of each of the quantitative variables in a Big Data set. Similar to measures of central tendency, the measures of variability are very powerful descriptive summary measures and yet simple to calculate, understand, and interpret. The most commonly used measures of variability are the range, variance, and standard deviation and these measures are presented below:

1. **Range:** *Range* is the difference between the largest and smallest numerical values of a quantitative variable in a data set including Big Data set and it is calculated as follows:

Range = Highest numerical Value - Lowest Numerical Value

The range is very easy to calculate and understand because it takes into account only two numerical values (the highest and lowest numerical values) from each of the quantitative variables in a data set including a Big Data set. Yet the range provides a quick summary of the variability and overall spread of the distribution of a quantitative variable in a data set. One of the key limitations of the range is that its value is based on only two values (the lowest and highest numerical values) of a variable in a data set, which makes it vulnerable to the extreme (outliers) values of a quantitative variable in a Big Data set. Also, it does not provide any information about how all the numerical values of the distribution of each of the quantitative variables in a data set is clustered or concentrated around the center of the distribution. Therefore, we need to have other measures of variability that takes into consideration every single numerical value of a quantitative variable in a Big Data set. The variance and the standard deviation are two such measures of variability.

2. **Variance:** *Variance* refers to the spread (dispersion) of the values of a quantitative variable around their mean. Specifically, it can be defined as the average squared deviations of the numerical values of a quantitative variable from its own mean. Similar to the mean of the numerical values of a data set, the variance takes into consideration every single numerical value of a variable in a quantitative data set. The formula for calculating the variance of a numerical data set is as follows:

$$s^2 = \sum \frac{\left(X - \bar{X}\right)^2}{\left(n - 1\right)}$$

where s^2 is the variance of a set of the numerical values of a quantitative variable, X, in a Big Data set; $\bar{X}$ is the mean of the numerical values of a quantitative variable in the Big Data set, X; and n is the number of the numerical values of variable, X.

The variance provides important information and insights about the spread of the numerical values of each of the variables in a Big Data set. Based on the metric of the variable, the larger the value of the variance the more variability and spread in the numerical values of the data. If the value of the variance is zero or close to zero, it means that all of the cases have the same value and absolutely no variability exists among the numerical values of a quantitative Big Data set.

3. **Standard Deviation:** *Standard deviation* is the square root of the variance. It is the best measure of the spread of the distribution of a set of numerical values of a variable and it is the most commonly used measure of variability (spread or dispersion). Similar to the variance, the value of the standard deviation is always positive because it is simply the square root of the variance, which always has a positive value. Like the variance and based on the metric of the variable, the higher the value of the standard deviation, the more spread are the numerical values of a variable in a quantitative Big Data set. In fact, it is the most widely used and reported by data analysts and researchers because it is more useful and meaningful measure of spread than the variance for the following main reason: Unlike the variance, which is stated in measurement units that are squared, the standard deviation is stated in terms of the original units of measurement of each of the variables in a Big Data set.

Descriptive Analytics Using Measures of Relationship

Pearson product-moment correlation coefficient, r, is the most commonly used tool for describing and measuring the degree and direction of the relationships between pairs of quantitative variables in a quantitative Big Data set. The value of the Pearson product-moment correlation coefficient ranges from -1.0 to +1.0; a value of a correlation coefficient of one indicates a perfect relationship; and a value of correlation coefficient of zero indicates no relationship between the correlated variables. Positive values of r indicate positive association between the pair of variables. As a substantive example, typically one would expect that the interpersonal communication skills of the employees of a company are strongly related to their work satisfaction, therefore, the value of the correlation coefficient will be close to +1.0.

On the contrary, negative values of r indicate that as the values of one variable increase the values of the other variable decrease. For example, more experienced employees, measured by the length of time (e.g., months or years) employed in a company, are less satisfied with their work environments. Such a relationship with a correlation coefficient of -1.0 or close to -1.0 is referred to as a high negative correlation. It is important to note that the larger the absolute value of the correlation coefficient (e.g., close to absolute 1.00) the greater the relationship between the two quantitative variables.

The relationships between a pair of quantitative variable s (e.g., the relationship between employees salary and job satisfaction) can be also presented graphically using *bivariate scatterplots (scatter charts)*. The scatterplot is created by allocating the *x-axis* to the numerical values of one variable and the *y-axis* to the numerical values of the other variable. The intersection of the individual's (e.g., employee's)

Figure 3. Scatterplots of bivariate data displaying different types of relationships

A. Negative Correlation   B. Positive Correlation   C. Weak Correlation

numerical values of both variables is represented by a dot on the graph (chart). In Figure 3, scatterplot "A" represents a strong negative relationship between two variables (e.g., the relationship between organizational climate and productivity or performance), which is possibly close to -1.0; Scatterplot "B" shows a strong positive relationship between the two variables, which is possibly close to +1.0; Scatterplot "C" shows a weak or no relationship between the two variables, possibly zero or close to zero.

PREDICTIVE ANALYTICS (MODELING)

Predictive analytics, also referred to as *predictive modeling*, are quantitative analytical tools that are used most often to make data-based informed enterprise and organizational decisions and future predictions of enterprise performance based on current and past historical data that includes performance indicators and factors that affect organizational productivity and performance (Evans & Lindner, 2012; Kalaian & Kasim, 2015). Kuhns and Johnson (2013) defined predictive modeling as "the process of developing a mathematical tool or model that generates an accurate prediction" (p. 2).

The main objective of predictive analytics and modeling is to:

- Build a predictive model from the current and past enterprise Big Data that includes dependent (outcome) and independent (predictor) variables, and
- Predict the unknown value of the dependent (outcome) variable (e.g., organizational performance, trends, risks, behavior patterns) from existing and past values of a set of exploratory independent (predictor) variables by analyzing and capturing the relationships between the dependent and independent variables in a Big Data set.

Organizational productivity and performance, consumer purchasing patterns, credit risks, credit limits, tax fraud, unemployment rates, and consumer attrition are examples of such future predictions that the enterprises and organizations are often interested in to make informed data-based decisions about future enterprise and organizational improvements and changes.

Predictive modeling is a complex data analytic process and building the most fitted predictive model is an important part of the data analytic process. The predictive analytics process includes:

1. Understanding company's predictive research problem and the massive data to be analyzed;

2. Managing and processing the data and preparing the data for analysis such as extracting the relevant information from a data set to be integrated and aligned with one or more data sets;
3. Analyzing the data and building the predictive analytic models;
4. Evaluating the accuracy and the fit of the predictive models; and
5. Deploying, interpreting, and tailoring the final specified predictive models to directly addressing the original predictive organizational research problems.

Identifying the most appropriate predictive analytic tools for analyzing Big Data sets, which can be utilized to answer a particular research oriented enterprise and business research questions, is one of the most difficult analytical tasks for data scientists and analysts, researchers and students conducting predictive modeling. In addition, the type and number of the dependent outcome) variables are two important primary factors to determine the appropriateness of the predictive modeling tool to predict, for example, future enterprise's or organization's productivity and performance. Provost and Fawcett (2013) stated that the success in today's data-driven businesses and enterprises requires being able to think about how to correctly apply the principles, concepts, and tools of predictive modeling to particular business- and enterprise-oriented predictive problems.

Specifically, the main objective of predictive modeling is to predict an unknown value of a dependent (outcome) variable from known values of a set of exploratory independent (predictor) variables by analyzing and capturing the relationships between the dependent and independent variables in any research problem. The results and findings of these analyses are then used to make future predictions such as predicting specific future trends, risks, and behavior patterns. Consumer purchasing patterns, credit risks, credit limits, tax fraud, and consumer attrition are examples of such predictions of future trends and consumer behavioral patterns that the businesses and enterprises often deal with (Kalaian & Kasim, 2015).

Simple Regression Analysis

Simple regression analysis is one of the predictive analytics tools for analyzing and modeling the relationship between a single continuous dependent (outcome) variable and a single continuous or categorical independent (predictor) variable to build a predictive model that can be used for making future organizational predictions. It is the simplest and the most basic regression analysis method in the predictive analytics toolbox because it includes only a single independent (predictor) variable and a single dependent variable.

The main goals of the simple linear regression analysis are to:

- Examine the relationships between a single dependent and a single independent variable to build and explain the best predictive model that represents the linear relationship between the dependent and independent variables; and
- Predict the value of a dependent (outcome) variable such as organizational performance given the specific values of a single independent (predictor) variable based on the best specified predictive regression model (Field, 2009; Kalaian & Kasim, 2015).

The following are examples of such independent variables (predictors), which had been explored and examined in previous published studies: Employee satisfaction measure (Imran, Majeed, & Ayub

(2015); Human Resources (Felicio, Couto, & Caiado, 2014; Okoye & Ezejiofor, 2013); Enterprise's information technology (IT) use (Mahmood & Mann, 2005; Lee, 2015); or Organizational climate (Patterson, et al, 2005).

In simple linear regression analysis, the linear relationship between a single dependent (outcome) variable and a single known independent (predictor) variable for n individuals (cases) is represented by the following simple linear regression model (Kalaian & Kasim, 2015):

$$Y_i = \alpha + BX_i + e_i$$

where,

- Y_i, is the value of the dependent (outcome) variable for the ith individual (e.g., employee, manger, executive, or leader in a company) and $i = 1, 2,..., n$ individuals. Company's performance and productivity are examples of such a dependent variable.
- X_i is the value of the independent (predictor) variable for individual, i $(i = 1, 2,..., n)$. Organizational climate, enterprise technology use, and human resources are examples of such independent variables.
- α, which is known as Y-intercept, is a constant that represents the intercept of the regression line with the Y-axis. That is, it is the value of the outcome (dependent) variable, Y_i, when the value of the independent (predictor) variable, X_i, is equal to zero.
- B is the regression coefficient of the independent variable, X, in the regression model and it represents the slope of the regression line, which can be interpreted as the amount of change in the dependent (outcome) variable for one unit change (e.g., one point, one year, one dollar) in the independent (predictor) variable, X. The value of the slope is positive when the numerical values of the independent (predictor) variable increase as the numerical values of the dependent (outcome) variable increase. Conversely, the value of the slope is negative when the numerical values of the independent variable increase as the numerical values of the dependent variable decrease.
- e_i, which is the error or residual of the regression equation, represents the amount by which the observed value of the dependent variable, Y_i deviates from its predicted value, $\hat{Y}_i$, for individual (case), i, in the estimated simple regression model (Kalaian & Kasim, 2015). It is represented as follows:

$$e_i = Y_i - \hat{Y}_i$$

1. **Linear Regression Line:** In simple linear regression, the bivariate scatterplot is often used to graphically portray the linear relationship between the predictor variable (X) and the dependent variable (Y). Enterprise and organizational climate and performance are examples of such independent and dependent variables, respectively. Viewing the bivariate scatterplots in Figure 3, we can envision many possible straight lines that can be drawn through the data points. But, only one of these straight lines would be the best-fitting regression line (Field, 2009; Mertler & Vannatta, 2013; Sprinthall, 2011). A straight regression line that represents the best fit of the regression

model is usually drawn through many scatterplot data points that lies closest to all the points and minimizes the sum of squared errors.

The regression line portrays the direction and the extent of the deviations of the actual data values (e.g., values of the organizational performance construct) from their predictive values ($\hat{Y}_i$), which are located on the regression line (Kalaian and Kasim, 2015). In Figure 4, graph "A" represents a linear regression line with a high and negative slope (*B*) value. An example of negative regression line might be that firm's hiring and firing practices have a negative effect on organizational productivity and performance. Graph "B" in Figure 4, represents a regression line with a high and positive slope (B) value. An example of positive regression line might be that organizational climate has a positive effect on company's productivity and performance. The regression line will be horizontally flat when the value of the slope is zero, which indicates that there is no relationship between the dependent and the independent variables.

2. **Assumptions of Simple Linear Regression Analysis:** As any predictive analytic tool, simple linear regression analysis is based on specific assumptions about the quantitative variables in the Big Data set (Kalaian & Kasim, 2015). Meeting these assumptions is a necessary requirement in order to achieve the best estimation of the parameters of the regression model such as the intercept and slope, which leads to a better fitted predictive model. These assumptions are:

    a.   The distribution of the numerical values of the dependent variable is normal;
    b.   The error terms (e_i) of the regression model are independently and normally distributed with mean equal to zero;
    c.   The relationship between the dependent and the single independent variable is linear;
    d.   The errors of fitting the regression model are not correlated with the single independent (predictor) variable; and
    e.   The distribution of the errors of the regression model for each value of the independent variable (*X*) has an approximately normal distribution with constant variance across all values of the independent (predictor) variable, *X*.

    As a result of testing the assumptions, if there is sufficient number of cases (this is not a problem in Big Data sets) and no violations of the assumptions are evident, then it is safe to interpret the linear regression analysis results (Field, 2009; Kalaian & Kasim, 2015; Tabachnik & Fidell, 2012). But, for example, if the relationship between the dependent and the independent variable appears to be nonlinear (curvilinear) then nonlinear regression methods should be used to analyze the data instead of the linear regression.

3. **Statistical Significance of the Coefficient of the Simple Linear Regression:** A *t-test* can be used to test whether or not the associated population parameter of the regression coefficient is equal to zero. In other words, it tests the null hypothesis (H_0: *B* = 0). In simple regression analysis, the t-test can be used to answer the following research question: What is the effect of the independent variable (e.g., organizational climate) on the dependent variable (e.g., organizational productivity or performance)? The t-test is computed by dividing the estimated regression coefficient, *b*, by the standard error (*S.E.*) of the estimated regression coefficient, *b*. Therefore, the t-statistic formula is represented as follows:

$$t = \frac{b}{S.E._{(b)}}$$

4. **Predictive Simple Linear Regression Models:** Predictive regression models are used to:
    a. Predict the values of the dependent variable given known numerical values of an independent (predictor) variable within the given range of the independent variable (X) values, and
    b. Evaluate the accuracy of predicting (that is, evaluating the fit of the estimated regression line to the data) the values of the dependent variable from known values of the independent variable. The predicted value ($\hat{Y}$) of the dependent variable (Y) in simple linear regression is represented as follows:

$$\hat{Y}_i = a + bX_i$$

where, "a" is the estimated intercept of the population parameter, α. "b" is the estimated regression coefficient of the population's regression coefficient parameter for the independent variable. The accuracy of the predicted value of the dependent variable (Y) is calculated by subtracting the corresponding predicted value of the dependent variable, $\hat{Y}$, from the original observed value of the dependent variable, Y. The closer the value of the difference to zero the more accurate is the prediction model. This difference is called the error of prediction (Y_e) and represented as:

$$Y_e = Y - \hat{Y}$$

5. **Coefficient of Determination (R^2):** One of the goals of simple regression is to measure the contribution of a single independent variable to the overall fit of the simple regression equation. The *coefficient of determination* (R^2) is such a commonly used measure and it is a descriptive measure of goodness-of-fit of the regression model. It is a measure of the proportion (percentage) of the total variance in the dependent variable (Y) that is accounted for and explained by the variation of a single independent variable in the simple regression model. The unexplained variance in the dependent variable is assumed to result from other factors not included in the specified regression model or from random error. Having high R^2 indicates that the specified regression model explains the variation in the dependent variable well, suggesting that the regression model can be used for predictive purposes.

    R^2 represents the squared correlation between the actual values of the dependent variable (Y) and the predicted values of Y obtained from the regression model. Its numeric value ranges from 0 to 1.0 and the closer the value of the R^2 statistic is to the value of 1.0, the better the fit of the estimated regression line to the bivariate data with a single independent (predictor) variable (Kalaian & Kasim, 2015; Nathans, Oswald, & Nimon, 2012).

MULTIPLE LINEAR REGRESSION ANALYSIS

The main goals of the multiple linear regression analyses where the researcher, data scientist, or data analyst have two or more independent variables in the regression model are to:

Figure 4. Regression lines fitted to bivariate data displaying different types of regression lines

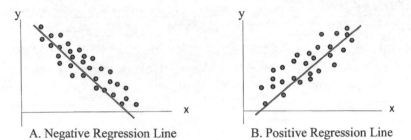

A. Negative Regression Line   B. Positive Regression Line

- Explore and understand the relationships between the dependent variable e.g., organizational performance or productivity) and the multiple independent (predictor) variables (e.g., organizational climate, leadership style, and technology use);
- Identify and explain the best model that captures and represents the linear relationships between a quantitative dependent variable and two or more quantitative independent variables;
- Predict the value of the dependent variable given the specific values of the multiple independent variables based on the best fitted model; and
- Examine the relative importance of the independent (predictor) variables by comparing the regression coefficients in the specified regression model.

In multiple linear regression analysis, which is an extension of the simple linear regression, the linear relationship between a dependent variable and two or more known independent (predictor) variables (X_1, X_2, ..., X_k) in the population is represented by the following linear model:

$$Y_i = \alpha + B_1 X_{i1} + B_2 X_{i2} + ... + B_k X_{ik} + e_i$$

where Y_i is the value of the dependent (outcome) variable for individual i ($i = 1, 2, ..., n$); α is the intercept of the regression model, which is the value of the dependent variable, Y, when all the predictors in the regression model have values equal to zero; B_1, B_2, ..., B_k are the regression coefficients for the corresponding k independent (predictor) variables, X_{i1}, $X_{i2, ...,}$ X_{ik}, respectively. Each of these coefficients (regression weights) represents the effects of its associated predictor, X_i, on the dependent variable, Y_i, while holding the other predictors in the model constant. Similar to the simple regression model, e_i represents the amount by which the observed value of the dependent variable deviates from the predicted value for an individual, i, from the estimated multiple regression model. The errors represent the "noise" term reflecting the other factors (variables) that influence the dependent (outcome) variable and are not accounted in the regression model (Kalaian & Kasim, 2015; Tabachnik & Fidell, 2012).

1. **Assumptions of Multiple Linear Regression:** Like any predictive analytical tool, multiple linear regression analysis is based on specific assumptions about the quantitative data in a Big Data set. Meeting these assumptions is necessary in order to achieve the best estimation of the parameters of the regression model such as the intercept and the multiple slopes, which leads to better fit of the regression model. These assumptions are:
   a. The distribution of the quantitative dependent variable is normal;

    b.   The relationship between the dependent variable and each of the multiple independent (predictor variables is linear;

    c.   The multiple independent (predictor) variables in the regression model are not correlated with each other;

    d.   The errors are not correlated with each of the independent (predictor) variables; and

    e.   The error terms (e_i) of the regression model are independent and identically normally distributed with mean equal to zero and a constant variance.

2.   **Statistical Significance of the Coefficients of the Multiple Regression:** As in simple regression analysis, in multiple-regression analysis, we are also interested in testing whether each of the multiple regression coefficients is statistically significant. A t-test can be used to test whether or not the associated population parameter of each of the multiple regression coefficients, which is adjusted (controlled) for all the other independent (predictor) variables in the regression model, is equal to zero (i.e., H_0: $B_i = 0$). For example, the regression model with two independent variables (e.g., organizational climate and leadership style), the value of the regression coefficient for organizational climate variable is controlled for the leadership style variable. The t-statistic is computed by dividing the each of the multiple estimated regression coefficients, b_i, by the standard error (*S.E.*) of the estimated regression coefficient, b_i. The formula for testing each of the regression coefficients is represented as follows:

$$t = \frac{b_i}{S.E._{(bi)}}$$

With a large sample sizes, which is not a problem with any Big Data set, a t-test value of 2.0 or greater for any of the regression coefficients in the regression model is statistically significant at a significance level of .05. This significant result leads to rejecting the null hypothesis of the specific regression coefficient (i.e., H_0: $B_i = 0$), which is adjusted (controlled) for the other variables included in the regression model. In multiple regression analysis, a significant regression coefficient indicates that the particular independent (predictor) variable has an effect on the dependent (outcome) variable controlling for the effects of the other predictors in the regression model.

Omnibus *F-test* can also be used to test the collective multiple regression coefficients in the regression model. It tests whether or not all of the regression coefficients, B_i, for all of the variables in the regression model are simultaneously equal to zero (i.e., H_0: $B_1 = B_2 = ... = 0$) (Kalaian & Kasim, 2015).

3.   **Predictive Multiple Linear Regression Models:** As in simple linear regression, predictive regression models are used to:

    a.   Predict the values of the dependent variable given known values of the independent (predictor) variables, and

    b.   Evaluate the degree of accuracy in prediction (that is, evaluating the fitting of the regression model to the data) of the unknown numerical values of a dependent variable from multiple known numerical values of the multiple independent variables (Field, 2009; George & Mallery, 2010). The predicted value $(\hat{Y})$ of the dependent variable (Y) in multiple linear regression is represented as follows:

$$\hat{Y}_i = a + b_1 X_{i1} + b_2 X_{i2} + ... + b_k X_{ik}$$

where, "a" is the estimated intercept of the population parameter, α; and b_1, b_2, ..., b_k are the estimated regression coefficients of the regression coefficient parameters, B_1, B_2, ..., B_k for the independent variables X_{i1}, X_{i2}, ..., X_{ik} respectively.

As in simple regression, the accuracy of the predicted values of any Y value can be found by subtracting the predicted value of the dependent variable, $\hat{Y}$, from its corresponding original numerical value of the dependent variable, Y. This difference is called the error of prediction (Y_e) and represented as follows:

$$Y_e = Y - \hat{Y}$$

4. **Evaluating the Adequacy of the Fitted Multiple Regression Model:** Once the regression model is specified and built, it is necessary to evaluate the goodness of fit of the model and test the statistical significance of the estimated regression parameters (Kalaian & Kasim, 2015). As it is presented earlier, a *t-test* is used to test each of the individual parameters of the regression model (the intercept and each of the multiple slopes). *F-statistic* is an omnibus (overall) test, which tests whether or not all of the regression coefficients, B_i for all of the variables in the regression model are simultaneously equal to zero (i.e., H_0: $B_1 = B_2 = ... = 0$). Using t-tests and the F-tests are the initial steps for assessing the significance of each of the individual independent (predictor) variables and the significance of the collective contribution of all the variables in the specified model respectively (Kalaian & Kasim, 2015). Beta weights (standardized regression coefficients) are also used as the initial steps to examine the contribution of each individual independent (predictor) variables to the regression equation. These initial significance tests and contribution assessments are often followed by examining the fit of the regression model to the quantitative Big Data.

    One of the key goals of model fitting in multiple-regression is to examine: (a) The overall contribution of all the independent variables in the regression model; and (b) The differential contribution of each independent variable to the overall fit of the best multiple regression model, while accounting for the contributions of the remaining independent variables in the regression equation. One such measure to examine the overall model fitting and the differential contribution of each of the individual independent variable to the regression model is the *coefficient of determination* (R^2).

    R^2 is a descriptive measure of goodness-of-fit. It is a measure of the proportion of the total variance in the dependent variable (Y) that is accounted for and explained by the linear combination of the multiple independent (predictor) variables in the regression model. The unexplained variance in the dependent variable is assumed to result from other independent variables not included in the model or from random error. R^2 represents the squared correlation between the actual values of the dependent variable (Y) and the linear combination of the predicted values of Y, which is $\hat{Y}$, obtained from the regression equation. Its numeric value ranges from 0 to 1.0 and the closer R^2 statistic is to the value 1.0, the better the fit of the estimated regression line to the data with multiple independent (predictor) variables (Kalaian & Kasim, 2015). A high value of R^2 indicates that the specified regression model with multiple (two or more) independent variables explains the variation in the dependent (outcome) variable well, suggesting that the regression model can be used for predictive purposes (Kalaian & Kasim, 2015).

CONCLUSION

Big Data analytics, which includes descriptive and predictive analytics tools are basic and advanced analytical techniques to assess the variables and explain the relationships or patterns among the variables in the existing (recent and past) data in efforts to predict the future enterprise and organizational performances, risks, trends, and behavior patterns. The uses and applications of Big Data analytics are becoming more common due largely to collecting massive amount of data, which is called "Big Data" and the increased need to transform the large quantities of data into intelligent information and knowledge such as trends, patterns, and relationships that can be used to make smart and informed data-based and analytical-based enterprise and organizational decisions and predictions.

Since Big Data analytics including descriptive and predictive analytics cover a wide-range of basic and advanced analytical techniques, all the analytical methods are impossible to be covered in a single chapter or even a book. Therefore, in this chapter, we chose to cover some of the important descriptive and predictive analytical tools that are most commonly used by data scientists and data analysts across a wide spectrum of disciplines and fields of study to accurately describe, visually represent, and accurately make informed enterprise and organizational performance decisions (e.g., performance growth) and future predictions. Hence, various descriptive analytical tools such as data visualization, measures of central tendency, measures of variability, and measures of relationships were covered in this chapter. Also, the most commonly used predictive analytical tools such as correlations and simple- and multiple-linear regression analyses were covered.

However, it is important to remind the reader that many of the basic and advanced descriptive analytical methods such as boxplots, bar charts, and stem-and-leaf plots are not covered in this chapter. Also, many important advanced predictive analytical methods such as logistic regression, polynomial regression, non-linear regression, discriminant analysis, structural equation modeling, multilevel modeling, and cluster analysis are not covered because comprehensively covering and including most of these descriptive and predictive analytical methods we end up with writing at least a book.

Generally, once the quantitative data is cleaned, conditioned, and structured; it can be analyzed using specific analytical software such as R, Excel, Minitab, SAS, or SPSS. But, all these analytical software packages have limited capacity in terms of the amount of data that can store, process, and analyze. In essence, these analytical software packages are useful for analyzing datasets with limited amount of data, but they may suffer from analytical performance issues with massive amount of data such as Big Data. Therefore, analyzing Big Data can be a big challenge and the massive amount of data needs to be divided into smaller blocks of data in order to use these analytical software packages.

Keep in mind that the ability to design, develop, and implement a Big Data analytical application is dependent on technical knowledge of the architecture of the underlying storage, processing, and computing platforms from both of the hardware and software perspectives (Loshin, 2013). Another option is to use *Apache Mahout* within the *Hadoop ecosystems* and *Graphlab* to analyze Big Data using high-performance platforms. These high-performance platforms are composed of collections of networked computers in which the massive amounts of data, processing, and analyzing can be distributed among a pool of resources (EMC Education Services, 2015).

The descriptive and predictive analytical tools can be used by data analysts and researchers to appropriately analyze their quantitative Big Data sets in order to answer the research questions of their study and draw valid and accurate conclusions. The conceptual overview also provides students, researchers, and analysts with the necessary skills to interpret the business and enterprise reports that employed one or more of the various descriptive and predictive analytics techniques. It is important to keep in mind that not every business and enterprise problem is a Big Data problem, and not every big data analysis and solution is needed and appropriate for all enterprises and organizations (Loshin, 2013).

REFERENCES

Carlberg, C. (2013). *Predictive analytics: Microsoft excel.* Pearson Education, Inc.

EMC Education Services. (2015). *Data Science and Big Data analytics: Discovering, analyzing, visualizing and presenting Data.* Indianapolis, IN: John Wiley & Sons.

Evans, J. R., & Lindner, C. H. (2012). Business Analytics: The Next Frontier for Decision Sciences. *Decision Line, 43*(2).

Felicio, J. A., Couto, E., & Caiado, J. (2014). Human capital, social capital and organizational performance. *Management Decision, 52*(2), 350–364. doi:10.1108/MD-04-2013-0260

Field, A. (2009). *Discovering statistics using SPSS* (3rd ed.). Thousand Oaks, CA: Sage Publications.

George, D., & Mallery, P. (2014). *IBM SPSS statistics 21 step by step: A simple guide and reference* (13th ed.). Boston, MA: Allyn and Bacon.

Hair, J. F. Jr. (2007). Knowledge creation in marketing: The role of predictive analytics. *European Business Review, 19*(4), 303–315. doi:10.1108/09555340710760134

Imran, R., Majeed, M., & Ayub, A. (2015). Impact of organizational justice, job security and job satisfaction on organizational productivity. *Journal of Economics. Business and Management, 3*(9), 840–845. doi:10.7763/JOEBM.2015.V3.295

Kalaian, S. A., & Kasim, R. M. (2015). Predictive analytics. In M. Tavana, S. B. Zhou, & S. K. Puranam (Eds.), *Handbook of research on organizational transformations through big data analytics* (pp. 12–29). Hershey, PA: IGI Global.

Kuhns, M., & Johnson, K. (2013). *Applied predictive modeling.* New York: Springer. doi:10.1007/978-1-4614-6849-3

Lee, M. (2015). Business intelligence, knowledge management, customer relations, and technological support in enterprise competitive competence. In M. Tavana, S. B. Zhou, & S. K. Puranam (Eds.), *Handbook of research on organizational transformations through big data analytics* (pp. 243–262). Hershey, PA: IGI Global.

Loshin, D. (2013). *Big data analytics: From strategic planning to enterprise integration with tools, techniques, NoSQL, and Graph.* Waltham, MA: Elsevier.

Mahmood, M. A., & Mann, G. J. (2005). Information technology investments and organizational productivity and performance: An empirical investigation. *Journal of Organizational Computing and Electronic Commerce, 15*(3), 185–202. doi:10.1207/s15327744joce1503_1

Maisel, L. S., & Cokins, G. (2014). *Predictive business analytics: Forward looking capabilities to improve business performance.* Hoboken, NJ: John Wiley & Sons, Inc.

Mertler, C. A., & Vannatta, R. A. (2013). *Advanced and multivariate statistical methods* (5th ed.). Glendale, CA: Pyrczak Publishing.

Nathans, L. L., Oswald, F. L., & Nimon, K. (2012). Interpreting multiple linear regression: A guidebook of variable importance. *Practical Assessment, Research & Evaluation, 17*(9). Available online http://pareonline.net/getvn.asp?v=17&n=9

Okoye, P. V. C., & Ezejiofor, R. A. (2013). The effect of human resources development on organizational productivity. *International Journal of Academic Research in Business and Social Sciences, 3*(10), 250–268. doi:10.6007/IJARBSS/v3-i10/295

Patterson, M. G., Michael, A., West, M. A., Shackleton, V. J., Dawson, J. F., Lathom, R., & Wallace, A. M. et al. (2005). Validating the organizational climate measure: Links to managerial practices, productivity and innovation. *Journal of Organizational Behavior, 26*(4), 379–408. doi:10.1002/job.312

Provost, F., & Fawcett, T. (2013). *Data Science for Business.* Sebastopol, CA: O'Reilly Media, Inc.

Richard, P. J., Devinney, T. M., Yip, G. S., & Johnson, G. (2009). Measuring organizational performance: Towards methodological best practice. *Journal of Management, 35*(3), 718–804. doi:10.1177/0149206308330560

Siegel, E. (2014). *Predictive Analysis: The power to predict who will click, buy, lie, or die.* Indianapolis, IN: John Wiley & Sons, Inc.

Sprinthall, R. C. (2011). *Basic statistical analysis* (9th ed.). Boston, MA: Allyn & Bacon.

Tabachnick, B. G., & Fidell, L. S. (2012). *Using multivariate statistics* (6th ed.). Pearson Education.

Chapter 6
A Framework to Analyze Enterprise Social Network Data

Janine Viol Hacker
University of Erlangen – Nuremberg, Germany

Freimut Bodendorf
University of Erlangen – Nuremberg, Germany

Pascal Lorenz
University of Haute Alsace, France

ABSTRACT

Enterprise Social Networks have a similar set of functionalities as social networking sites but are run as closed applications within a company's intranet. Interacting and communicating on the Enterprise Social Networks, the users, i.e. a company's employees, leave digital traces. The resulting digital record stored in the platform's back end bears great potential for enterprise big data engineering, analytics, and management. This book chapter provides an overview of research in the area of Enterprise Social Networks and categorizes Enterprise Social Network data based on typical functionalities of these platforms. It introduces exemplary metrics as well as a process for the analysis of ESN data. The resulting framework for the analysis of Enterprise Social Network data can serve as a guideline for researchers in the area of Enterprise Social Network analytics and companies interested in analyzing the data stored in the application's back end.

INTRODUCTION

Companies increasingly use internal social networking services in order to improve knowledge sharing and collaboration among employees. Belonging to the category of Enterprise 2.0 tools (McAfee, 2006b), these so-called Enterprise Social Networks (ESN) are closed applications within a company's intranet that include features such as a profile page, a newsfeed, search options and different communication channels (Koch, Richter, & Schlosser, 2007; Richter, 2010)

DOI: 10.4018/978-1-5225-0293-7.ch006

An extensive body of research deals with the analysis of social media data, e.g. data generated in online social networks, forums, Wikis or blogs. ESN enable a digitization of social relations and communication within the company (Behrendt, Richter, & Trier, 2014). The analysis of ESN data, however, is a new stream in social media research. To date, only few studies deal with the analysis of the big data accumulated in the back end of ESN. Behrendt, Richter & Trier (2014), for instance, identify data dimensions as well as exemplary data collection and data analysis methods used in social media research. Focusing on ESN, Behrendt, Richter, & Riemer (2014) provide starting points for structuring digital traces, i.e. records of user activities. Both articles ground their analysis frameworks in existing studies.

Taking a different approach, it is the aim of this book chapter to show the spectrum of available data dimensions in ESN based on the functionalities of ESN platforms, to derive exemplary metrics based on the available data and to provide ESN data analysts with guidelines for actual data analysis projects. The resulting framework for the analysis of ESN data will support researchers and practitioners interested in e.g. analyzing ESN platform behavior, community health, monitoring adoption processes and identifying social roles or key actors on ESN.

The book chapter starts of providing background information on Enterprise 2.0, ESN and research on ESN. In addition, basics in the area of social network theory and social network analysis are explained. Based on the standard set of ESN functionalities, data dimensions and exemplary metrics are derived. Next, a data analysis process according to the Cross-Industry Standard Process for Data Mining (CRISP-DM) is described for the case of ESN data analysis. Finally, an overview of data analysis features of the three leading ESN platforms IBM Connections, Microsoft Yammer and Jive is provided and set into relation with the previously introduced set of data dimensions and metrics. Directions for future research as well as implications for research and practice conclude the chapter.

BACKGROUND

The following sections give an overview of Enterprise 2.0, the functionalities typically implemented in ESN and discuss directions in ESN research. Moreover, basic information on social networks and social network analysis is provided.

Enterprise 2.0 and Enterprise Social Networks

The term Enterprise 2.0 refers to the "use of emergent social software platforms within companies, or between companies and their partners or customers" (McAfee, 2006a). Adopting principles and technologies of Web 2.0 (Osimo et al., 2010), the focus on user interaction and the collective creation of content by all users instead of individuals.

Social software includes applications such as wikis and group editors, blogs, social bookmarking services and social tagging, SNS and instant messaging services (Koch & Richter, 2009, p. 11). Boyd and Ellison (2007) define SNS as "web-based services that allow individuals to:

1. Construct a public or semi-public profile within a bounded system,
2. Articulate a list of other users with whom they share a connection, and
3. View and traverse their list of connections and those made by others within the system".

Organized around people, SNS are primarily used to create and maintain relationships with other users.

Unlike public and open SNS, ESN are closed applications implemented behind the company's firewall. Yellow pages applications, as e.g. "Blue Pages" in the case of IBM, can be recognized as a very early form of corporate social networking (Koch & Richter, 2009, p. 60). Extending the concept of an employee directory, the application "Fringe" allows users to tag other people's profiles and thus facilitates the collective maintenance of interest and expertise profiles (Farrell, Lau, Nusser, Wilcox, & Muller, 2007). Subsequently, earlier versions of some corporate SNS, e.g. Yammer, showed a lot of similarity to public microblogging services by allowing users to post short updates into a message stream and to follow other users' updates (e.g., Riemer, Diederich, Richter, & Scifleet, 2011). In the following, vendors of corporate SNS extended their platforms by adding collaboration and Web 2.0 features. Being referred to as enterprise social networking applications (Richter & Riemer, 2013), platforms such as Communote, Yammer, and Jive nowadays include document management and social networking, e.g. profile pages, as well as collaboration features.

IBM, Accenture Ltd. and the SAP AG launched their corporate SNS in the years of 2006 and 2007 (Richter & Riemer, 2009) and can be regarded as early adopters of ESN. According to a report by BITKOM (2013) on the use of Enterprise 2.0 applications in 161 German companies in the Internet & Telecommunications sector, 79% of the large companies and 67% of the small and medium sized companies used an ESN in 2013.

As to the employed ESN platforms, a consolidation of the market with a few dominant solutions, i.e. IBM Connections, Jive and Microsoft Office 365, can be observed according to a report by Forrester Research (Koplowitz, 2014). While ESN platforms offered by different vendors have converged in terms of functionality, the platforms still differ regarding their integration possibilities and analytics features (Koplowitz, 2014). Grouped into the categories of ESN functionality as defined by Richter (2010), Table 1 gives an overview of the features generally provided by ESN (Drakos, Mann, & Gotta, 2014; Koplowitz, 2014; Kurzlechner, 2011).

ESN have become a prominent research topic in the field of information systems (Viol & Hess, 2016). In this regard, research on ESN has investigated implementation strategies (Richter, Behrendt, & Koch, 2012; Richter & Stocker, 2011) and adoption mechanisms (Richter & Riemer, 2009; Riemer & Johnston, 2012; Riemer, Overfeld, Scifleet, & Richter, 2012) as well as explored for which purpose and how employees use ESN (DiMicco et al., 2008; Richter & Riemer, 2009; Riemer & Richter, 2012). For instance, Geyer et al. (2008) investigate how people create and reuse shared lists on the ESN Beehive. They find that users socialize more around lists than photos, and use lists as a medium for self-representation. Moreover, DiMicco, Geyer, Millen, Dugan, & Brownholtz (2009) explore how people use ESN to create new and maintain existing relationships and Steinfield, DiMicco, Ellison, & Lampe (2009) show how the use of ESN contributes to social capital formation. Other researchers looked into the potential benefits of organizational social networking from a knowledge management perspective (Riemer & Scifleet, 2012; Schneckenberg, 2009). The MYGROUP system (Atzmueller, 2012, 2014), for instance, aims to enhance interactions and knowledge exchange between the individual team members by localizing members and monitoring their social contacts, by integrating activity streams from different applications as well as through the provision of contact recommendations. More recently, researchers have started to derive metrics to measure the success of ESN implementation (Richter, Heidemann, Klier, & Behrendt,

Table 1. ESN features

ESN Feature	Description	Category of ESN Functionality
User profile	Entering, maintenance and display of personal information (name, contact details, position etc.), e.g. by creating a profile page.	Identity management
Activity stream	Display of updates from colleagues/followed topics, integration of a newsfeed.	Network awareness
Search	Searching the content stored in the ESN, e.g. searching for people or topics.	(Expert) search
Community/group capabilities	Creation and participation in public or restricted groups. Groups may be used to e.g. organize the work of project teams or to discuss topics of interest of a subset of a company's staff. Groups enable discussion threads, content sharing, content storing etc.	Exchange
Discussion threads	Initiation of discussions using status updates in the ESN main stream, participation in discussions by commenting on a user's post.	
Content liking/rating/sharing	Possibility to react on a user's post by using a "Like Button", rating a user's contribution or by sharing a file or post by another user with one's own network.	
Tagging	Mentioning of other users or topics in messages, e.g. comments or status updates.	
Bookmarks	Saving, organizing and sharing of bookmarked content, e.g. conversations or (external) websites.	
File sharing	Uploading and sharing of files such as reports.	
Blog	Creation of a blog to share or store knowledge, e.g. to keep everyone informed within a project group.	
Wiki	Use of a Wiki to collaboratively author content together with other users or to store knowledge such as meeting protocols.	
Social analytics	Provision of recommendations of colleagues a user may want to add to their network, e.g. users with similar interests.	Context awareness
Export possibilities	Possibility to export data stored in the back end of the ESN.	Supporting features
Integration possibilities	Integration with other enterprise applications, provision of interfaces.	

2013). In this regard, Muller, Freyne, Dugan, Millen, & Thom-Santelli (2009) propose a measurement concept called *Return on Contribution* to determine the value of enterprise social media applications. As to ESN data analytics, Perer, Guy, Uziel, Ronen, & Jacovi (2011) developed an application supporting relationship discovery in ESN. While Trier & Richter (2015) develop a theoretical framework to assess the deep structure of social networking which they apply in a qualitative case analysis, Behrendt, Richter, & Trier (2014) derive data dimensions in ESN research and discuss the application of a mixed methods approach in this context. Furthermore, Berger, Klier, Klier, & Richter (2014) investigate the structural characteristics of value adding users in ESN using qualitative text analysis and Social Network Analysis (SNA). Finally, Behrendt, Richter, & Riemer (2014) introduce dimensions for structuring digital traces, i.e. records of user activities, in order to identify informal networks.

A comprehensive framework and guidelines for the analysis of ESN data are not provided in the existing literature. The growing interest in ESN data analytics points to the relevance and need for such as framework. It is the aim of this book chapter to address this gap.

Figure 1. Different types of social networks

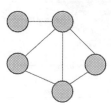 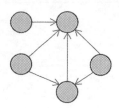 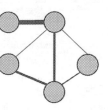 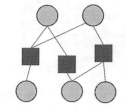

| Undirected, unweighted, one-mode social network | Directed social network | Weighted social network | Two-mode social network |

Social Networks and Social Network Analysis

A social network "consists of a finite set or sets of actors and the relation or relations defined on them" (Wasserman & Faust, 1994, p. 20). Nodes, i.e. actors, are described as social entities, e.g. individual, corporate, or collective social units. The transfer of immaterial or material resources, such as information and knowledge between them happens along relational ties (called edges). Social networks are characterized by the following attributes:

- **Directed and Undirected Social Network Graphs:** In a directed network (Wasserman & Faust, 1994, pp. 140), actors are connected with arrows. An arrow pointing from actor A to actor B could mean that actor A asked actor B for advice, for instance. Undirected relationships between actors, e.g. employees, are shown as lines without arrows. A connection between actor and actor B means that they are associated, e.g. by working in the same department.
- **Weighted and Unweighted Social Network Graphs:** In a weighted graph (Wasserman & Faust, 1994, pp. 140), the edge between actors are valued. Closely related to the concept of tie strength (Granovetter, 1973), the thickness of an edge in a valued graph often corresponds to the strength of a relationship between two actors. For instance, in a graph showing communication between employees, the line between two actors will be thicker the more often they talk to each other. Unweighted graphs, on the other hand, simply show connections between people without an indication of tie strength.
- **One-Mode and Two-Mode Networks:** A one-mode network (Wasserman & Faust, 1994, pp. 249) contains one set of actors, for instance, the relations between employees of a company. A two-mode network includes two sets of entities, e.g. showing connections between persons and events.

Figure 1 shows the different types of networks. It is possible to combine the different characteristics of social network graphs. For instance, networks can be directed and weighted or undirected and unweighted. Social network analysis (SNA) offers measures to characterize entire networks and individuals (Freeman, 1978; Wasserman & Faust, 1994) .

Networks and network analysis have been important topics in organizational science and management research. Organizational science researchers have sought to detect informal relationships in companies and investigated coordination and communication mechanisms, for instance (Raab, 2010). Management researchers have considered organizational and leadership questions from a network perspective

(Wald, 2010). Most commonly, the collection of network data in these studies was based on interviews, questionnaires and observation. More recently, researchers started to use email logs (e.g. Hansen, Shneiderman, & Smith, 2010) and sensor data (Fischbach, Schoder, & Gloor, 2008) to construct datasets to study organizational networks.

POSSIBLE DATA ANALYSIS DIMENSIONS AND METRICS

Having introduced the typical set of ESN functionalities in the last sections, the following paragraphs give an overview of relevant data dimensions, the accumulated ESN data, and develop exemplary metrics.

Data Dimensions

Two recent publications provide starting points for the structuring of ESN data. Behrendt, Richter, & Trier (2014) develop a data category framework including the data dimensions *activities*, *content*, *relations* and *experiences*. In this regard, *activities* refers to usage data, *content* describes different kinds of

Figure 2. Actors and actions in ESN

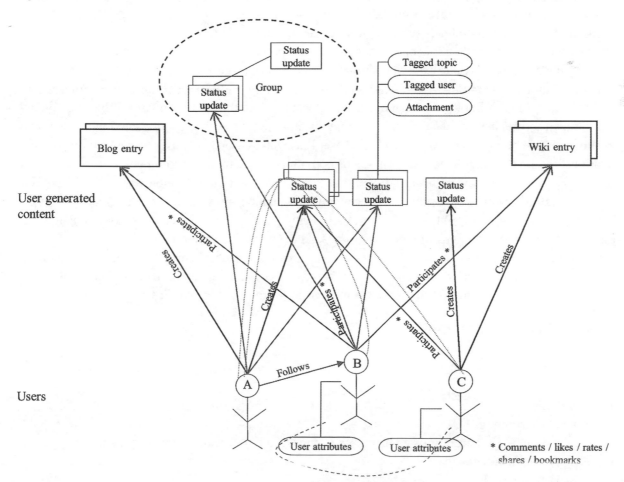

user-generated data, *relations* refers to the structural data based on different kinds of relationships and the category *experiences* describes information reported by the users of the ESN. For each category, they name exemplary data collection methods, e.g. log files or structured content export, as well as exemplary data analysis methods, e.g. web analytics or text mining. Behrendt, Richter, & Riemer (2014) structure ESN data along the dimensions *Who*, *How*, *When*, *Where*, *What* and *Whom*. While the dimension *Who* describes the ESN user, the dimensions *How*, *When* and *Where* are based on records of user activity. *What* describes the different types of user-generated content and *Whom* refers to different types of direct and indirect social relations emerging on the platform. Both studies based their category frameworks on existing work.

Taking a different approach, this book chapter derives relevant data dimensions based on functionalities of ESN platforms. Figure 2 provides an overview of ESN actors and typical actions.

The two main entities on an ESN platform are the ESN users and the content they create. At a basic level, an individual user is characterized by the information displayed on their profile page. The content generated by users can take different forms, i.e. users can create status updates, blog entries and wiki entries. These may include a tagged topic, a tagged user or an attachment such as a file or link. Users can generate content on the platform's main stream or in subcommunities, such as public or private groups. Besides initiating content, e.g. by creating a status update, users can contribute to the content created by other users. Commenting on a status update or blog entry as well as editing a Wiki entry can be regarded as a direct contribution on the content created by another user. Activities such as liking, rating, sharing or bookmarking content by other users can be subsumed as content processing.

Relationships, i.e. social network ties, between users can be distinguished into explicit and implicit connections. In this regard, following another user, i.e. the connection between user A and user B in Figure 2, is the most direct form of an explicit relationship comparable to a friendship declaration on Facebook. Other explicit ties emerge through the content users interact on. Activities such as commenting on, liking, rating, sharing or bookmarking another user's post result in this kind of relationship. Even though users may not (yet) have declared a follower relationship, they have directly interacted with each other as shown by the blue lines between user A and user B as well as user A and user B respectively. Implicit relationships, on the other hand, can be based on common user attributes or common usage patterns. For instance, people who show high similarity in their profile data or have overlapping sets of colleagues or group membership could be assumed to have an implicit relationship as shown by the green dashed line between user A and user C in Figure 2. Also, participation in the same threads or creation of content on the same topic (without interacting directly) may lead to an implicit relationship.

Considering the content of messages, relationships can emerge between posts created on the ESN, too. For instance, messages containing the same topic tags or a frequent combination of particular topic tags could point to a connection between the messages and the discussed topics respectively.

Accumulated ESN Data

Generally, the data accumulated in the back end of ESN platforms can be distinguished into

- User data,
- Data describing groups, blogs or wikis,
- Data about the messages posted on the main stream, within groups, blogs or wikis,
- Data on attachments and
- Data on topics tagged in messages.

Table 2. ESN data categories and exemplary data points

Data Category	Exemplary Data Points
User data	<ul><li>ID</li><li>Name</li><li>Job title</li><li>Department</li><li>Location</li><li>Address</li><li>Report-to chain</li><li>Skills</li><li>Interests</li><li>Follower relationships</li><li>Date of joining/quitting</li></ul>
Group/blog/wiki data	<ul><li>ID</li><li>Name</li><li>Description</li><li>Creator ID</li><li>Access options/rights management</li><li>Date of creation/deletion</li></ul>
Messages data	<ul><li>ID</li><li>ID of the thread/group/blog/wiki the message belongs to</li><li>Author information</li><li>Message content</li><li>Date of creation/deletion</li></ul>
Attachment data	<ul><li>ID</li><li>Name</li><li>Description</li><li>Uploader information</li><li>ID of the thread/group/blog/wiki the file was uploaded to</li><li>Date of upload/deletion</li></ul>
Topic tag data	<ul><li>ID</li><li>Name</li><li>Creator information</li><li>Date of creation/deletion</li></ul>

Depending on the ESN platform design, the data points within these categories may vary. Table 2 provides an overview of the data that is available according to the common ESN features (see Table 1).

Exemplary Metrics

The data accumulated in the ESN back end enables the calculation of metrics describing the overall activity on the platform, individual metrics for each user in terms of their platform engagement as well as the characterization of substructures, e.g. groups. Table 3 provides an overview of exemplary metrics at the different levels of analysis.

Similar metrics can be created to characterize activities with regard to other platform elements, e.g. wikis or blogs. To be able to better understand and compare different metrics, average values and standard deviations should be calculated for each metric. Depending on the focus of the analysis, more detailed metrics, e.g. *average length of a discussion in the top ten groups*, or ratios, e.g. *# first messages/# comments* can be implemented. Moreover, the metrics can be calculated for different periods of time, e.g. in 3 month intervals, to enable trend analysis.

Table 3. Exemplary metrics according to different levels of analysis

Level of Analysis	Metric	Description
Overall	# users	Number of users
	# active users	Number of users who have posted at least one piece of content (e.g. a status update, a comment etc.) within a defined period of time
	# messages	Number of messages posted (includes first messages and replies)
	# groups	Number of groups
	# messages in groups	Number of messages posted in groups
	# blogs	Number of blogs
	# blog posts	Number of posts across all blogs
	# wikis	Number of wikis
	# wiki entries	Number of entries across all wikis
Activities by users	# messages created by a user	Number of messages created by a user
	# status updates created by a user	Number of status updates (first messages) created by a user
	# comments created by a user	Number of comments created by a user
	# conversations initiated by a user	Number of status updates (first messages) of a user that received at least one comment
	# groups started by a user	Number of groups started by a user
	# groups contributed to by a user	Number of (unique) groups a user has contributed to
	# blog posts created by a user	Number of blog posts created by a user
	# wiki entries created by a user	Number of wiki entries created by a user
	# attachments posted by a user	Number of attachments posted by a user
	# (unique) topic tags used by a user	Number of unique topic tags used in posts by a user
	# comments received by a user	Number of comments/replies received by a user
	Avg # words/characters per message created by a user	Average number of words/characters per message created by a user
Activities in a group	# contributors per group	Number of contributors in a group
	# messages per group	Number of messages (includes first messages and replies) posted in a group
	# status updates per group	Number of status updates (first messages) posted in a group
	# comments per group	Number of comments on status updates posted in a group
	# conversations	Number of status updates (first messages) in a group that received at least one comment
	# attachments per group	Number of attachments posted in a group

Beyond the metrics listed in Table 3, the calculation of social network metrics and visualization of social network graphs are powerful tools to better understand platform engagement. In this regard, the available data bears many options to conceptualize the edges of the social network graph (cf. Behrendt, Richter, & Riemer, 2014). Table 4 shows exemplary types relationships than can be found in ESN and gives information on the characteristics of the respective social network graphs.

Table 4. Identifiable types of relationships on ESN

Type of Relationship	Description	Social Network Characteristics
Following	Edges between users are based on following another user's updates.	One mode, directed, unweighted
Comments	Edges between users are based on who comments on whose messages.	One mode, directed, weighted
Common conversation participation	Edges between users are based on the common participation in conversations (e.g. threads or discussions).	One mode, undirected, weighted
Users and topic tags	Edges between users and topics occur if users create or use a topic tag.	Two mode, undirected, weighted
User tags	Edges between users are based on who tags whom in a post.	One mode, directed, weighted
Questions	Edges between users indicate that a user asks another user a question.	One mode, directed, weighted

Using a social network analysis tool, it is possible to calculate social network metrics, such as the degree centrality, betweenness centrality or closeness centrality of individual actors, for the different networks. Again, average values and standard deviations should be calculated to have a reference for individual values.

DATA ANALYSIS PROCESS

Having determined possible ESN data dimensions and metrics, following a data mining process is suggested to structure the steps of the ESN data analysis. In this regard, the Cross-Industry Standard Process for Data Mining (CRISP-DM) is one commonly employed process (Chapman et al., 2000). The CRISP-DM reference model consists of six phases representing a cyclical process (*Figure 3*). The six phases are defined as:

1. **Business Understanding:** The first step involves the definition of the business objectives, the assessment of the situation in terms of resources as well as the determination of the data mining goals. This knowledge is then documented in a project plan.
2. **Data Understanding:** Within the second phase, an initial set of data is collected. The analysts familiarize themselves with the data by describing and exploring it. These activities are important to gain first insights into the data and to figure out data quality problems.
3. **Data Preparation:** The third phase results in the construction of a final dataset. Prior to that, the data may need to be cleaned, transformed or reformatted to be compatible with a modeling tool.
4. **Modeling:** The fourth phase involves the selection of a modeling technique, e.g. a cluster analysis or the development of association rules. The selection is followed by generating a test design, building the model and assessing the model.

Figure 3. CRISP-DM reference model
Adapted from Chapman et al. (2000, p. 10).

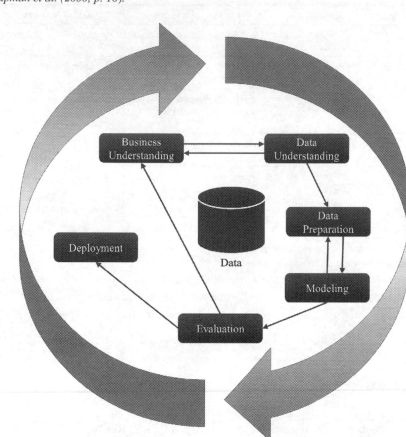

5. **Evaluation:** Within the fifth phase, the quality of the built model is assessed in terms of the business objectives set in the first phase. The steps to create the model are reviewed and amended, if necessary.
6. **Deployment:** The final phase involves the creation of a deployment plan as well a plan for the monitoring and maintenance. A final report is generated for documentation purposes.

The following paragraphs discuss the process of analyzing ESN data according to the phases of the CRISP-DM reference model (Chapman et al., 2000).

Business Understanding

Within the first phase, the data analyst needs to collect background information on the company, i.e. the customer, whose ESN dataset is to be analyzed in the subsequent steps (Chapman et al., 2000). This is particularly important if the data analyst is not employed by the company but acts as an external consultant. Besides doing general research on the company, the following questions should be addressed within interviews or a workshop:

- What are the business objectives that the company wants to achieve based on the results of the ESN data analysis?
- What are secondary questions that the company would like to address?
- Are they conflicts between the objectives of the customer?
- What outcome of the project is successful from a business point of view?

It is the task of the data analyst to elicit the customer requirements in this step. Moreover, it is important for the data analyst to get a better understanding of the ESN and its use in the organization. For instance, the data analyst should find out since when the ESN has been used, who initiated the roll-out as well as how and for what purpose it is used in general. This background knowledge is important to better understand and interpret the results of the subsequent analysis.

Besides the determination of the business objectives, the required resources in terms of personnel, data, computing resources and software need to be defined (Chapman et al., 2000). As a business objective, a company might want to *increase the success of project work*. To do the analyses regarding this business objective, it would be necessary to collect both ESN data and project related data. As to software, a data mining tool, such as RapidMiner (RapidMiner Inc., 2015), as well as a Social Network Analysis tool, e.g. UCINET (Borgatti, Everett, & Freeman, 2002) or Gephi (Bastian, Heymann, & Jacomy, 2009) would be required. Moreover, possible constraints and risks, e.g. privacy concerns, of the analysis need to be considered.

Next, the data mining goals are to be determined. Using the above example, a possible data mining goal is "Predict the success of a project based on the communication data accumulated on the ESN" with a certain level of predictive accuracy. The findings of the first phase should be documented in a project plan.

Data Understanding

The second phase involves the collection and description (Chapman et al., 2000) of a first ESN dataset. To better understand the data at hand, some basic metrics, e.g. the metrics listed in the category *overall* in Table 3 should be calculated. Depending on the format of collected ESN data, it can be imported and processed in a spreadsheet software or database. Basic metrics and statistics can then be calculated using Pivot tables or SQL statements. For instance, one may want to compare the *number of registered users* with the *number of active users* to get an idea of the actual adoption of the ESN. Other descriptive statistics such as the *number of new users over time*, the *number of posts per department* or *location* as well as the identification of peaks in the volume of posts lead to first insights into the dataset and point to subsets of the data that could be particularly interesting. Moreover, the data analyst should carefully examine the quality of the dataset to identify missing or irregular values.

Data Preparation

Based on the findings of the previous phase, a suitable subset of the collected ESN data is selected (Chapman et al., 2000). Referring back to the above example (see Business Understanding), this subset could concern data on groups on the ESN dedicated to specific projects within a period of one year. Next, this subset is cleaned (Chapman et al., 2000) which may include the inserting of default values or the deletion of implausible records. Moreover, values such as dates or textual values might have to be converted and reformatted, e.g. from a data type feasible for spreadsheets into one that can be processed in a database.

Based on this cleaned ESN raw data, the dataset to be used in the modeling phase is constructed. This step involves the implementation and calculation of metrics comparable to those listed in Table 3. As to the example, it would be necessary to develop and implement customized metrics characterizing the communication behavior at the level of the individual user and at the group level. As in the previous step, the metrics can be calculated using a spreadsheet tool or SQL statements when using a database. The calculation of SNA metrics is done using the aforementioned tools. Finally, the different metrics describing the same object, i.e. an individual ESN user, need to be merged in one table. Due to integrating values from multiple sources and tools, it may again be necessary to reformat the metrics for the processing in a data mining software in the next phase.

Modeling

The selection of a modeling technique is the first step within the modeling phase (Chapman et al., 2000). Regarding the above example, one could use a decision tree data mining model to predict project success. Hence, the calculated metrics would serve as attributes while a measure of project success would be the target value. Having decided for a modeling technique, it is necessary to generate a test design in order to evaluate the model's quality and validity. As to decision tree learning, the dataset will be split into a train and test set with the model being built on the train set and the model's quality be assessed on the test set (Han, Kamber, & Pei, 2012). The model is then run and assessed by the data analyst. The assessment is done based on the previously defined success criteria and focuses on the technical aspects. If several models have been created, the data analyst will compare and rank them according to the evaluation criteria. The analyst may also rerun the model using revised parameter settings.

Evaluation

While the assessment in the previous phase focused on technical aspects (Chapman et al., 2000), the evaluation of the data mining project in this phase also considers the business objectives defined in phase 1 (see Business Understanding). The data mining results are assessed and the models meeting the business objectives become approved models. Moreover, the data mining process as such and findings that are not closely related to the business objectives are reviewed. At this point, it may be necessary to go back to the previous phase to e.g. start another iteration of the modeling. If the results of the data mining project are satisfactory, the project can enter the deployment phase.

Deployment

The last phase includes the creation of a deployment strategy as well as a monitoring and maintenance plan (Chapman et al., 2000). In this regard, the use of the data mining results within the day-to-business should be planned, for instance, how and to what extent the results can inform management decisions. It should also be planned if and when the models are to be revised or run again. As to the above example, the metrics and hence the model could be extended if a new version of the employed ESN platform is released. The monitoring and maintenance plan should summarize the steps to be taken if that occurs. The deployment phase also includes the creation of a final report and the documentation of experience, i.e. what went right or wrong.

DATA ANALYTICS FEATURES PROVIDED BY SELECTED ESN PLATFORMS

Having given an overview of relevant ESN data dimensions and introduced the process of analyzing ESN data, the subsequent paragraphs discuss data analysis features provided by selected ESN platforms. The platforms, i.e. *IBM Connections*, *Yammer* and *Jive*, are included in reports of the technology and market research companies Gartner and Forrester Research. Both Gartner's report *Magic Quadrant for Social Software in the Workplace* (Drakos et al., 2014) and *The Forrester Wave* (Koplowitz, 2014) classify the selected platforms as leading solutions on the enterprise social platform market.

IBM Connections

IBM first released an application especially designed for social business in June 2007. This platform was extended step-by-step in the following years by adding new functionalities. As of August 2014, IBM Connections was ranked number one in worldwide market share for enterprise social software for the fifth consecutive year (IBM, 2014). Moreover, IBM Connections has been recognized as a *Leader* for the seventh consecutive year in the Gartner Magic Quadrant for Social Software in the Workplace (Gotta, Drakos, & Mann, 2015).

The current version 5.0 of the platform includes a homepage, profiles, communities, blogs and micro-blogs, bookmarks, mail, a task management system (activities), wikis, file sharing and document management, forums, social analytics, polls and survey and document collaboration (McIntyre, 2014). Users can easily customize the platform's frontend by using built-in widgets or creating custom widgets. IBM Connections also provides a mobile application and enables the communication with external partners. The platform is well integrated with other IBM products and allows for combinations with third party products, too.

According to a survey on the use and adoption of IBM Connections among end-user organizations around the world (Sampson, 2014), the platform is highly used for "social" activities such as distributing team and organizational updates, building knowledge together as well as sharing and learning best practice. Longer-term customers increasingly use IBM Connections to find expertise, too.

As to analytics features, IBM Connections provides social analytics information that helps users to grow their network. New contacts can be discovered through the "Do You Know", the "Things in Common" and "Who Connects Us" widgets (Ambler et al., 2014).

For administrators and designated users, IBM Connections provides tools for viewing global and community metrics (Kuang & Zhi Gang, 2012). These metrics are collected and maintained by the application IBM Cognos Business Intelligence which also enables the generation of reports that can directly be viewed in IBM Connections.

The global metrics inform about overall platform usage and can be seen by administrators and users who have been granted access by the administrator. Community metrics inform about the activity of a particular community and can be viewed by community owners and designated users.

Global metrics and community metrics are run within the following themes (Kuang & Zhi Gang, 2012):

- **People:** Metrics in this category report on the people who visit IBM Connections (Kuang & Zhi Gang, 2012). Exemplary metrics include *Number of unique authenticated visitors* and *People with the most new followers*. It is possible to calculate these metrics for individual applications, e.g. Wikis, as well as to compare activity across different applications. The metrics can be visualized using different types of diagrams, e.g. in trend charts or pie charts.

- **Participation:** The participation theme tracks actions in IBM Connections, such as uploading files or posting a status update (Kuang & Zhi Gang, 2012). It runs reports for all components of IBM Connections regarding the *number of visits, number of unique contributors, number of new status updates* and *number of new updates*. An exemplary metric is the *number of new files* report for the files application.
- **Content:** The content theme considers information shared on IBM Connections (Kuang & Zhi Gang, 2012), e.g. using comments or files. Within this theme, a *most followed content* report and a *most active apps* report can be run. The "most followed content" report shows the top 10 followed content items in a list, including e.g. the most followed wiki entry and forum entry. The "most active apps" report ranks the components of IBM Connections, e.g. communities, files, and bookmarks, by usage, i.e. based on visits, postings, and updates.

Additionally, it is possible to run individual reports for each of the global apps in IBM Connections, i.e. activities, blogs, bookmarks, communities, files, forums and wikis. With regard to blogs, for instance, the available metrics include *most active blogs*, the *number of new blogs*, the *number of new entries*, *the number of new entry comments*, the *number of unique authenticated visitors* as well as the *number of visits* (Kuang & Zhi Gang, 2012). Hence, the metrics allow for the identification of the most active content.

When working with reports, users can select the metrics to be displayed and set the date range of a report. IBM Connections also enables the grouping of reports by user by selecting a category, e.g. focusing on a geographical area or certain roles. It is possible to switch between different types of views, e.g. table format and chart format, as well as to drill up and drill down on the data (Kuang & Zhi Gang, 2012).

Microsoft Yammer

Launched in 2008, Yammer includes profiles, a news stream, collaborative work spaces, different means to connect with and communicate with other users, e.g. by sharing updates in the main stream or by sending private messages to other users. Moreover, Yammer provides search functionalities, possibilities to share content and to collaborate on documents with other users (Yammer, 2015). Also, users can recognize the work of others by praising them. People can join Yammer using their work email address. Networks on Yammer then emerge based on a common domain name. Yammer was acquired by Microsoft in 2012 and is now becoming the "social layer" across other Microsoft products (Drakos et al., 2014), e.g. Skype.

As to analytics, Yammer provides leaderboards that allow users to identify important colleagues in their network. Leaderboards show people with the most messages, replied-to messages, and liked messages (Yammer, 2015).

For administrators, Yammer offers more advanced analytics features (Microsoft, 2015):

- **Network Analytics:** Provides usage metrics and member statistics and helps administrators to better understand how employees are using the ESN. It reports on the overall activity on the network, member engagement, the number of messages, groups and top 5 groups, the number of uploaded files and file views as well as on the creation and views of notes (Ross, 2014).
- **Data Export:** Enables administrators to export all messages, notes, files, topics, users, and groups in separate .csv files or a .zip file containing all data using the data export API. Information on mentions, i.e. who tags whom, following and sharing are currently not included. The .csv files can be used to run metrics and generate reports.

Beyond Microsoft Yammer's internal analytics features, external vendors, e.g. GoodData, enable the creation of Yammer Analytics Dashboards. These include information on the overall employee engagement, community management and usage, enable the identification of influencers and champions and provide employee morale and sentiment analysis (GoodData Corporation, 2015).

Jive

Jive was first launched as Clearspace in 2006 and provides a wide range of social and collaboration capabilities. These include people profiles displaying a user's contact information as well as information on skills, recognition, activity and endorsements (Jive Software, 2015c). Jive further includes advanced search features, group capabilities, and discussion spaces that enable users to ask questions and brainstorm ideas, for instance. Jive enables collaborative work on documents, spreadsheets and slide decks. The blogs applications allows users to inform their co-workers and to share ideas. Activity streams can be used to keep up to date with what is happening in the organization. Users can customize activity streams according to their interests and needs.

Jive facilitates different possibilities to create, rate, like or mark content as well as the participation in discussions. Moreover, users can earn points for contributions or give role badges to other users. Jive provides the following analytics features (Jive Software, 2015a, 2015b, 2015c):

- **Impact Metrics:** Allow individual users to better understand how others engage with their content (Jive Software, 2015a). The different metrics, i.e. *impact*, *global reach*, *sentiment*, and *email*, are available for different content types, such as blog posts, discussions and documents. While *impact* provides information as to how others react to the content posted by a user considering their social actions, e.g. bookmarks, comments, and shares, *global reach* indicates how widely a user's content is viewed in the community. *Sentiment* conveys how well a user's content resonates with the community and *email* indicates how many users receive notifications when a particular user updates the content.
- **Community Manager Reports:** Offer user, content, group and space leaderboards and participation trends (Jive Software, 2015b). There are two types of reports: While global reports show data for the entire community, it is also possible to create reports for particular groups and spaces. Global reports can be created to assess *community health, profile completion, and user-to-user interactions*. The community health report, for instance, includes metrics such as *active users*, *new registrations*, and *number of content items created*, *number of comments and replies given*, *number of likes*, *number of views given to content*, and *number of correct answers* provided within the report time. Global reports are also available *for views of answered questions*, *correct and helpful events*, and the *top successful search queries*, for instance. As to reports for particular groups and spaces, Jive offers e.g. reports on *content creation*, *answered questions*, *daily activity*, and *user* as well as *content leaderboards*.

Comparison of the Data Analytics Features and Application

Each of the three leading ESN platforms offers a set of analytics features that provide insights for different types of platform users. While IBM Connections and Yammer include features reinforcing network and context awareness based on social analytics features and leaderboards, Jive offers better insights in terms of how other users engage with the content posted by someone via the impact metrics and news stream analytics. Hence, the users' ability to understand and reinforce their reputation and popularity is improved. Beyond the reports for platform users, the three introduced platforms offer a considerable amount of metrics and reports accessible to platform administrators. In this regard, IBM Connections seems to provide the biggest number of metrics characterizing user behavior in general, participation and content. Yammer offers basic usage metrics and member statistics. Jive offers detailed reports for community managers and is particularly strong in analyzing usage data generated in Q&A forums.

The analytics features included in three platforms enable answering questions like "Who are the platform's top users in terms of created messages?" or "Which groups are particularly popular?" using leaderboards and dashboards. However, it is up to the community manager to interpret and make sense of this data. While community managers can customize the reports to some extent, e.g. by filtering for specific applications and periods of time, it does not seem possible to create particular ratios and calculate metrics for individual users, such as *number of threads initiated/number of all threads* in a certain period of time.

ESN data analysts can take the analyses further by exporting the accumulated data and using it to implement customized metrics. Since IBM Connections and Jive are installed, run and administered within a company's IT architecture, it is possible to export the platform data by backing up the content stored in the according databases. Yammer data can be exported by administrators using the data export API. Having this data, ESN data analysts are able to run analyses as described above, e.g. develop a predictive model of team success.

ESN data analytics bears great potential to usefully inform organizational decision-making and thus, to better meet business goals. Exemplary objectives of introducing ESN are to improve *knowledge transfer*, to *support networks of experts*, to *improve employee communication*, to create more *transparency* as to what is happening in an organization, as well as to *support innovation management* (Richter, Stocker, Müller, & Avram 2011). The related business objectives are to e.g. reduce the time and thus cost to identify experts in an organization as well as to increase the number of innovative ideas. As to the objectives of introducing ESN, the following exemplary reports and metrics can be derived:

- **Assess Knowledge Transfer across Function of the Organization:** The metrics and reports implemented in Jive provide information as to the number of correct answers given and views of answered questions given, and thus, indicate instances of (successful) knowledge transfer in the organization.
- **Identify and Support Experts:** The people theme in IBM Connections and the leaderboards implemented in Yammer determine the number of messages and followers for individual users. Metrics in this category are helpful to identify key users who may have certain expert knowledge. Networks of experts can further be supported through social analytics features, i.e. by recommending contacts with specific expertise to the platform users.
- **Understand What Is Happening in the Organization:** The content theme implemented in IBM Connections can be used to identify the most followed content in different areas, such as forum or wiki entries. On the other hand, the community health report implemented in Jive includes information as to how often a piece of content has been liked or viewed. These reports help community managers to identify important topics in the organization.

The existing reports facilitate valuable insights into the ESN user activity. However, to provide comprehensive insights, the findings from ESN data analytics need to be combined with other internally available reports. For instance, to find out whether employee-to-employee communication has improved, one would need to consider the traffic on the ESN as well as the development of the number of sent emails in the last months.

FUTURE RESEARCH DIRECTIONS

Using an ESN, employees leave digital traces that are stored in the back end of these platforms. These digital traces include quantitative data, such as log data and interaction data, as well as qualitative data, e.g. the content of messages posted on the platform (Behrendt, Richter, & Trier, 2014). Taken together, employee interactions result in the generation of rich data that bears great potential as well as challenges for enterprise big data engineering, analytics, and management.

ESN are still a recent phenomenon and data analytics are an emerging trend within the field of ESN research. In this regard, this book chapter offers a state-of-the-art analysis as well as a framework for the analysis of ESN data. A number of future research directions within the domain of ESN data analytics can be suggested:

1. **Use Cases:** Which questions for the analysis of ESN data are interesting from a research and practice point of view? Existing studies have sought to identify valuable staff, measure the success of ESN and performed relationship discovery based on ESN data. To broaden the scope of ESN data analytics, basic research could collect potential use cases and research questions and assess their relevance and feasibility for research and practice. This is of particular relevance as to the business objectives that should be satisfied using ESN.
2. **Metrics and Tie Design:** The metrics developed in this book chapter only represent a segment of the metrics that are possible. In combination with the previous point, it would be interesting to come up with metrics and combinations of metrics to address specific use cases. In this regard, tie design for social network analysis, i.e. the different types of relationships that can be constructed based on the data, is a relevant topic on its own. Also, it is necessary to find reduced sets of metrics that are especially helpful to address a number of use cases in order to make the data analysis process more efficient.
3. **Tool Support for the Data Analysis Process:** As to the actual data analysis, tools and combinations of tools that support the different steps of the data analysis process best should be identified. This also includes the development of recommendations (or tool support) regarding the import and export of data from one tool, e.g. an SNA tool, to another one, such as a data mining tool, as these steps are particularly error-prone.
4. **Ethics:** As for other means of monitoring the actions of employees, it is important to assess to what extent collecting and analyzing ESN data is ethical and conform to legal and company specific requirements. Privacy concerns of employees should be addressed very carefully. Finding a suitable way to communicate a planned ESN data analysis project seems important since this could significantly affect employee engagement on the platform.

CONCLUSION

With the advent of ESN in companies, the data accumulated in the back end of these applications is a promising for research in the field of enterprise big data engineering, analytics, and management. This book chapter provided an overview of Enterprise 2.0 and research in the area of ESN in particular. Based on the typical set of ESN functionalities, data dimensions were derived and different metrics developed accordingly. Moreover, a standard data mining process was adapted for the use case of analyzing ESN data. Finally, the data analytics features of leading ESN platforms were introduced and discussed in terms of the previously identified data analysis dimensions and the data analysis process.

For researchers in the area of ESN analytics, the book chapter provides a framework and guideline for the analysis of ESN data. Moreover, it points to a number of directions for future research in the context of ESN.

As to practitioners, many companies are about to introduce ESN and are interested in getting a better understanding of what is happening on the platforms. The book chapter provides starting points on how to make use of the data accumulated in the back end of ESN. For instance, companies could create success measures based on the derived metrics, monitor the process of adoption or investigate community health. Moreover, the book chapter can help improve existing dashboard functionalities of ESN solutions by informing the design of applications and plug-ins focusing on the analysis of ESN data.

REFERENCES

Ambler, H., Nichols, A., Slavens, B., Benitez, L., Schimmer, R., & Livingston, S. (2014). *IBM Connections 5.0 Reviewer's Guide.* Retrieved April 27, 2015, from http://public.dhe.ibm.com/software/dw/lotus/connections/connections5/connections5reviewersguide.pdf

Atzmueller, M. (2012). Mining social media: Key players, sentiments, and communities. *Wiley Interdisciplinary Reviews: Data Mining and Knowledge Discovery, 2*(5), 411–419.

Atzmueller, M. (2014). Data Mining on Social Interaction Networks. *Journal of Data Mining & Digital Humanities.*

Bastian, M., Heymann, S., & Jacomy, M. (2009). Gephi: an open source software for exploring and manipulating networks. In *Proceedings of the Third International Conference on Weblogs and Social Media (ICWSM 2009).* San Jose, CA: The AAAI Press.

Behrendt, S., Richter, A., & Riemer, K. (2014). Conceptualisation of Digital Traces for the Identification of Informal Networks in Enterprise Social Networks. In *ACIS 2014 Proceedings.* Auckland: AIS.

Behrendt, S., Richter, A., & Trier, M. (2014). Mixed methods analysis of enterprise social networks. *Computer Networks, 75*(Part B), 560–577.

Berger, K., Klier, J., Klier, M., & Richter, A. (2014). "who is Key...?" - Characterizing Value Adding Users in Enterprise Social Networks. In M. Avital, J. M. Leimeister, & U. Schultze (Eds.), *22st European Conference on Information Systems.* Tel Aviv: AIS.

BITKOM. (2013). *Einsatz und Potenziale von Social Business für ITK-Unternehmen*. Retrieved April 29, 2015, from http://www.bitkom.org/files/documents/Studie_SocialBusiness_Potenziale.pdf

Borgatti, S. P., Everett, M. G., & Freeman, L. C. (2002). *UCINET 6 for Windows: Software for Social Network Analysis*. Analytic Technologies.

Boyd, d. m., & Ellison, N. (2007). Social Network Sites: Definition, History, and Scholarship. *Journal of Computer-Mediated Communication, 13*(1), 210–230.

Chapman, P., Clinton, J., Kerber, R., Khabaza, T., Reinartz, T., Shearer, C., & Wirth, R. (2000). *CRISP-DM 1.0: Step-by-step data mining guide*. Retrieved April 28, 2015, from http://www.crisp-dm.org/CRISPWP-0800.pdf´

DiMicco, J. M., Geyer, W., Millen, D. R., Dugan, C., & Brownholtz, B. (2009). People Sensemaking and Relationship Building on an Enterprise Social Network Site. In *2009 42nd Hawaii International Conference on System Sciences* (pp. 1–10). IEEE.

DiMicco, J. M., Millen, D. R., Geyer, W., Dugan, C., Brownholtz, B., & Muller, M. (2008). Motivations for Social Networking at Work. In *Proceedings of the 2008 ACM Conference on Computer Supported Cooperative Work* (pp. 711–720). New York: ACM.

Drakos, N., Mann, J., & Gotta, M. (2014). *Magic quadrant for social software in the workplace*. Retrieved April 28, 2015, from https://www.jivesoftware.com/discover-jive/analyst-reports/gartner-magic-quadrant/

Farrell, S., Lau, T., Nusser, S., Wilcox, E., & Muller, M. (2007). Socially augmenting employee profiles with people-tagging. In *Proceedings of the 20th annual ACM symposium on User interface software and technology - UIST '07* (p. 91). New York: ACM Press.

Fischbach, K., Schoder, D., & Gloor, P. a. (2008). Analyse informeller Kommunikationsnetzwerke am Beispiel einer Fallstudie. *Wirtschaftsinformatik, 51*(2), 164–174.

Freeman, L. C. (1978). Centrality in social networks conceptual clarification. *Social Networks, 1*(3), 215–239.

Gartner. (2013). *Magic Quadrant for Social Software in the Workplace*. Retrieved April 28, 2015, https://www.jivesoftware.com/discover-jive/analyst-reports/gartner-magic-quadrant/

Geyer, W., Dugan, C., DiMicco, J. M., Millen, D. R., Brownholtz, B., & Muller, M. (2008). Use and reuse of shared lists as a social content type. In *Proceeding of the twenty-sixth annual CHI conference on Human factors in computing systems - CHI '08* (p. 1545). New York: ACM Press.

GoodData Corporation. (2015). *GoodData Yammer Analytics Dashboard*. Retrieved April 28, 2015, from http://www.gooddata.com/bi-solutions/enterprise-analytics/yammer-analytics

Gotta, M., Drakos, N., & Mann, J. (2015). *Magic Quadrant for Social Software in the Workplace*. Retrieved December 3, 2015, from https://www.ibm.com/services/forms/signup.do?source=gts-LITS-WebOrganic-NA&S_PKG=ov35194

Granovetter, M. S. (1973). The strength of weak ties. *American Journal of Sociology, 78*(6), 1360–1380.

Han, J., Kamber, M., & Pei, J. (2012). *Data mining: concepts and techniques* (3rd ed.). Waltham: Morgan Kaufmann/Elsevier.

Hansen, D. L., Shneiderman, B., & Smith, M. A. (2010). Visualizing Threaded Conversation Networks: Mining Message Boards and Email Lists for Actionable Insights. In A. An, P. Lingras, S. Petty, & R. Huang (Eds.), *Active Media Technology SE - 7* (Vol. 6335, pp. 47–62). Berlin: Springer.

IBM. (2014). *IBM Named Worldwide Market Share Leader in Enterprise Social Software for Fifth Consecutive Year.* Retrieved April 27, 2015, from http://www-03.ibm.com/press/us/en/pressrelease/43703.wss

Jive Software. (2015a). *Jive 7.0 Community User Help: Using Impact Metrics.* Retrieved December 4, 2015, from https://docs.jivesoftware.com/jive/7.0/community_user/index.jsp?topic=/com.jivesoftware.help.sbs.online/user/WhatareImpactMetrics.html

Jive Software. (2015b). *Jive Analytics: Community Manager Reports.* Retrieved December 4, 2015, from https://docs.jivesoftware.com/cloud_int/comm_mgr/jive.help.analytics/#user/AboutReportsv3.html

Jive Software. (2015c). *Jive features.* Retrieved April 28, 2015, from https://www.jivesoftware.com/products-solutions/jive-n/#tab-features

Koch, M., & Richter, A. (2009). *Enterprise 2.0: Planung, Einführung und erfolgreicher Einsatz von Social-Software in Unternehmen.* München: Oldenbourg.

Koch, M., Richter, A., & Schlosser, A. (2007). Produkte zum IT-gestützten Social Networking in Unternehmen. *Wirtschaftsinformatik, 49*(6), 448–455.

Koplowitz, R. (2014). *The Forrester Wave: Enterprise Social Platforms, Q2 2014.* Retrieved April 28, 2015, from https://www.jivesoftware.com/discover-jive/analyst-reports/forrester-wave-social/

Kuang, H., & Zhi Gang, L. (2012). *Using the Metrics application in IBM Connections 4.0. IBM Connections wiki.* Retrieved April 27, 2015, from http://www-10.lotus.com/ldd/lcwiki.nsf/dx/Using_the_Metrics_application_in_IBM_Connections_4.0

Kurzlechner, W. (2011). Social Software: IBM, Microsoft und Jive im Vergleich. *CIO Magazin.* Retrieved April 28, 2015, from http://www.cio.de/a/ibm-microsoft-und-jive-im-vergleich,2298192

McAfee, A. P. (2006a). *Enterprise 2.0, version 2.0. Andrew McAfee's Blog.* Retrieved April 28, 2015, from http://andrewmcafee.org/2006/05/enterprise_20_version_20/

McAfee, A. P. (2006b). Enterprise 2.0: The Dawn of Emergent Collaboration. *MIT Sloan Management Review, 47*(3), 21–28.

McIntyre, S. (2014). *IBM Connections: Components.* Retrieved April 28, 2015, from http://ibmconnections.com/features/components/

Microsoft. (2015). *Monitoring your Yammer data.* Retrieved April 27, 2015, from https://support.office.com/en-au/article/Monitoring-your-Yammer-data-Yammer-admin-guide-8c4651fa-12c2-4ced-b4ea-2200c0a630ed?ui=en-US&rs=en-AU&ad=AU

Muller, M. J., Freyne, J., Dugan, C., Millen, D. R., & Thom-Santelli, J. (2009). Return On Contribution (ROC): A Metric for Enterprise Social Software. In I. Wagner, H. Tellioğlu, E. Balka, C. Simone, & L. Ciolfi (Eds.), *ECSCW'09: Proceedings of the 11th European Conference on Computer Supported Cooperative Work* (pp. 143–150). London: Springer London.

Osimo, D., Szkuta, K., Foley, P., Biagi, F., Thompson, M., Bryant, L., . . . Ritzek, J. (2010). *Enterprise 2.0 study D4 Final report*. Retrieved from http://enterprise20eu.files.wordpress.com/2010/09/e20d3.pdf

Perer, A., Guy, I., Uziel, E., Ronen, I., & Jacovi, M. (2011). Visual social network analytics for relationship discovery in the enterprise. In *2011 IEEE Conference on Visual Analytics Science and Technology (VAST)* (pp. 71–79). IEEE.

Raab, J. (2010). Netzwerke und Netzwerkanalyse in der Organisationsforschung. In C. Stegbauer & R. Häußling (Eds.), *Handbuch Netzwerkforschung*. Wiesbaden: VS Verlag für Sozialwissenschaften.

RapidMiner Inc. (2015). *RapidMiner Studio*. Retrieved April 28, 2015, from https://rapidminer.com/

Richter, A. (2010). *Der Einsatz von Social Networking Services in Unternehmen. Der Einsatz von Social Networking Services in Unternehmen*. Wiesbaden: Gabler.

Richter, A., Behrendt, S., & Koch, M. (2012). APERTO: A Framework for Selection, Introduction, and Optimization of Corporate Social Software. *All Sprouts Content*, Paper 488.

Richter, A., Heidemann, J., Klier, M., & Behrendt, S. (2013). Success Measurement of Enterprise Social Networks. In Wirtschaftsinformatik Proceedings 2013.

Richter, A., & Riemer, K. (2009). Corporate Social Networking Sites – Modes of Use and Appropriation through Co-Evolution. In ACIS 2009 Proceedings.

Richter, A., & Riemer, K. (2013). The Contextual Nature Of Enterprise Social Networking: A Multi Case Study Comparison. In *ECIS 2013 Completed Research*. Retrieved from http://aisel.aisnet.org/ecis2013_cr/94

Richter, A., & Stocker, A. (2011). Exploration & Promotion: Einführungsstrategien von Corporate Social Software. In Wirtschaftinformatik Proceedings 2011.

Richter, A., Stocker, A., Müller, S., & Avram, G. (2011). Knowledge Management Goals Revisited– A Cross-Sectional Analysis of Social Software Adoption in Corporate Environments. In ACIS 2011 Proceedings.

Riemer, K., Diederich, S., Richter, A., & Scifleet, P. (2011). Short Message Discussions: On The Conversational Nature Of Microblogging In A Large Consultancy Organisation. In PACIS 2011 Proceedings.

Riemer, K., & Johnston, R. B. (2012). Place-making: A Phenomenological Theory of Technology Appropriation. In ICIS 2012 Proceedings.

Riemer, K., Overfeld, P., Scifleet, P., & Richter, A. (2012). Eliciting the Anatomy of Technology Appropriation Processes: A Case Study in Enterprise Social Media. In ECIS 2012 Proceedings.

Riemer, K., & Richter, A. (2012). *SOCIAL-Emergent Enterprise Social Networking Use Cases: A Multi Case Study Comparison*. Retrieved April 27, 2015, from http://ses.library.usyd.edu.au/handle/2123/8845

Riemer, K., & Scifleet, P. (2012). Enterprise social networking in knowledge-intensive work practices: a case study in a professional service firm. In ACIS 2012 Proceedings.

Ross, R. (2014). *Yammer Analytics – Basic Reports*. Retrieved April 28, 2015, from http://blogs.perficient.com/microsoft/2014/03/yammer-analytics-basic-reports/

Sampson, M. (2014). *Use and Adoption of IBM Connections: State of the Market 4Q2014*. Retrieved from April 28, 2015, https://michaelcollabguy.files.wordpress.com/2014/11/use-and-adoption-of-ibm-connections-by-michael-sampson.pdf

Schneckenberg, D. (2009). Web 2.0 and the empowerment of the knowledge worker. *Journal of Knowledge Management, 13*(6), 509–520.

Steinfield, C. W., DiMicco, J. M., Ellison, N. B., & Lampe, C. (2009). Bowling online. In *Proceedings of the fourth international conference on Communities and technologies - C&T '09* (p. 245). ACM.

Trier, M., & Richter, A. (2015). The deep structure of organizational online networking - an actor-oriented case study. *Information Systems Journal, 25*(5), 465–488.

Viol, J., & Hess, J. (2016). Information Systems Research on Enterprise Social Networks – A State-of-the-Art Analysis. In MKWI 2016 Proceedings.

Wald, A. (2010). Netzwerkansätze in der Managementforschung. In C. Stegbauer & R. Häußling (Eds.), *Handbuch Netzwerkforschung*. Wiesbaden: VS Verlag für Sozialwissenschaften.

Wasserman, S., & Faust, K. (1994). *Social network analysis: methods and applications*. Cambridge, UK: Cambridge University Press.

Yammer. (2015). *Yammer Full Feature List*. Retrieved April 27, 2015, from https://about.yammer.com/product/feature-list/

KEY TERMS AND DEFINITIONS

Data Analysis Process: The data analysis process includes the (1) preparation and pre-processing of the data, the (2) actual data analysis and a (3) validation and interpretation of the results.

Enterprise 2.0: Enterprise 2.0 refers to the use of Web 2.0 tools and technologies within companies, e.g. blogs, wikis and Enterprise Social Networks.

Enterprise Social Network: An Enterprise Social Network (ESN) is a Social Networking Site run behind a company's firewall, i.e. an internally used Social Networking Site. ESN typically include features such as profiles, message exchange, a news stream, discussion threads, blogs and wikis.

Social Analytics: Social Analytics describes the analysis of user profile data and the patterns of relationships emerging based on communication in (e.g.) ESN. Based on Social Analytics, users of Enterprise Social Networks are recommended colleagues who they may want to add to their networks.

Social Network Analysis: Social Network Analysis (SNA) describes the process of collecting and analyzing network data. The analysis includes the calculation of social network measures, e.g. centrality measures to characterize individual users, as well as the visualization of the network. This process is usually supported by SNA tools.

Social Networking Site: A Social Networking Site (SNS) is a web-based application where users can create a profile, connect and communicate with other users and share as well as consume content. SNS can be distinguished into public and closed SNS and differ in terms of their focus.

Chapter 7
Big Data Analytics Using Local Exceptionality Detection

Martin Atzmueller
University of Kassel, Germany

Dennis Mollenhauer
University of Kassel, Germany

Andreas Schmidt
University of Kassel, Germany

ABSTRACT

Large-scale data processing is one of the key challenges concerning many application domains, especially considering ubiquitous and big data. In these contexts, subgroup discovery provides both a flexible data analysis and knowledge discovery method. Subgroup discovery and pattern mining are important descriptive data mining tasks. They can be applied, for example, in order to obtain an overview on the relations in the data, for automatic hypotheses generation, and for a number of knowledge discovery applications. This chapter presents the novel SD-MapR algorithmic framework for large-scale local exceptionality detection implemented using subgroup discovery on the Map/Reduce framework. We describe the basic algorithm in detail and provide an experimental evaluation using several real-world datasets. We tackle two algorithmic variants focusing on simple and more complex target concepts, i.e., presenting an implementation of exceptional model mining on large attributed graphs. The results of our evaluation show the scalability of the presented approach for large data sets.

INTRODUCTION

With the exponential growth of the available data, e.g., due to ubiquitous applications and services, large-scale data mining provides many challenges. Efficient and scalable methods need to be developed that on the one hand provide the handling of such large data, on the other hand support an efficient and scalable analysis approach. In this chapter, we focus on subgroup discovery for local exceptionality detection on large datasets. During data exploration, the data analyst, for example, might be interested in

DOI: 10.4018/978-1-5225-0293-7.ch007

partitions of the data that show some specific exceptional characteristics, and respective descriptions of these partitions. An exploratory analysis approach for identifying such a subset of the data with a concise description is given by subgroup discovery (e.g., Klösgen 1996; Wrobel 1997; Atzmueller 2015) – here, also specifically the variant of exceptional model mining (Leman 2008; Duivestein 2016) as an approach for modeling complex exceptionality criteria. Intuitively, subgroup discovery aims at identifying such an exceptional subgroup of the whole dataset, e.g., concerning notable different distribution of some target concept, where the subgroup typically also should be as large as possible. Exceptional model mining especially focuses on complex target properties; it considers specific model classes, such as a correlation model between two variables, linear regression, or complex graph properties.

Overall, subgroup discovery is a broadly applicable data mining technique which can be applied for descriptive data mining as well as predictive data mining. We can obtain an overview on the relations in the data, for example, for automatic hypotheses generation, for attribute construction, or for obtaining a rule-based classification model. The basic idea is to identify subgroups covering instances of the dataset, which show some interesting, i.e., unexpected, deviating or exceptional behavior, concerning a given target concept. This notion can be flexibly formalized using a quality function. We can estimate, for example, the deviation of the mean of a numeric target concept in the subgroup compared to the whole dataset; more complex functions utilizing graph-structured data consider, e.g., the density of a certain subgraph compared to the expected density of a null model given by a random edge assignment approach.

In this chapter, we present the novel SD-MapR algorithmic framework for large-scale subgroup discovery: Based on data projection techniques of the FP-Growth (Han et al. 2000) and the Parallel FP-Growth (PFP) algorithm (Li et al. 2008) for large-scale frequent pattern mining, SD-MapR employs the Map/Reduce framework (Dean & Ghemawat 2008) for large-scale data processing. The basic idea of SD-MapR is the construction of projected databases such that the subgroup discovery task can be independently deployed on several computation clusters in a divide-and-conquer manner, inspired by the PFP algorithm. For local exceptionality detection, we propose the efficient subgroup discovery algorithms SD-Map* (Atzmueller & Lemmerich 2009), GP-Growth (Lemmerich et al. 2012), and COMODO (Atzmueller et al. 2015a) which can be applied for instantiating SD-MapR. Specifically, we present specific adaptations of the SD-Map* and the COMODO (Atzmueller et al. 2015a) algorithms for implementing SD-MapR.

The remainder of this chapter is structured as follows: In the next section, we introduce some preliminaries on local exceptionality detection using subgroup discovery and exceptional model mining, the respective state-of-the-art algorithms, and the Map/Reduce framework. After that, we describe the novel SD-MapR algorithmic framewrok in detail. Next, we provide a comprehensive evaluation of the presented algorithms using ubiquitous data, and show the scalability and performance for large-scale datasets. Finally, we conclude with a summary and point out interesting options for future work.

BACKGROUND

This section first briefly introduces the background concerning mining locally exceptional patterns. We focus especially on approaches for local exceptionality detection based on subgroup and exceptional model mining, and briefly introduce these. After that, we summarize the basics of the Map/Reduce framework. Next, we briefly sketch an approach for local exceptionality detection on Map/Reduce, i.e., the PFP algorithm and the underlying FP-Growth algorithm. Furthermore, we summarize the algorithmic methods that are used in the evaluation, i.e., the SD-Map/SD-Map*, GP-Growth and COMODO algorithms for local exceptionality detection targeting subgroup discovery with exceptional model mining techniques.

Local Exceptionality Detection, Subgroup Discovery, and Exceptional Model Mining

A core idea in local pattern detection (Morik 2002) is to consider only partial relations in the data, in contrast to global modeling approaches that try to fit global models to the whole data.

Subgroup discovery (cf. Kloesgen 1996; Wrobel 1997; Atzmueller 2015) is a general and broadly applicable approach for local exceptionality detection. The interestingness of a subgroup is usually defined by a certain property of interest formalized by a quality function. According to the type of the property of the subgroup, that we are interested in, we can distinguish between simple concepts such as a minimal frequency/size of the subgroup (also known as support for association rules), a deviating target share (confidence) of a binary target property of the subgroup, or a significantly different subgroup mean of a numeric target concept. More complex target concepts consider sets of target variables. In particular, exceptional model mining (Leman et al. 2008; Atzmueller 2015; Duivestein et al. 2016) focuses on more complex quality functions, considering complex target models, e.g., given by regression models or Bayesian networks with a deviating behavior for a certain subgroup. In the context of ubiquitous data and mining social media (e.g., Atzmueller et al. 2012), interesting target concepts are given, e.g., by densely connected structures (communities), see (Atzmueller et al. 2015a), exceptional spatio-semantic distributions (Atzmueller et al. 2015b), or class association rules (Atzmueller et al. 2015c). Using a quality function, a set of subgroups is then identified using a given subgroup discovery algorithm, i.e., the top-k subgroups, or those above a minimal quality threshold. Furthermore, also constraints and other forms of background knowledge can be provided for selecting patterns and/or restricting the search space etc. (e.g., Atzmueller 2007).

Subgroups are described by the features common to the covered set of instances. This provides a direct interpretation in terms of their features, i.e. attribute-value pairs, also called selectors. Essentially, a subgroup description is given by a selection expression in a certain pattern language, e.g., as a conjunction of selectors. Due to the exponential search space given by all possible combinations of feature-value pairs (selection expressions) efficient methods, e.g., (Wrobel 1997, Atzmueller & Puppe 2006, Atzmueller & Lemmerich 2009) are crucial for constraining the search space and optimizing the search process (Atzmueller 2015). Here, we distinguish between heuristic methods - mainly based on beam search (e.g., Lavrac et al. 2004; Duivestein et al. 2016) and exhaustive approaches like SD-Map/ SD-Map* (e.g., Atzmueller & Puppe 2006, Atzmueller & Lemmerich 2009, Atzmueller 2015). Often, branch-and-bound methods can be implemented using optimistic estimate functions (Grosskreutz et al. 2008, Atzmueller & Lemmerich 2009). Also, special data structures like FP-Trees (Han et al. 2000) can be applied for increasing efficiency (e.g., Atzmueller & Puppe 2006), also with respect to handling large datasets, as we will see below.

Map/Reduce

Map/Reduce (Dean & Ghemawat 2008) is a paradigm for scalable distributed processing of big data, with a prominent implementation given by the Hadoop framework[1]. Its core ideas are based on the functional programming primitives map and reduce. Whereas map iterates on a certain input sequence of key-value pairs, the reduce function collects and processes all values for a certain key. The Map/Reduce paradigm is applicable for a certain computational task, if this task can be divided into independent computational tasks, such that there is no required communication between these. Complex tasks can then be split up into different Map/Reduce phases, such that the output of the reducers in one phase is provided as the input to the mappers of the next phase. During these phases, the individual jobs are run on the computing nodes and the input dataset is split into independent chunks such that these are processed by the map tasks in parallel. The Map/Reduce framework sorts the output of the maps for obtaining the input for the subsequent reduce tasks. Then, large tasks can be split up into subtasks according to a typical divide-and-conquer strategy.

FP-Growth

The FP-Growth algorithm (Han et al. 2000) has been proposed as an efficient approach for frequent pattern mining. It avoids multiple scans of the whole dataset for evaluating candidate patterns by constructing a special data structure, the so-called FP-Tree. This extended prefix tree structure contains the relevant data in a compressed way. Each tree node contains a reference to a selector and a frequency count. Selectors on a path from a node to the root are interpreted as a conjunction. Additionally, links between nodes referring to the same selector are maintained.

The FP-Tree is built by sorting the selectors of each data record according to their descending frequency in the dataset. Then, each data instance is inserted into the FP-Tree. The order of the selectors increases the chance of shared prefixes between the data records, thus decreasing the size of the FP-Tree. Most importantly, the resulting FP-Tree contains the complete condensed frequency information for the complete dataset.

For mining frequent patterns, FP-Growth starts with creating an FP-Tree for the initial dataset.

Patterns containing exactly one selector are evaluated by the frequencies collected during the first pass over the dataset. Then, the algorithm recursively extends those patterns by adding further selectors in a depth-first manner, building conditional trees conditioned on the current pattern prefix. Each node corresponds to a conditional data instance built from the selectors referred to by its parent nodes. In this way, FP-Growth enables a compact and efficient mining of the condensed tree structure. We refer to (Han et al. 2000) for a more detailed discussion.

PFP

Parallel FP-Growth (Li et al. 2008) is a variant of the frequent pattern mining algorithm FP-Growth, which uses the Map/Reduce paradigm to parallelize the computation. PFP splits the data into independent shards. A modified version of FP-Growth is applied parallel on these shards and the results are aggregated in a post-processing step.

The frequent pattern mining process is split into five steps and three Map/Reduce passes. The first step is the sharding of the input database: Here the input data is split into shards of item sets. These shards are distributed on different computing units; this step is usually done by the Map/Reduce infrastructure. The second step counts the support of all items in the database in parallel with a Map/Reduce pass. This implicitly yields the vocabulary of the data set, which is usually unknown for huge databases. The result is called the F-List. In the third step the F-List is divided into groups identified by a *gid*. The F-List is small and the grouping can be done on a single computer in a few seconds. The fourth step is using one

Map/Reduce pass: The Mapper generates the group dependent records. This is done by ordering the items in a record according to the frequency descending, i.e., that the most common item is the left most item. Now the items are replaced by their corresponding *gid*. For each *gid* in the record, a group dependent record is created, by selecting all items from the left most occurrence of the gid. This group dependent record is written to the output as value along with its gid as key. The Map/Reduce infrastructure groups these group dependent records, and for each group one and only one Reducer is called, with a list of all group dependent records belonging to the group. These group dependent records are used to construct the group dependent FP-Tree. On this FP-Tree an adapted version of the FP-Growth algorithm is executed. There are two adaptations compared to classical FP-Growth: The growth step is only called for the items which are in the group and only the top-k results are stored and written to the output. After computing all groups, the results are collected and post-processed in a Map/Reduce step.

SD-Map/SD-Map* and GP-Growth

For efficient local exceptionality detection using subgroup discovery, there are several exhaustive algorithms. SD-Map* (Atzmueller & Lemmerich 2009) is based on the efficient SD-Map algorithm (Atzmueller & Puppe 2006) utilizing an extended FP-Tree data structure, cf. (Han et al. 2000), i.e., an extended prefix-tree-structure that stores information for pattern refinement and evaluation, complemented by optimistic estimate pruning.

SD-Map* applies a divide and conquer method, first mining patterns containing one selector and then recursively mining patterns of size 1 conditioned on the occurrence of a (prefix) 1-selector. For the binary case, an FP-Tree node stores the subgroup size and the true positive count of the respective subgroup description. In the continuous case, it considers the sum of values of the target variable, enabling us to compute the respective quality functions value accordingly. Therefore, all the necessary information is locally available in the FP-Tree structure.

For extending the FP-Tree structure towards multi-target concepts, we utilize the concept of valuation bases introduced by (Lemmerich et al. 2012). Then, all information required for the evaluation of the respective quality functions is stored in the nodes of the FP-Tree, as the basis of the GP-Growth algorithm extending SD-Map/SD-Map*. With this technique, a large number of single and multi-target concept quality functions can be implemented (cf. Lemmerich et al. 2012; Atzmueller 2015).

In particular, for enabling multi-target quality functions using exceptional model mining techniques as sketched above, we focus on detecting patterns with respect to a local model derived from a set of attributes. The interestingness can then be defined, e.g., by a significant deviation from a model that is derived from the total population or the respective complement set of instances within the population.

In general, a model consists of a specific model class and certain model parameters which depend on the values of the model attributes in the instances of the respective pattern cover. The applied quality measure then determines the interestingness of a pattern according to its model parameters. We can consider, for example, the slope of a linear regression model induced on the subgroup, and the total population (or the complement of the subgroup, respectively) in order to identify deviating subgroups regarding certain target variables. We could consider, for example, wins and losses of certain players in a game: Then, assuming a linear regression model, wins could be indicated by the values on the x-axis while losses could be indicated by the values on the y-axis. Then, we could derive the slope of the line corresponding to the total population. Let us assume that this would be close to the diagonal. In that case, interesting subgroups would be those, that have a slope that deviates from the diagonal, i.e., where the points are, e.g., either in the top-left or bottom-right quadrant.

The algorithmic framework implemented by SD-Map* and GP-Growth enables optimistic estimate pruning: When determining the top-k subgroups, the current subgroup hypothesis (and all its further specializations by adding further selectors) can be pruned, if its optimistically estimated quality is below the worst quality of the top-k patterns identified so far. In that way, significant efficiency gains can be obtained, depending on the applied quality function and its optimistic estimate.

COMODO

The COMODO algorithm (Atzmueller & Mitzlaff 2011; Atzmueller et al. 2015a) for description-oriented community detection aims at discovering the top-k communities (described by community patterns) with respect to a number of standard community evaluation functions. The method itself is based on algorithmic principles of SD-Map* and GP-Growth in the context of community detection on attributed graphs, targeting dense structures that are described by a concise description. Essentially, COMODO is a fast branch-and-bound algorithm utilizing optimistic estimates (cf. Wrobel 1997; Grosskreutz et al. 2008) which are efficient to compute. This allows COMODO to prune the search space significantly. COMODO utilizes an extended FP-Tree structure, called the community pattern tree in order to efficiently traverse the solution space. The tree is built in two scans of the graph data set and is then mined in a recursive divide-and-conquer manner, cf. (Atzmueller & Lemmerich 2009, Lemmerich et al. 2012). The FP-Tree contains the frequent FP-nodes in a header table, and links to all occurrences of the frequent basic patterns in the FP-Tree structure. In addition, COMODO also stores additional information about the graph structure into a compiled graph representation as a set of edge data records, i.e., about the degrees of the individual nodes in order to apply several standard community quality functions, e.g., the Modularity quality function (Newman 2006).

In (Atzmueller et al. 2015a) the approach is demonstrated on data sets from three social systems namely, i.e., from the social bookmarking systems BibSonomy[2], delicious[3], and from the social media platform last.fm[4]. However, the presented approach is not limited to such systems and can be applied to any kind of graph-structured data for which additional descriptive features (node labels) are available, e.g., certain activity in telephone networks or interactions in face-to-face contacts (cf. Atzmueller et al. 2012). Since COMODO applies exceptional model mining techniques for implementing subgroup discovery for complex targets, we can also extend this formalization for even more complex model classes. Then, in order to handle community quality functions that include both the structure of the covered subgroups and additional parameters of these, we can combine, for example, a structural community quality function like the Modularity with an exceptional model like the slope model (linear regression). COMODO already enables such extensions since it includes ideas of the GP-Growth algorithm (valuation bases for model modularization) and the application of selectable community (pattern) quality functions. As we will see below in the evaluation, structural and model parameters can be suitably combined. Then, we can also model more complex discovery processes with respect to local exceptional pattern detection for answering advanced analytical questions.

METHOD

SD-MapR is a framework for implementing subgroup discovery and exceptional model mining algorithms for large datasets using the Map/Reduce framework. Below, we describe this algorithmic framework for efficient large-scale local exceptionality detection. We provide an outline of SD-MapR, and discuss its implementation concerning the SD-Map/SD-Map* and the COMODO algorithms. These algorithms allow exhaustive subgroup discovery in complex datasets. SD-Map/SD-Map* can be applied for binary and numerical target concepts, while COMODO – by integrating techniques of the GP-Growth algorithm, can apply complex quality functions for local exceptionality detection on attributed graphs. In particular, we also describe a novel extension of a community quality function that includes local exceptionality measures on numeric properties of the covered subgraph – in addition to considering structural aspects. In the next section, we will discuss evaluation results of these adaptations in detail.

Overview

SD-MapR is based on the idea of partitioning the data onto different computing units, such that on each of these a respective Map/Reduce job can be run. Existing approaches rely on shared memory (using multiple cores) for each processing unit (cf. Lemmerich et al. 2010), or do not distribute the data but the search space of subgroup discovery (Trabold and Grosskreutz 2013) also relying on central memory and node-to-node communication. In contrast to these, SD-MapR provides an implementation directly utilizing the Map/Reduce paradigm, such that computation can be effortlessly distributed in this efficient programming model.

The SD-MapR approach enables subgroup discovery for simple and complex target concepts – relating to exceptional model mining. Using techniques of the GP-Growth algorithm like valuation bases for modularizing the quality computation of a subgroup, complex quality functions can then be efficiently implemented. The next section describes some examples of that – from simple shares to a hybrid quality function including structural measures on a graph with statistical properties of the covered subgroup.

SD-MapR

Essentially, the SD-MapR algorithmic framework applies the data partitioning technique of the PFP algorithm for distributing the data on the Map/Reduce infrastructure, complemented by a specific subgroup discovery algorithm that runs on the local computation nodes. After the individual results on these nodes have been obtained, they need to be recombined. After an initial generic preprocessing and data integration step (Convert), where the data is loaded, transformed and partitioned into the Hadoop filesystem, SD-MapR consists of the following three phases:

1. **Count and Group (Obtain Frequent Selectors and Partition These):** First, acquire initial subgroup statistics (optionally: pruning bounds) by parallel counting; obtain frequency statistics on the individual selectors contained in the dataset, and use these for generating a list of frequent selectors. Second, group the frequent selectors into disjoint sets according to the technique of the PFP algorithm; divide the frequent selectors into a given number of groups.
2. **SD (Parallel Projection-Driven Subgroup Discovery):** Build group-projected databases, i.e., by applying adapted grouping steps of the PFP algorithm such that the database is split into indepen-

dent (projected) databases. Apply a (potentially adapted) subgroup discovery algorithm on those projected databases, e.g., SD-Map/SD-Map* or GP-Growth-based variants. Collect the resulting patterns.

3. **Combine (Merge Results):** Aggregate the individual patterns into the global result set of patterns, e.g., in a top-k approach, select the k best patterns from the result set.

These phases are implemented using three Map/Reduce steps, utilizing the basic structure of the PFP algorithm for data partitioning, parallel pattern discovery, and result aggregation.

For local exceptionality detection, the algorithmic step (2) provides for some flexibility regarding the specific implementation of the pattern discovery step. Due to their efficiency, pattern-growth-based algorithms like SD-Map/SD-Map* can be applied, since they only require two passes through the utilized (projected) databases for building their core mining structure, which can be implemented efficiently in the Map/Reduce infrastructure. Also, algorithms for complex target concepts, i.e., for subgroup discovery applying exceptional model mining techniques, like the COMODO algorithm can also be implemented. In particular, the applied algorithm and technique for estimating the local exceptionality can be selected and configured according to the specific objectives of the analysis. Thus, there is a wide range of quality functions (Kloesgen 1996; Atzmueller 2015): These can range from simple methods, e.g., comparing means in subgroups to the total population (e.g., Wrobel 1997), spatial distributions (e.g., Atzmueller & Lemmerich 2013; Atzmueller et al. 2015b) to more complex ones, e.g., including components from a linear regression between two variables (Duivestein 2016), and the structural assessment of a complex network/graph (Atzmueller et al. 2015a). In the next section, we evaluate instantiations with the mentioned algorithms (SD-Map*, COMODO) in the context of real-world datasets, also exemplifying the flexibility of the applicable quality functions.

RESULTS

For the evaluation of the SD-MapR algorithmic framework, SD-MapR was instantiated using the SD-Map* and the COMODO algorithms – that were adapted to the characteristics of Map/Reduce. In particular, SD-Map/SD-Map* and COMODO were reimplemented for efficiency on Map/Reduce, such that the construction of the FP-Trees was performed in a rather memory-efficient way – by scanning the (projected) databases on disk, i.e., in a one-pass iteration on disk instead of processing the projected database in-memory, as provided by the Hadoop framework. The implementation was performed based on the VIKAMINE system (Atzmueller & Puppe 2005, Atzmueller & Lemmerich 2012), for which extensions for Map/Reduce were created.

In the following, we first outline the characteristics of the applied datasets. After that, we present results of our evaluation and discuss them in detail.

Datasets

We performed the evaluation using four datasets. For subgroup discovery using a binary target concept, we applied two real-world datasets in the social media domain, i.e., using data from the music platform last.fm and from the social photo sharing system Flickr. In addition, we utilized synthetic data generated using the Quest data generator. For detecting community patterns in an exceptional model mining approach, we applied a dataset from a large-scale online game. Below, we summarize the characteristics of the applied datasets.

1. **last.fm ("The Million Song Dataset", Bertin-Mahieux et al. 2011):** The dataset contains 505,216 songs and one song-tag relation. Each song is tagged with at least one tag. In total, 552,897 tags are contained. The tags are power-law distributed (cf. Bertin-Mahieux et al. 2011). For subgroup discovery, each tag is represented by a binary attribute. For evaluation, the dataset was replicated 1, 5, 10, 50 and 100 times.

2. **MIRFLICKR-1M (Huiskes & Lew 2008):** In this dataset, each picture is tagged with at least one tag. For subgroup discovery, all tags (binary attributes) and license data (owner, title, license – as nominal attributes) were utilized. In total, the dataset contained 906,280 attributes. In contrast to the tagging data, the license information yields very dense attributes. For evaluation, the dataset was replicated 1, 5, 10, 50 and 100 times.

3. **Quest – IBM Quest Synthetic Data Generator (Agrawal & Srikant 1994):** The Quest data generator is typically applied for creating synthetic market basket transaction data, e.g., for testing association rule mining algorithms. Typically, the generation yields baskets with similar sizes. There are different parameters that can be supplied for generating the transactions, where we applied the numbers in brackets for generation:

    a. Total number of transactions (3, 10, 30 million),
    b. Total number of different items (100 000),
    c. Average length of a transaction (15),
    d. Number of item patterns (100 000).

4. **Massive Multiplayer Online Game – Fleetgraph (Attributed Graph Data):** We crawled the data from a massive multiplayer online game and constructed a graph with the players as nodes; an edge was created between two players if they were co-engaged in a battle a certain number of times as discussed below.

    a. **Raw Data:** We collected the raw data from several websites, obtaining about 24.7 million textual battle reports, with a raw size of 79 GB. In addition, we collected the character profiles for the players using the game's API, e.g., game party, participating alliance, information about solar systems and structure of the game universe, information about the game items like ships and weapons, etc. This resulted in a dataset with a total size of about 500 MB.
    b. **Graph Construction:** Here, an edge is created between two players if they were co-engaged in a battle, a certain minimal number of times (support), i.e., using a certain minimal support threshold. In addition, the graph is labeled using information about the participating players: We label the edge with the intersection of the attributes of the participating players. Overall, for attributing the graph about 8,000 selectors and additional derived numerical indicators can be used, e.g., the number of times a player participated in a battle in a certain alliance.

Exceptional Tags: Instantiating SD-MapR Using SD-Map/SD-Map*

For the evaluation, we applied the three datasets (1-3) outlined above. Below, we show several runtime examples, selecting certain tags as binary targets (last.fm: tag rock, MIRFLICKR-1M: tag mcity, Quest: randomly selected tag for each run). Here, with respect to the selected target, a subgroup (pattern) should have a frequency of the target that deviates from the overall frequency in the database the most. We weight the difference of the target frequency in the subgroup and the total database by the square root of the size of the subgroup, thus applying the simplified binomial quality function (Atzmueller 2015) which is a standard quality function often applied in a subgroup discovery setting for a binary target variable. For running Map/Reduce, we used a twelve node Hadoop cluster. Each node had an AMD DualCore Opteron 2218 CPU with 2.6 GHz, 16 GB RAM, and 1 TB local storage on a 7200 rpm hard disk. Each node was configured to execute two mappers and two reducers, resulting in a total of 24 available slots.

Figure 1 shows the runtime of the SD-MapR instantiation on the last.fm dataset using different parameters for group partitioning (G) and reducers (R). Overall, we observe that the configuration with G=2500 groups and R=100 reducers provides both the most efficient data partitioning and computation of the local exceptionality detection task. Figure 2 shows a detailed view on the computational phases: In the phases that we outlined above for the SD-MapR framework, the mentioned *Convert* phase (pre-processing and data integration) also includes the transformation of a dataset into a binary transaction oriented dataset, during the write operations to the Hadoop HDFS. With a growing problem size, we observe a linear performance speedup. The SD-Map phase takes the most effort, which is explained by the effort on the extended pattern-tree construction. The overall sublinear performance of the SD-Map step is explained by the restricted size of the FP-Tree which is limited by the number of available selectors/patterns. Similar results are observed in Figures 3 and 4 for the MIRFLICKR-1M dataset. For larger datasets, we also observe a high impact on the SD-Map phase which can be explained by a more complex tree structure. Finally, Figure 5 shows the individual performance results on the Quest dataset. Again, we observe a stable linear scale up of the algorithm, also for significantly larger datasets. Overall, the runtime develops always linearly, which shows the huge potential of the approach for handling large datasets. SD-MapR provides the mechanisms for processing and mining large datasets in order enable large-scale local exceptionality detection. As we will see below, this also works well for more complex data, i.e., complex structured graph data.

Figure 1. SD-MapR/SD-Map* runtime on the last.fm dataset

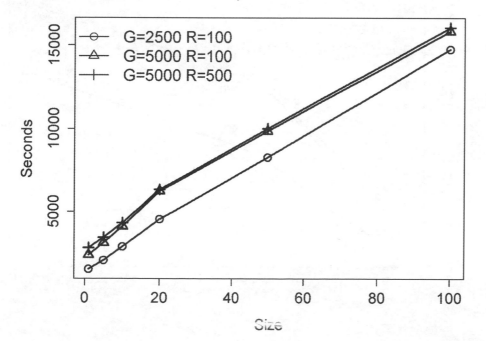

Figure 2. Runtime of the individual SD-MapR/SD-Map* phases on the last.fm dataset

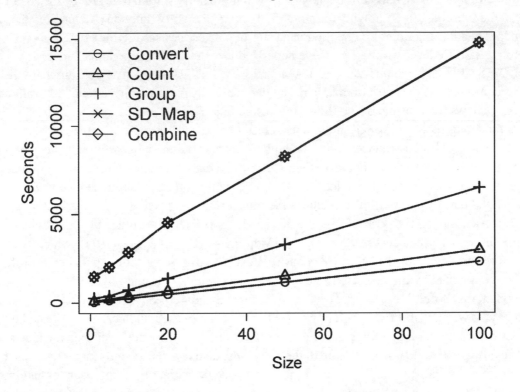

Figure 3. SD-MapR/SD-Map* runtime on the MIRFLICKR-1M dataset

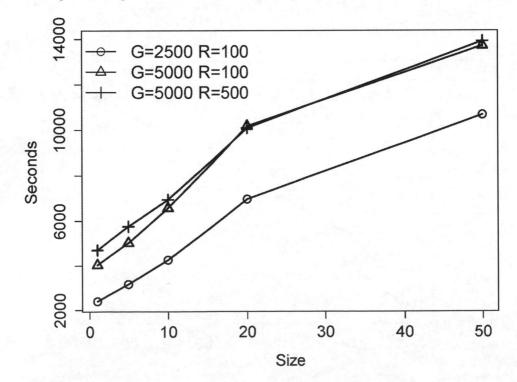

Figure 4. Runtime of the individual SD-MapR/SD-Map* phases on the MIRFLICKR-1M dataset

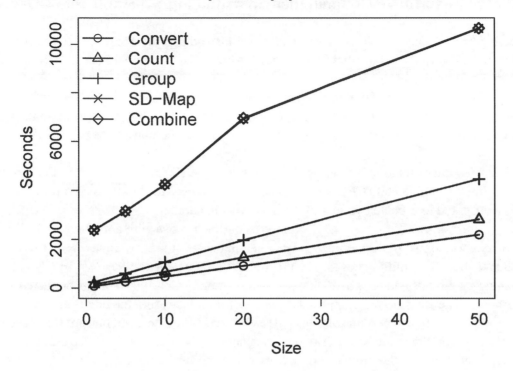

Figure 5. Runtime of the individual SD-MapR/SD-Map* phases on the generated Quest dataset

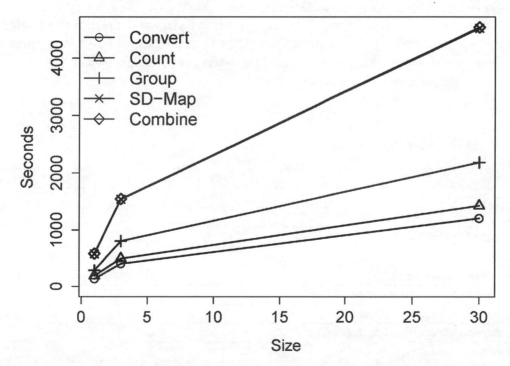

Exceptional Descriptive Communities: Instantiating SD-MapR with COMODO

For detecting exceptional descriptive communities we instantiated the SD-MapR framework with an adaptation of the COMODO algorithm (Atzmueller & Mitzlaff 2011, Atzmueller et al. 2015a). Here, the focus is on detecting densely connected groups (communities) in a network/graph, where the covered nodes of the graph have a concise description in terms of assigned features. In our context of a massive online multiplayer game, we can, for example, focus on players that collaborate (forming their connections) and that are active in certain solar systems (properties of the players, respectively nodes in the network/graph).

We conducted the evaluation of this dataset on a three node Hadoop 1.2.1 cluster. Each node had 8 cores on an Intel Xeon E5-2690 CPU with 2.9 GHz and 64 GB of RAM allocated. Furthermore, each node was configured to execute two map and reduce slots in parallel.

For the evaluation, we computed the fleetgraph as outlined above with a minimum edge support of 10, i.e., we connected two players if they collaborated in battles at least 10 times. With this constraint, the graph had about 37.2 million edges. The preprocessed input edge data set was 14 GB in total. The computation time for this dataset was 18 hours. The execution of COMODO on the projected databases lasted 17 hours. The steps before completed in one hour. For answering the question, whether we can find groups that are active in certain solar systems and/or spatial regions, and that are very successful or unsuccessful, we combined the Modularity quality function (on the graph) with the exceptional model mining slope function (on the number of wins/losses). Then, we applied SD-MapR/COMODO on a graph constructed from three month of battle reports. Table 1 shows exemplary results which revealed groups of players which fought in SecureSpace, where players can only interact rather regulated, i.e., they can only fight consensual or in formal wars without consequences. Also these systems (S1 – S3) are relatively close to each other in the universe. A closer look on the groups showed that the individuals in these groups were primarily in two large alliances which had a war in the time frame selected and most battles took places in very few systems. Overall, the communities are rather large, which shows the good connectivity of players in the game, and their relation to different alliances when cooperating.

Furthermore, we performed a speedup evaluation.

Table 1. Top ten exceptional communities solarsystem

Description	# Member
Primary SecureSpace	7671
Primary SecureSpace, KillInRegion R1	5485
Primary SecureSpace, KillInSystem S1	3643
Primary SecureSpace, KillInSystem S2	3756
Primary SecureSpace, KillInSystem S3	3783
Primary SecureSpace, KillInRegion R1, KillInSystem S1	3602
Primary SecureSpace, KillInRegion R1, KillInSystem S3	3754
Primary SecureSpace, KillInRegion R1, KillInSystem S2	3702
KillInRegion R1, KillInSystem S1	3852
KillInSystem S1	3853

Figure 6. SD-MapR/COMODO speedup on the attributed graph dataset (massive multiplayer online game)

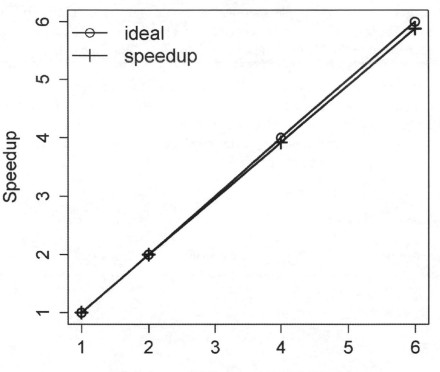

Figure 6 shows the speedup using different mappers and reducers. In our configuration, we also observe a speedup that is linear with growing problem size, which demonstrates the applicability of the approach for large datasets. Thus, SD-MapR/COMODO is scalable for large-scale (exceptional) community detection tasks.

CONCLUSION

In this chapter, we presented the novel SD-MapR algorithmic framework for large-scale local exceptionality detection. We demonstrated the implementation using subgroup discovery methods that were instantiated utilizing the Map/Reduce framework. We outlined the basic algorithm and evaluated several scenarios using both real-world and synthetic datasets – ranging from structured tabular data to complex network data, i.e., in the form of attributed graphs. In summary, our evaluation results proved the scalability of the presented approach for large data sets.

FUTURE RESEARCH DIRECTIONS

For future research, we envision a large-scale processing and local exceptionality detection in heterogeneous data, including structured, semi-structured and unstructured (textual data) which is a typical requirement in many Big Data scenarios (McAfee et al. 2012). For that, information extraction (Cowie & Lehnert 1996) approaches, for example, statistical (e.g., McCallum et al. 2000) or rule-based methods (e.g., Atzmueller et al. 2008; Atzmueller & Nalepa 2009; Kluegl et al. 2009) can be applied. Here, also the detailed inspection of the patterns (Atzmueller & Puppe 2008) and the option of generating explanations (Roth-Berghofer 2004; Roth-Berghofer et al. 2005; Atzmueller & Roth-Berghofer 2010) for the discovered patterns are important future directions. In addition, data quality (e.g., Wang & Strong 1996) is an important aspect for large-scale data mining. Here, quality measures for the extracted relations (e.g., Atzmueller et al. 2005b) and the assessment and validation of the data, e.g., checking expected relations (Atzmueller et al. 2005a) can then provide critical tools for estimating the data quality and for implementing strategies for increasing that.

ACKNOWLEDGMENT

This work has been partially supported by the German Federal Ministry of Education and Research (Bundesministerium für Bildung und Forschung, BMBF), project "FEE", under the sponsorship reference number 01IS14006.

REFERENCES

Agrawal, R., & Srikant, R. (1994). *Quest synthetic data generator*. IBM Almaden Research Center.

Atzmueller, M. (2007). *Knowledge-Intensive Subgroup Mining -- Techniques for Automatic and Interactive Discovery. Dissertations in Artificial Intelligence-Infix (Diski), (307)*. IOS Press.

Atzmueller, M. (2015). *Subgroup Discovery – Advanced Review*. WIREs. *Data Mining and Knowledge Discovery*, *5*(1), 35–49. doi:10.1002/widm.1144

Atzmueller, M., Baumeister, J., & Puppe, F. (2005a). Quality Measures and Semi-Automatic Mining of Diagnostic Rule Bases.*Proc. 15th International Conference on Applications of Declarative Programming and Knowledge Management*. Springer. doi:10.1007/11415763_5

Atzmueller, M., Doerfel, S., Hotho, A., Mitzlaff, F., & Stumme, G. (2012). *Face-to-Face Contacts at a Conference: Dynamics of Communities and Roles. Modeling and Mining Ubiquitous Social Media, LNCS 7472*. Heidelberg, Germany: Springer Verlag.

Atzmueller, M., Doerfel, S., & Mitzlaff, F. (2015a). Description-Oriented Community Detection using Exhaustive Subgroup Discovery. *Information Sciences*, *329*, 965–984. doi:10.1016/j.ins.2015.05.008

Atzmueller, M., Kibanov, M., Hayat, N., Trojahn, M., & Kroll, D. (2015c) Adaptive Class Association Rule Mining for Human Activity Recognition. In *Proceedings of the International Workshop on Mining Ubiquitous and Social Environments* (MUSE2015).

Atzmueller, M., Kluegl, P., & Puppe, F. (2008). Rule-Based Information Extraction for Structured Data Acquisition using TextMarker. In *Proc. LWA 2008*. University of Wuerzburg.

Atzmueller, M., & Lemmerich, F. (2009) Fast Subgroup Discovery for Continuous Target Concepts. *Proc. 18th International Symposium on Methodologies for Intelligent Systems (ISMIS 2009)*. Springer Verlag. doi:10.1007/978-3-642-04125-9_7

Atzmueller, M., & Lemmerich, F. (2012). VIKAMINE - Open-Source Subgroup Discovery, Pattern Mining, and Analytics. In *Proc. ECML/PKDD 2012: European Conference on Machine Learning and Principles and Practice of Knowledge Discovery in Databases*. Springer. doi:10.1007/978-3-642-33486-3_60

Atzmueller, M., & Lemmerich, F. (2013). Exploratory Pattern Mining on Social Media using Geo-References and Social Tagging Information. *International Journal of Web Science*, *1/2*(2), 2013.

Atzmueller, M., Mueller, J., & Becker, M. (2015b). *Exploratory Subgroup Analytics on Ubiquitous Data. Mining, Modeling and Recommending 'Things' in Social Media, LNCS 8940*. Heidelberg, Germany: Springer Verlag.

Atzmueller, M., & Nalepa, G. J. (2009). A Textual Subgroup Mining Approach for Rapid ARD+ Model Capture.*Proc. 22nd International Florida Artificial Intelligence Research Society Conference (FLAIRS)*. AAAI Press.

Atzmueller, M., & Puppe, F. (2005). Semi-Automatic Visual Subgroup Mining using VIKAMINE. *Journal of Universal Computer Science*, *11*(11), 1752–1765.

Atzmueller, M., & Puppe, F. (2006). SD-Map – A Fast Algorithm for Exhaustive Subgroup Discovery. In *Proc. PKDD 2006*. Springer.

Atzmueller, M., & Puppe, F. (2008). A Case-Based Approach for Characterization and Analysis of Subgroup Patterns. *Journal of Applied Intelligence*, *3*(28), 210–221. doi:10.1007/s10489-007-0057-z

Atzmueller, M., Puppe, F., & Buscher, H.-P. (2005b). Profiling Examiners using Intelligent Subgroup Mining.*Proc. 10th International Workshop on Intelligent Data Analysis in Medicine and Pharmacology (IDAMAP-2005)*.

Atzmueller, M., & Roth-Berghofer, T. (2010). The Mining and Analysis Continuum of Explaining Uncovered.*Proc. 30th SGAI International Conference on Artificial Intelligence (AI-2010)*.

Bertin-Mahieux, T., Ellis, D. P., Whitman, B., & Lamere, P. (2011). The million song dataset. In *ISMIR 2011: Proceedings of the 12th International Society for Music Information Retrieval Conference* (pp. 591-596). University of Miami.

Cowie, J., & Lehnert, W. (1996). Information extraction. *Communications of the ACM*, *39*(1), 80–91. doi:10.1145/234173.234209

Dean, J., & Ghemawat, S. (2008). MapReduce: Simplified Data Processing on Large Clusters. *Communications of the ACM*, *51*(1), 107–113. doi:10.1145/1327452.1327492

Duivesteijn, W., Feelders, A., & Knobbe, A. (2016). Exceptional Model Mining. *Data Mining and Knowledge Discovery*, *30*(1), 47–98. doi:10.1007/s10618-015-0403-4

Grosskreutz, H., Rüping, S., & Wrobel, S. (2008) Tight Optimistic Estimates for Fast Subgroup Discovery. In *Proceedings of the ECML/PKDD*. Springer Verlag. doi:10.1007/978-3-540-87479-9_47

Han, J., Pei, J., & Yin, Y. (2000) Mining Frequent Patterns without Candidate Generation. In *ACM SIGMOD International Conference on Management of Data*. ACM Press.

Huiskes, M. J., & Lew, M. S. (2008, October). The MIR Flickr retrieval evaluation. In *Proceedings of the 1st ACM international conference on Multimedia information retrieval* (pp. 39-43). ACM. doi:10.1145/1460096.1460104

Klösgen, W. (1996). Explora: A Multipattern and Multistrategy Discovery Assistant. In Advances in Knowledge Discovery and Data Mining. Palo Alto, CA: AAAI Press.

Kluegl, P., Atzmueller, M., & Puppe, F. (2009) Meta-Level Information Extraction. *The 32nd Annual Conference on Artificial Intelligence*. Springer. doi:10.1007/978-3-642-04617-9_30

Lavrac, N., Kavsek, B., Flach, P., & Todorovski, L. (2004). Subgroup Discovery with CN2-SD. *Journal of Machine Learning Research*, 5, 153–188.

Leman, D., Feelders, A., & Knobbe, A. (2008) Exceptional Model Mining. In *Proceedings of ECML/PKDD*. Springer Verlag. doi:10.1007/978-3-540-87481-2_1

Lemmerich, F., Becker, M., & Atzmueller, M. (2012). Generic Pattern Trees for Exhaustive Exceptional Model Mining. In *Proceedings of ECML/PKDD*. Springer Verlag. doi:10.1007/978-3-642-33486-3_18

Li, H., Wang, Y., Zhang, D., Zhang, M., & Chang, E. (2008). PFP: Parallel FP-Growth for Query Recommendation. *Proc. 2008 ACM conference on Recommender systems*. ACM. doi:10.1145/1454008.1454027

McAfee, A., Brynjolfsson, E., Davenport, T. H., Patil, D. J., & Barton, D. (2012). Big data. *The management revolution. Harvard Business Review*, 90(10), 61–67. PMID:23074865

McCallum, A., Freitag, D., & Pereira, F. C. (2000, June). *Maximum Entropy Markov Models for Information Extraction and Segmentation* (Vol. 17). ICML.

Morik, K. (2002). Detecting Interesting Instances. In Pattern Detection and Discovery (LNCS), (vol. 2447, pp. 13-23). Springer. doi:10.1007/3-540-45728-3_2

Newman, M. E. J. (2006). Modularity and Community Structure in Networks. *Proceedings of the National Academy of Sciences of the United States of America*, 103(23), 8577–8582. doi:10.1073/pnas.0601602103 PMID:16723398

Roth-Berghofer, T., Cassens, J., & Sørmo, F. (2005). *Goals and Kinds of Explanations in Case-Based Reasoning*. Wissensmanagement.

Roth-Berghofer, T. R. (2004). Explanations and case-based reasoning: Foundational issues. In *Advances in case-based reasoning* (pp. 389–403). Springer Berlin Heidelberg. doi:10.1007/978-3-540-28631-8_29

Trabold, D., & Grosskreutz, H. (2013). Parallel Subgroup Discovery on Computing Clusters—First results. In *2013 IEEE International Conference on Big Data* (pp. 575-579). IEEE doi:10.1109/BigData.2013.6691625

Wang, R. Y., & Strong, D. M. (1996). Beyond accuracy: What data quality means to data consumers. *Journal of Management Information Systems*, 12(4), 5–33. doi:10.1080/07421222.1996.11518099

Wrobel, S. (1997) An Algorithm for Multi-Relational Discovery of Subgroups. In *Proceedings of the 1st European Symposium on Principles of Data Mining and Knowledge Discovery*. Heidelberg, Germany: Springer Verlag. doi:10.1007/3-540-63223-9_108

ENDNOTES

[1]   http://hadoop.apache.org
[2]   http://www.bibsonomy.org
[3]   http://delicious.com/
[4]   http://www.last.fm/

Chapter 8
Statistical Features for Extractive Automatic Text Summarization

Yogesh Kumar Meena
MNIT Jaipur, India

Dinesh Gopalani
MNIT Jaipur, India

ABSTRACT

Automatic Text Summarization (ATS) enables users to save their precious time to retrieve their relevant information need while searching voluminous big data. Text summaries are sensitive to scoring methods, as most of the methods requires to weight features for sentence scoring. In this chapter, various statistical features proposed by researchers for extractive automatic text summarization are explored. Features that perform well are termed as best features using ROUGE evaluation measures and used for creating feature combinations. After that, best performing feature combinations are identified. Performance evaluation of best performing feature combinations on short, medium and large size documents is also conducted using same ROUGE performance measures.

INTRODUCTION

Day by day the information content on World Wide Web is exponentially increasing (BIG Data) along with the increase in the number of web users. In current scenario volume of information available on World Wide Web exceeded the textual information available in the printed form in libraries. The rapid growth of online information services makes it difficult to retrieve the relevant information quickly. While searching a particular information content, many a times information system users realize that the extracted information using currently available popular tools, that is present in the form of text, is not relevant to their information need at all, even after reading the whole list of text documents. They perhaps only waste their valuable time in reading the irrelevant text document. This problem can be

DOI: 10.4018/978-1-5225-0293-7.ch008

solved if users can be provided with a summary of the given text document. However, due to a large volume of available text data, that too dynamic in nature, it is very cumbersome for human experts to summarize all the documents manually. This issue leads to the requirement of an automated system that summarize the given text document automatically. This system that condenses the text document automatically and preserving its overall information content using a computer is termed as Automatic Text Summarization (ATS) system. There are numerous applications of automatic text summarization such as a snippet in information retrieval systems, news headlines as replacement to full story of news, electronic program guide in television systems. ATS is widely used for various domains such as business, news, legal and medical domains.

The researchers have classified text summarization systems (Hovy & Lin, 1995; Jones, 1997; Mani & Maybury, 1999; Gupta & Lehal, 2010; Lloret & Palomar, 2012; Nenkova & McKeown, 2012) on the basis of three main perspectives namely input, purpose and output. The third aspect which is most popular among these (i.e. output) considers summarization systems as either extractive or abstractive, and is mostly used by researchers. In extractive automatic text summarization (EATS), a subset of sentences from the original text document is selected for the final summary. Whereas abstractive automatic text summarization (AATS), sentences are fused and regenerated using natural language resources or rules. Abstractive text summarization requires deep knowledge resources, lexical/language resources, parsers and language generators. Because of these resource requirements, it is practically infeasible to use abstractive methods for automatic text summarization. Therefore, researches mainly focused on extractive text summarization instead of abstractive text summarization. The research work carried out is also focused on extractive automatic text summarization.

A typical extractive text summarization process completes in three steps namely pre-processing, sentence scoring, and summary generation. The first step in text summarization is preprocessing the input text document. Preprocessing mainly includes the sentence segmentation, stemming, stopword removal and special symbol removal. In the step which is sentence scoring, a score is assigned to each sentence of the document based on certain specific criteria. In literature various features are defined for sentence scoring such as term frequency, numerical data inclusion, sentence location, etc. After calculating each sentence score, rank is assigned to each sentence based on these scores. The sentences with the higher score are considered more important than the sentences with lower scores and are assigned high ranks consequently. After assigning a rank to each sentence, in third step, top ranked sentences are selected to generate the summary. Total number of sentences in the summary depends on the required length of it.

This chapter is focused on statistical features used in extractive approaches. In this chapter performance of these features is analyzed individually. After that, features that perform well termed as best features using ROUGE evaluation measures are used for creating feature combinations. After that, best performing feature combinations are identified. A deep performance evaluation of best performing feature combinations on short, medium and large size documents is also conducted using same ROUGE performance measures.

The rest of the chapter is organized as follows: After discussing challenges of ATS, background methods are presented followed by features used for sentence scoring. . Next, author discusses generic summarization process used for ATS. This is subsequently followed by evaluation matrices for ATS, followed by proposed impact analysis. Features and their combinations are properly analyzed before the chapter is finally concluded.

GENERAL CHALLENGES IN TEXT SUMMARIZATION

Major issues (Jones, 1998, Mani & Maybury, 1999) in generating automatic extractive text summaries are listed below:

1. **Redundancy:** Extractive text summaries are generated by selecting top scoring sentences from the text document. This sometimes led to the selection of redundant sentences in the final summary.
2. **Cohesion:** Sometimes, top scoring sentences becomes totally different from each other. Each neighboring sentence contains totally different terms without any of context in between. It becomes an issue, because if sentence are not cohesive then it becomes difficult to interpret the intended gist of text.
3. **Coherence:** Textual relationship beyond more than one sentence and through a discourse, if not meaningful then there is no meaning of generated summary. As selected sentences on the basis of some scoring function might not produce quality summary due to lack of coherence in between the selected ones.
4. **Anaphora:** Scoring function do not reproduce sentence as they only select the sentences as it is from the original text, therefore referring pronouns in the resulted summary creates issues in terms of interpretation and resolution.
5. **Coverage:** Extractive summaries do not guarantee that all inherent topics or themes are present in the finally produced summary as selection is purely on the basis of score of sentences obtained using some scoring methodology.

BACKGROUND AND ISSUES

Work in the area of EATS started in the early 1950s, however as of now; no such system is available that can generate summaries as efficient as experts. In early stage, pioneered features such as term frequency (Luhn, 1958), sentence location (Baxendale, 1958), cue words and title similarity (Edmundson, 1969) were proposed for text summarization process. As the time progressed, new features were added for the text summarization process like tf-isf, gain, etc. The basic methodology behind these summarization processes is to assign score to each of the sentences present in the text by using either a single feature or linear sum of features. However, applying features alone do not improve the quality of text summaries significantly, as each feature processes sentences in a different aspect. In literature many feature based statistical, graph based, lexical, machine learning and evolutionary methods for extractive summarization are proposed by researchers.

The key component of the statistical approaches(Rush et al.,1971; Pollock & Zamora, 1975; Brandow et al., 1995; Salton, 1983; Church & Gale, 1995; Hovy & Lin, 1997; Hovy & Lin, 1998; Baldwin & Morton, 1998; Radev et al., 2001; Nobata et al., 2001; Mori, 2002; Nobata et al., 2002; Pingali et al., 2005; Liu et al., 2009) of extractive text summarization is assigning weights to words or sentences based on certain statistics such as frequency of appearance of words in the text. Statistical approaches are simple to use as no knowledge source is required in these approaches. However problems with these approaches are similar to extractive text summarization approaches such as problem of ambiguous references i.e. anaphors (such as pronouns which refers to some words that appears earlier in the text) and cataphors (ambiguous words which signals to word that appears later in the text).

In graph based approaches (Michalcea & Tarau, 2004), sentence scores are generated based on the relationship among the sentences. Although graph based approaches work well as graph based approaches do not rely only on the local context of a text unit (vertex), rather take into account information recursively drawn from the entire text (graph). However graph based approaches also have the issue of ambiguous references. In addition to this issue, graph based approaches also have an issue of the requirement of multiple iterations as these approaches require multiple iterations to converge.

Later machine learning methods and evolutionary methods (Kupiec, 1995; Hirao et al., 2002; Varma et al., 2005; Fattah & Ren, 2009; Prasad & Kulakarni, 2010; Xiaoyan et al., 2010; Abuobieda et al., 2013; Abuobieda et al., 2012; Wang & Maches, 2013; Mendoza et al., 2014) were proposed with the increase number of features. These methods, used to identify a suitable set of features and their applicable weights. On the trained data the performance, most of the times, is optimal; however applying the same process to unknown data may result in the generation of poor quality summaries. This issue of generation of poor quality summaries for unknown data is known as the generalization issue. Although machine learning algorithms allow to test performance with a high number of features in an easy way, however at the same time, all these approaches require labelled corpus of sentences. This requirement of labelled corpus becomes a critical issue while summarization because it is difficult to mark summary sentences similar to abstracts, manually. Also these methods are not able to resolve the issue of coherence and cohesiveness.

Semantic methods such as feature based semantic similarity and lexical chains were proposed to alleviate the issue of coherence and cohesiveness. In lexical chain based approaches, lexical chains are constructed after the pre-processing step. Thereafter in the next step, scoring of the chains is conducted. For this purpose various matrices are applied such as chain length, chain distribution in the text, text span covered by the chain, density, graph topology (diameter of the graph of the words) and number of repetitions. The main issue with lexical chain based methods is the requirement of knowledge sources on hand such as WordNet to find semantically related words and chains, and secondly interpretation of semantic information such as semantic similarity threshold. These practical issues limits and puts constraints on the usefulness of semantic methods.

In order to improve the performance of extractive text summarization systems, the information-rich sentences need to be selected to produce the final summary. Hence sentence selection is the most important step of extractive text summarization process. For the purpose a numerical measure of usefulness may be assigned to each of the sentences in the given text. Information rich sentences are then selected according to the specified heuristics. Aforesaid weight assigning process by using a specific heuristic is termed as sentence scoring. For the final summary, sentences are selected on the basis of their scores computed using different scoring methods. Therefore, the overall performance of extractive text summarization system mainly depends on the sentence scoring methods employed to score the sentences. Several other factors like pre-processing, also influences the quality of text summaries.

From early 1960s, researchers are continuously trying to analyze the feature from different perspectives in order to generate efficient text summaries. Rafael et al., 2013 assessed a broader set of features that includes term frequency, tf-isf, upper case, proper noun, word co-occurrence, lexical similarity, cue word, numerical data, sentence length, sentence position, title similarity, aggregate similarity, bushy path and textrank. They tested each and every algorithm for three different datasets. It was concluded that term frequency, tf-isf, sentence length, lexical similarity and text rank are better features for sentence scoring as compared to the rest of the features listed. Later Rafael et al., 2014 analyzed the performance of previously proposed algorithms using different combinations. The proposed methodology was termed as context based summarization and three groups of features were created namely word level, sentence level and graph level. All combinations of intra-group and inter-group word level, sentence level and graph level features are tried to test their impact on sentence scoring. This approach concluded that word frequency; title similarity and sentence location are the best features specifically for News domain. However, in all assessments listed above impact analysis of features such as sentence entropy, sentence to sentence cohesion etc. has not been carried out and a single evaluation measure ROUGE-1 for extracting best feature combinations is used. Moreover, some semantic features are also analyzed with statistical features. However, lack of abundant knowledge sources makes it difficult to use semantic features. This motivated to use exhaustive set of features for impact analysis other than semantic features (due to lack of knowledge sources) and evaluation measures (ROUGE-1, ROUGE-2, ROUGE-L and ROUGE-W).

FEATURE ENGINEERING

A typical sentence scoring module of extractive automatic text summarization requires various features to score sentences. A number of statistical and linguistics features have been proposed by researchers for the aforesaid scoring process. These features are categorized into three groups of categories according to their processing level. The categories are word level scoring, sentence level scoring and graph based scoring and these are described as following:

1. **Word Level Scoring:** The features used for word level scoring methods score each term present in the given text according to a particular criterion. Sentence score is computed as the sum of each term present in a given sentence.
2. **Graph Level Scoring:** The sentence score in case of graph level scoring method is calculated using the relationship of a sentence with other sentences. If two sentences are linked via some defined parameter, then an edge is established in between them. Their weights are used to generate sentence scores.
3. **Sentence Level Scoring:** The features used for sentence level scoring methods use sentence level statistics for computing score for a given sentence.

All features are summarized in Table 1.

GENERIC SUMMARIZATION PROCESS

A typical extractive text summarization process completes in three steps namely pre-processing, sentence scoring and summary generation. The details of process flow are discussed in the following subsection. Whole generic text summarization process flow consisting of three steps is shown in Figure 1.

1. **Pre Processing:** First step in text summarization is preprocessing the input text document. Preprocessing mainly includes the following steps sentence segmentation, stemming (Porters, 1980), stopword removal and special symbol removal.
2. **Feature Based Scoring:** After preprocessing, the next step in generic text summarization is sentence scoring. In this step, a score is assigned to each sentence of the document based on certain specific

Table 1. Feature algorithms

S. No.	Short Name	Author, Year	Feature Algorithm Name	Level
1	FA1	Salton, 1997	Bushy Path	Graph Level
2	FA2	Neto et al., 2002	Cosine Similarity With Title	Sentence Level
3	FA3	Edmundson, 1969	Cue Words	Word Level
4	FA4	Neto et al., 2002	Depth of Sentence in the Tree	Sentence Level
5	FA5	Mori, 2002	Gain	Word Level
6	FA6	Torres et al., 2002	Hamming Distance	Sentence Level
7	FA7	Torres et al., 2002	Hamming Weight	Sentence Level
8	FA8	Torres et al., 2002	Interaction Between the Sentences	Sentence Level
9	FA9	Erkan et al., 2004	LexRank	Graph Level
10	FA10	Torres et al., 2002	Named Entity	Word Level
11	FA11	Lin, 1999	Numerical Data	Sentence Level
12	FA12	Salton, 1997	Aggregate Similarity	Graph Level
13	FA13	Torres et al., 2002	Sentence Entropy	Sentence Level
14	FA14	Baxendale, 1958	Sentence Location1	Sentence Level
15	FA15	Nobata et al., 2002	Sentence Location2	Sentence Level
16	FA16	Neto et al., 2002	Sentence to Centroid Cohesion	Sentence Level
17	FA17	Neto et al., 2002	Sentence to Sentence Cohesion	Sentence Level
18	FA18	Torres et al., 2002	Sum of Probability	Sentence Level
19	FA19	Torres et al., 2002	Sum of Hamming Weights of Words by Frequency	Sentence Level
20	FA20	Luhn, 1958	Term Frequency	Word Level
21	FA21	Mihalcea et al., 2004	TextRank	Graph Level
22	FA22	Brandow et al., 1995	TFIDF	Word Level
23	FA23	Edmundson, 1969	Title Similarity	Sentence Level
24	FA24	Torres et al., 2002	Total Terms in Sentence	Sentence Level
25	FA25	Liu et al., 2009	Word Co-occurrence	Sentence Level

Figure 1.

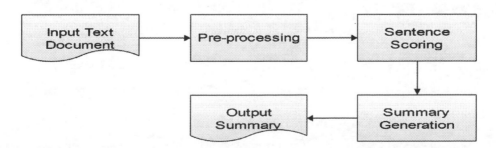

criteria. Various features are defined for sentence scoring such as term frequency, numerical data inclusion, sentence location, etc. After calculating each sentence score, rank is assigned to each sentence based on these scores of the sentences. The sentences with the higher score are considered as more important than the sentences with lower scores. Ranks are assigned to each sentence in the given text according to their scores.

3. **Summary Generation:** After assigning a rank to each sentence, the final step in generic text summarization is summary generation. In this step, top ranked sentences are selected to generate the summary. The number of sentences to be selected depends on the required length of the summary.

Evaluation Matrices

Automatic evaluation of text summaries is a challenging and difficult task. The gold summaries provided by human experts and summary generated by automatic text summarization systems usually do not match exactly. Lin, 2004 proposed Recall-Oriented Understudy for Gisting Evaluation (ROUGE) measures for evaluation of text summarization systems. ROUGE measures are the only available commonly used measures for the purpose of automatic evaluation. ROUGE-1 and ROUGE-2 are versions of ROUGE-N, where N is 1 and 2, respectively. ROUGE-L and ROUGE-W are computed using longest common sub-sequences.

Proposed Impact Analysis

As discussed earlier, extractive text summarization in general completes in three steps namely: pre-processing, sentence scoring and summary generation. Process flow to analyze the impact of feature combinations is shown in Figure 2. Pre-processing is applied on the text document using the process described earlier. Each sentence is then scored using all the features one by one. After sentence scoring, summary is generated using each feature. ROUGE-1 evaluation measure as described in previous section is then applied on the summary and relevant features are further used for generation of feature combinations. These relevant features are termed as prominent features. For each feature combination, a summary is generated. ROUGE evaluation measures (ROUGE-1, ROUGE-2, ROUGE-L, ROUGE-W) are further applied to get the better performing feature combinations which are termed as best feature combinations.

Figure 2.

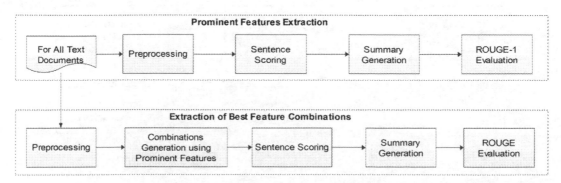

RESULTS AND DISCUSSIONS ON DUC 2002 DATASET

Document Understating Conference (DUC) 2002 dataset is used for experimental evaluation of proposed impact analysis. This dataset contains News data along with their gold summaries (manual summaries provided by humans). Sixty reference documents sets, each of them consisting of approximately ten documents for the evaluation task are provided in DUC 2002. For each document, DUC 2002 provides two abstractive summaries as gold summaries with about hundred words each.

After summary generation using a specific sentence scoring ROUGE-1, ROUGE-2, ROUGE-L and ROUGE-W scores are computed for each document. Initially, for each feature algorithm precision, recall and f-Measure value is calculated for each document. Thereafter, features that perform well are identified and termed as prominent features. These feature algorithms are then used for generating feature combinations. The feature algorithm combinations which perform well are termed as best feature combinations.

Using prominent feature algorithms, different feature algorithm combinations are generated for sentence scoring. Initially, Best forty combinations for each evaluation measure ROUGE-1, ROUGE-2, ROUGE-L and ROUGE-W are selected. Combinations which are present in the lists of best performing combinations, for each of the four evaluation measures are selected as final best feature algorithm combinations. These combinations are listed in Table 2. The list comprised of features algorithms busy path, cosine similarity with title, depth of the sentence in the tree, lexrank, aggregate similarity, sentence location1, sentence to sentence cohesion and title similarity. Despite having better performance individually, sentence entropy did not produce higher ROUGE scores in combinations with other feature algorithms. All best combinations are renamed as COMB with number in the same order of their respective rank for ROUGE-2 F-measure, for the purpose of comparison in graphical form. For example: first best performing combinations is renamed as COMB1.

Pre-processing is an important step of any text processing system. Final results are very much sensitive to this pre-processing. Comparison of results obtained using ROUGE-1 evaluation measure on all documents for single feature algorithms, with stemming and without stemming is shown in Figure 3.

It is observed that results using stemming are better as compared to results without stemming. The fact that stemming use the root forms of the words, enhances the performance. Comparing terms using their stemmed version gives more number of matches, which ultimately improves the results. Comparison of results obtained using ROUGE-2 evaluation measure on all documents for single feature algorithms, with stemming and without stemming is shown in Figure 4. Here also, the performance of stemmed version is better as compared without non-stemmed version.

Precision, Recall and F-Measure comparisons of best feature algorithm combinations for all documents set using ROUGE-1 and ROUGE-2 are presented in Figure 5 and Figure 6 respectively. Results are sorted on the basis of f-measure. It is observed that their are notable variations in ROUGE scores of precision and recall for some of the combinations. This is primarily due to the size of summary to be produced i.e. compression rate.

In proposed experiments, the compression rate is hundred words. At the time, total words in the summary exceed the limit beyond hundred words, the variation in between precision and recall is visible. More the limit exceeds, more the difference is reported in precision and recall. The smooth curve shows that COMB1 performs better as compared to all other feature algorithm combinations. ROUGE-L and ROUGE-W comparisons for the similar group are shown in Figure 7 and Figure 8, respectively.

Similar to ROUGE-1 and ROUGE-2, it is observed that COMB1 performs better in case of ROUGE-L and ROUGE-W evaluation as well. COMB1 comprised of feature algorithms aggregate similarity (Salton,

Table 2. Best feature algorithm combinations details

S. No.	Combination ID	Features in Combination
1	COMB1	Aggregate Similarity + LexRank + Sentence Location1
2	COMB2	LexRank + Sentence Location1
3	COMB3	Aggregate Similarity + LexRank + Sentence Location1 + Sentence to Sentence Cohesion
4	COMB4	Bushy Path + LexRank + Sentence Location1 + Sentence to Sentence Cohesion
5	COMB5	LexRank + Sentence Location1 + Sentence to Sentence Cohesion + Sentence to Centroid Cohesion
6	COMB6	LexRank + Sentence Location1 + Sentence to Sentence Cohesion
7	COMB7	Depth of the Sentence in the Tree + LexRank + Sentence Location1
8	COMB8	Aggregate Similarity + LexRank + Sentence Location1 + Sentence to Sentence Cohesion + Sentence to Centroid Cohesion
9	COMB9	Depth of the Sentence in the Tree + LexRank + Sentence Location1 + Sentence to Centroid Cohesion
10	COMB10	LexRank + Sentence Location1 + Sentence to Sentence Cohesion + Term Frequency
11	COMB11	Aggregate Similarity + Depth of the Sentence in the Tree + LexRank + Sentence Location1 + Sentence to Sentence Cohesion
12	COMB12	Depth of the Sentence in the Tree + LexRank + Sentence Location1 + Term Frequency
13	COMB13	Aggregate Similarity + Depth of the Sentence in the Tree + LexRank + Sentence Location1
14	COMB14	Aggregate Similarity + LexRank + Sentence Location1 + Sentence to Sentence Cohesion + Term Frequency
15	COMB15	Sentence Location1 + Sentence to Sentence Cohesion
16	COMB16	Aggregate Similarity + Depth of the Sentence in the Tree + LexRank + Sentence Location1 + Sentence to Centroid Cohesion
17	COMB17	Aggregate Similarity + Frequential Sum of Probability + LexRank + Sentence Location1 + Sentence to Sentence Cohesion
18	COMB18	Aggregate Similarity + Sentence Location1 + Sentence to Sentence Cohesion
19	COMB19	Aggregate Similarity + Depth of the Sentence in the Tree + LexRank + Sentence Location1 + Term Frequency
20	COMB20	Depth of the Sentence in the Tree + Sentence Location1 +Term Frequency
21	COMB21	Aggregate Similarity + Sentence Location1
22	COMB22	Similarity + Depth of the Sentence in the Tree + Hamming distance + LexRank + Sentence Location1

1997), lexrank (Erkan, 2004) and sentence location1. This is primarily due to using graph based feature algorithms such as aggregate similarity (Salton, 1997) and lexrank (Erkan, 2004) which focuses on the sentences which have more number of interlinks. In rest of the other combinations, feature algorithms such as depth of the sentence in the Tree (Neto et al., 2002), frequential sum of probability (Torres et al., 2002), hamming distance (Torres et al., 2002) sentence to sentence cohesion (Neto et al., 2002)}, term frequency (Luhn, 1958) and title similarity (Edmundson, 1969) are present other then the three features present in COMB1.

All the best twenty two feature algorithm combinations differ slightly in ROUGE scores. Comparing with individual feature algorithms, these feature algorithm combinations performs better as shown in Figure 9. It is clearly visible that all best feature algorithm combinations performs better as compared to all individual algorithms. Similar to individual feature algorithms, it is not a good idea to use a single feature algorithm combination for summary generation. As different feature algorithm combinations have different inherent properties. In comparison with work carried out by Rafael et al. (Rafael et al., 2013; Rafael et al., 2014) reported best combination is COMB1 contains two graph level and one sentence

Figure 3.

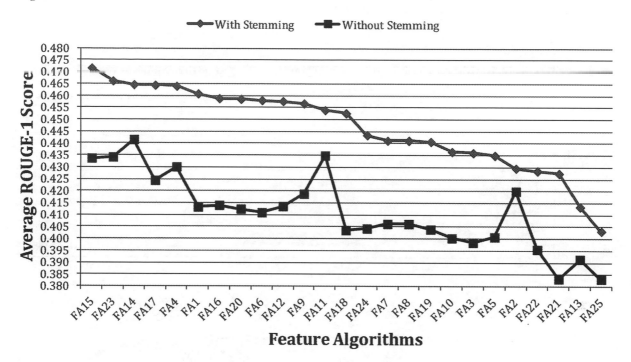

Figure 4.

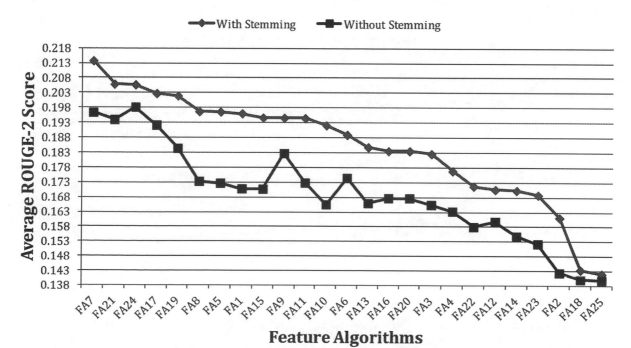

Figure 5.

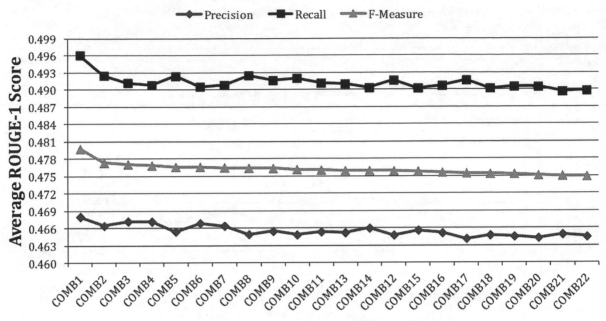

Figure 6.

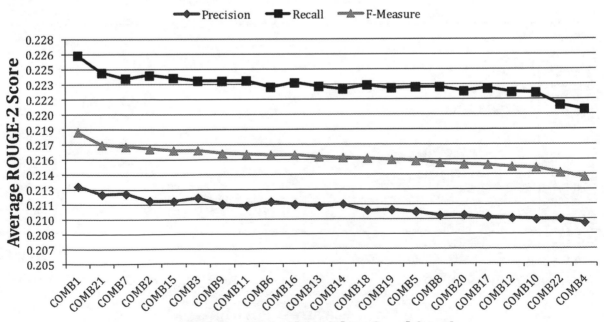

Figure 7.

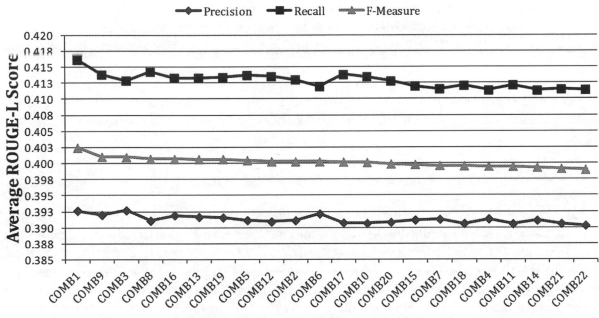

Best Feature Algorithm Combinations

Figure 8.

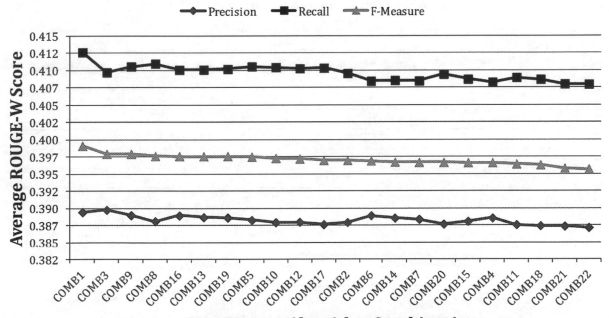

Best Feature Algorithm Combinations

level features. Moreover, no dependent features such as cue words (Edmundson, 1969), named entity (Nobata et al., 2002) etc. are present in the reported best combinations.

Comparisons in between ROUGE-1 scores for short size, medium size, large size and all set of documents are shown in Figure 10. It is observed from the figure that performance of summarization system decreases as the size of document increases. This degradation is due to increase in the number of sentences because as the number of sentences increases, probability of selection of informative sentences decreases.

ROUGE-2 scores comparisons for short size, medium size, large size and all set of documents are shown in Figure 11. Here also performance decreases with the increase in the size of input text document.

CONCLUSION

In this chapter performance of various individual features algorithms such as bushy path, cosine similarity, cue words etc. is tested using ROUGE evaluation measures. It is observed that single feature algorithms only use specific feature strengths that are not capable of generating efficient summaries. Stemming impact is also analyzed while pre-processing of input text document; it is observed that with stemming performance improves significantly. Thereafter, feature algorithm combinations are generated using best performing single feature algorithms using ROUGE evaluation measures. A feature algorithm combination which performs well for all ROUGE evaluation measures are reported as best feature algorithm combinations. Their performance is investigated on short, medium and large size documents. It is observed that performance degrades as the size of document increases.

Figure 9.

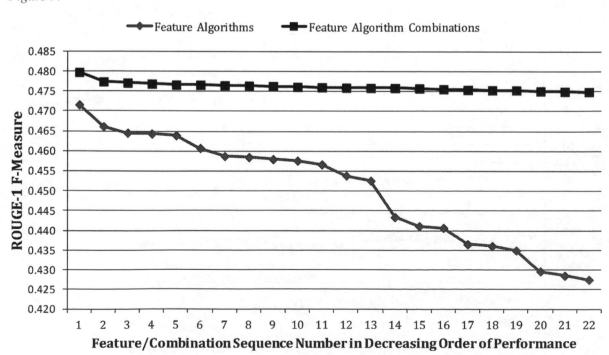

Figure 10.

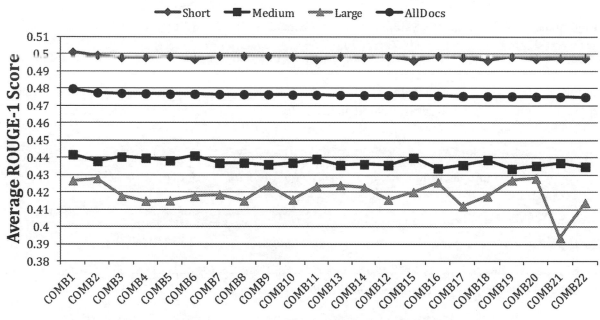

Figure 11.

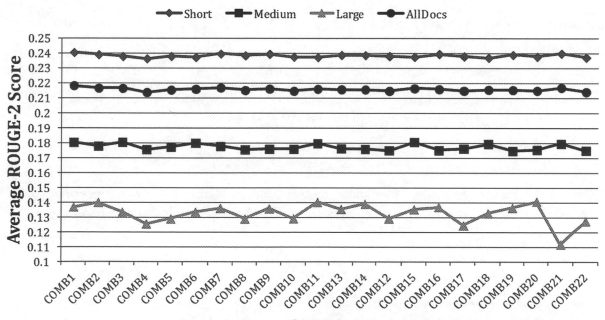

REFERENCES

Abuobieda, A., Salim, N., Binwahlan, M. S., & Osman, A. H. (2013). Differential evolution cluster-based text summarization methods. *Computing, Electrical and Electronics Engineering (ICCEEE), 2013 International Conference on,*. doi:10.1109/ICCEEE.2013.6633941

Abuobieda, N., Salim, A., Albaham, A., Osman, Y., & Kumar. (2012). Text summarization features selection method using pseudo genetic-based model. In *International Conference on Information Retrieval Knowledge Management (CAMP)*. doi:10.1109/InfRKM.2012.6204980

Aliguliyev, R. M. (2009). A new sentence similarity measure and sentence based extractive technique for automatic text summarization. *Expert Systems with Applications*, *36*(4), 7764–7772. doi:10.1016/j.eswa.2008.11.022

Baldwin, B., & Morton, T. S. (1998). Dynamic co reference based summarization. In *Proceedings of the Third Conference on Empirical Methods in Natural Language Processing (EMNLP-3)*.

Barzilay, R., & Elhadad, M. (1997). Using Lexical Chains for Text Summarization. In *Proceedings of the ACL/EACL'97 Workshop on Intelligent Scalable Text Summarization* (pp. 10–17).

Baxendale, P. B. (1958). Machine-made index for technical literature: An experiment. *IBM Journal of Research and Development*, *2*(4), 354–361. doi:10.1147/rd.24.0354

Binwahlan, M. S., Salim, N., & Suanmali, L. (2009). Swarm Based Text Summarization. In *Proceedings of the International Association of Computer Science and Information Technology - Spring Conference. IACSITSC '09* (pp. 145-150). doi:10.1109/IACSIT-SC.2009.61

Binwahlan, M. S., Salim, N., & Suanmali, L. (2010). Fuzzy swarm diversity hybrid model for text summarization. *Information Processing & Management*, *46*(5), 571–588. doi:10.1016/j.ipm.2010.03.004

Brandow, R., Mitze, K., & Rau, L. F. (1995). Automatic condensation of electronic publications by sentence selection. *Information Processing & Management*, *31*(5), 675–685. doi:10.1016/0306-4573(95)00052-I

Carpineto, C., Osinski, S., Romano, G., & Weiss, D. (2009). A survey of Web clustering engines. *ACM Computing Surveys*, *41*(3), 1–38. doi:10.1145/1541880.1541884

Church, K., & Gale, W. A. (1995). Inverse document frequency (idf): A measure of deviations from poisson. In *Proceedings of the Third Workshop on Very Large Corpora*.

Conroy, J., & O'leary, D. (2001). Text summarization via hidden Markov models. In *Proceedings of the 24th annual international ACM SIGIR conference on Research and development in information retrieval* (pp. 406-407). New Orleans, LA: ACM.

Dehkordi, P.-K., Kumarci, F., & Khosravi, H. (2009). Text Summarization Based on Genetic Programming. *Proceedings of the International Journal of Computing and ICT Research*, *3*, 57–64.

Edmundson, H. P. (1969). New methods in automatic extracting. *Journal of the ACM*, *16*(2), 264–285. doi:10.1145/321510.321519

Fattah, M. A., & Ren, F. (2009). Ga, mr, ann, pnn and gmm based models for automatic text summarization. *Computer Speech & Language, 23*(1), 126–144. doi:10.1016/j.csl.2008.04.002

Garcia, H. R., & Ledeneva, Y. (2013). Single Extractive Text Summarization Based on a Genetic Algorithm. In J. Carrasco Ochoa, J. Martínez Trinidad, J. Rodríguez, & G. Baja (Eds.), *Pattern Recognition* (Vol. 7914, pp. 374–383). Springer Berlin Heidelberg. doi:10.1007/978-3-642-38989-4_38

Gupta, V., & Lehal, G. S. (2010). A survey of text summarization extractive techniques. *Journal of Emerging Technologies in Web Intelligence, 2*(3), 258-268.

Hirao, T., Sasaki, Y., Isozaki, H., & Maeda, E. (2002). NTT's Text Summarization system for DUC-2002. In *Workshop on Text Summarization(In conjunction with the ACL 2002 and including the DARPA/NIST sponsored DUC 2002 Meeting on Text Summarization).*

Hovy, E., & Lin, C.-Y. (1998). Automated text summarization and the summarist system. In *Proceedings of a Workshop onAssociation for Computational Linguistics.*

Jezek, K., & Steinberger, J. (2008). Automatic Text Summarization (The state of the art 2007 and new challenges). In Znalosti 2008 (pp. 1-12).

Jones, K. S. (1998). Automatic summarising: Factors and directions. In *Advances in Automatic Text Summarization* (pp. 1–12). MIT Press.

Kogilavani, A., & Balasubramanie, P. (2010). Clustering and Feature Specific Sentence Extraction Based Summarization of Multiple Documents. *International Journal of Computer Science and Information Technology, 2*(4), 99–111. doi:10.5121/ijcsit.2010.2409

Kupiec, J., Pedersen, J., & Chen, F. (1995). A trainable document summarizer. In *Proceedings of the 18th annual international ACM SIGIR conference on Research and development in information retrieval.* Seattle, WA: ACM.

Lewandowski, D. (2005). Web searching, search engines and Information Retrieval. *Inf. Serv. Use, 25*(3-4), 137-147.

Lin, C.-Y. (2004). Rouge: a package for automatic evaluation of summaries. In *Proceedings of the ACL-04 Workshop on Text Summarization Branches Out* (pp. 74-81).

Lin, C.-Y., & Hovy, E. (1997). Identifying topics by position. In *Proceedings of the fifth conference on Applied natural language processing (ANLC '97).* Association for Computational Linguistics. doi:10.3115/974557.974599

Litvak, M., Last, M., & Friedman, M. (2010). A new approach to improving multilingual summarization using a genetic algorithm. In *Proceedings of the 48th Annual Meeting of the Association for Computational Linguistics* (pp. 927-936). Uppsala, Sweden: Association for Computational Linguistics.

Liu, X., Webster, & Kit, C. (2009). An Extractive Text Summarizer Based on Significant Words. In *Proceedings of the 22nd International Conference on Computer Processing of Oriental Languages. Language Technology for the Knowledge-based Economy* (ICCPOL '09). Springer-Verlag.

Lloret, E., & Palomar, M. (2012, January). Text summarization in progress: A literature review. *Artificial Intelligence Review, 37*(1), 1–41. doi:10.1007/s10462-011-9216-z

Luhn, H. P. (1958). The automatic creation of literature abstracts. *IBM Journal of Research and Development, 2*(2), 159–165. doi:10.1147/rd.22.0159

Mani, I., & Maybury, M. T. (1999). Advances in Automatic Text Summarization. MIT Press.

Marcu, D. (1998). Improving summarization through rhetorical parsing tuning. In *Proceedings of The Sixth Workshop on Very Large Corpora* (pp. 206-215).

Meena, Y. K., & Gopalani, D. (2014). Analysis of Sentence Scoring Methods for Extractive Automatic Text Summarization. *International Conference on Information and Communication Technology for Competitive Strategies (ICTCS-2014)*. ACM. doi:10.1145/2677855.2677908

Mendoza, M., Bonilla, S., Noguera, C., Cobos, C., & Leon, E. (2014). Extractive single-document summarization based on genetic operators and guided local search. *Expert Systems with Applications, 41*(9), 4158–4169. doi:10.1016/j.eswa.2013.12.042

Mihalcea, R., & Tarau, P. (2004). Textrank: Bringing order in to texts. In Proceedinngs of EMNLP 2004. Barcelona, Spain: Association for Computational Linguistics.

Mori, T. (2002). Information gain ratio as term weight: the case of summarization of ir results. In *Proceedings of the 19th International Conference on Computational Linguistics*. Association for Computational Linguistics. doi:10.3115/1072228.1072246

Nenkova, A., & McKeown, K. (2012). A Survey of Text Summarization Techniques. In C. C. Aggarwal & C. Zhai (Eds.), *Mining Text Data* (pp. 43–76). Springer, US. doi:10.1007/978-1-4614-3223-4_3

Neto, J. L., Freitas, A. A., & Kaestner, C. A. A. (2002). Automatic text summarization using a machine learning approach. In Advances in Artificial Intelligence (LNCS), (vol. 2507, pp. 205-215). Springer Berlin Heidelberg. doi:10.1007/3-540-36127-8_20

Nobata, C., Sekine, S., Isahara, H., & Grishman, R. (2002). Summarization System Integrated with Named Entity Tagging and IE pattern Discovery. *Proceedings of Third International Conference on Language Resources and Evaluation (LREC 2002)*.

Nobata, C., Sekine, S., Murata, M., Uchimoto, K., Utiyama, M., & Isahara, H. (2001). Sentence extraction system assembling multiple evidence. In *Proceedings of the Second NTCIR Workshop Meeting*.

Ono, K., Sumita, K., & Miike, S. (1994). Abstract generation based on rhetorical structure extraction. In *Proceedings of the 15th conference on Computational linguistics* (Vol. 1, pp. 344-348). Kyoto, Japan: Association for Computational Linguistics. doi:10.3115/991886.991946

Pingali, J. J., & Varma, V. (2005). Sentence extraction based on single document summarization. In *Workshop on Document Summarization*.

Pollock, J. J., & Zamora, A. (1975). Automatic Abstracting Research at Chemical Abstracts Service. *Chemical Information and Computer Sciences, 15*(4), 226–232.

Porselvi, A., & Gunasundari, S. (2013). Survey on web page visual summarization. *International Journal of Emerging Technology and Advanced Engineering, 3*, 26–32.

Porter, M. F. (1980). An algorithm for suffix stripping. *Program, 14*(3), 130–137. doi:10.1108/eb046814

Prassad, R., Shardanand, & Kulkarni, U. (2010). Implementation and evaluation of evolutionary connectionist approaches to automated text summarization. Journal of Computer Science, 1366-1376.

Radev, D., Blair-Goldensohn, S., & Zhang, Z. (2001). Experiments in single and multi-document summarization using MEAD. In *First Document Understanding Conference.*

Rafael, F., Freitas, F., De Souza, C. L., Dueire, L. R., Lima, R., Franca, G., … Favaro, L. (2014). A Context Based Text Summarization System. *2014 11th IAPR International Workshop on Document Analysis Systems (DAS).*

Rush, J. E., Salvador, R., & Zamora, A. (1971). Automatic abstracting and indexing. ii. production of indicative abstracts by application of contextual inference and syntactic coherence criteria. *Journal of the American Society for Information Science, 22*(4), 260–274. doi:10.1002/asi.4630220405

Salton, G., Fox, E. A., & Wu, H. (1983). Extended Boolean information retrieval. *Communications of the ACM, 26*(11), 1022–1036. doi:10.1145/182.358466

Salton, G., Singhal, A., Mitra, M., & Buckley, C. (1997, March). Automatic text structuring and summarization. *Information Processing & Management, 33*(2), 193–207. doi:10.1016/S0306-4573(96)00062-3

Shen, D., Sun, J.-T., Li, H., Yang, Q., & Chen, Z. (2007). Document summarization using conditional random fields. In *Proceedings of the 20th international joint conference on Artifical intelligence* (pp. 2862-2867). Hyderabad, India: Morgan Kaufmann Publishers Inc.

Svore, K., Vanderwende, L., & Burges, C. (2007). Enhancing single-document summarization by combining RankNet and third-party sources. In *Proceedings of the EMNLP-CoNLL* (pp. 448-457).

Torres, M., Juan-Manuel, P. M., & Meunier, J.-G. (2002). Condenses de textes par des methodes numeriques. In *JADT* (Vol. 2, pp. 723–734). JADT.

Wong, K.-F., Wu, M., & Li, W. (2008). Extractive summarization using supervised and semi-supervised learning. In *Proceedings of the 22nd International Conference on Computational Linguistics* (Vol. 1, pp. 985-992). Manchester, UK: Association for Computational Linguistics. doi:10.3115/1599081.1599205

Xiaoyan, C., Wenjie, L., You, O., & Hong, Y. (2010). Simultaneous ranking and clustering of sentences: a reinforcement approach to multi-document summarization. In *Proceedings of the 23rd International Conference on Computational Linguistics* (COLING '10). Association for Computational Linguistics.

KEY TERMS AND DEFINITIONS

Abstractive Summarization: Extraction of sentences by merging and fusing from the original text.
Extractive Summarization: Retrieval of sentences as its is from the original text.
Precision: Ratio of the relevant sentences retrieved divided by total sentences retrieved.

Recall: Ratio of the relevant sentences retrieved divided by total sentences relevant sentences.

Sentence Features: Any of various abstract entities that specify or combine to specify phonological, morphological, semantic, and syntactic properties of linguistic forms and that act as the targets of linguistic rules and operations.

Stemming: The process of reducing the words to its root form or word stem.

Stopword: Commonly or frequently used words (such as "is") that needs to be ignored at most of the times of processing of text either searching or retrieving.

Text Summarization: A process of condensing the text document automatically by computer system such that the produced summary is no longer than a specified threshold [typically one-third of the size of original text] and covers all the information contents of it.

Section 3
Case Studies and Application Areas

Chapter 9
Data Modeling and Knowledge Discovery in Process Industries

Benjamin Klöpper
ABB Corporate Research Center, Germany

David Arnu
RapidMiner GmbH, Germany

Marcel Dix
ABB Corporate Research Center, Germany

Dikshith Siddapura
ABB Corporate Research Center, Germany

ABSTRACT

Dispersed data sources, incompatible data formats and a lack of non-ambiguous and machine readable meta-data is a major obstacle in data analytics and data mining projects in process industries. Often, meta-information is only available in unstructured format optimized for human consumption. This contribution outlines a feasible methodology for organizing historical datasets extracted from process plants in a big data platform for the purpose of analytics and machine learning model building in an industrial big data analytics project.

INTRODUCTION

Driven by the development of the Internet and Internet of Things, the amount of data we are generating every day from these systems has exploded during last years. This is why big data analytics has become increasingly important for many companies, who try to mine their data to better understand their business and thereby make better business decisions. For example, credit card companies who handle millions of credit card transactions every day make heavy use of big data analytics and machine learning algorithms, such as anomaly detection algorithms, to automatically detect anomalies in card uses of their customers and thereby are able to better protect against credit card fraud. There are many more popular examples for the use of big data analytics and machine learning today from B2C and B2B sectors.

And it turns out that also in the industrial domain we are dealing with big data, and there is great potential for big data analytics: Industrial automation has led to plants being increasingly IT-centric and data-intense. Today, a typical process plant like a paper mill, a hot-rolling mill or a petro-chemical plant generates a large amount of documents and data throughout its entire life-cycle: e.g. measurement values, alarm and event logs, shift book logs, laboratory results (during plant operation), as well as I/O and tag

DOI: 10.4018/978-1-5225-0293-7.ch009

lists, piping and instrumentation diagrams (P&ID), control logic, alarm configurations (during planning and commissioning), and maintenance notification, repair and inspection reports (during maintenance). The continuous stream of process data such as measurements and alarms is inconsistent large databases (e.g. information management systems) for many years. For instance, a refinery produces more than 300 GB measured values per year, produced by more than 60.000 sensors with sampling rates between 1 and 60 seconds (Kloepper et al., 2015). This results in truly big data that perfectly suffice the notorious big data criteria (high volume, high velocity and high variety) and corresponding big data challenges as well as opportunities to exist also in the industrial domain.

The increasing degree of automation and use of IT was essential to assure profitable operation. However, this development also lead to an increasing loss of operator experience and an increasing risk to overburden operators–especially in the case of abnormal/critical plant situations. Here, data analytics and machine learning approaches could be used to better understand plant dynamics, and thereby better support operators how to handle the plants. The availability of historic big data in plants makes big data analytics and machine learning interesting also in the plant automation industry. This is essentially the motivation of the public-funded project "FEE"[1]. One of the main goals of the project is to develop prediction models, such as logistic regression or anomaly detection models, for the early detection and decision support for critical situations in the production environment, so that the operator has more time to develop a sustainable intervention plan and gets better guidance how to intervene in a given plant situation. This would essentially result in a paradigm shift in the state-of-the-art of today's industrial control systems from reactive to a more *proactive/predictive* operation of plants. In summary this section should highlight that there is great potential and value in "learning" from historic plant data, to improve the future performance of the plant.

A TYPICAL DATA ANALYTICS PROJECT IN PROCESS INDUSTRIES

From a business model perspective, such a prediction feature for industrial control systems could be delivered to plant operators as a product (e.g. as a control system product extension), as a service (e.g. a data analytics consultation service for existing plants), or a combination of both (as so-called product-service-system or PSS, cf. Mont, 2001). In either way, the underlying development project to create prediction models in process industries will deal with similar tasks which are illustrated in Figure 1 and explained in the following. As we will see in this chapter, a key challenge in industrial data analytics is: understanding the customer problem and data, in order to prepare this data for the prediction model development.

As depicted in Figure 1, in a typical data analytics project in process industries we can distinguish between two types of users. The project customer, which is the plant operator, knows the process very well. The lack of meta-data is not an issue as he has a full understanding of the process and works everyday with the diverse IT infrastructure. He knows precisely where in the plant the potential for improvement by data analytics projects is. However, he lacks the competency in data analytics and data mining to realize the improvements.

The data analyst, which can be e.g. the plant manufacturer who provides additional data analytics services, works at the plant only for the duration of the data analytics project. He might be specialized in projects in the process industry, and thus has sufficient domain and application understanding, allowing him to leverage material that is provided to him by the process engineer. However, he suffers heavily from the lack of metadata when exploring the available data and performing the tasks of data curation.

Figure 1. A typical (big) data analytics workflow in process industries; experience has shown that the steps for understanding and preparing the data (dark red steps) are not only important but also very involved and time consuming (can make up 50%-80% of the overall effort), which have to be carried out even before any model development (or analytics/search engine development respectively) can be done.

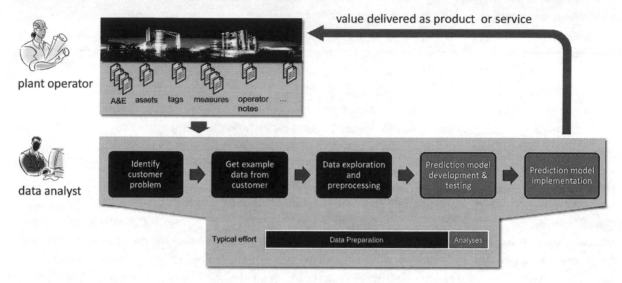

At the start of a project, the plant operator and the data analyst collaborate to identify problems that can be addressed by means of data analytics. This work helps the data analyst to understand the plant and the process application. The customer will also provide an extract of some historical plant data from his IT systems (e.g. of the last 6 months) that should contain examples where the specified problem has occurred in the past. Extracting thousands of signals for long periods from the process plant can result in very long response times of today's process information systems and can there introduce performance problems for concurrent users (e.g. process engineers) who rely on these systems in their everyday work. Consequently, the export is often limited to only a subset of measurement points and only a few months' worth of data. Still, it is not uncommon that the exported dataset results in several hundreds of files (e.g. CSV files), summing up to several gigabytes. In some cases, the data analyst is also provided the piping and instrumentation diagrams (P&IDs) to support his understanding of the data.

Following the identification and selection of specific problem the overall data situation has to be explored. The purpose of this data exploration step is to get a better understanding for the data related to the given customer problem and an ETL ("extract, transform, load") strategy to transform the dataset into a standard format that can be used later by the data analytics tools. If the data analyst discovers short comings within the provided data set, e.g. missing measurement points or an insufficient number of relevant examples, he has to request an update or more data from the process engineers. This procedure considerably slows down the data exploration and preparation process. Furthermore, the data analyst has to handle large amounts of data in flat files (thousands of signals are common) and has to manually identify the relevance of each measurement based on the physical position depicted in dozens or even hundreds of PDF documents.

Meta-information about the collected data is optimized for human understanding and is therefore not machine-readable. Especially in the matching, exploring, understanding, and cleaning-up the provided data, the data analysts heavily suffers from the lack of provided meta-data. Information from different sources should be considered, or "mashed-up" during analysis. For example, while analyzing an alarm of an asset, the metadata about the asset is mentioned in asset inventory files, the alarm is mentioned is alarm log files, the measurements related to the process variable are mentioned in measurement log files. Information regarding the actions taken is mentioned in the operator notes which are semi-structured in nature (manual notes which can contain spelling mistakes and non-uniform ways of naming things such as assets). The information regarding the alarm threshold and process idle states are mentioned in operational manual which is unstructured in nature, too. In process industries, for exchange of information and standardization, the naming of measurements and alarm follow industry naming standard. For example, (the now replaced) DIN 19227-1 is a standard used in German speaking countries. According to the standard, the tag name is alphanumeric. The characters in the name identify the measuring variable as well as signal processing, organizational information, and the signal flow path. The number in the name indicates the instrumentation and control tag number. For example, in the measurement tag "P1234", the "P" indicates that it is a "pressure" signal, and the number "1234" is the sensor number. Here, a common data quality issue is that naming conventions are not used uniformly: a common aberration is inconsistent usage (e.g. P-1234, P1234A, P 1234) caused due to spelling errors during manual entry. Another example for a common aberration is to encode additional values or strings (e.g. 01:P1234 which adds the string "01:"). Such encoded values are often used to convey additional information regarding the plant operations which the plant operator understands. However, when the datasets are exported for analytics purposes and handed to the data analyst, this information is not always explicitly communicated. The analyst is unaware of the importance of these encoded values; hence the data dependency is established by manual annotations.

As of today, this "mashing-up" of data is processed manually, as the data dependency between different entities in process industry datasets is not captured at data level, but free-text mentions in the description of the tuples in the file. These relations cannot be simply established based on string search or regular expressions as the entities' names may have incorrect representation and encoded values as below. Figure 2 illustrates these issues with help of a realistic example.

These typical examples for data quality issues in process industries should highlight the big challenges involved with extracting example datasets from customers and organizing them in a big data platform for analytics purposes. However, it should also be noted that this challenge is not specific to process industries. Today, most effort in data mining projects is typically spent on these data understanding and preparation tasks. The estimates range from 50%-80% of effort (Fan and Geerts, 2012; Dasu and Johnson, 2003), as illustrated in Figure 1. Data mining methodologies and tools such as a search tool for plant data exploration could help the data scientist in better managing these data preparation steps. In the following section we will describe a methodology to transform such data extracts into a standard data format, in order to organize that data in a data store that should serve as basis in the subsequent steps of the analytics project, such as the "data exploration" step. We will also highlight an example application – a data exploration tool – that could built on this data store, and in this context we will shortly refer to the "Lambda Architecture" for big data analytics systems.

Figure 2. A common challenge in preparing the datasets from industrial customer plants: linking datasets that have been exported from different data sources/systems of the plant. This linking poses a challenge especially due to unstructured data in some of the datasets (e.g. free texts with spelling mistakes or inconsistent naming). In the example of figure 2, the list of assets should link to a list of sensors for that asset, however, there asset name such as "K123" appear with inconstant writing in the data.

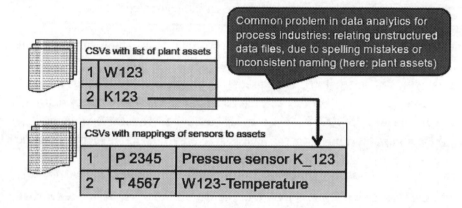

KNOWLEDGE DISCOVERY OF INDUSTRIAL PLANT DATA

Overview

Before being able to analyze data with help of a data analytics system, some example dataset first has to be extracted from the customer plant, and stored within that analytics system, which is not a trivial task as discussed in the previous section. The following methodology describes a feasible sequence of steps how storing and organization the data can be organized in a typical data analytics project in process industries.

An overview of the proposed methodology is depicted in Figure 3. As shown there, given a dataset without any metadata, the first task is to perform a data profiling. The end result of the data profiling step is a better understanding of the data and an ETL strategy for transforming data into a standard data model. The next step is to perform ETL to transform the dataset into the data model and store the dataset in a data store. Here, we have performed statistical testing to make sure no data quality issues are introduced during the transformation step. After the data is stored in the data store, the next step is to establish relational dependencies between multiple relations by applying similarity algorithms. The use of similarity algorithms is essential due to the issues related to unstructured data described above. This is an iterative process based on application accuracy needs. We perform use-case tests to ascertain the success of the entity resolution phase. Now the dataset is prepared for analytical tasks. The analyst can query the data and perform various analyses or searches. This is the final step is to build a search engine to facilitate document analysis and search. The process involves reading the data from several sources and constructing an index. As mentioned above, such a search tool could be useful in the next analysis stages such as the more domain-specific data exploration step e.g. to identify the interesting parts of the data for feature extraction and the later model building.

The data store that has been established for the subsequent data analysis steps relates best to the so-called *batch layer* of the *Lambda Architecture* for big data systems by Marz and Warren (2015). The Lambda Architecture describes a system specifically designed to handle the challenges of big data

Figure 3. The proposed methodology how to transform industrial plant data into a standard data model to be stored as masterdata for analytics purposes
Note: in the Lambda Architecture for big data systems by Marz and Warran (2015) the issue of storing the masterdata would essentially concern the design of the so-called batch layer.

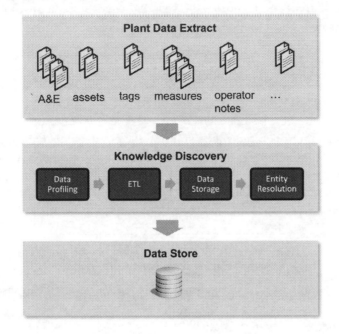

applications. So-called batch views are calculated that preprocess the data. The batch views are usually realized in a classic big data environment like Hadoop, which offers parallelization and high reliability as integrated design features. The batch views will be stored in a co-called serving layer, which will handle the users' search query request. Updating the batch views might take some time so that queries to the serving layer might be already outdated as new data continuously arrives. Therefore a speed layer is added, that should handle real-time analysis of arriving data until it is processed by the batch layer. The original purpose of the Lambda Architecture was for large-scale web service based systems, such as search engines, but has turned out to be well suited also in the industrial domain e.g. to build a search tool (or engine) for the data exploration in an industrial analytics project as described here.

In the following sections we will discuss the different methodology steps of Figure 3 in more detail.

Data Profiling

Data profiling involves taking samples of the data examining the structure and fields in each dataset in order to determine the characteristics of the relations and attributes. The task involves determining the data type of the attribute, range of the attribute, foreign keys in multiple relations and identifying data quality issues involving possible missing values, duplicates and data format violations.

The end result of this process is better understanding of the dataset and an ETL strategy to transform the dataset into standard format. Note that the dataset from two different companies may not have the same data quality issues hence this step is repeated for each dataset, at least for the first time the dataset is processed.

The aim of the process is to develop a strategy on how to transform a raw dataset into a standard format. There is no standard check-list describing the steps needed to be performed. Often the experience of the analyst is the guide to the process. Naumann (2014) provides a classification of data profiling tasks based on the input data source, and identifies the key challenges in data profiling. The most common tasks performed in this step are:

1. Identify and classify the data quality issues.
2. Prioritize the data cleaning task.
3. Determine whether the data quality issues can be solved in a domain independent manner.
4. For example, imputation of missing values in measurement depends on the operation that needs to be performed while other operations, like splitting the composite attribute into atomic attributes, can be done in a domain independent way as this operation is performed on strings at a syntactic level.
5. Determine the attributes on which the relational dependency can be specified that ensure maximum coverage.

As an example, when examining a dataset holding an inventory of the "assets" in the plant (e.g. containments, coolers, filters, distillers, etc.), the naming of assets found in customer data often does not strictly follow an industry standard as mentioned above. Hence we would like to answer questions such as:

*   Are there any duplicate assets in the data?
*   What is the minimum, maximum and average length and distribution of asset names?
*   Can we capture the asset names in a simple regular expression?

For example, upon a pattern analysis carried out for a customer dataset it was ascertained that asset names can be captured based on regular expressions, and string search is not possible as the asset names have spelling errors in free text.

Data Modeling

Industrial process plants always differ; there are no two of the same plants in the word. However, we can identify common model elements that plants are typically comprised of, such as assets (e.g. a reactor column) and tags (e.g. a pressure sensor mounted to that column). An asset can have one or more tags. A tag can produce a series of measurements over time, and measurement can cause alarms when a predefined measurement threshold is exceeded (e.g. when a temperature measured was too high).

Hence, it is possible to describe a general or "global data model" for analytical purposes for process industries. Such a global model is defined only once, and to be applicable for different customers (therefore, not illustrated explicitly in Figure 3). The goal of having a global data model is for the analytics system and algorithms to be built on top of the data store to be easily transferable to other customers without having to modify these algorithms - i.e. to be as generalizable as possible. The model captures the relationships between data entities and mandatory fields that are required for matching the metadata information to process variables to answer queries of type "what is the asset name of process variable 'X'". Often relationships between entities have to be represented as weak links, when fields include free text and content has no specific format. This is true especially in case of fields that contain manual notes made by operators or service engineers, as mentioned above. One of the more trivial ways to establish a link is by assigning a probability based on the temporal closeness of two fields that appear to be weakly linked.

ETL

The next step is to populate the model. The task performed typical involves *extracting* data from several sources and performing different *transformations* like field transformation (e.g. split a composite attribute to atomic attributes and remove inconsistencies in the data) and *loading* the data into data store. Hence, this step is commonly referred to "Extract, Transform, Load" or "ETL".

The above mentioned problem of "encoded values and inconsistent usage" is handled in the ETL stage. The information encoded in the attributes is useful for plant operations and doesn't contribute significantly in the analysis process. Hence, for the analysis purpose, we standardize the encoded values and inconsistent usage and remove extraneous information that doesn't contribute in the further analysis steps. The similar steps are followed for inconsistent usage.

Data Storage

The data needs to be stored in a persistent storage system suitable for running analytical methods. As most relations in process industry datasets are typically semi-structured, a relational view on the data can help the data scientist to reduce the ETL time. In order to take advantage of big data file systems such as Hadoop HDFS as basis for a big data analytics system, technologies such as Apache Hive on top of HDFS can help the data analyst in still being able to interact with the data in a relational way.

Entity Resolution

One of the common tasks in data cleaning is entity resolution or data-deduplication. Entity resolution is an important step in the methodology in order to deal with the above-named issues of unstructured data. We want to identify similar or nearly similar entities. This helps us to decrease data redundancy by eliminating duplicates in the relation. Similarity algorithm can help to establish the relational dependency between related entities in multiple relations. The similarity between entities can be calculated based on similarity measures.

There are several similarity algorithms that are developed for entity resolution to capturing various problems occurring in the data (cf. Elmagarmid et al., 2007). The algorithms can be classified as domain based and domain independent. The domain based algorithms depend on the domain information to define the threshold at which the two candidates are considered similar. Conversely, domain independent algorithms are applied on the strings and are further classified based on whether they operate on single word string or multi-word strings. There are also hybrid methods that use combined similarity measures. Cohen et al. (2003) and Moreau et al. (2008) compare several algorithm and Cohen et al. conclude that there is no single best algorithm that works in all cases and choice of algorithm is based on data characteristics and the application accuracy needs. In our case we make use of the N-Gram cosine similarity and Jaro-Winkler algorithms, as they provide the best similarity score for the short strings (Elmagarmid et al., 2007) considering that entity names in process plant data, such as asset names and tag names, are typically short strings.

Entity resolution can be carried out in a domain independent manner as relational dependencies between the data objects in process industries is often logged only as a free text (e.g. in manual operator notes), and fuzzy matching on the string can be carried out in domain independent model. The entity resolution is carried out in two steps: firstly, choosing an algorithm, and secondly, defining the threshold value. The referential dependency between two assets are established when similarity algorithm returns a score above the threshold value. The choice of the algorithm and the threshold depends on the data characteristics and the application accuracy needs.

ETL Test

The complex transformation of data can introduce new data quality issues not present in the raw dataset. To avoid this problem we recommend adding tests and check points at intermediate steps of the knowledge discovery process. This helps us to validate the output of transformation and revert back to the last successful checkpoint if the current transformation test fails.

Some of the common tests includes checking whether the number of records matches before and after the transformation, checking that all the atomic attributes generated from composite attribute adhere to the domain format. The exact test depends on the transformation being performed on the dataset.

CONCLUSION AND FURTHER RESEARCH

Big data analytics and machine learning has become very popular in many industries, and also in the industrial automation domain there is great potential in mining historic plant data to better understand plant dynamics and to better support operators how to handle the plants. However, data analytics in process plants turns out to be also a very tedious tasks suffering from the lack of appropriately provided meta-data. Any effort to improve this situation has to consider the brown-field situation in these industries and should leverage existing data and information as extensively as possible. Cost pressure does not allow for large data annotation and cleaning efforts.

In this chapter we have outlined a scenario and steps how a data analytics project in the industrial domain can look like, and what challenges it will typically face, especially with regard to understanding the customer's problem and data. We have seen that understanding and preparing the customer datasets is not only an important task - even before any model development can take place – it is also a very time consuming and painful task. The aim of the presented methodology for knowledge discovery in process industries is to streamlining this process based on the typical data quality issues found in industrial plants. This reduces the time of manual metadata matching, and data scientists can focus on the more interesting subsequent steps in a data analytics and machine learning project such as feature extraction and prediction model building. First applications within the public-funded project FEE, where we have used our methodology, for example, to build a proof-of-concept (PoC) for a search engine for industrial plant data, support the usefulness of this methodology. Nevertheless, the work towards big data analytics and machine learning based operator support systems (OSS) in industrial plants has to be continued: e.g. advanced data linking procedures, the integration into a plant's IT infrastructure, or user defined queries for a search engine, are some examples for possible further research directions.

ACKNOWLEDGMENT

The underlying project of this contribution was sponsored by the German Federal Ministry of Education and Research (Bundesministerium für Bildung und Forschung, BMBF), under the sponsorship reference number 01IS14006. The authors are responsible for the contents of this contribution.

REFERENCES

Kloepper, B., Dix, M., Siddapura, D., & Taverne, L. (2015). *Integrated Search for Hetereogenous Data in Process Industry Applications - A Proof of Concept.32nd IEEE International Conference on Data Engineering*, Helsinki, Finland.

Mont, O. K. (2001). *Clarifying the concept of product–service system*. The International. *Journal of Cleaner Production, 10*(3), 237–245. doi:10.1016/S0959-6526(01)00039-7

DIN 192271. (n.d.). *Control technology; graphical symbols letters for process control engineering; symbolic representation functions*. Deutsche Institut für Normung e. V. Std.

Fan, W., & Geerts, F. (2012). Foundations of data quality management. *Synthesis Lectures on Data Management, 4*(5), 1–217. doi:10.2200/S00439ED1V01Y201207DTM030

Dasu, T., & Johnson, T. (2003). *Exploratory data mining and data cleaning*. New York, NY: John Wiley & Sons.

Marz, N., & Warren, J. (2015). *Big Data: Principles and best practices of scalable realtime data systems*. Shelter Island, NY: Manning Publications Co.

Naumann, F. (2014). Data profiling revisited. *SIGMOD Record, 42*(4), 40–49. doi:10.1145/2590989.2590995

Elmagarmid, A. K., Ipeirotis, P. G., & Verykios, V. S. (2007). Duplicate record detection: A survey. *Knowledge and Data Engineering. IEEE Transactions, 19*(1), 1–16.

Cohen, W., Ravikumar, P., & Fienberg, S. (2003). A comparison of string metrics for matching names and records. In Kdd workshop on data cleaning and object consolidation, (vol. 3, pp. 73–78).

Moreau, E., Yvon, F., & Cappé, O. (2008). Robust similarity measures for named entities matching. In *Proceedings of the 22nd International Conference on Computational Linguistics*. Association for Computational Linguistics. doi:10.3115/1599081.1599156

KEY TERMS AND DEFINITIONS

Batch Layer: It represents the lowest layer in the Lambda Architecture. It is responsible for storing and preprocessing the masterdata to enable faster queries of that data.

CSV: Comma Separated Values. A standard file format often used in an industrial analytics project for exporting example datasets from the plant's data systems.

ETL: Extract, Transform, Load. Describes steps needed when loading datasets into a data store (e.g. a batch layer) for analytics purposes. Sometimes the order of steps is changed e.g. to ELT.

FEE: German project acronym. Stands for "Frühzeitige Erkennung und Entscheidungsunterstützung für kritiscche Situationen im Produktionsumfeld", which can be translated to "Early detection and decision support for critical situations in production environments".

Lambda Architecture: A reference architecture handle the challenges of big data applications, proposed by Marz and Warren (2015).

OSS: Operator support system.

P&ID: Piping and Instrumentation Diagram. It illustrates the schematic layout of the physical components in an industrial plant.

ENDNOTE

[1]   "FEE" is a German acronym for "Frühzeitige Erkennung und Entscheidungsunterstützung für kritiscche Situationen im Produktionsumfeld" which can be translated to "Early detection and decision support for critical situations in production environments". The project is sponsored by the German Federal Ministry of Education and Research (Bundesministerium für Bildung und Forschung, BMBF). Project website: http://fee-projekt.de/

Chapter 10
Data Preparation for Big Data Analytics:
Methods and Experiences

Andreas Schmidt
University of Kassel, Germany

Martin Atzmueller
University of Kassel, Germany

Martin Hollender
ABB Corporate Research Center, Germany

ABSTRACT

This chapter provides an overview of methods for preprocessing structured and unstructured data in the scope of Big Data. Specifically, this chapter summarizes according methods in the context of a real-world dataset in a petro-chemical production setting. The chapter describes state-of-the-art methods for data preparation for Big Data Analytics. Furthermore, the chapter discusses experiences and first insights in a specific project setting with respect to a real-world case study. Furthermore, interesting directions for future research are outlined.

INTRODUCTION

In the age of the digital transformation, data has become the fuel in many areas of research and business—often it is already regarded as the fourth factor of production. Prominent application domains include, for example, industrial production, where the technical facilities have typically reached a very high level of automation. Thus, many data is typically acquired, e.g., via sensors, in alarm logs or entries into production management systems regarding currently planned and fulfilled tasks. Data in such a context is represented in many forms, e.g., as tabular metric data, also including time series. In the latter example, this data can be structured according to time and different types of measurements. With

DOI: 10.4018/978-1-5225-0293-7.ch010

respect to textual data collected in logs or production documentation, however, we can easily see that this data does not exhibit the rich structure as in the case of the sensor data. Therefore, this unstructured data first needs to be transformed into a data representation that exhibits a higher degree of structuring, before it can be utilized in the analysis. However, this is also true for structured data, since metric data, for example, can also contain falsely recorded measurements leading to outliers and non-plausible values. Therefore, appropriate data preprocessing steps are necessary in order to provide for a consolidated data representation, as outlined in the data preparation phase of the Cross Industry Standard Process for Data Mining (CRISP-DM) process model (Shearer, 2000).

This chapter discusses state-of-the-art approaches for data preprocessing in the context of Big Data and reports experiences and first insights about the preprocessing of a real world dataset in a petrochemical production setting. We start with an overview on the project setting, before we outline methods for processing structured and unstructured data. After that, we summarize experiences and first insights using the real-world dataset. Finally, we conclude with a discussion and present interesting directions for future research.

CONTEXT

Know-how about the production process is crucial, especially in case the production facility reaches an unexpected operation mode such as a critical situation. When the production facility is about to reach a critical state, the amount of information (so called shower of alarms) can be overwhelming for the facility operator, eventually leading to loss of control, production outage and defects in the production facility. This is not only expensive for the manufacturer but can also be a threat to humans and the environment. Therefore, it is important to support the facility operator in a critical situation with an assistant system using real-time analytics and ad-hoc decision support.

The objective of the BMBF-funded research project "Frühzeitige Erkennung und Entscheidungsunterstützung für kritische Situationen im Produktionsumfeld"[1] (short FEE) is to detect critical situations in production environments as early as possible and to support the facility operator with a warning or even a recommendation how to handle this particular situation. This enables the operator to act proactively, i.e., before the alarm happens, instead of just reacting to alarms.

The consortium of the FEE project consists of several partners, including application partners from the chemical industry. These partners provide use cases for the project and background knowledge about the production process, which is important for designing analytical methods. The available data was collected in a petrochemical plant over many years and includes a variety of data from different sources such as sensor data, alarm logs, engineering- and asset data, data from the process-information-management-system as well as unstructured data extracted from operation journals and operation instructions (see Figure 1). Thus, the dataset consists of various different document types. Unstructured / textual data is included as part of the operation instructions and operation journals. Knowledge about the process dependencies is provided as a part of cause-effect-tables. Information about the production facility is included in form of flow process charts. Furthermore, there is information about alarm logs and sensor values coming directly from the processing line.

Figure 1. In the FEE project, various data sources from a petrochemical plant are preprocessed and consolidated in a big data analytics platform in order to proactively support the operator with an assistant system for an automatic early warning

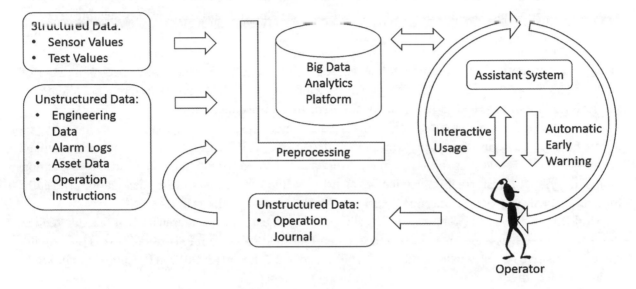

METHODS

In this chapter, we share our insights with the preprocessing of a real world, industrial data set in the context of big data. Preprocessing techniques can be divided into methods for structured and unstructured data. Different types of preprocessing have been proposed in the literature and we will give an overview of the state-of-the-art methods. We first give a brief description of the most important techniques for structured data. After that, we focus on preprocessing techniques for unstructured data, and provide a comprehensive view on different methods and techniques with respect to structured and unstructured data. Specifically, we also target methods for handling time-series and textual data, which is often observed in the context of Big Data. For several of the described methods, we will briefly discuss examples for special types of problems that need to be handled in the data preparation phase for Big Data analytics, by sharing some experiences in the FEE project. In particular, this section focuses on the Variety dimension concerning Big Data - thus we do not specifically consider Volume but mainly different data representations, structure, and according preprocessing methods (Figure 1).

Preprocessing of Structured Data

Preprocessing techniques for structured data have been widely applied in the data mining community. Data preparation is a phase in the CRISP-DM standard data mining process model (Shearer, 2000) that is regarded as one of the key factors for good model quality. In this section, we give a brief overview of the most important techniques that are widely used in the preprocessing of structured data.

When it comes to the application of a specific machine learning algorithm, one of the first steps in data preparation is to transform attributes to be suitable for the chosen algorithm. Two well-known techniques that are widely used are numerization and discretization: Numerization aims at transforming non-numerical attributes into numeric ones, e.g. for machine learning algorithms like SVM and Neural Networks. Categorical attributes can be transformed to numeric ones by introducing a set of dummy variables. Each dummy variable represents one categorical value and can be one or zero meaning the value is present or not. Discretization takes the opposite direction by transforming non-categorical attributes into categorical ones, e.g. for machine learning algorithms like Naive Bayes and Bayesian Networks. An example for discretization is binning, which is used to map continuous values to a specific number of bins. The choice of bins has a huge effect on the machine learning model and therefore manual binning can lead to a significant loss in modeling quality (Austin and Brunner, 2004).

Another widely adopted method for improving the numerical stability is the centering and scaling of an attribute. By centering the attribute mean is shifted to zero while scaling is transforming the standard deviation to one. By applying this type of preprocessing, multiple attributes are transformed to a common unit. This type of transformation can lead to significant improvements in the model quality especially for outlier sensitive machine learning algorithms like k-nearest neighbors.

Modeling quality can also be affected by skewness in the data. Two data transformations that reduce the skewness are Box and Cox (1964), and Yeo and Johnson (2000). While Box and Cox is only applicable for positive numeric values, the approach by Yeo and Johnson (2000) can be applied to all kinds of numerical data.

The transformations described so far are only affecting individual attributes, i.e., the transformation of one attribute does not have an effect on the value of another attribute. They can also be applied to a subset of the available attributes. In contrast to that there also exist data transformations that are affecting multiple attributes. The spatial sign (Serneels et al., 2006) transformation is well known for reducing the effect of outliers by projecting the values to a multi-dimensional sphere.

Another data preprocessing technique that is having an effect on multiple attributes is feature extraction. A variety of methods have been proposed in literature and we will only name Principle Component Analysis (Hotelling, 1933), short PCA, as the most popular one. PCA is a deterministic algorithm that transforms the data into a space where each dimension (Principle Component) is orthogonal, i.e., not correlated, but still captures most of the variance of the original data. Typically, PCA is applied to reduce the number of dimensions by using a cutoff for the number of Principle Components. PCA can only be applied to numerical data, which is typically centered and scaled beforehand.

Another popular preprocessing method for reducing the number of attributes is feature reduction. It is apparent that attributes with variance close to zero are not helping to separate the data in the machine learning model. Therefore, attributes with variance near zero are often removed from the dataset. Highly correlated attributes capture the same underlying information and can therefore be removed without compromising the model quality. Feature reduction is typically used to decrease computational costs and support the interpretability of the machine learning model.

A special case of feature reduction is feature selection where a subset of attributes is selected by a search algorithm. All kinds of search and optimization algorithms can be applied and we will only name Forward Selection and Backward Elimination. In Forward Selection, search starts with one attribute adding one attribute at a time as long as model quality improves with respect to an optimization criterion. Backward Elimination has the same greedy approach starting with all attributes removing one attribute at a time. In addition to feature reduction, the feature selection method has also the motivation of preventing overfitting by disregarding a certain amount of information.

Finally yet importantly, feature generation is a preprocessing technique for augmenting the data with additional information derived from existing attributes or external data sources. Of all the presented methods feature generation is the most advanced one, because it enables the induction of background knowledge into the model. Complex combination of the data has been considered in Forina et al. (2009).

So far, only the preprocessing of attributes has been covered. When it comes to the attribute values, there is a lot of effort in order to eliminate missing values. The most obvious approach is to simply remove the respective attribute, especially when the fraction of missing values is high. In the case of numeric data, another approach is to "fill in" missing values utilizing the attribute mean, which is not changing the centrality of the attribute. Approaches that are more sophisticated use a machine learning model to impute the missing values, e.g., by using a k-nearest neighbors model (Troyanskaya et al. 2001). Alternatively, one can also not address the missing value problem and simply select a machine learning model that can deal with missing values, e.g., Naïve Bayes and Bayesian Networks.

In the case of supervised learning, one can also face the problem of unevenly distributed classes leading to an overfitting of the model to the most frequent classes. Popular methods for balancing the class distribution are under- and over-sampling. When performing under-sampling the number of the frequent classes is decreased. The dataset gets smaller and the distribution of classes becomes more similar. In contrast to that over-sampling is increasing the number of infrequent classes by replication. The dataset gets bigger and again the distribution of classes becomes more similar. This problem can also be addressed in the training phase of the machine learning model by using instance-weighting. Instance weighting is a technique for dealing with unevenly distributed classes by introducing a penalty for misclassification giving the infrequent classes more weight.

Preprocessing of Time Series Data

Numerical process values like flows, pressures and temperatures are typically digitized with a limited resolution like, for example, 16 bit. Sampling rates of one value per second are well mastered by today's Distributed Control Systems (DCS). Some processes like metal rolling mills require faster sampling rates whereas in other areas one value in ten minutes might be sufficient. Modern smart instruments implement sophisticated self-diagnosis mechanisms telling about the quality and reliability of the measured signal. It is almost certain to assume that in a larger plant with many thousands of sensors, some of the sensors will deliver wrong signals. It is the task of the maintenance department to make sure that all sensors are well calibrated and properly functioning, but some of the sensors might not have highest priority or the next scheduled maintenance might be relatively far away.

Usually the operators and the plant engineers will make sure that the key signals they monitor in their trend displays are available in high quality. However, data analysts are often also interested in other signals that were not in the focus so far. Quite often the deadbands for exception-based storage are chosen much too wide for such signals (the next value is only stored once the deadband is left) (Hollender, 2010). Consequently, some parts of the signals have been filtered out and the signal might not be suitable for the intended analysis (Thornhill 2004). If such problems are discovered, the configured deadbands need to be optimized and new data needs to be collected with the new settings. If large amounts of data are required, this might mean to wait several months until the new data is available.

Typical pre-processing problems for the data analyst include:

1. Outliers (e.g. the signal jumps to maximum value for several samples and then returns to the previous range). Many algorithms for outlier detection and removal exist (Liu 2004).
2. Frozen signals (signal stops moving, typically the current value will stay at the last known good value in case of an error). After maintenance has fixed the problem, the signal starts moving again. The intervals where a signal is frozen need to be identified and excluded from the analysis.
3. Noise like electromagnetical interference needs to be filtered out. Low pass and Median filters can be used for this.
4. Sampling rate is either too high (unnecessary calculation load) or too low (not enough information contained in the signals). The Nyquist-Shannon sampling theorem says that the sampling frequency should be twice the highest frequency of interest. This also means that for slow phenomena in the area of days or weeks it does not make sense to work with one second samples. A typical down sampling algorithm is to take the average of the values inside an interval.
5. Exception-based sampling means that the distance between samples varies. Most analysis algorithms require equidistant sampling rates. An interpolation is required to get to an equidistant sampling rate

Many big data algorithms assume 100% clean and valid data. One single outlier can completely destroy complex calculations. It is therefore very important to have an adequate preprocessing in place to either remove or at least identify intervals with measurement problems.

It is very important to carefully take the quality attributes of a signal into account. For example these attributes can contain the results of a self diagnosis in an intelligent field device or if a cable is broken. However, a less than perfect quality attribute does not always mean that a signal cannot be used because it might only be indication that a maintenance should be performed.

Data reconciliation (Crowe, 1996) uses mathematical models of the process to discover and remove errors in the measured signals.

Preprocessing of Unstructured Data

Structured Data deals with data in a pre-defined fixed format. In contrast to that, unstructured data involves free formats, e.g., the text that an operator has written into a digital operating journal. Techniques for the preprocessing of unstructured data have been proposed in the research areas of Information Retrieval and Natural Language Processing and have been widely adopted in the Text Mining community.

Typically, unstructured data is organized into multiple documents containing free text. The preprocessing of unstructured data starts with a tokenization step. For each document, the text is cleaned by removing non-word characters, e.g., punctuation and special characters, and then split at each whitespace to create a set of words for the document. The union of all words in the document collection yields the dictionary.

One of the most commonly used representations for a document is the bag-of-words model. In this model, a document is represented by a multiset of words, i.e., a set of words with corresponding frequencies. The order of the words is not taken into account, which means that this type of model is not able to capture the relation between words, e.g. the co-occurrence of words in a sentence.

A popular implementation of the bag-of-words model is the vector space model (Salton 1975) where each document is represented by vector containing weighted frequencies of the words. Each dimension of the vector corresponds to a term and the value of the vector component is given by a weighting scheme. Multiple types of weighting schemes have been proposed in literature and two of the most popular ones are TF (Luhn 1957), short for term frequency, i.e., giving a high weight to frequent terms, and TF-IDF (Sparck 1972), short for term frequency combined with inverted document frequency, i.e., giving a high weight to frequent terms that only occur in few documents. Finally, a document-term-matrix is obtained by using the document vectors as rows in the matrix. The TF can be computed in a single run having linear time complexity. For IDF a second run over all terms is required. With D documents, T terms and the use of appropriate data structures TF-IDF can be computed in O (D+T), making it applicable for big data applications.

When working with unstructured data, especially with text data, one has to deal with two types of problems:

1. **High Dimensionality of the Data:** With a vector representation, each term in the dictionary becomes a dimension in a vector space. Typically, the dictionary size is large and thus the vector space has a high dimensionality.
2. **Sparsity of the Data:** The distribution of terms corresponds to a power law distribution. There are a few, very frequent terms while most of the terms occur only a single time. This so-called "long tailed" distribution results in a high sparsity, because most of the vector components will be zero when words are absent.

In order to deal with these two types of problems techniques have been proposed to reduce the size of the dictionary, either by removing unimportant terms, e. g. words that do not hold any information in the domain context, or by mapping semantically related words to a common notation, i.e., equivalence classes of terms.

When it comes to the application of machine learning algorithms to unstructured data, one has to deal with upper and lower case terms. One way to model case-insensitivity is to simply substitute all upper case letters according to their lower case counterpart. This operation is appropriate for big data applications, because it can be performed in linear time.

Another popular preprocessing technique coming from the information retrieval community is the filtering of stop words (Rijsbergen, 1979). Hans Peter Luhn introduced the term "stop word" in 1958 for non-keywords, i.e., words with a lack of content that do not help to distinguish information in the documents. This involves articles such as "a" and "the", pronouns such as "that" and "my", as well as language-dependent frequent words. Typically, stop words are filtered by using a standard stop word list for the corresponding language. In the FEE project, a German stop word list is being used. Filtering of stop words is also appropriate for big data because of linear time complexity.

One of the challenges in the preprocessing of unstructured data is to make use out punctuations and numbers. This is a problem related to the natural language processing community and involves advanced analysis of sentences, terms and term order, e.g. segmentation methods, POS tagging and named entity recognition. As a simplification, one can just ignore punctuations and numbers by removing the corresponding characters. This operation can also be performed in linear time and is appropriate for big data applications.

Semantic relations of words can be identified by stemming and lemmatization. Stemming refers to the process of removing pre- and suffixes by applying a set of rules. A popular algorithm for stemming is the porter stemmer algorithm (Porter, 1980). With stemming, the result is not guaranteed to have a valid form. Typical problems of stemming are over-stemming, i.e., too many characters are removed leading to an overlap in semantically non-related terms, and under-stemming, i.e., not enough characters are removed so that semantically related terms are not overlapping. A more complex approach is lemmatization, which only tries to map inflectional forms of terms to their base form.

Another technique for the reduction of words is the index term selection (Witten 1999). The idea behind this technique is to use only the most representative words of each document in order to reduce the dimensionality of the vector space model even further. The most representative words can be determined by an information measure on the word frequencies relative to the frequencies in the document collection, i.e., how well the documents can be separated by the words. Only the most separating words are then used to create the vector space.

Finally, one can also use matrix factorization techniques for the reduction of dimensions in the vector space. One of the most popular techniques is Latent Semantic Analysis (Deerwester 1990), which projects the original vectors to a vector space with "latent" semantic dimensions. Dimensions in the latent vector space correspond to concepts, which are shared by co-occurring terms. The dimensionality reduction is performed with respect to keeping the greatest variation in the dimensions and is closely related to PCA (see section Preprocessing of Structured Data).

EXPERIENCES AND LESSONS LEARNED

One key aspect prior to an analysis is the anonymization of the data. In order to protect personal data of individuals from further analytics, person names should be made unrecognizable. One way to achieve this is to simply remove those names from the document. This follows the principle "privacy by design" which means that anonymization should be performed as early as possible, so that person names cannot be the subject of further analytics any more. When it comes to automated anonymization, it is also a requirement to convert the files from binary to text formats. One should take into consideration that such a conversion could cause a loss of information. For example, in the case of graphical documents, it is obvious that the visual information cannot be captured by a text format. Such documents have to be manually anonymized by hand (e.g., by blackening person names). For text processing documents (e.g., word format) most of the information can be preserved by choosing an html format over a plain text format. This way, the document structure (e.g., headlines, bold words) is still available for analytical processing such as generating warnings for abnormal situations.

An assistant system that generates early warnings for abnormal situations actually has to solve two types of tasks. At first, the system has to identify events based on the long history of data. A burst in the frequency of the alarm logs, for example, could be an indicator for an unexpected situation, which corresponds to an event. Secondly, after identifying events, the system needs to extract features that help to predict this type of event as early as possible. Coming back to the frequency of alarm logs example, small fluctuations in the frequency distribution could be an indicator for a specific event characterized by a burst in the alarm log frequency.

In our analysis, we focused on unstructured data, i.e., free text entered by operators into the system, but we found that text data could also be part of the sensor data as well. For example, a sensor value is only recorded when it is within a specific range of electricity current, e.g. 24mA. An electricity current above the threshold cannot be recorded and will result in a specific error code translated to a label, e.g. the character string "bad value". There exists a variety of error codes for sensor data and one has to consider how to deal with these error values.

When analyzing free text entered into the system by an operator one has also to consider two types of situations. Text messages that are really typed by the operator, e.g. because the text is about irregular situation in the production facility, and text messages that are just copied from a template, e.g. the text is about a standard procedure like weekly maintenance work. Both situations show different characteristics and should be considered separately. In the former case, the free text is prone to typos and different spellings of the words, e.g. abbreviations and acronyms. In an industrial environment, there also exist some special wordings and a domain-specific vocabulary that has to be taken into account. One of the key challenges when working with industrial text data is to define a semantical relatedness between the words due to the lack of domain-specific concept hierarchies.

In the FEE project, we tried to overcome this problem by using two approaches. First, we used stemming (see section "Preprocessing of Unstructured Data") in order to find semantically related words by removing of prefixes and suffixes. Furthermore, we used a micro-worker approach, where ordinary persons should mark similar words in order to improve the set of related words. We found that the micro-worker approach was difficult due to the lack of domain-specific knowledge by the micro-workers. With stemming, there is also the problem of over- and under-stemming making it necessary to manually inspect stemming results.

Concerning numerical data, methods like outlier detection can help to check the data quality and to ensure meaningful episodes, e.g., in the case of time series. In addition, value imputation methods can be helpful, e.g., in the case of missing values. Advanced methods for data preprocessing, like filter approaches of course can result in a loss of information and should therefore always be targeted with respect to the analytical goals.

Having different data sources in FEE project, we also had to deal with different file formats. All the binary formats were converted to text formats in order to be able to further process the files with standard command line tools. For Excel documents, we choose the CSV format and Word / PDF documents were converted to HTML format in order to keep as much information about the formatting as possible. With the PDF documents, we found that text spanning multiple lines is divided by line when converted to a text format. This could lead to artefacts that have to be further processed, e.g. by dense-based clustering, to connect associated character strings again.

We also like point out, that when dealing with data from different data sources one has to consider the time dependency of the data. In a production environment, there are multiple production applications that have been introduced and expanded over multiple years. These systems are typically not synchronized by a local time server making it necessary to inspect time offsets between different data sources. We found that log entries in the operation journals had an offset of approximately one hour when compared to events in the sensor data (see Figure 2). Reasons for time offsets can be found in differing time zones as well as data types not capable of dealing with daylight saving time. Furthermore operators do not have time for documentation when a critical situation is about to happen, because they have to react to bring the system to a stable state again. Therefore, most of the documentation for critical situations is done after the event has happened.

Figure 2. Log entries in the operation journals had an offset of approximately one hour when compared to events in the sensor data. Reasons for time offsets can be found in differing time zones as well as data types not capable of dealing with daylight saving time. Furthermore operators do not have time for documentation when a critical situation is about to happen, because they have to react to bring the system to a stable state again. Therefore, most of the documentation for critical situations is done after the event has happened.

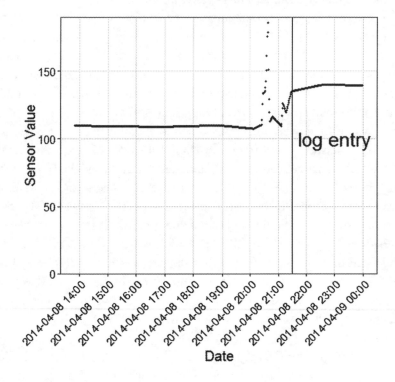

CONCLUSION

In this chapter, we have discussed several methods and techniques for data preprocessing in the context of Big Data. We have reported experiences and first insights about the preprocessing of a real world dataset in a petro-chemical production setting.

Overall, the principle "privacy by design" is extremely important in a big data environment in order to protect personal data of individuals from further analytics. We also identified two types of tasks that have to be addressed separately in order to create an assistant system for early warnings.

Our experiences show that unstructured data can be found in various places in a production environment containing shift reports, alarm data and even some error codes in the sensor data. For structured data, always the relation between filtering and information loss needs to be balanced. Furthermore, one simple, but important preprocessing techniques for the analysis of natural language text is the mapping of different notations of the same word to a common form, i.e., to a common terminology so that the different entities can be correctly resolved.

Furthermore, we have found that the conversion of file formats can lead to further preprocessing steps, especially when the data is fragmented. Finally, it is important to consider that data is not always coming from one system, making it necessary to check for time offsets and the reasons behind it, connecting that to the business and data understanding phases of CRISP-DM (Figure 2).

FUTURE RESEARCH DIRECTIONS

Future work will include the analysis of extraordinary characteristics in the industrial real world dataset. One algorithm that can be applied for exploratory analysis is Exceptional Model Mining (Atzmueller, 2015, Leman, Feelders, & Knobbe, 2008), as a variant of subgroup discovery (Kloesgen 1996, Wrobel, 1997, Atzmueller, 2015) focusing on complex target properties. For that, there are fast implementations available, e.g., (Atzmueller & Lemmerich 2012, Atzmueller & Puppe, 2006). This technique can both be applied in the modeling phase as well as in the preprocessing phase, e.g., for attribute construction and data aggregation. Here, also knowledge-based approaches (e.g., Atzmueller 2007) can be utilized.

Furthermore, we plan to apply techniques from information extraction (Grishman, 1997) to the unstructured/textual information for event detection (Melton & Hripcsak, 2005), e.g., using rule-based techniques (Atzmueller & Kluegl & Puppe, 2008, Kluegl et al. 2009). By applying NLP techniques, for example, we will analyze the potential of extracted information for indicating upcoming events. Then, by using advanced methods for information extraction, we can closely link unstructured as well as structured data, also with respect to data quality. The latter is a major issue that can also targeted using the techniques described above, including appropriate measures (cf. Atzmueller et al., 2005). Furthermore, Exceptional Model Mining can be applied on the given multi-dimensional dataset in order to detect implausible correlations, which can then indicate problematic episodes. Here, techniques for profiling expected relations, e.g., (Atzmueller et al., 2005) can be a good starting point for future research, which can also be supported by appropriate visualization, inspection and explanation methods, see e.g., (Atzmueller & Puppe, 2008, Atzmueller & Roth-Berghofer, 2010).

ACKNOWLEDGMENT

The underlying project of this contribution was sponsored by the German Federal Ministry of Education and Research (Bundesministerium für Bildung und Forschung, BMBF), under the sponsorship reference number 01IS14006. The authors are responsible for the contents of this contribution.

REFERENCES

Atzmueller, M. (2007). *Knowledge-Intensive Subgroup Mining -- Techniques for Automatic and Interactive Discovery. Dissertations in Artificial Intelligence-Infix (Diski), (307).* IOS Press.

Atzmueller, M. (2015). *Subgroup Discovery – Advanced Review. Data Mining and Knowledge Discovery, 5*(1), 35–49. doi:10.1002/widm.1144

Atzmueller, M., Baumeister, J., & Puppe, F. (2005). Quality Measures and Semi-Automatic Mining of Diagnostic Rule Bases.*Proc. 15th International Conference on Applications of Declarative Programming and Knowledge Management.* Springer. doi:10.1007/11415763_5

Atzmueller, M., Kluegl, P., & Puppe, F. (2008). Rule-Based Information Extraction for Structured Data Acquisition using TextMarker. In *Proc. LWA 2008*. University of Wuerzburg.

Atzmueller, M., & Lemmerich, F. (2012). VIKAMINE - Open-Source Subgroup Discovery, Pattern Mining, and Analytics. In *Proc. ECML/PKDD 2012: European Conference on Machine Learning and Principles and Practice of Knowledge Discovery in Databases*. Springer. doi:10.1007/978-3-642-33486-3_60

Atzmueller, M., & Puppe, F. (2006). SD-Map – A Fast Algorithm for Exhaustive Subgroup Discovery. In *Proc. PKDD 2006* (LNAI), (vol. 4213, pp. 6–17). Springer.

Atzmueller, M., & Puppe, F. (2008). A Case-Based Approach for Characterization and Analysis of Subgroup Patterns. *Journal of Applied Intelligence*, *3*(28), 210–221. doi:10.1007/s10489-007-0057-z

Atzmueller, M., Puppe, F., & Buscher, H.-P. (2005). Profiling Examiners using Intelligent Subgroup Mining. *Proc. 10th International Workshop on Intelligent Data Analysis in Medicine and Pharmacology (IDAMAP-2005)*.

Atzmueller, M., & Roth-Berghofer, T. (2010). The Mining and Analysis Continuum of Explaining Uncovered. *Proc. 30th SGAI International Conference on Artificial Intelligence (AI-2010)*.

Austin, P., & Brunner, L. (2004). Inflation of the Type I Error Rate When a Continuous Confounding Variable Is Categorized in Logistic Regression Analyses. *Statistics in Medicine*, *23*(7), 1159–1178. doi:10.1002/sim.1687 PMID:15057884

Box, G., & Cox, D. (1964). An Analysis of Transformations. *Journal of the Royal Statistical Society. Series B. Methodological*, 211–252.

Crowe, C. M. (1996). Data reconciliation—progress and challenges. *Journal of Process Control*, *6*(2), 89–98. doi:10.1016/0959-1524(96)00012-1

Deerwester, S. C., Dumais, S. T., Landauer, T. K., Furnas, G. W., & Harshman, R. A. (1990). Indexing by latent semantic analysis. *JAsIs*, *41*(6), 391–407. doi:10.1002/(SICI)1097-4571(199009)41:6<391::AID-ASI1>3.0.CO;2-9

Grishman, R. (1997). Information extraction: Techniques and challenges. In *Information Extraction: A Multidisciplinary Approach to an Emerging Information Technology*. Springer. doi:10.1007/3-540-63438-X_2

Hollender, M. (2010). *Collaborative Process Automation Systems*. ISA.

Hotelling, H. (1933). Analysis of a complex of statistical variables into principal components. *Journal of Educational Psychology*, *24*(6), 417–441. doi:10.1037/h0071325

Klösgen, W. (1996). Explora: A multipattern and multistrategy discovery assistant. In Advances in Knowledge Discovery and Data Mining, (pp. 249–271). AAAI.

Kluegl, P., Atzmueller, M., & Puppe, F. (2009). Meta-Level Information Extraction. *The 32nd Annual Conference on Artificial Intelligence*. Springer. doi:10.1007/978-3-642-04617-9_30

Leman, D., Feelders, A., & Knobbe, A. J. (2008). Exceptional model mining. In ECML/PKDD (LNCS), (vol. 5212, pp. 1–16). Springer. doi:10.1007/978-3-540-87481-2_1

Liu, H., Shah, S., & Jiang, W. (2004). On-line outlier detection and data cleaning. *Computers & Chemical Engineering*, *28*(9), 1635–1647. doi:10.1016/j.compchemeng.2004.01.009

Luhn, H. P. (1957). A statistical approach to mechanized encoding and searching of literary information. *IBM Journal of Research and Development*, *1*(4), 309–317. doi:10.1147/rd.14.0309

Melton, G., & Hripcsak, G. (2005). Automated detection of adverse events using natural language processing of discharge summaries. *Journal of the American Medical Informatics Association*, *12*(4), 448–457. doi:10.1197/jamia.M1794 PMID:15802475

Porter, M. (1980). An Algorithm for Suffix Stripping. *Program*, *14*(3), 130–137. doi:10.1108/eb046814

Rijsbergen, C. V. (1979). *Information Retrieval*. Butterworth-Heinemann Newton.

Salton, G., Wong, A., & Yang, C. S. (1975). A Vector Space Model for Automatic Indexing. *Communications of the ACM*, *18*(11), 613–620. doi:10.1145/361219.361220

Serneels, S., Nolf, E., & Espen, P. (2006). Spatial Sign Pre-processing: A Simple Way to Impart Moderate Robustness to Multivariate Estimators. *Journal of Chemical Information and Modeling*, *46*(3), 1402–1409. doi:10.1021/ci050498u PMID:16711760

Shearer, C. (2000). The CRISP-DM Model: The New Blueprint for Data Mining. *Journal of Data Warehousing*, *5*(4), 13–22.

Sparck Jones, K. (1972). A statistical interpretation of term specificity and its application in retrieval. *The Journal of Documentation*, *28*(1), 11–21. doi:10.1108/eb026526

Thornhill, N. F., Choudhury, M. S., & Shah, S. L. (2004). The impact of compression on data-driven process analyses. *Journal of Process Control*, *14*(4), 389–398. doi:10.1016/j.jprocont.2003.06.003

Witten, I. H., Moffat, A., & Bell, T. C. (1999). *Managing gigabytes: compressing and indexing documents and images*. Morgan Kaufmann.

Wrobel, S. (1997). An algorithm for multi-relational discovery of subgroups. In Principles of Data Mining and Knowledge Discovery (LNCS), (vol. 1263, pp. 78–87). Springer. doi:10.1007/3-540-63223-9_108

Yeo, I., & Johnson, R. (2000). A new family of power transformations to improve normality or symmetry. *Biometrika*, *87*(4), 954–959. doi:10.1093/biomet/87.4.954

KEY TERMS AND DEFINITIONS

Anonymization: Process of removing personal information from a document to protect the identity of a person.

CRISP-DM: The Cross Industry Standard Process for Data Mining describes the common phases of a data mining workflow.

Dummy Variable: A variable that holds the information about one categorical value which either can be present (1) or absent (0).

Stop Words: Frequent words with a lack of content, like pronouns and prepositions, that do not help to distinguish documents from each other. Typically, stop words are filtered during the processing of natural language text.

TF-IDF: Weighting of terms according to the term frequency (TF) and inverted document frequency (IDF). Frequent terms that only occur in a few documents get the highest weight.

Unstructured Data: Data that is not organized in a pre-defined format. Typically, this involves natural language text.

Vector Space Model: A model that represents text documents in a vector space where each dimension corresponds to a term.

ENDNOTE

[1]   http://www.fee-projekt.de

Chapter 11
Semantification of Large Corpora of Technical Documentation

Sebastian Furth
denkbares GmbH, Germany

Joachim Baumeister
denkbares GmbH, Germany & University of Würzburg, Germany

ABSTRACT

The complexity of machines has grown dramatically in the past years. Today, they are built as a complex functional network of mechanics, electronics, and hydraulics. Thus, the technical documentation became a fundamental source for service technicians in their daily work. The technicians need fast and focused access methods to handle the massive volumes of documentation. For this reason, semantic search emerged as the new system paradigm for the presentation of technical documentation. However, the existent large corpora of legacy documentation are usually not semantically prepared. This fact creates an invincible gap between new technological opportunities and the actual data quality at companies. This chapter presents a novel and comprehensive approach for the semantification of large volumes of legacy technical documents. The approach especially tackles the veracity and variety existent in technical documentation and makes explicit use of their typical characteristics. The experiences with the implementation and the learned benefits are discussed in industrial case studies.

INTRODUCTION

In the mechanical engineering domain, the growth of complex products including a number of different technologies can be experienced. In the past, mechanical engines typically could be simply maintained and repaired using mechanical tools. Today's machines, however, are designed as a combination of mechanical components, electrics, hydraulics, and electronics. Consequently, today's service technicians need an increased competence for their daily repair and maintenance work. Technical documentation tries to support the service technician with relevant information on the respective machine. However,

DOI: 10.4018/978-1-5225-0293-7.ch011

as a result of the rising complexity of the products the corpora of technical documentation become extremely large (Volume; typically up to 12,000 pages for a single machine). Terabytes of data are a common dimension, as the documentation usually not only needs to cover different skill levels of users, configurations and aspects of a product but also targets different markets and their respective languages. Hence, documentation exists for each variant of a machine and every relevant market (Variety; different kinds, content structures and languages of documentation). In order to provide efficient customer support fast and effective access to the relevant information becomes a critical success factor.

In recent years, well-established semantic technologies (Antoniou & van Harmelen, 2008; Horrocks, Parsia, Patel-Schneider, & Hendler, 2005; Sauermann, et al., 2006) have been applied to facilitate this task. A typical example is *Semantic Search* (Guha, McCool, & Miller, 2003) that—in contrast to traditional search technologies—uses ontologies to connect content with semantic information. This connection can then be exploited in order to improve the search results. *Semantic Navigation* is another example of advanced technologies enabling users to browse multi-modal content by following automatically generated semantic links. However, the incorporation of these technologies in enterprise applications has just started and only a small amount of technical documentation is already semantically enriched. Thus, the service staff usually still has to deal with large quantities of rather loosely organized legacy information. Examples of such information include operation manuals, installation guides, and repair manuals. In order to make the large volumes of legacy information accessible for semantic technologies, connections between the traditional content and semantic information must be created. This is typically done in a process called *Ontology Population* (Buitelaar & Cimiano, 2008), where a given ontology structure is filled by instances. These instances describe for example the main subject (in terms of ontology concepts) of a document. This kind of ontology population can be regarded as a form of the *Entity Integration* task in Big Data, and is vaguely related to *Subject Indexing* (Albrechtsen, 1993; Hutchins, 1978), which in turn can be considered as part of the more general problem of *Document Classification*.

Creating these instances in a manual step requires an in-depth analysis of the original content by humans, which is usually error-prone, time-consuming, and very cost-intensive for large scale corpora. In recent years, however, *Text Analytics* approaches have been adapted in order to automate the population of such ontologies.

BACKGROUND

In the field of Information Extraction and Text Analytics, established methods exist for the extraction of semantic information from natural language texts. Most of these methods are based on supervised Machine Learning approaches that require a sufficient amount of training data for decent results. In real-world scenarios such training data is often not available, and the creation with respect to a cost-benefit ratio is not reasonable.

The chapter presents a holistic approach for the automatic semantification of large volumes of technical documentation that does not require training data. The approach is holistic, as it is a complete process that covers all steps necessary for the semantification of existing technical documents. In this chapter, semantification is defined as the identification and annotation of the main subjects for a given document. For instance, the chapter of a repair manual is identified and annotated by ontological subjects representing the main content of the chapter in focus. The typical goal of the presented semantification approach is the subsequent use of the enriched documents within a semantic search application, e.g., when service staff is searching for the repair instructions of a special assembly.

The approach tackles multiple challenges, such as varying data quality (Veracity; very old/scanned input documents or missing domain information), different document types and formats (Variety), terminology extraction, segmentation, semantic annotation, and reviewing. It uses standard techniques for the preprocessing and the structural enrichment of the documents. The core of the approach is semantic annotation based on domain ontologies and an adapted version of Explicit Semantic Analysis (Gabrilovich & Markovitch, 2007) that has originally been developed for the computation of semantic relatedness between texts. The analysis is powered by a Semantic Interpreter that is based on sets of domain terms, domain concepts, and weighted semantic relations between them. This allows for the easy adaptation to new corpora and domains.

The approach has already been applied to the technical service documents of different mechanical engineering companies. Two case studies present the experiences made. As a decent terminology is the basis for the semantification approach, the first case study covers the definition of a comprehensive domain terminology on basis of different data sources (Variety) for an engineering company for special purpose vehicles. The case study describes how the approach facilitated the definition of a terminology with more than 50,000 terms in a couple of days. The second case study covers the actual semantification of the technical documentation of a German manufacturer for harvesting machines. The corpus contains about 9,000 legacy PDF documents with up to 2,000 pages per document. The presented approach achieved satisfying results on this corpus (average f-measure of 83% on samples). A specialized review tool facilitated the quick review and correction of large quantities of the automatically generated semantic annotations. Experiments with domain experts showed that the average correction time per section is about 20 seconds; this allows for the complete review of large technical service documents in a matter of minutes. Both case studies cover a variety of different machine and document types and thus underline the flexibility of the presented approach.

Structure of the Chapter

The remainder of this chapter will first state some prerequisites of the presented approach—giving a brief introduction to the different types of technical documents and their characteristics, and introducing the required knowledge representations with an emphasis on the definition of a domain terminology. Afterwards the holistic approach of semantifying documents will be described: special emphasis will be on the method used for the actual annotation of the documents. Two case studies show the practical applicability of the approach and serve as a recommendation for similar projects. The chapter closes with a suggestion of future research opportunities and a discussion of the overall coverage.

PREREQUISITES

The chapter does not focus on the technical handling of large amounts of data (Volume) but emphasizes on dealing with Veracity and Variety in large corpora of technical documentation. Thus, the chapter covers a comprehensive description of the semantification process that aims at the identification and annotation of the main subjects for given technical documents.

The process assumes that the identifiable subjects can be derived from a domain ontology – or similarly structured sources, like hierarchically organized corporate master data that is available from modern enterprise information systems – and relies on a well-defined terminology, providing terms for these subjects. The following sections describe how the content of technical documentation can be hierarchically structured, from different document types to segments within documents and finally to tokens and terms contained in the segments. See Figure 1 depicting this hierarchical structure with an example. Introducing the set of identifiable subjects and the elements of technical documentation in general will expand this brief overview in the following section. Visualization techniques of the used terminology within the documentation will also be discussed.

Identifiable Subjects

The presented approach relies on the assumption that the problem domain can be described in a domain ontology, e.g. considering the technical domain, such an ontology could describe the structural decomposition and functionalities of a machine. Then the set of identifiable subjects S would typically comprise components or functions. As such compontents or functions are then the entities that are modeled in a corresponding domain ontology, they can be derived from it in forms of ontological concepts.

Definition 1: Identifiable Subjects. Let $\mathcal{O}$ be a domain ontology, consisting of ontological concepts $o_k \in \mathcal{O}$. Then the set of identifiable subjects $S \subseteq \mathcal{O}$ is defined as a set of ontological concepts $S = \{o_1,\ldots,o_n\}$.

Characteristics of Technical Documentation

In this section, the domain of technical documentation will be described in more detail. The understanding of the different types and uses of the technical documentation is helpful to fully understand the motivation of the later introduced semantic technologies.

Figure 1. The elements of technical documentation

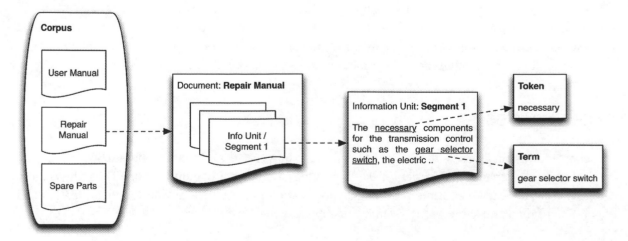

Tasks of the Technical Documentation

The main task of technical documentation is the support and training of a service technician during the daily work. Here, the documentation is used to teach entire function systems but also to fill knowledge gaps of the technician on-site. Therefore, technical documentation needs to work as a teaching textbook but also as a lexicon. The service technician is supported by the documentation during the following tasks:

1. Operation of the machine,
2. Maintenance of the machine,
3. Localization of specific components,
4. Diagnosis of problems,
5. Repair of damage.

Types of Technical Documentation

Documentation manuals support the described tasks. The organization of the manual into one large file or into multiple documents varies from company to company. For larger and complex machines the companies tend to organize the technical documentation into multiple documents, each covering a specific aspect. The main aspects and their corresponding manuals are introduced in the following.

- **User Manual:** The operation of each machine function is described in detail for a non-technical user. For instance, for driving machines the use of the "gear stick" is described, i.e., how to select an appropriate gear for the current driving speed. Also, simple and frequent maintenance tasks accomplishable by end-users are explained.
- **Repair Manual:** The repair manual is written for the technical user, typically service technicians, and it describes the repair of all relevant components of the machines. In such a manual, the exchange and adjustments of mechanical parts are explained. Following the example, the repair manual would describe the replacement of a defective "gear stick". Depending of the manufacturer of the machine, different levels of detail are used in the manual, ranging from the description of the exchange of only larger components to the repair of elements of detailed sub-components. For electronic parts and software, the reading, update, and calibration of the particular entities are described.
- **Technical Function:** For the diagnosis of malfunctions, the service technician needs to have a thorough understanding of the functional dependencies and interrelations of the components. The technical function manual describes for each technical function the connections between components. For instance, for a driving machine the components "gear stick", "CAN bus", and "transmission" are connected in a functional dependency. Typically, also the electrics and hydraulics of a machine are documented in such a manual, e.g., by printing circuit diagrams.
- **Spare Parts Catalog:** Spare parts catalogs provide a detailed view of parts located in particular components. Service technicians use such catalogs to locate specific parts, but also to order new parts in exchange for defective ones. Typically, the catalogs are defined hierarchically, starting from top-level components (e.g., a "cabin") and then navigating to detailed components contained in the top-level components (e.g., a "gear stick" in a "cabin").

The corpus of given documents is formalized in the following definition.

Definition 2: Document Corpus. Let $\mathcal{D}$ be the universal set of possible documents and let $d_i \in \mathcal{D}$ be a document. Then a corpus $\mathcal{C} \subseteq \mathcal{D}$ is defined as a set of documents $\mathcal{C} = \{d_i, \ldots, d_n\}$.

In the following, the different corpora $\mathcal{C}_1$ and $\mathcal{C}_2$ are refered to by explicitly naming them. A corpus consists of a set of documents, where a document itself contains terms (possibly) referring to a terminology.

Terminology and Terms in Technical Documentation

Every document in a corpus is further structured into so-called information units. An information unit consists of terms and tokens.

Information Units and Characteristics

Each document can be broken down in atomic *information units*. Such an information unit represents a self-contained block of information to be used by the service technician, e.g. a chapter, section or even a specialized fine-grained structure like a table containing measurement values for a certain signal. The information unit typically consists of textual content combined with multi-media (images, video, mixed-reality) content.

Definition 3: Information Unit. Let $d_i \in \mathcal{D}$ a document in a given corpus $\mathcal{C} \subseteq \mathcal{D}$. Then, d_i can be split into the non-empty partition of segments $d_{i,j}$ so that $d_i = \left[d_{i,1}, \ldots, d_{i,m}\right]$. A segment $d_{i,j}$ is called an information unit.

Examples of information units are: a complete exchange sequence of a component in a repair manual, the description of a specific function in an operation manual, and the entry of a spare parts catalog describing all elementary parts of a component.

The manual and its information units, respectively, are often organized in a hierarchy, where top-level components are main headings and detailed components are the headings of an information unit. Also, in globally acting companies the information units are available in multiple languages.

In modern information systems, metadata is attached to the particular information units. Such metadata may include applicability notes on specific machines, components codes, and the version history of the unit. Besides metadata the used terminology in the textual content is of interest: In recent years some effort was undertaken in the standardization of the terminology used in the documents, leading to a relatively controlled vocabulary in newer documents. These characteristics can be exploited by Text Analytics approaches but also raise new challenges.

The persistence format of the documentation is also of interest for the later semantification: Older documentation systems publish the manuals as monolithic PDF documents (often including many thousands of pages). Those PDF documents are usually less easily accessible. More advanced systems publish the manuals on basis of XML/HTML technologies. Then, a manual comprises a tree of XML/HTML documents. Often the leaf elements of such a tree represent the corresponding information units.

Domain Terminology

The set of identifiable subjects S that has been derived from a domain ontology $\mathcal{O}$ consisting of ontological concepts o_k has already been defined. Additionally, the domain terminology as a set of (human-readable) terms that are associated to these ontological concepts gets defined. In the context of technical documents such terms typically comprise the officially used label of a component, abbreviations, special identifiers like drawing numbers or alternative names. Thus, every concept instance o_k can have one or more relations $r_{k,m}$ to term concepts b_m, forming the connection between a concept and a related term. Each concept instance o_k and term instance b_m has a human-readable label l_p. The union of these labels represents the *terminology*, which is the basis for the semantic annotation method presented later in this chapter.

Definition 4: Domain Terminology. Let $\mathcal{O}$ be a domain ontology, consisting of ontological concepts $o_k \in \mathcal{O}$ and term concepts $b_m \in \mathcal{O}$ that are connected using relation instances $r_{k,m} \in \mathcal{O}$. And let all concepts o_k and term concepts b_m have a human-readable label l_p. Then the domain terminology is defined as the union of all labels $\mathcal{T} = \bigcup_p l_p$.

It is worth noting that related terms have a relation to the given set of concepts but are not necessarily included in the set of identifiable subjects. Typical examples are abbreviations, or assuming that the given set of concepts covers all assemblies of a machine, related terms are all parts the assemblies consist of.

If such a terminology is not available, term concepts b_m need to be extracted from various sources (see Figure 2) and connected to the set of identifiable subjects S.

Figure 2. Extracting terminology from different sources

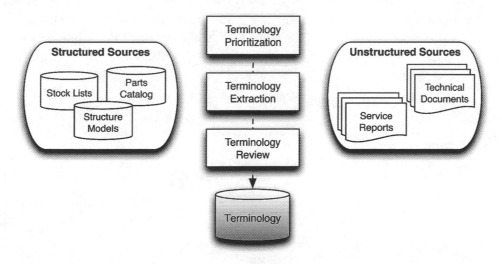

Term Sources

In the mechanical engineering domain, typical examples for term sources are stock lists or technical structure models. Figure 3 shows an excerpt of a stock list, that contains terms (highlighted) and a lot of additional information (e.g. identifiers, amounts etc.) about the parts of a specific machine. Referring back to the gear stick example, the figure shows some of the parts a gear stick consists of. Assuming that the gear stick is an identifiable subject (concept) and all its parts are not, the labels of the parts (e.g. "knob") can be used as related terms for the gear stick concept.

Another valuable terminology source is the corpus itself. In recent years controlled vocabularies were introduced for the authoring process. However, older documents often use varying vocabularies because of different writing styles or translation processes. Therefore especially the older technical documents in the corpus are a promising source for the extraction of terms. Automatic Term Extraction (ATE) methods can be used to extract term candidates from textual resources automatically. Popular examples are the C-Value/NC-Value method (Frantzi, Ananiadou, & Mima, 2000), TermEx (Sclano & Velardi, 2007) and GlossEx (Park, Byrd, & Boguraev, 2002) that combine linguistic and statistical measures to extract ranked lists of terms. For further reading at this point please refer to the evaluations of ATE methods from Pazienza et al. (2005) or Zhang et al. (2008).

Visualization and Review

Found terms in a corpus need to be reviewed and probably revised by a human expert. Here, visualization methods can help to guide the review process.

Visualization of the Term Coverage

The term sources usually vary in forms of term quality and connectability to the set of concepts. The connectability describes the level of difficulty for the establishment of a relation $r_{k,m}$ between a concept o_k and a term concept b_m. While a high quality of terms from structured sources can be assumed, the terms extracted using ATE methods need a dedicated quality measure. Thus the quality of these terms is usually expressed as a confidence value computed by an ATE method. These confidence values typically consider the termhood (degree to which a linguistic unit is related to domain-specific concepts) and unithood (strength and stability of word combinations or collocations) of a term, as defined by Kageura and Umino (1996).

Figure 3. Excerpt of a stock list, showing the contained terminology

Catalogue sequence number	Item sequence number	Reason for selection	Quantity per next higher assembly	Manufacturer	Part number	2000M PAS Segment						
						Description of parts	Unit of issue	2000M PCS Segment	Special storage	Fitment code	Physical security/pilferage code	Calibration marker
B5000001 064	00A	1	1	A434	1954343534079	GEAR SELECTOR SWITCH	EA		0		U	
B5000001 065	00A	1	6	99008	O40328A2P	NUT,PLAIN,HEXAGON	EA		0		U	
B5000001 066	00A	1	6	99008	7069200HV	WASHER,FLAT	EA		0		U	
B5000001 067	00A	1	3	11871	2700109-060000.007.0	MOUNT,RESILIENT,GENERAL PURPOSE	EA		0		U	
B5000001 068	00A	1	1	33518	278M531SCHW	KNOB	EA		0		U	

The connectability cannot be measured easily, but there exists a guiding principle that terms from highly structured sources like stock lists are easier to connect to existing concepts. These sources often reference global identifiers, which allow for the automatic association of the terms with the concepts. Other, rather unstructured term sources often need manual work. A good example for the latter one are the term candidates generated by ATE methods. These terms are usually not connected to the concepts of the ontology. In most cases a domain expert needs to establish these connections manually. Usually the availability of domain experts is low and their employment expensive. Therefore, the manual integration of a term source needs to be evaluated carefully under the cost-benefit ratio (Lidwell, Holden, & Butler, 2003).

A large terminology is crucial for the performance of the semantic annotation. In general the more terminology is available, the better is the semantic annotation. However some term sources contribute more to the performance than others, as they fit better into the terminology used in the documents that shall be annotated. Hence a good strategy is to prefer these term sources during the integration process. Albeit the priorization of term sources according to their contribution capabilities is not a trivial task. Usually even technical writers and editors have to guess, when they are asked to prioritize term sources according to the expected compliance with a corpus.

Objective metrics can support the technical editors in their cognitive selection process. An example for such a metric is the *term coverage*, which expresses the proportion of terms among all tokens in a text.

Definition 5: Token. Let $\mathcal{D}$ be the universal set of all documents and let $\mathcal{L}$ be the universal set of all possible literals. Then the function $to : \mathcal{D} \to 2^{\mathcal{L}}$ extracts the set of all literals for a given document. The literal $t \in to\left(d_i\right)$ is called a token of document d_i, where $d_i \in \mathcal{D}$.

It is worth noting, that the function *to* is also applicable to information units, i.e., parts of the document.

Definition 6: Term Candidates. Let $\mathcal{L}$ be the universal set of all possible literals. Then the term candidates T of a problem domain as a set of literals, i.e. $T \subseteq \mathcal{L}$.

Definition 7: Term Coverage. Let $T \subseteq \mathcal{L}$ be the term candidates of the problem domain extracted from a term source, and let $C = \left\{d_i, ..., d_n\right\}$ be the inspected corpus. Then the term coverage function *tcov* is defined as

$$tcov = \frac{|T|}{\left|\bigcup_{i=1,...,n} to\left(d_i\right)\right|} .$$

A high term coverage implies that the term source fits the document well. In practice, the threshold for a high coverage is set to 0.3 with a fuzzy range ± 0.05. The approach presented in this chapter provides tool support based on different metrics to guide the term source selection. The metrics are visualized using the city metaphor (See Figures 4 and 5), where a document corresponds to a city and districts and houses represent the hierarchical segment structure. The houses' areas are adapted in accordance to the number of tokens in a segment, while their height and color indicate the respective term coverage. High and greenish houses represent a good term coverage (see Figure 4), reddish ones a low coverage respectively (see Figure 5).

Figure 4. Term city showing a term source with high coverage

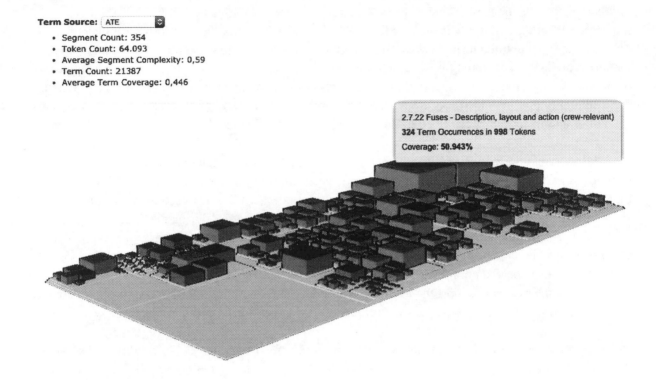

Term Source: ATE

- Segment Count: 354
- Token Count: 64.093
- Average Segment Complexity: 0,59
- Term Count: 21387
- Average Term Coverage: 0,446

2.7.22 Fuses - Description, layout and action (crew-relevant)
324 Term Occurrences in **998** Tokens
Coverage: **50.943%**

Figure 5. Term city showing a term source with low coverage

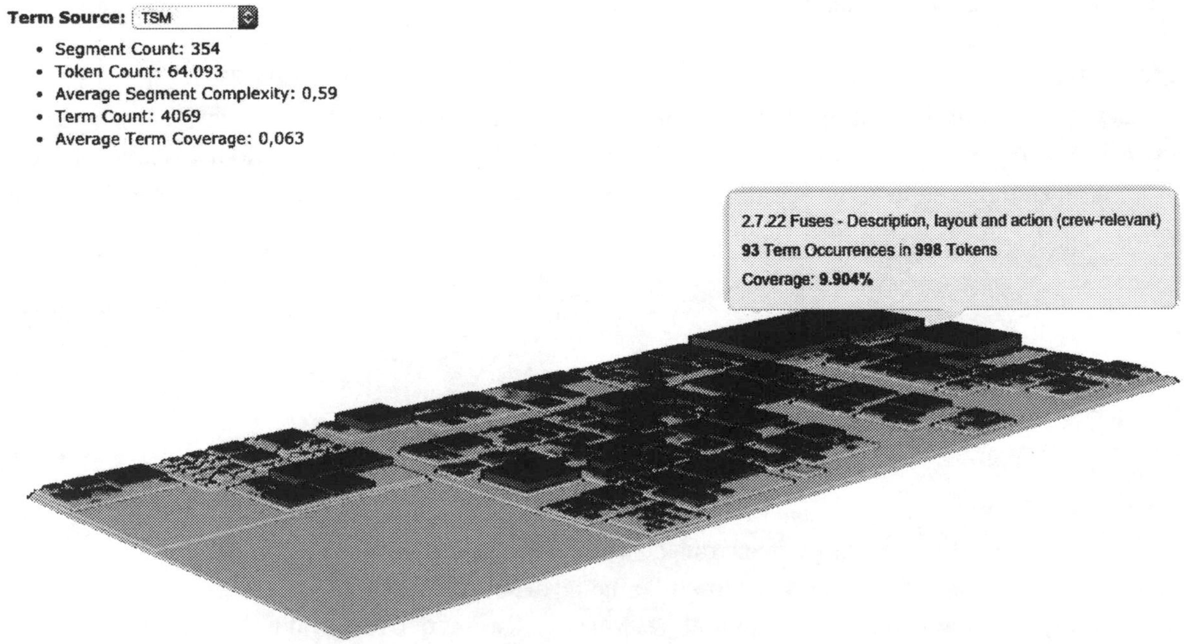

Term Source: TSM

- Segment Count: 354
- Token Count: 64.093
- Average Segment Complexity: 0,59
- Term Count: 4069
- Average Term Coverage: 0,063

2.7.22 Fuses - Description, layout and action (crew-relevant)
93 Term Occurrences in **998** Tokens
Coverage: **9.904%**

Term Review

After selecting the corpus, i.e., the term sources that shall be integrated in the terminology, automatic methods are used to establish connections $r_{k,m}$ between the identifiable subjects o_k and the term concepts b_m. Depending on the term source the methods used for the integration are either general fuzzy string matching methods or more elaborate methods based on ontology alignment approaches or even domain-specific heuristics. Cheatham and Hitzler (2013) examined several string similarity metrics (Needleman & Wunsch, 1970; Levenshtein, 1966; Smith & Waterman, 1981) for their ontology alignment abilities. For a comprehensive survey of alignment methods please refer to (Euzenat & Shvaiko, 2012). Either way, a technical writer or domain expert should carefully review the established connections, as they directly influence the performance of the semantic annotation. Since the review of many thousand terms is a cumbersome and error-prone task, the presented approach proposes the use of dedicated tool support. A term review tool (see Figure 6) has been developed that visualizes the established connections between concepts and terms and additionally offers user-friendly editing functionality. The tool is table-based, where each line displays a term and its connections to concepts. It distinguishes related concepts and concepts (identifier). The latter one is used when the term is an identifier for a concept, the former one when the term is somehow related to a concept. The tool additionally provides a list of text occurrences for each term, in order to cover different meanings of a term in the corpus. The provided confidence value and status information express the quality of the term and the status of the semantic connection respectively. The status "unclear" is used for terms, which have connections that have not yet been reviewed or do not have any connections at all. The status "confirmed" is used for reviewed connections and can automatically be set if the confidence value exceeds a certain threshold.

A technical editor or domain expert can edit the semantic connections by drag-and-dropping the suggested concepts, by deleting one or by adding new connections. Semantic typing with autocompletion (Hyvönen & Mäkelä, 2006) supports the process of adding new connections by providing concept suggestions on the basis of the entered verbalization of the concept that he has in mind. The autocompletion consideres all previously established connections between terms and concepts for its suggestions.

Figure 6 shows an excerpt of a term review. In the first row the term "Fan for drive electronics" is reviewed. The term was found in a term source called "LCDP tables", has several textual occurrences in the underlying corpus, and has automatically been marked as confirmed, because of its high confidence

Figure 6. Tool support for the term review

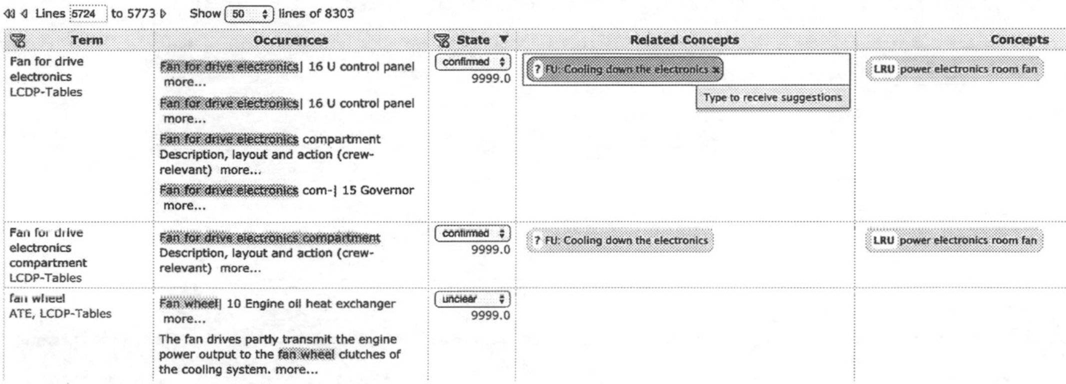

value. The term is related to the concept "FU: Cooling down the electronics" (a concept representing a function of the machine) and serves as an identifier (synonym) for the concept "power electronics room fan", which is a component in the machine.

SEMANTIFICATION OF TECHNICAL DOCUMENTS

The documentation of technical machinery typically yields large corpora. New authoring systems enable the attachment of semantic annotations within the authoring process. Legacy corpora, however, need to be enriched by such metadata in order to make the contained documents accessible for semantic technologies. In the following the process as depicted in Figure 7 will be detailed. It represents the transformation of a corpus $C = \{d_i, ..., d_n\}$ of legacy documents d_i into information units (segments) $d_{i,j}$, and the identification of the most relevant subjects (concepts) for each information unit. The following sections assume that a terminology is available as defined earlier in this chapter.

Data Selection

Basically the approach presented here allows for the batch processing of the legacy documents. However, depending on the quality requirements of the semantification an explicit review phase may be necessary. The (manual) review of semantified documents is cost-sensitive and therefore a prioritization of the legacy documents is recommended. In the data selection phase the documents contained in the corpus are therefore grouped in disjunct priority lists (see Figure 8).

Definition 8: Priority List. Let C be the corpus of technical documents and let .. be a document. Then a priority list $P_b \subseteq C$ is defined as a set of documents $P_b = \{d_1,...,d_n\}$ so that $\forall b \forall c P_b \cap P_c = \varnothing$ with $b \neq c$ and $\bigcup_b P_b = C$.

The creation of the priority lists is usually a rather manual task as corporate aspects such as market penetration of the corresponding product or customer satisfaction needs to be taken into account. Real world projects showed that workshops with different stakeholders for the definition of the priority lists are indispensable. It is not necessary to define priority lists on the document level. In recent projects, these lists were defined on the machine and document type level, e.g. including repair manuals of a specific machine type into a specific priority list.

Figure 7. Overview of the semantification process

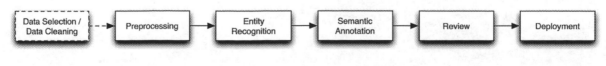

Figure 8. Prioritization of documents on priority lists

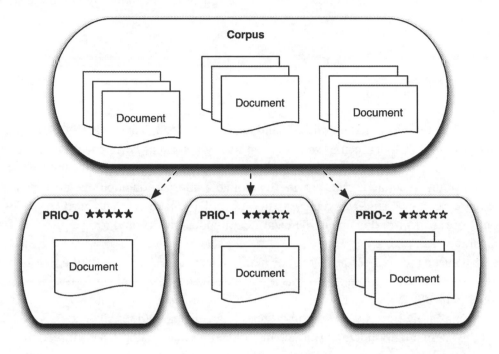

Data Cleaning

The documents selected for semantification might not be in a processable state, i.e., documents may be damaged, use unsupported encodings or do not contain text at all (e.g. scanned legacy documents). Therefore the semantification process contains an explicit data-cleaning step that checks the processability of the selected documents.

Definition 9: Processable Documents. Let $\mathcal{C}$ be the complete corpus of technical documents and let $d_i \in \mathcal{C}$ be a document. Then the function $pcorp : \mathcal{C} \to \mathcal{C}_p$ extracts all processable documents from the corpus by examining each document d_i using the function $pdoc : d \to BOOLEAN$ so that $\mathcal{C}_p \subseteq \mathcal{C}$.

The function *pdoc* checks every document for processability, which for instance can be realized by using heuristics. Here, a file-size-token-ratio-heuristic can be used to identify scanned documents. The documents identified as not processable $\mathcal{C}_{np} = \dfrac{\mathcal{C}}{\mathcal{C}_p}$ need manual review before they can be processed. Depending on their importance the review might also result in an exclusion of the respective documents.

Preprocessing

The next phase of the process consists of a series of preprocessing steps, which transform an original document d_i into structurally enriched information units (segments) $d_{i,j}$ (see Figure 9). The preprocessing is necessary to prepare the input documents for the semantic annotation. In detail the steps of this process phase are:

1. The conversion,
2. The segmentation of the input documents, as well as
3. The addition of structure to the segments.

As stated before the presented approach mainly addresses documents in PDF format. To simplify the further processing all documents are converted to XML format. Different PDF conversion tools have been evaluated. The reference implementation of the presented approach uses the Xpdf-based tool "pdf2xml"[1], since the generated XML provides exploitable information about the document's original structure. Figure 10 shows an XML representation of a PDF document. The XML provides detailed information about a specific document, the pages, contiguous blocks, and texts as well as formatting information about each token.

In order to achieve the goal of identifying the main subjects for each segment, the first step is to split the input documents d_i into information units $d_{i,j}$ as described earlier. Technical documents are often structured hierarchically, e.g., a section describing the replacement of a component typically has subsections for the disassembly step and the assembly step. Semantic annotations shall be provided for different levels of the segmentation hierarchy. Referring to the previous example the subsections describing the disassembly and assembly of a gear stick would be annotated with respective context annotations "assembly" and "dissassemly", while their parent section receives the more general context annotation "replacement". Depending on the data quality of the input documents different segmentation methods are used. Besides established methods—based on lexical or statistical analysis (Reynar, 1999; Hearst, 1997; Choi, 2000; McCallum, Freitag, & Pereira, 2000; Borkar, Deshmukh, & Sarawagi, 2001; Kan, Klavans, & McKeown, 1998)—the reference implementation employs dedicated algorithms that exploit the PDF outline (provided as PDF bookmarks) and/or formatting information.

Definition 10: Segmentation. Let $\mathcal{C}$ be the complete corpus of technical documents, $d_i \in \mathcal{C}$. Let $\mathcal{I}$ be the universal set of all information units $d_{i,j} \in \mathcal{I}$. Then a sequence of information units $d_{i,j} \in d_i$ forms a document, s.t. a function $segment : \mathcal{D} \rightarrow 2^{\mathcal{I}}$ can split the document d_i to information units $d_{i,j}$.

Each segment $d_{i,j}$ is enriched with structure using established methods from Natural Language Processing like Tokenization, Part-of-Speech Tagging and Parsing, and specialized algorithms for the

Figure 9. Converting documents to enriched segments

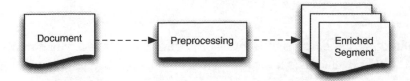

Figure 10. XML representation of a PDF document

```xml
<?xml version="1.0" encoding="UTF-8"?>
<DOCUMENT>
  <METADATA>
    <PDFFILENAME>0002983211.pdf</PDFFILENAME>
  </METADATA>
  <PAGE width="595" height="842" number="4" id="p4">
    <MEDIABOX x1="0" y1="0" x2="595" y2="842"/>
    <CROPBOX x1="0" y1="0" x2="595" y2="842"/>
    <BLEEDBOX x1="0" y1="0" x2="595" y2="842"/>
    <ARTBOX x1="0" y1="0" x2="595" y2="842"/>
    <TRIMBOX x1="0" y1="0" x2="595" y2="842"/>
    <BLOCK id="p4_b3">
      <TEXT width="78.4398" height="13.0712" id="p4_t3" x="28.1971" y="21.952">
        <TOKEN sid="p4_s102" id="p4_w13" font-name="OKMKFK+Helvetica-Bold" symbolic="yes" serif="yes" fixed-width=
          "yes" bold="yes" italic="no" font-size="14.1311" font-color="#000000" rotation="0" angle="0" x="28.1971"
          y="21.952" base="32.0981" width="78.4398" height="13.0712">Zentralelektrik</TOKEN>
      </TEXT>
    </BLOCK>
    <BLOCK id="p4_b5">
      <TEXT width="35.4944" height="9.18618" id="p4_t5" x="288.975" y="81.7164">
        <TOKEN sid="p4_s110" id="p4_w21" goto="p-4 249 207" font-name="okmkgk+helvetica" bold="no" italic="no" font-
          size="9.931" font-color="#000000" rotation="0" angle="0" x="288.975" y="81.7164" base="88.8468"
          width="23.8642" height="9.18618">(Abb.</TOKEN>
        <TOKEN sid="p4_s111" id="p4_w22" goto="p-4 249 207" font-name="okmkgk+helvetica" bold="no" italic="no" font-
          size="9.931" font-color="#000000" rotation="0" angle="0" x="315.577" y="81.7164" base="88.8468"
          width="8.89321" height="9.18618">4)</TOKEN>
      </TEXT>
    </BLOCK>
    <BLOCK id="p4_b6">
      <TEXT width="120.191" height="10.1705" id="p4_t6" x="288.975" y="233.819">
        <TOKEN sid="p4_s112" id="p4_w23" font-name="okmkfk+helvetica-bold" symbolic="yes" serif="yes" fixed-width=
          "yes" bold="yes" italic="no" font-size="10.9951" font-color="#000000" rotation="0" angle="0" x="288.975"
          y="233.819" base="241.714" width="40.2783" height="10.1705">Monitor</TOKEN>
        <TOKEN sid="p4_s113" id="p4_w24" font-name="okmkfk+helvetica-bold" symbolic="yes" serif="yes" fixed-width=
          "yes" bold="yes" italic="no" font-size="10.9951" font-color="#000000" rotation="0" angle="0" x="332.276"
          y="233.819" base="241.714" width="25.5966" height="10.1705">(CIS)</TOKEN>
        <TOKEN sid="p4_s114" id="p4_w25" font-name="okmkfk+helvetica-bold" symbolic="yes" serif="yes" fixed-width=
          "yes" bold="yes" italic="no" font-size="10.9951" font-color="#000000" rotation="0" angle="0" x="360.985"
          y="233.819" base="241.714" width="48.1816" height="10.1705">einbauen</TOKEN>
      </TEXT>
    </BLOCK>
    <BLOCK id="p4_b7">
      <TEXT width="215.404" height="9.18618" x="294.828" y="252.938" id="p4_t7">
        <TOKEN sid="p4_s115" id="p4_w26" font-name="okmkgk+helvetica" bold="no" italic="no" font-size="9.931" font-
          color="#000000" rotation="0" angle="0" x="294.828" y="252.938" base="260.069" width="8.34701"
          height="9.18618">1.</TOKEN>
        <TOKEN sid="p4_s116" id="p4_w27" font-name="okmkgk+helvetica" bold="no" italic="no" font-size="9.931" font-
          color="#000000" rotation="0" angle="0" x="308.837" y="252.938" base="260.069" width="85.059"
          height="9.18618">Steckverbindungen</TOKEN>
        <TOKEN sid="p4_s117" id="p4_w28" font-name="okmkgk+helvetica" bold="no" italic="no" font-size="9.931" font-
          color="#000000" rotation="0" angle="0" x="396.71" y="252.938" base="260.069" width="10.5398"
          height="9.18618">(R</TOKEN>
        <TOKEN sid="p4_s118" id="p4_w29" font-name="okmkgk+helvetica" bold="no" italic="no" font-size="9.931" font-
          color="#000000" rotation="0" angle="0" x="410.099" y="252.938" base="260.069" width="16.6056"
          height="9.18618">und</TOKEN>
        <TOKEN sid="p4_s119" id="p4_w30" font-name="okmkgk+helvetica" bold="no" italic="no" font-size="9.931" font-
          color="#000000" rotation="0" angle="0" x="429.518" y="252.938" base="260.069" width="10.4891"
          height="9.18618">N)</TOKEN>
        <TOKEN sid="p4_s120" id="p4_w31" font-name="okmkgk+helvetica" bold="no" italic="no" font-size="9.931" font-
          color="#000000" rotation="0" angle="0" x="442.818" y="252.938" base="260.069" width="47.9062"
          height="9.18618">aufstecken</TOKEN>
        <TOKEN sid="p4_s121" id="p4_w32" font-name="okmkgk+helvetica" bold="no" italic="no" font-size="9.931" font-
          color="#000000" rotation="0" angle="0" x="493.538" y="252.938" base="260.069" width="16.694"
          height="9.18618">und</TOKEN>
      </TEXT>
    </BLOCK>
```

identification of structural elements like headlines, lists, and tables. The result of the enrichment is stored for each information unit $d_{i,j}$ in forms of annotations $\mathcal{A}_{i,j}$.

Definition 11: Annotation. Let $d_{i,j} \in \mathcal{I}$ be an information unit. Then the set of annotations for this information unit is defined as $\mathcal{A}_{i,j} = \{a_1, \ldots, a_n\}$ where each annotation is described as a tuple of relevant information.

Definition 12: Enrichment. Let $d_{i,j} \in \mathcal{I}$ be an information unit and the set $\mathcal{A}_{i,j}$ the corresponding annotations. Then a function $enrich : \mathcal{I} \rightarrow 2^A$ creates annotations $\mathcal{A}_{i,j} = \{a_1, \ldots, a_n\}$ for an information unit $d_{i,j}$.

The detection of structural elements is motivated by the fact, that the conversion of the documents from PDF to XML does not recognize such elements. However, having access to these elements is beneficial during the subsequent process phases, e.g. terms in headlines can be weighted higher as term matches in the body of a segment. The algorithms operate on the formatting information contained in the converted XML documents, e.g. a table detection algorithm exploits the x and y attributes of the TEXT and TOKEN tags, while a headline detector considers the font-name, font-size as well as the formatting information bold and italic.

Entity Recognition

For each information unit $d_{i,j}$ the next step is to identify occurrences of terminology terms $t \in \mathcal{T}$, since the semantic annotation algorithm is based on these terms. That way, the domain terminology $\mathcal{T}$ is the basis for an *entity recognition* (Nadeau & Sekine, 2007) step. As the terminology $\mathcal{T}$ is a controlled vocabulary and the approach precisely knows what entities (terms) it wants to recognize. In consequence, it is possible to use a dictionary-based entity recognition method identifying all occurrences of terminology terms in the information unit. The identified occurrences are represented in a bag of terms $e_{i,j}$.

Definition 13: Entity Recognition. Let $\varepsilon = \{e_{i,j}\}$ be the universal set of bags of terms, where each $e_{i,j} = \langle t_1, \ldots, t_n \rangle$ is a vector representing a bag of terms recognized in an information unit $d_{i,j} \in \mathcal{I}$ and each t_i is an element of the domain terminology $\mathcal{T}$. Then the entity recognition is defined as a function $er : \mathcal{I} \rightarrow \varepsilon$ that transforms an information unit $d_{i,j} \in \mathcal{I}$ to a bag of terms $e_{i,j} \in \varepsilon$.

At the moment the lookup of terms in the reference implementation is based on word stems produced by a standard Porter stemmer (Porter, 1980). Regarding multi-word terms, the reference implementation allows order independent matches, i.e., all permutations as well as non-contiguous matches. It thus ignores non-matching tokens between tokens belonging to a term.

Coming back to the gear stick example, Figure 11 shows the entity recognition process for an information unit that is about the components of the transmission control. The resulting bag of words contains all terms from the information unit, e.g. "components", "transmission control", "gear selector switch" or "electric".

Figure 11. Transformation of an information unit to a bag of terms using entity recognition methods

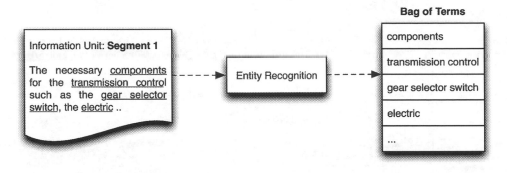

Automated Semantic Annotation

After the entity recognition step a bag of identified terms $e_{i,j} = \langle t_1, \ldots, t_n \rangle$ for each information unit $d_{i,j}$, is available that may indicate different identifiable subjects o_k. For each information unit the task is now the determination of the main subjects (ontological concepts) $\mathcal{S}' \subset \mathcal{S} \subseteq \mathcal{O}$ based on the recognized terms. Therefore the reference implementation employs an approach derived from Explicit Semantic Analysis proposed by (Gabrilovich & Markovitch, 2007). The method was originally developed for the determination of semantic relatedness of texts and is based on a semantic interpreter, which copes with a fixed set of concepts, representing each of them as an attribute vector of words. For an experiment Gabrilovich et al. derived concepts from a subset of Wikipedia articles, where each concept corresponded to the title of a Wikipedia article. The words had been extracted from the article text and weights were assigned by using the TFIDF weighting scheme (Salton & Buckley, 1988). The semantic interpreter is realized as an inverted index that maps each word into a list of concepts in which it appears. When confronted with an input document, the relevance of the concepts contained in the index can be computed by using the semantic interpreter. For each word in the input document the inverted index is asked for the corresponding concepts and their TFIDF weights. Figure 13 shows an excerpt of a semantic interpreter for the gear stick example. Lets consider that the semantic interpreter is asked for the concepts related to the term t_1 "transmission", it would return o_1 "transmission" and o_2 "gear box" and their associated weights. The relevance of the concepts is simply computed by aggregating the weights retrieved from the semantic interpreter for all terms $t_x \in e_{i,j}$. The result is a weighted vector of concepts, where the top-ranked concept is most relevant for the underlying document (See Figure 12 for an example in the gear stick context). The semantic relatedness of texts can then be determined by comparing the computed weighted concept vectors.

Building the Semantic Interpreter

The presented approach also uses a semantic interpreter. However its purpose is not the determination of semantic relatedness of texts but the identification of the main subjects of an information unit. Instead of TFIDF weights it uses available domain knowledge to manually specify the weights, e.g. assuming the set of identifiable subjects $\mathcal{S}'$ corresponds to a hierarchy of assemblies, then terms $t \in \mathcal{T}$ for the direct predecessors and successors of an assembly are weighted higher than the transitive ones. With

Figure 12. Determination of the main subjects on basis of the discovered terminology

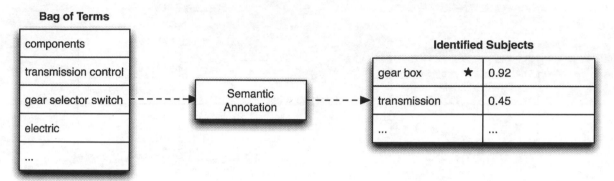

Figure 13. An excerpt of a semantic interpreter showing the gear stick example.

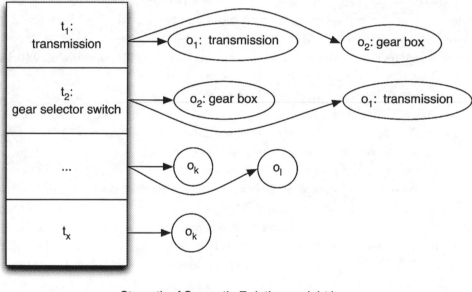

the availability of a spare parts catalog, it is possible to determine the weight of the parts' labels (part of the terminology) as a function of the components they are used in: Special parts that are used in only one component of the machine, receive the highest weight. In contrast, general parts (e.g., bolts) used in many components receive a very low weight. In the following, let $\mathcal{S} = \left\{ s_x \right\}$ be the set of identifiable subjects (concepts), $\mathcal{T} = \left\{ t_z \right\}$ be the set of terms, k_x be an inverted index entry for term t_z, where the weight k_x represents the strength of the association between term t_z and concept s_x.

Using Document Characteristics for Term Weighting

To determine the main subject of a segment, the approach exploits the bag of terms representation $e_{i,j}$ of each information unit $d_{i,j}$. The bag of terms corresponds to the result of the dictionary-based entity recognition method used in a preceding process phase. In contrast to Gabrilovich and Markovitch (2007) document characteristics are also taken into account by weighting the terms. Several document specific information aspects like relevance in the document (segment frequency; corresponds to the document frequency in other corpora), formatting (bold, italics, underscoring) or the position in the segment (headline) are considered. For the latter one the approach exploits the set of annotations $\mathcal{A}_{i,j}$ that has been created in the preprocessing phase. In the following let $e_{i,j} = \left\{ t_z \right\}$ be the bag of terms representing the information unit $d_{i,j}$, and let v_z be its weight vector, where v_z is the weight of term t_z.

Ranking Concepts

For all information units the semantic interpreter derives a ranked list of concepts. The algorithm given as pseudo code in Listing 1 does the ranking.

The algorithm basically iterates through all terms t_z in a bag of terms $e_{i,j}$, asks for the inverted index entry $\langle k_x \rangle$ of all concepts c_x related to term t_z, and sums up the product of term weight v_i and relation strength k_x—the result is called *weighted relatedness*. The temporary results are saved in a map, which gets sorted for the final result in descending order on the weighted relatedness score. This score expresses the relevance of the concepts for the segment, i.e. a higher score means higher relevance.

The described algorithm produces a ranking of relevant concepts. Now, the next is to identify the most relevant concepts—that are refered to as *sprint group*; an analogy to the sprint group in cycling races that offsets from the peloton.

For the determination of the sprint group two different strategies are proposed. The first one simply uses a threshold; the second one is based on statistical outlier tests. The basic approach for determining the sprint group is taking the score of the most relevant concept. Based on this score all concepts that are within a specified threshold, e.g. 90% of the highest score are added to the sprint group. Basically this yields good results, but there are scenarios where it does not fit. An example for such a scenario is

Listing 1. An algorithm for the term-based ranking of concepts

```
getRankedConcepts (e_i, j, ⟨v_z⟩)
 Map<Concept, Double> ranking
    for each t_z in e_i,j
        ⟨k_x⟩ = SemanticInterpreter.get(t_z)
        for each k_x
            wtdrelatedness = k_x * v_z
            ranking.update(s_x, wtdrelatedness)
 ranking.sort(WeightedRelatedness, DESC)
 return ranking
```

a result where all concepts have low scores, i.e., no concept is actually relevant for the segment. Using the basic approach the majority of the concepts would enter the sprint group. Statistical outlier tests can tackle this issue. Using such tests it can be determined whether scores exist that offset from the rest. A simple test is for example to compute the interquartile range ($IQR = Q_{75} - Q_{25}$) and then to treat all scores that are higher than $Q_{75} + \alpha * IQR$ as outliers. In principle, more sophisticated outlier tests like Grubbs' test for outliers (Grubbs, 1969) can also be applied.

Review

Depending on the requirements on data quality, a manual review of the results of the semantic annotation by domain experts might be necessary. As the availability of domain experts is a crucial element in this step, the usage of an appropriate interactive review tool (see Figure 14) that helps to improve the review time is proposed.

For this task such a review tool needs to fulfill at least the following requirements: (1) Display the hierarchical segmentation of a specific document, (2) display the main subjects for each segment and (3) allow the addition and deletion of subjects. The usage of a visual component and the highlighting of critical annotations are also recommended in order to optimize the review effort. The visual component should be able to display the semantic similarity of identified subjects. This can help to overview the document, since the subject in a sequence of information units is often constant or at least semantically

Figure 14. A tool for the manual review of semantic annotations, containing the hierarchical segmentation (left), a visual report (top right) and a detail view (bottom right)

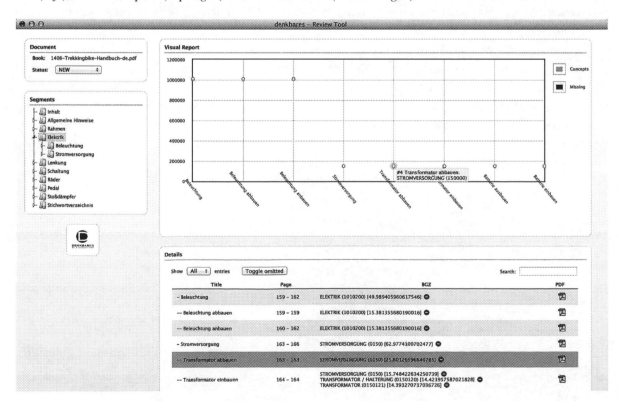

similar. An example for this claim is a technical document that covers the mounting and unmounting of assemblies. In such a document the probability is high that the corresponding segments of a specific assembly are in a sequence. In the visual component characteristic patterns like the *semantic staircase* as displayed in Figure 14 can be expected. Additionally, information units without any annotations or with many semantically unrelated annotations should be automatically detected and highlighted.

There exist various metrics for the computation of semantic similarities. Examples for approaches based on WordNet (Fellbaum, 1998) were proposed among others by Jiang and Conrath (1997) or Lin (1998). These metrics might be adapted due to the specificity of the used terminology.

Figure 14 shows a sample review tool. In the left the title of the current document is displayed and a status for the document ("new", "in progress", "reviewed") can be specified by the reviewer. Below, the hierarchical segmentation of the document is displayed in a tree view element. The tree view can be used for checking and navigating through the segmentation. Clicking on an element in the tree view loads the information regarding the semantic annotations for the selected segment. The loaded information is displayed in the right part of the application. In the upper part a visual component ("Visual Report") displays the results based on semantic similarity. In the example taxonomic information for the computation of semantic similarity is used. Missing annotations are indicated using a red placeholder. At the bottom of the right part detailed information ("Details") about the semantic annotations are available. They can be accessed by scrolling the view or by clicking on a data point in the visual component. For a thorough review it may be necessary to look up the text of a segment, therefore the tool provides direct access to the text in the original document. The detail view also provides possibilities for the addition and removal of concepts supported by semantic typing with autocompletion (Hyvönen & Mäkelä, 2006).

Deployment

The final step in the proposed process is concerned with post-processing tasks. Such tasks typically handle the resource preparation for the target applications, evaluate the results or apply measurements to the extracted data. A typical scenario is the generation of proprietary XML files that contain information about the information units and the discovered subjects. In some cases additional meta data, that can be derived from the provided domain ontology or other meta data are also incorporated and deployed.

SOLUTIONS AND RECOMMENDATIONS (CASE STUDIES)

The presented approach has already been applied to corpora of several German mechanical engineering companies. In the following the definition of a domain terminology for an engineering company for special purpose vehicles is described. Afterwards the semantification procedure for an engineering company for harvesting technology is presented. Both case studies might serve as recommendations for similar scmantification projects.

Defining a Domain Terminology for Special Purpose Vehicles

In the following case study the applicability of the terminology definition process that was presented at the beginning of the chapter shall be presented. In preparation of an ongoing semantification project an existing domain ontology had to be enhanced by providing a supplementary terminology. The ontology in focus covers a special purpose vehicle and contains about 35,000 identifiable concepts representing components, user interface elements, functions and locations. All concepts have German and English labels. The supplementary terminology should provide additional identifiers as well as related terms for the provided set of concepts.

The Data Set

Different term sources that varied in forms of their structure, the term quality, and their connectability were considered. In total about 60,000 term candidates were extracted from these sources.

- **Technical Structure Model:** The technical structure model represents the structural decompositions of the vehicle in forms of components and was provided in XML format. The quality of the about 8,000 contained terms was high, as they were extracted directly from XML attributes representing German and English labels. The connectability was also considered high as additional XML attributes were available, that reference different types of id numbers.
- **Spare Parts and Stock Lists:** Spare parts and stock lists were provided as data base dumps and data sheets and contained about 45,000 terms. The terms were extracted using SQL statements and custom parsers for the data sheets. Due to the similar character of this source to the structure models, the term quality and connectability was also high.
- **Technical Documentation:** Despite these rather structured term sources the technical documentation for the vehicle were also considered. Different ATE methods were employed to extract about 9,000 term candidates together with associated confidence values from these documents. The threshold for the confidence value had been defined to be 0.35 and all terms with a confidence value below were ignored – about 5,000 terms remained. The corpus contains a document that describes the components and functions of the particular vehicle in detail and therefore contains a lot of tables, images with associated explanations (see Figure 15) and other structures that evidently contain high quality terms.

Dedicated extraction rules (Chiticariu, Li, & Reiss, 2013; Kluegl, Atzmueller, & Puppe, 2009) extracted about 2,000 of such terms from the document. The connectability of the terms extracted by ATE methods and extraction rules was rather low.

Prioritization and Review

About 50,000 terms (95%) were connected automatically from the structured sources (technical structure models, spare parts and stock lists) to the existing set of concepts by exploiting referenced global identifiers. In contrast only about 1,500 terms (20%) extracted from the technical documents could be connected automatically using fuzzy string matching techniques.

In the project the access to the domain expert— who is able to connect the remaining terms to the correct concepts—was limited (5 days). The goal was to maximize the cost-benefit ratio, i.e. connecting those terms first, that support best the target scenario – the semantification of a corpus of technical documents.

As described in the Prerequisites section such terms usually have a high coverage. For all term pools coverage metrics were computed and visualized using the term cities. As expected the terms extracted

Figure 15. Example of structured content that has been accessed using extraction rules

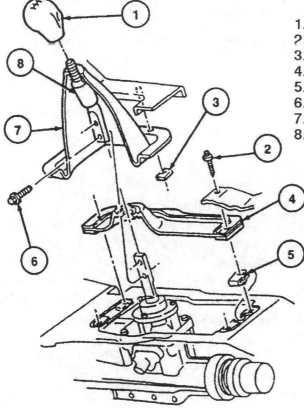

1. Gearshift lever knob
2. Lower dust boot retaining screw
3. Upper dust boot retaining clip
4. Lower gearshift lever boot
5. Retaining clip
6. Gearshift lever retaining screw
7. Upper gearshift lever boot
8. Gearshift lever

directly from the technical documents had the highest coverage. While the coverage for the terms from the technical structure models was reasonable, it was low for the spare parts and stock lists. The term sources were priorizied as follows, considering the term cities and the term quality of the different sources:

1. Terms extracted by dedicated extraction rules.
2. Terms from the technical structure model.
3. Terms extracted using ATE methods.
4. Terms from the spare parts list.
5. Terms from the stock list.

The expert was able to connect all terms of the three top prioritized term sources to their respective concepts. Tool support in form of the presented term review tool (see Figure 6) was provided. The expert confirmed that the provided text occurrences in conjunction with the semantic autocompletion ability were a noticeable simplification of the task. He connected all the remaining 500 terms from the structure model and about 5,000 terms that have been extracted from the technical documentation within 5 workdays. So the average connection time per term was 26 seconds (5,500 terms in 5 days with 8 working hours). The expert was asked to connect some of the remaining terms without the help of the term review tool. In order to complete the task, he was forced to look up text occurrences manually.

Instead of entering new concepts with the help of the semantic typing component—instead a data sheet containing the URI and the original labels of the concepts had been provided. The connection of the terms took 2 minutes and 23 seconds on the average.

Semantifying the Technical Documentation for Harvesting Technology

The second case study reports on an actual semantification project for harvesting machines. The task was to split a corpus of legacy technical documents to information units and determine for each the most important concepts.

The Data Set

A domain ontology described in OWL (Hitzler, Krötzsch, Parsia, Patel-Schneider, & Rudolph, 2012) and RDFS (Brickley & Guha, 2014) as well as a decent terminology has already been available in the company and were supplied in forms of two ontologies serialized in the Turtle (Beckett, Berners-Lee, & Prud'hommeaux, 2014) format. The first ontology describes relations of assemblies, products, and machines, e.g. that the cylinder block assembly is part of the engine assembly, which itself is a part of a certain product or machine—in the following this ontology will be refered to as *core ontology*. The second ontology describes in detail which parts are build in a special assembly, e.g. that a certain valve is part of the cylinder head—it is called the *parts ontology*. Assemblies and parts have had labels attached as literals using the RDFS property rdfs:label and language attributes. SPARQL (Harris & Seaborne, 2013) queries were employed to extract concepts (assemblies) and terms. Concepts were represented using their URI while the labels described above were used as terms.

The technical document corpus in focus contains about 9,000 PDF documents, covering different machines. Each document has up to 2,000 pages and is of a certain type, e.g. repair manual, operation manual, circuit diagram or installation guide. The documents address different target groups ranging from maintenance staff to end-users what influences the structure and the level of detail.

Processing the Corpus

The corpus of technical documents ran through the complete process as described earlier. The documents were provided in the PDF format and got converted to XML. Then a segmentation algorithm used the included PDF bookmarks to segment the documents. Structure was added to the produced segments, using a standard whitespace tokenizer and a maximum-entropy part-of-speech tagger. Then a dictionary-based entity recognition algorithm annotated all occurrences of terms extracted from the core and parts ontologies. A semantic interpreter with domain-specific weights identified the main subjects of each segment.

The $\langle k_x \rangle$ values indicating the strength of the association between term t_z and concept s_x were computed differently for assembly and part terms. For terms extracted from the core ontology weight was defined as

$$k_x = \frac{1}{\# edges\ between\ concepts},$$

i.e., the label of the concept in focus will get the maximum weight of 1, which means that this label indicates the concept best. Predecessors and successors in the assembly hierarchy got lower weights, e.g. the parents and children got the weight 0.5, grandparents and grandchildren the weight 0.33.

This approach was not feasible for terms from the parts ontology, because there are parts that are semantically different but have the same label (e.g. "valve" or "screw"). The more parts have the same label, the less suitable are they for the inference of a particular concept, i.e. their weight should be adapted accordingly. The weight for terms from the parts ontology were defined as:

$$k_x = \frac{1}{concept\ frequency},$$

where *concept frequency* is the number of concepts that have a part represented by a particular label. This procedure shifts the focus from concepts to labels for terms from the parts ontology. The maximum weight of 1 is assigned to parts that have a unique label and are built in only one assembly. Parts with common labels that are used in a variety of assemblies get lower weights, e.g. parts with the label "screw" are built in more than 500 assemblies, so the weight is as low as 0.002.

The described standard procedure for computing the sprint group and filtering outliers from the concept ranking were applied as described above. The resulting concept sprint groups were reviewed using the review tool depicted in Figure 14. The reviewed documents were used as the basis for the computation of the f-measure of the presented semantic annotation approach. On the average the presented approach yield an f-measure of 83%. As the availability of a domain expert is critical, the time needed for a correction was also determined. The time a user worked with the provided review tool was logged together with a count of the changes he made, leading to an average correction time of 20 seconds per correction.

The reviewed results were finally converted into an XML format compatible with the target application.

FUTURE RESEARCH DIRECTIONS

Future research directions might cover the integration of the presented approach in authoring systems and processes. Thus, the text analytics abilities would also be available for supporting technical writers during the creation or update of technical documentation. The presented review tool might be extended in a way that it makes use of the corrections made to other documents to suggest possibly errornous annotations. On a more fundamental level the intermediate transformation of proprietary file formats (PDF) to the XML format could be replaced by a standardized ontological representation of technical documentation. This representation should not only cover the geometrical representation of a technical document in forms of pages, sections etc. but also describe the logical structure. This would be a big step in reducing the veracity and variety of the underlying data.

CONCLUSION

Advanced technical documentation makes use of semantic metadata and thus enables new applications such as semantic search and navigation. Legacy corpora of technical documentation, however, are usually characterized by a high veracity and variety in the data together with a lack of semantically enriched documents.

This chapter presented a holistic approach for the semantification of large corpora of legacy technical documents. The approach requires no training data but makes use of existing background knowledge and appropriate review techniques. A vital part of the approach is a process tackling the arising challenges, such as different file formats, varying data quality, terminology extraction, semantic annotation, and focused reviews. For the remaining tasks—preprocessing and the structural enrichment of the documents—standard NLP technologies are employed. The core of the presented approach is the semantic annotation that is based on Explicit Semantic Analysis and domain ontologies. In real-word projects the applicability and easy adaptation of this approach to a variety of corpora was experienced.

The described approach was implemented in two domains, both the technical corpora of mechanical engineering companies. The approach achieved successful results in both corpora with an average f-measure of 83%. Within the approach, also a tool for the manual review and correction of automatically applied semantic annotations was developed. Experiments with domain experts showed that the average correction time is 20 seconds, that allows for the complete review of a large technical document in a couple of minutes.

In research there exist many approaches for information extraction of textual resources. To the best of the authors' knowledge there is no other holistic approach for the problem of the semantification of technical documents, although there exist alternatives for the single steps of the presented approach. The approach uses standard methods for the terminology extraction, preprocessing, structural enrichment, and entity recognition. Therefore, the focus was on the remaining tasks for which adapted methods were implemented: semantic annotation, and the review.

Regarding the semantic annotation, which in this case is the identification of the main subject for a segment or document, latent approaches exist, e.g., Latent Dirichlet Allocation (Blei, Ng, & Jordan, 2003) or Latent Semantic Analysis (Deerwester, Dumais, Furnas, Landauer, & Harshman, 1990). In the presented approach the goal is the identification of a concrete (or explicit) concept, so the latent approaches do not fit for the problem. Efforts have been made to make the topics discovered by the latent approaches more explicit, e.g. Ramage et al. (2009) proposed Labeled LDA that constraints LDA by defining one-to-one correspondence between LDA's latent topics and user defined tags. Andrzejewski and Zhu (2009) proposed the usage of supervision in form of Topic-in-Set knowledge to improve the recovery of original topics using LDA. Chemudugunta et al. (2008) proposed the combination of semantic concepts and unsupervised statistical learning to tag web pages with concepts from a known set of concepts without the need for labeled documents.

Regarding the review of semantic annotations the authors are not aware of a comparable tool for the review of the main subject of a segment or document. Ontosophie (Celjuska & Vargas-Vera, 2004) is a system for the population of event ontologies and uses supervised machine learning for learning extraction rules. These rules also compute a confidence value, which is used to determine whether a human reviewer needs to accept extracted information. The idea of the presented review tool is to guide a human reviewer through an entire book and highlight critical annotations for rapid correction.

REFERENCES

Albrechtsen, H. (1993). Subject analysis and indexing: From automated indexing to domain analysis. *The Indexer*, *18*, 219–219.

Andrzejewski, D., & Zhu, X. (2009). Latent Dirichlet Allocation with topic-in-set knowledge.*Proceedings of the NAACL HLT 2009 Workshop on Semi-Supervised Learning for Natural Language Processing*, (pp. 43-48). doi:10.3115/1621829.1621835

Antoniou, G., & van Harmelen, F. (2008). A Semantic Web Primer (2nd ed.). Cambridge, MA: MIT Press.

Beckett, D., Berners-Lee, T., & Prud'hommeaux, E. (2014, February 25). *Turtle - Terse RDF Triple Language*. Retrieved May 15, 2015, from http://www.w3.org/TR/turtle/

Blei, D. M., Ng, A. Y., & Jordan, M. I. (2003). Latent Dirichlet Allocation. *Journal of Machine Learning Research*, *3*, 993–1022.

Borkar, V. R., Deshmukh, K., & Sarawagi, S. (2001). Automatic Segmentation of Text into Structured Records. In S. Mehrotra, & T. K. Sellis (Ed.), *SIGMOD Conference* (pp. 175-186). ACM. doi:10.1145/376284.375682

Brickley, D., & Guha, R. (2014, February 14). *RDF Schema 1.1*. Retrieved May 15, 2015, from http://www.w3.org/TR/rdf-schema/

Buitelaar, P., & Cimiano, P. (2008). *Ontology learning and population: bridging the gap between text and knowledge* (Vol. 167). IOS Press.

Celjuska, D., & Vargas-Vera, M. (2004). Ontosophie: A semi-automatic system for ontology population from text.*Proceedings of the 3rd International Conference on Natural Language Processing (ICON)*.

Cheatham, M., & Hitzler, P. (2013). String similarity metrics for ontology alignment. In The Semantic Web - ISWC 2013 (pp. 294-309). Springer. doi:10.1007/978-3-642-41338-4_19

Chemudugunta, C., Holloway, A., Smyth, P., & Steyvers, M. (2008). *Modeling documents by combining semantic concepts with unsupervised statistical learning*. Springer. doi:10.1007/978-3-540-88564-1_15

Chiticariu, L., Li, Y., & Reiss, F. R. (2013). *Rule-Based Information Extraction is Dead! Long Live Rule-Based Information Extraction Systems!*. EMNLP.

Choi, F. Y. (2000). *Advances in domain independent linear text segmentation*. ANLP.

Deerwester, S., Dumais, S. T., Furnas, G. W., Landauer, T. K., & Harshman, R. (1990). Indexing by latent semantic analysis. *Journal of the American Society for Information Science*, *41*(6), 391–407. doi:10.1002/(SICI)1097-4571(199009)41:6<391::AID-ASI1>3.0.CO;2-9

Euzenat, J., & Shvaiko, P. (2007). *Ontology Matching*. Heidelberg, Germany: Springer.

Fellbaum, C. (Ed.). (1998). *WordNet: An Electronic Lexical Database*. Cambridge, MA: MIT Press.

Frantzi, K., Ananiadou, S., & Mima, H. (2000). Automatic recognition of multi-word terms. the C-value/NC-value method. *International Journal on Digital Libraries*, *3*(2), 115–130. doi:10.1007/s007999900023

Gabrilovich, E., & Markovitch, S. (2007). Computing semantic relatedness using Wikipedia-based explicit semantic analysis.*Proceedings of the 20th international joint conference on artificial intelligence.*

Grubbs, F. E. (1969). Procedures for Detecting Outlying Observations in Samples. *Technometrics, 11*(1), 1–21. doi:10.1080/00401706.1969.10490657

Guha, R., McCool, R., & Miller, E. (2003). Semantic search.*Proceedings of the 12th international conference on World Wide Web*, (pp. 700-709).

Harris, S., & Seaborne, A. (2013, March 21). *Webpage.* Retrieved May 15, 2015, from SPARQL 1.1 Query Language: http://www.w3.org/TR/sparql11-query/

Hearst, M. A. (1997). TextTiling: Segmenting text into multi-paragraph subtopic passages. *Computational Linguistics, 23*(1), 33–64.

Hitzler, P., Krötzsch, M., Parsia, B., Patel-Schneider, P. F., & Rudolph, S. (2012, December 11). *OWL 2 Web Ontology Language: Primer.* Retrieved May 15, 2015, from http://www.w3.org/TR/owl2-primer/

Horrocks, I., Parsia, B., Patel-Schneider, P., & Hendler, J. (2005). Semantic Web Architecture: Stack or Two Towers? In F. Fages & S. Soliman (Eds.), *Principles and Practice of Semantic Web Reasoning (PPSWR)* (pp. 37–41). Springer. doi:10.1007/11552222_4

Hutchins, W. J. (1978). The concept of aboutness in subject indexing.*Aslib Proceedings, 30*(5), 172–181. doi:10.1108/eb050629

Hyvönen, E., & Mäkelä, E. (2006). Semantic autocompletion. In The Semantic Web - ASWC 2006 (pp. 739-751). Springer. doi:10.1007/11836025_72

Jiang, J. J., & Conrath, D. W. (1997). Semantic similarity based on corpus statistics and lexical taxonomy. *Proceedings of ROCLING X.* Taiwan.

Kageura, K., & Umino, B. (1996). Methods of automatic term recognition: A review. *Terminology, 3*(2), 259–289. doi:10.1075/term.3.2.03kag

Kan, M.-Y., Klavans, J. L., & McKeown, K. (1998). Linear Segmentation and Segment Significance. *CoRR.*

Kluegl, P., Atzmueller, M., & Puppe, F. (2009). Textmarker: A tool for rule-based information extraction.*Proceedings of the Biennial GSCL Conference*, (pp. 233-240).

Levenshtein, V. (1966). Binary Codes Capable of Correcting Deletions, Insertions, and Reversals. *Soviet Physics, Doklady, 10*(8), 707–710.

Lidwell, W., Holden, K., & Butler, J. (2003). *Universal Principles of Design.* Rockport Publishers.

Lin, D. (1998). An information-theoretic definition of similarity. *ICML, 98*, 296–304.

McCallum, A., Freitag, D., & Pereira, F. (2000). *Maximum Entropy Markov Models for Information Extraction and Segmentation. In Proceeding 17th International Conforence on Machine Learning* (pp. 591–598). San Francisco, CA: Morgan Kaufmann.

Nadeau, D., & Sekine, S. (2007). A survey of named entity recognition and classification. *Lingvisticae Investigationes*, *30*(1), 3–26. doi:10.1075/li.30.1.03nad

Needleman, S. B., & Wunsch, C. D. (1970). A general method applicable to the search for similarities in the amino acid sequence of two proteins.*Journal of Molecular Biology*, *48*(3), 443–453. doi:10.1016/0022-2836(70)90057-4 PMID:5420325

Park, Y., Byrd, R. J., & Boguraev, B. K. (2002). Automatic glossary extraction: beyond terminology identification.*Proceedings of the 19th international conference on Computational linguistics-Volume 1*, (pp. 1-7). doi:10.3115/1072228.1072370

Pazienza, M., Pennacchiotti, M., & Zanzotto, F. (2005). Terminology Extraction: An Analysis of Linguistic and Statistical Approaches. In S. Sirmakessis (Ed.), *Knowledge Mining Series: Studies in Fuzziness and Soft Computing*. Springer Verlag. doi:10.1007/3-540-32394-5_20

Porter, M. (1980). An Algorithm for Suffix Stripping. *Program*, *14*(3), 130–137. doi:10.1108/eb046814

Ramage, D., Hall, D., Nallapati, R., & Manning, C. D. (2009). Labeled LDA: A supervised topic model for credit attribution in multi-labeled corpora.*Proceedings of the 2009 Conference on Empirical Methods in Natural Language Processing* (pp. 248-256). doi:10.3115/1699510.1699543

Reynar, J. C. (1999). Statistical Models for Topic Segmentation. In R. Dale & K. W. Church (Eds.), *ACL. Association of Computer Linguistics*. doi:10.3115/1034678.1034735

Salton, G., & Buckley, C. (1988). Term-Weighting Approaches in Automatic Text Retrieval. *Information Processing & Management*, *24*(5), 513–523. doi:10.1016/0306-4573(88)90021-0

Sauermann, L., Grimnes, G. A., Kiesel, M., Fluit, C., Maus, H., & Heim, D. et al.. (2006). Semantic Desktop 2.0: The Gnowsis Experience.*Proceedings of the 5th International Semantic Web Conference, LNCS 4273*, (pp. 887-900). doi:10.1007/11926078_64

Sclano, F., & Velardi, P. (2007). Termextractor: a web application to learn the shared terminology of emergent web communities. In Enterprise Interoperability II (pp. 287-290). Springer. doi:10.1007/978-1-84628-858-6_32

Smith, T., & Waterman, M. (1981). Identification of Common Molecular Subsequences. *Journal of Molecular Biology*, *147*(1), 195–197. doi:10.1016/0022-2836(81)90087-5 PMID:7265238

Zhang, Z., Iria, J., Brewster, C. A., & Ciravegna, F. (2008). A comparative evaluation of term recognition algorithms.*Proceedings of The sixth international conference on Language Resources and Evaluation*.

KEY TERMS AND DEFINITIONS

Annotation: Let $d_{i,j} \in \mathcal{I}$ be an information unit. Then the set of annotations for this information unit is defined as $\mathcal{A}_{i,j} = \left\{ a_1, \ldots, a_n \right\}$ where each annotation is described as a tuple of relevant information.

Document Corpus: Let $\mathcal{D}$ be the universal set of possible documents and let $d_i \in \mathcal{D}$ be a document. Then a corpus $\mathcal{C} \subseteq \mathcal{D}$ is defined as a set of documents $\mathcal{C} = \{d_i, \dots, d_n\}$.

Domain Terminology: Let $\mathcal{O}$ be a domain ontology, consisting of ontological concepts $o_k \in \mathcal{O}$ and term concepts $b_m \in \mathcal{O}$ that are connected using relation instances $r_{k,m} \in \mathcal{O}$. And let all concepts o_k and term concepts b_m have a human-readable label l_p. Then the domain terminology is defined as the union of all labels $\mathcal{T} = \bigcup_p l_p$.

Enrichment: Let $d_{i,j} \in \mathcal{I}$ be an information unit and the set $\mathcal{A}_{i,j}$ the corresponding annotations. Then a function $enrich : \mathcal{I} \rightarrow 2^A$ creates annotations $\mathcal{A}_{i,j} = \{a_1, \dots, a_n\}$ for an information unit $d_{i,j}$.

Identifiable Subjects: Let $\mathcal{O}$ be a domain ontology, consisting of ontological concepts $o_k \in \mathcal{O}$. Then the set of identifiable subjects $\mathcal{S} \subseteq \mathcal{O}$ is defined as a set of ontological concepts $\mathcal{S} = \{o_1, \dots, o_n\}$.

Information Unit: Let $d_i \in \mathcal{D}$ a document in a given corpus $\mathcal{C} \subseteq \mathcal{D}$. Then, d_i can be split into the non-empty partition of segments $d_{i,j}$ so that $d_i = [d_{i,1}, \dots, d_{i,m}]$. The segment $d_{i,j}$ is called an information unit.

Priority List: Let $\mathcal{C}$ be the corpus of technical documents and let $d_i \in \mathcal{C}$ a document. Then a priority list $\mathcal{P}_b \subseteq \mathcal{C}$ is defined as a set of documents $\mathcal{P}_b = \{d_1, \dots, d_n\}$ so that $\forall b \forall c \mathcal{P}_b \cap \mathcal{P}_c = \varnothing$ with $b \neq c$ and $\bigcup_b \mathcal{P}_b = \mathcal{C}$.

Segmentation: Let $\mathcal{C}$ be the complete corpus of technical documents, $d_i \in \mathcal{C}$. Let $\mathcal{I}$ be the universal set of all information units $d_{i,j} \in \mathcal{I}$. Then a sequence of information units $d_{i,j} \in d_i$ forms a document, s.t. a function $segment : \mathcal{D} \rightarrow 2^{\mathcal{I}}$ can split the document d_i to information units $d_{i,j}$.

ENDNOTE

[1]   A copy of pdf2xml can be downloaded from https://sourceforge.net/projects/pdf2xml

Chapter 12

Application of Complex Event Processing Techniques to Big Data Related to Healthcare:
A Systematic Literature Review of Case Studies

Fehmida Mohamedali
University of West London, UK

Samia Oussena
University of West London, UK

ABSTRACT

Healthcare is a growth area for event processing applications. Computers and information systems have been used for collecting patient data in health care for over fifty years. However, progress towards a unified health care delivery system in the UK has been slow. Big Data, the Internet of Things (IoT) and Complex Event Processing (CEP) have the potential not only to deal with treatment areas of healthcare domain but also to redefine healthcare services. This study is intended to provide a broad overview of where in the health sector, the application of CEP is most used, the data sources that contribute to it and the types of event processing languages and techniques implemented. By systematic review of existing literature on the application of CEP techniques in Healthcare, a number of use cases have been identified to provide a detailed analysis of the most common used case(s), common data sources in use and highlight CEP query language types and techniques that have been considered.

INTRODUCTION/BACKGROUND

With the rising popularity of the Internet and the digital world, information is shared instantaneously and businesses have become increasingly global. This has given rise to "Big Data". Big data is the measurement of large, complex data, specifically data that falls into the "4V's model"; high Volume, high

DOI: 10.4018/978-1-5225-0293-7.ch012

Velocity, high Variety and high Veracity resulting from sensors, cameras, social media, smart phones and other consumer and monitoring devices in use daily.

Big data is a perfect fit for dealing with the technology challenges faced by the health care industry. Health data generated by wearable sensor devices, Wi-Fi enabled scales and smart phones could provide a far more accurate picture of individual's health and the treatment(s) they receive.

In terms of big data for healthcare, *Volume* refers to the rapidly expanding size of the sets of data that is generated in every area of activity in a healthcare enterprise, from revenue, to patient data, to supply and operations. *Variety* includes the diversity of data collected. In a hospital, for instance, data includes patient records containing a variety of information like lab reports, scans, x-rays, prescription details and other medical data. Apart from having access to patient data relating to diagnosis and treatment, other data such as patient scheduling and workflow, data resulting from healthcare administration and hospital hygiene are also available. Exposure to such rich and contrasting elements of data is challenging and requires the use of special techniques to synthesise and process these large sets of data in a reasonable time frame. With the advent of sensor technology, Radio Frequency Identification (RFID), personal health monitors, wireless network of wearable devices and other healthcare monitoring devices, there is significant *Velocity* of incoming healthcare data. Finally, *Veracity*, data assurance and quality issues are of acute concern in healthcare as important decisions depend on having accurate information. The quality of healthcare data, especially unstructured data, is highly variable and needs utmost care.

Big data technologies deal with petabytes of records, files, transactional data either arriving as streams or in batches. The rise of technologies such as social and mobile are contributing to increase in unstructured and semi structured data. These datasets are so huge that they cannot be processed and managed using traditional methods like Relational Data Base Systems (RDBMS). Such data warehouses are not able to handle the processing demands of big data that need to be updated frequently or even continuously.

COMPLEX EVENT PROCESSING (CEP)

Complex event processing refers to the processing of representations of events possibly, thousands of events, in a form that is suitable for automated processing. An event is simply "something that happens" in real life. Event objects as these representations are called include data such as where and when the event happened, how long it took and if it was caused by other events.

Business enterprises are swamped by 100,000 to 100 million events per second, originating in their application systems, sensors, social applications, the Web and other sources. RFID readers, bar code scanners, and other devices detect the presence of objects and send events through Internet-based event-processing networks (EPNs) to CEP-enabled servers that maintain virtual representations for each object. Within healthcare, CEP engines can analyse events and related data which come from various sources (health sensors, environment sensors etc.) in real-time and provide insights for a better healthcare.

The CEP technology is aimed to provide applications with a flexible and scalable mechanism for constructing condensed, refined views of the data. It correlates the data (viewed as events streams) in order to detect and report meaningful predefined patterns, thus supplying the application with an effective view of the accumulated incoming data (events), and allowing the application to react to the detections by executing actions (Magid, Adi, Barnea, Botzer & Rabinovich, 2008).

CEP encompasses methods, techniques, and tools for processing events from a variety of sources in real time; while they occur in a continuous and timely manner. It derives valuable higher-level knowledge from lower-level events. This is referred as complex events; combination of several events.

Key concepts in event processing are events and patterns. An event is any action that is happening and an event pattern, in essence, is any particular configuration or arrangement of events that can be recognised by a machine. Event patterns can be specified using an event query language.

EVENT QUERY LANGUAGES

Unlike database queries, event queries are evaluated continuously as the events happen. These events are everywhere but need to be collected and combined in real-time in such a way so that they can be used for detection of interesting situation(s), which if relevant, can be modelled into patterns that represent topics of interest or certain situations of interest which need to be detected in real-time.

Patterns are dependent upon several factors such as user's needs, changes in the event sources, environment etc. and therefore, must be dynamically verified. This in turn entails that the description of a complex situation must be maintained over time, i.e., changed/adapted to new conditions etc.

Event Query Languages are specialised languages used to specify event queries. Each query in an event query language has its semantics determined by the language, corresponding to an event query. The most important features of an Event Query Language are the patterns it can detect.

Broadly speaking, there are five categories of languages used to express event queries:

1. Composition-operator-based languages (sometimes also called composite event algebras or event pattern languages).
2. Stream query languages (usually based on SQL).
3. Logic languages.
4. Production rule languages.
5. Timed (finite) state machine languages.

Production rule is not an event query language as such. The rules are usually tightly coupled with a host programming language (e.g., Java) and specify actions to be executed when certain states are entered. They do not operate on streams, but on data structures called working memories: mutable sets of objects capable of carrying data, called facts.

The timed state machine language uses established technology to model event queries in a graphical way. Since states in a state machine are reached by particular sequences of multiple events occurring over time, they implicitly define complex events. Though timed state machines provide intuitive visualisation of complex events their expressivity is limited. Negation and composition of events are cumbersome and they do not support aggregation. To overcome deficits of the theoretical automata, state machines are usually combined with languages of other styles. (Eckert, Bry, Brodt, Poppe, & Hausmann, 2011)

The first three language types listed above are *explicitly* developed for specifying event queries. These are described briefly below.

Composition-Operator-Based Languages

The general idea behind composition-operator-based languages is the composition of complex event queries using simpler event queries. Composition-operator-based languages have their origins in active database systems.

The expressivity of these languages is determined by their supported operators, such as conjunction, disjunction, sequences, negation, counting, and applicability of constraints. Examples of constraints where A and B below represent events are:

- **Relative Temporal Constraints:** B happens within one hour of A.
- **Absolute Temporal Constraints:** A and B happen at the same day.
- **Conditions on Data:** A and B agree on their ID attribute.

Nesting of expressions makes it possible to express more complicated queries. Currently, very few CEP products are based on composition operators e.g. IBM Active Middleware Technology (AMiT) and ruleCore being two of them.

Stream Query Languages

Data stream query languages are about querying data streams; however, the data are usually events. Their main idea is to use a relational query language for querying streams. In most cases this is Sequential Query Language (SQL), the industry standard language for querying databases. However, relational query languages are not capable of querying streams by themselves; they can only query relations. Streams change over time, and for every time instant, there is a set of events in the stream, which is converted into a relation. Data stream query languages therefore use, at every time instant, the following pattern:

- Convert snapshots of the input streams to relations.
- Apply query from relational query language to relation(s).
- Convert the result (a relation) back to a stream.

Instead of retrieving all events from a stream at a given time, it is also possible to retrieve only selected events by applying a window. Basic windows are tuple windows, retrieving only the last n events and time windows for retrieving only the events that entered the stream in the last n time units. Thus, data streams, which contain events as tuples, are converted into relations and SQL evaluate these relations and the results are converted into data stream. The process is done at every time point of a fixed discrete time axis.

CQL (Continuous Query Language) is based on the database query language SQL for registering continuous queries against streams and updatable relations. SQL-based data stream query languages are currently the most successful approach and are supported in several efficient and scalable industry products, including Oracle CEP, Coral8, StreamBase, Aleri and the open-source project Esper. However, it should be noted that while stream query languages are very suitable for aggregation of event data, and offer a good integration with databases, it is not well known for expressing negation and temporal relationships.

Logic Languages

Logic languages express event queries in logic-style formulae. It combines declarative and object-oriented programming by merging the syntaxes of Prolog and Java. Prova is used as a rule-based backbone for distributed web applications in biomedical data integration. One of the key advantages of Prova is its separation of logic, data access, and computation.

Another example is XChange[EQ] which identifies and supports data extraction, event composition, temporal (and other) relationships between events, and event accumulation. Its language design enforces a separation of the four querying dimensions. A further example of this language style is Reaction RuleML combining derivation rules, reaction rules and other rule types such as integrity constraints into the general framework of logic programming (Paschke & Kozlenkov, 2009).

Ontologies: Semantic and Knowledge-Based

While Event Processing Languages facilitate the use of event queries in order to detect patterns, it should be noted that there are many complex real-world events that cannot be processed by existing event processing systems. They are too complex to be understood and processed by such systems.

To improve the quality of event processing and to derive intelligent higher-level knowledge from lower-lever events, ontological background knowledge about events and their relationship to other non-event concepts is used. Complex events can be inferred from raw primitive events based on their incoming sequence, their syntax and semantics.

Use of background knowledge about events and their relations to other concepts in the application domain can improve the expressiveness and flexibility of complex event processing systems. Huge amounts of domain background knowledge stored in external knowledge bases can be used in combination with event processing in order to achieve more knowledgeable complex event processing. The value of decision support is largely dependent on the amount and quality of knowledge about that domain. This is a critical factor when complex event processing is used in environments that are rich in domain and background knowledge, e.g. in a hospital setting.

Ontologies formally model knowledge about a domain and allow reasoning over this knowledge. It consists of a set of classes, properties and relationships between the classes and individuals, which are used to represent the concepts of a domain. Additionally, ontology contains information about the meaning of these concepts and about the logical conclusions that can be drawn from them. The most common use of ontologies is to standardise the terminology in a domain and to facilitate knowledge sharing. Additionally, if an ontology captures the formal semantics of concepts, i.e., if it formally defines the meaning of concepts, the semantics can be accessed and processed by machines. An automated reasoner can then analyse concepts and their meaning and compute inferences. (Binnewies & Stantic, 2012)

The use of semantic web technologies is widely used to manage background knowledge and mix different data streams to execute reasoning processes. Therefore, the combination of event processing for dealing with volume of data and semantics to manage several streams and background ontologies can improve the recognition of important situations in a timely manner (Aggarwal, 2014)

The key properties of ontologies can be summarised as:

- **Structured:** Facilitate interoperability between events published by different sources by providing a shared understanding of the domain in question.

- **Formal:** The explicit representation of the semantics of complex event patterns through ontologies will enable CEP systems to provide a qualitatively new level of services such as verification, justification, and gap analysis.
- **Allow Inference:** Add expressiveness and reasoning capabilities.

Therefore, ontology rules provide a way to define behaviour in relation to a system model and allow for shared conceptualisation and agreed upon understanding of a domain.

RESEARCH APPROACH

This main focus of this article is to derive a holistic view of existing literatures related to the application of CEP techniques in healthcare. It will aim to systematically review existing literature in order to answer formulated research questions to support research topic.

A systematic literature review is a means of evaluating and interpreting all available research relevant to a particular research question or topic area. It aims to present a fair evaluation of research topic by using a reliable, rigorous and systematic methodology.

For this research, the SLR was split into three phases: Planning, Conducting and Reporting as illustrated below in Figure 1.

Figure 1. Systematic literature review

Research Questions

The main aim of conducting the systematic literature review (SLR) was to identify use cases, determine main sources of big data contributing to the application of CEP and to obtain an overview of the techniques implemented within the healthcare domain. The following research questions were formulated:

RQ1: What are the most common areas within the healthcare sector where the applications of CEP techniques have been widely implemented?

RQ2: What has been the main data source types contributing to the processing of big data in healthcare?

RQ3: What are the most used CEP query languages and techniques?

The answers to the above 3 RQs will provide an overview of key application areas of CEP within healthcare and give an insight of the effectiveness of the application of CEP languages and techniques.

Search Resources

Search was carried out for relevant articles published in English within journals and conference papers dating from 2010 onwards to ensure that findings were most up to date. With regards to search resources, all electronic databases that were accessible through the University of West London's library subscription were used.

Electronic Databases Used:

- ACM (Association for Computing Machinery Digital Library),
- IEEE (Institute of Electrical and Electronic Engineers Xplore Digital Library),
- Springer,
- ScienceDirect,
- Google Scholar.

Search Strings

Search was initially carried out using a combination of search terms in order to address the RQs stated above. The defined search string was ("CEP" or "Complex Event Processing") and ("healthcare" or "Health care").

Inclusion and Exclusion: Initial Search Criteria

After checking the relevance of retrieved papers, it became apparent that for some of the papers, the search keyword "CEP" was misrepresented as "Community Engagement Planning". This was excluded from the search by using the not operator in the search criteria.

It was also noted that some papers were not specifically mentioning CEP techniques in use and hence, the keyword "techniques" was added in the search criteria using the + operator.

The Table 1 summarises the results obtained for published papers using the above search criteria.

Table 1. Search results

	ACM	IEEE	Springer	Science Direct	Google Scholar
("CEP" or "Complex Event Processing") and ("healthcare" or "Health care") Year >2009; Language = English	86	167	58	295	131
Exclude: "Community Engagement Planning" **Include:** "Techniques"	61	22	41	113	123

Data Collection: Selection of Papers

In order to select a paper for further evaluation, the systematic review was split into two phases.

In the first phase, for each paper, the title, year, author(s), URL and abstract was catalogued using Microsoft Excel. The papers were grouped according to the electronic database used. The following is a snippet from Excel to illustrate recording of data extracted from each of the papers for further review (Figure 2).

Inclusion and Exclusion Criteria: Literature Review

Some papers appeared in more than one electronic database and thus duplicates were removed but a note made of databases that had cited them.

For the second phase of systematic review, the abstract for each of the papers listed in the spreadsheet was carefully reviewed independently by the two authors to specifically look for examples of use cases in healthcare where CEP was addressed. This was to judge whether the papers were appropriate for this research.

Figure 2. Excel snippet: summary of papers recorded

	A	B	C	D	E	F	G
1	Database resource	Title	Year	Author(s)	URL	Abstract/Summary	Reference
2	ACM	An Approach for Dynamic Personal Monitoring based on Mobile Complex Event Processing	2013	Yongchun Xu , Nenad Stojanovic , Ljiljana Stojanovic , Dusan Kostic	http://dl.acm.org.ezproxy.uwl.ac.uk/citation.cfm?id=2536853.2536868&coll=DL&dl=ACM&CFID=650086504&CFTOKEN=26496744	In this paper we present a novel approach for dynamic remote activity monitoring based on mobile complex event processing that has been used in a use case in the eHealth domain. Using complex event processing (CEP) in mobile environment enables a more flexible and efficient processing of personal sensor data and environment data, which are detected by sensors embedded in a mobile device. The main advantages of our approach are: an efficient combination of the mobile and server-side event processing through the semantic event model, optimal usage of mobile resources through dynamic management of mobile event processing and modelling of complex situations by using more expressive knowledge representation formalism. We present the settings for the use case and the results from the	Yongchun Xu , Nenad Stojanovic , Ljiljana Stojanovic , Dusan Kostic , (2013) , An Approach for Dynamic Personal Monitoring based on Mobile Complex Event Processing , ACM , http://dl.acm.org.ezproxy.uwl.ac.uk/citation.cfm?id=2536853.2536868&coll=DL&dl=ACM&CFID=650086504&CFTOKEN=26496744 , Accessed: 04/03/2015
3	ACM	Using Mobile-based Complex Event Processing to realize Collaborative Remote Person Monitoring	2014	Yongchun Xu , Nenad Stojanovic , Ljiljana Stojanovic , Aleksandar Stojadinovic	http://dl.acm.org.ezproxy.uwl.ac.uk/citation.cfm?id=2611286.2611306&coll=DL&dl=ACM&CFID=650086504&CFTOKEN=26496744	In this paper we present an application of the mobile-based distributed complex event processing for the collaborative remote person monitoring, a novel approach for the e-Health and Fitness domain that represents a kind of breakthrough for these domains. Indeed, so far remote monitoring has been focused on one individual person: the monitored person is equipped (wears) a sensor that sends data to the user's smartphone for storage, local (simple) analysis and upload to the server, where the data can be visualized and analyzed on request in off-line mode. Our, new, approach extends this processing pipeline with a) real-time feedback from the server-side processing in order to enable the detection of very complex situations and b) distribution of processing between several nodes (persons) in order to enable collaboration in detecting mentioned complex situations. The approach is applied in the development of the commercial solution for remote patient monitoring used in monitoring of the physical activities of grouped cardio patients in order to support collaborative detection of complex situations. In this paper we present the theoretical background of the approach and detail some most innovative elements. In addition we discuss the results from an ongoing piloting of this technology in a real healthcare	Yongchun Xu , Nenad Stojanovic , Ljiljana Stojanovic , Aleksandar Stojadinovic , (2014) , Using Mobile-based Complex Event Processing to realize Collaborative Remote Person Monitoring , ACM . http://dl.acm.org.ezproxy.uwl.ac.uk/citation.cfm?id=2611286.2611306&coll=DL&dl=ACM&CFID=650086504&CFTOKEN=26496744 , Accessed: 04/03/2015
4	ACM	MCEP: A Mobility-Aware Complex Event Processing System	2014	BEATE OTTENWALDER, BORIS KOLDEHOFE, and KURT ROTHERMEL	http://dl.acm.org.ezproxy.uwl.ac.uk/citation.cfm?id=2659232.2633688&coll=DL&dl=ACM&CFID=650086504&CFTOKEN=26496744	With the proliferation of mobile devices and sensors, complex event proceesing (CEP) is becoming increasingly important to scalably detect situations in real time. Current CEP systems are not capable of dealing efficiently with highly dynamic mobile consumers whose interests change with their location. We introduce the distributed mobile CEP (MCEP) system which automatically adapts the processing of events according to a consumer's location. MCEP significantly reduces latency, network utilization, and processing overhead by providing on-demand and opportunistic adaptation algorithms to dynamically assign event streams and computing resources	BEATE OTTENWALDER, BORIS KOLDEHOFE, and KURT ROTHERMEL , (2014) , MCEP: A Mobility-Aware Complex Event Processing System , ACM , http://dl.acm.org.ezproxy.uwl.ac.uk/citation.cfm?id=2659232.2633688&coll=DL&dl=ACM&CFID=650086504&CFTOKEN=26496744 , Accessed: 04/03/2015

Each author classified each paper, in terms of selection for further review, as "Definitely", "Possibly" or "Not Selected". The final list of papers selected for review was established by applying the following rules:

Rule 1: Paper is selected if it has been classified with at least one "Definitely".
Rule 2: Paper is selected if it has been classified with two "Possibly".
Rule 3: Paper classified with two "Not Selected" is not chosen.
Rule 4: If an article was classified as one "Possibly" and one "Not Selected", then the title, abstract and keywords were reviewed again.

The filtered papers were then read in detail by the authors of this research independently to give a fair and consistent evaluation of content for further analysis. The primary aim was to look for detailed examples of use cases within the healthcare domain, the sources of data that contributed to the example and a guide to CEP techniques that were implemented.

A following list gives a summary of Inclusion and Exclusion criteria employed for selecting relevant papers.

Inclusion of papers:

- Published after 2009.
- Publication in English.
- Include CEP representing "Complex Event Processing".
- Include "techniques".
- Health care use cases.
- Data sources used in healthcare sector for CEP.
- Examples of CEP techniques in use within healthcare sector.

Exclusion of papers:

- Published before 2010.
- Not published in English.
- Exclude CEP representing "Community Engagement Planning".
- Exclude papers if no reference to techniques.
- No health care related use cases.
- Data sources not related to health care use cases.
- Use of CEP techniques not applied to healthcare scenarios.

Figure 3 represents 25 papers that were finally selected and reviewed using the two phases of systematic review.

Analysis of Findings

For each of the 25 papers read, examples of use cases, data sources in use and specific CEP techniques employed were summarised and recorded in a list using Microsoft Excel spreadsheet. This data was then

Figure 3. Papers reviewed (25)

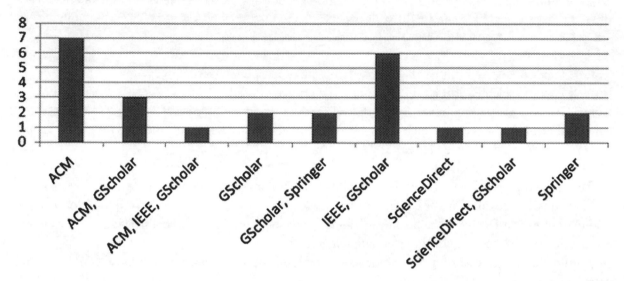

analysed using Pivot reporting tools to generate a range of reports and charts to give a clearer picture of common areas of CEP applications in healthcare and in turn provide answers to RQs outlined.

RQ1: What are the most common areas within the healthcare sector where the application of CEP techniques has been widely implemented?

Within the 25 papers reviewed, there was a wide variety of applications within the healthcare domain where the use of CEP was addressed. Some examples included remote monitoring of personal health and fitness to encourage healthier lifestyles, patient flow management system to monitor states in care processes, detection of hygiene care violation for preventing infections in hospital setting and Telecare/ Telemedicine to reduce the amount of personal care devoted to early dementia sufferers by means of the remote monitoring of their condition to reduce the pressure on NHS resources and to promotes good quality independent living.

All examples of use cases discussed in papers were categorised using number coding (1 to 7) to represent specific areas within healthcare. The count for the number of papers representing each category was recorded as shown in Box 1.

Box 1.

Category	Use Cases	No. of Papers
1	Personal Health and Fitness	4
2	Emergency Medical Assistance; Patient Safety	4
3	Patient Flow Management	3
4	Hygiene Compliances-prevention of infections	5
5	Remote Healthcare-Telecare, Telemedicine etc	5
6	Foodborne Disease Outbreak	1
7	Hosp. Processes, Transportation of drugs/vaccines	3

The analysis of results above show that the most widely used example where CEP is commonly used is "Category 4 for Hygiene Compliances-prevention of infections" and "Category 5 for Remote Healthcare-Telecare, Telemedicine etc."

Category 4 included examples of applications for detecting potential threads of infection, monitor hygiene compliance of healthcare workers and reporting of contaminated medical equipment in a hospital. The HyReminder system for tracking healthcare workers for hygiene compliance was repeatedly mentioned. Other examples in this category were of tracking inventory of medical equipment for quality assurance and monitoring transport of RFID tagged medical goods to prevent damage.

Category 5 was allocated to remote healthcare which included examples on improving support for the elderly/disabled in their home while reducing overall cost, use of information logistics processing in telemedicine for patients coping with obesity, remote monitoring and care devoted to early dementia sufferers.

It was decided to consider each of the identified use case again and group them into Clinical and Non-Clinical to determine if the application of CEP techniques had fully integrated within the healthcare sector. The use cases identified from the 25 reviewed papers revealed 4 cases that fell under the category of Clinical and the remaining 21 cases as Non-Clinical (Figure 4).

In this study, clinical applications relate to applications directly related to patient's physiological data within hospital settings, where else, non-clinical applications include wellness management, activity monitoring, remote healthcare, hospital services (equipment, administration etc.) and the use of smart environments.

As illustrated in the chart, 84% (21 examples) of cases identified from reviewed papers are non-clinical covering a broader scope and not restricted to patient physiological data.

RQ2: What has been the main data source types contributing to the processing of big data in healthcare?

Figure 4. Clinical and non-clinical groups of use cases

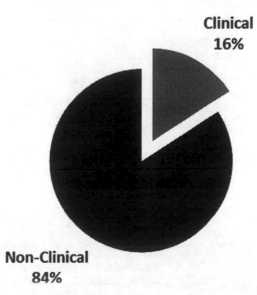

Big data in healthcare offers a wide variety of data types. This can range from data related to patient healthcare and well-being, clinical decision support systems (medical imaging, laboratory and pharmaceutical data and other administrative data), sensor data from medical devices that monitor vital signs, social media, web pages, GPS (Global Positioning System) and RTLS (Real Time Location System) data resulting from tracking devices/patients/staff at precise locations etc.

The range of data sources encountered in the applications reviewed were categorised into 4 groups as shown in the table below and count of papers using a source from a particular group has been given. However, it should be noted that there are examples of use cases where a combination of data sources have been in use.

For example, for the patient flow monitoring system to reduce waiting times in hospitals, RTLS tags are assigned to patients and key care providers. These tags use Wi-Fi and infra-red signals to reach location accuracy of about 10 cm. This location data, along with data from existing hospital systems is triangulated using CEP to infer the current patient state and wait time (Badreddin & Payton, 2013). Therefore, the data source category for this paper is a combination of A and D.

The main types of data sources discussed in the papers were categorised as shown in Box 2.

Table 2. CEP query language and ontologies in use

	Both (Semantic + Background Knowledge)	Background Knowledge	Semantic	Total Cases
Disease Outbreak				1
RBL	1			
Emergency Medical Assistance				4
RBL, SQ	1			
RBL	2			
CO, RBL	1			
Hygiene Compliances				5
RBL, SQ			3	
CO, RBL, SQ			2	
Patient Flow Management				3
RBL		3		
Personal Health & Fitness				4
RBL, SQ	3		1	
Remote Healthcare				5
RBL, SQ	1			
RBL	4			
Hosp. Processes, Transportation of medical goods				3
RBL, SQ		1		
RBL	1			
CO, RBL, SQ	1			
Total Cases Reviewed	15	4	6	25

Box 2.

Data Sources	Category	No. of Papers
Sensor Technology		
Personal and Environmental sensors	A	20
RFID, Wearable Sensors, RTLS		
External Web Sources	B	5
Healthcare IT systems	C	6
GPS Technology	D	3

The analysis of results above show that the main data source type contributing to the processing of big data in healthcare is Category A – Use of sensor technology: Personal and Environmental sensors, RFID, Wearable sensors, RTLS. This category is repeated again in combination with other data sources for some use cases, thus illustrating its popularity as a key data source producer.

Advances in RFID and sensor technology provide fast data collection with precise identification of objects with unique IDs that can be used for identifying, locating, tracking and monitoring physical objects. With RFID technology, it is possible to create a physically linked world in which every object is numbered, identified, catalogued and tracked. Use of this technology, is being gradually adopted and deployed in a wide area of healthcare applications, such as tracking of medical equipment, medical goods for transportation, locating hospital staff and monitoring patient's checking-in/out. This is achieved by using software applications to map objects and their behaviours in the physical world into the virtual counterparts and their virtual behaviours in the applications by semantically interpreting and transforming RFID/sensor data.

RQ3: What are the most used CEP query language types and techniques?

From the papers reviewed, it can be stated that with the use of CEP techniques it is possible to express causal, temporal, spatial and other relationships between events which specify patterns within event streams in real-time. Thus, by discovering associations and understanding patterns and trends within the data related to healthcare, the application of CEP techniques has the potential to improve care, save lives and lower costs.

In order to address the RQ3 above, all 25 papers were collectively reviewed to obtain a holistic view of the various CEP query language types, ontologies and techniques that have been implemented in the use cases explored (Figure 5).

Each of the 25 papers grouped within the use case category (as determined from RQ1) was explored further to determine the type of query language and application of ontologies in use. Event processing techniques were represented using coded letters and the application of ontologies, whether semantic, knowledge based or both was determined and broadly analysed as illustrated in the Table 2.

Event Processing Techniques:

CO: Composition Operators.
SQ: Stream Query.
RBL: Rule Based Logic.

Figure 5. Overview of CEP techniques considered

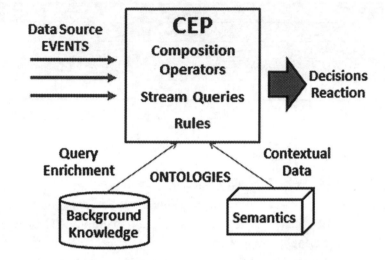

Ontologies: Semantic, Background Knowledge, Both.

For example, from the table, we can deduce that within the category of Disease Outbreak, there was one paper where the event processing language in use was RBL (Rule Based Language) and the application of ontologies was both semantics and background knowledge to capture contextual data and background knowledge for query enrichment respectively.

Therefore, from the analysis summarised in the table, it is seen that the combination of composition operators and/or stream query language together with rule based logic all contribute to CEP techniques.

This can be confirmed by reviewing the example of RFID enabled hospital to track movements of medical staff, patients and any equipment carrying RFID tags to accurately track patient flow and asset flow in real time.

The RFID tracking system consistently generates data about the location and time of tagged items, which is in low-level semantics and not directly useful. CEP has been introduced to process and correlate such data by processing multiple streams of data continuously and identifying meaningful events in real-time. At the lowest level, raw readings from location tracking systems are captured by RFID readers and then filtered (smoothing and aggregation) to remove noisy and redundant data. The filtered RFID events along with data from other embedded sensors or devices are then passed on to the CEP engine for further processing. In addition, data from other information systems or database is used for complex event pattern matching. Finally, CEP rules stored in the rule base, allow the CEP engine to detect complex events in order to signify critical situations.

The above example is demonstrated using open source software Drools 5.0, which include Drools expert and Drools fusion, as CEP engine to provide an integrated platform for modelling rules, events, and processes. (Yao, Chu & Li, 2011)

The use of ontologies has played a significant part in many examples when reviewing CEP techniques. As explained earlier, the use of ontologies offer a way of defining behaviour in relation to a system model by providing a shared conceptualisation and agreed upon understanding of the example/

case in question. In this research, ontology has been classified into Semantic and Knowledge-based (Background Knowledge).

Semantic ontology is used where CEP techniques have used conceptualisation of the application domain to allow reasoning on events in combination with other non-event concepts using formalised vocabularies/syntax and declarative rules. In the example of hygiene compliances, semantics repository is responsible for maintaining the contextual knowledge model that capture relevant information about the environment into which the application is deployed. In this example, the physical layout of the hospital and the positioning of rooms and sanitisers are referred to as static semantics whereas hygiene performance status of a Health Care Worker (HCW) that is dynamically updated based on their behaviours over time is dynamic semantics. (Wang, Rundensteiner & Ellison, 2010).

Knowledge-based ontology is used where CEP techniques have been used to enrich the incoming event data stream with background knowledge from an external knowledge base, so that the event processing engine has more knowledge about events and their relations to other concepts within the application domain. A paper reviewed on the use of RFID event streams in hospitals for patient monitoring systems demonstrate continuous tracking of patient's physiological data such as heart rate, blood pressure, blood oxygen saturation levels etc. Other data such as patient's medical records where needed to correlate and signify actionable information for decision making. For example, performing a surgery requires extensive information sharing in order to detect emergency situations and react to them promptly. (Yao, Chu & Li, 2011).

SUMMARY OF FINDINGS:

From the results obtained in addressing the three RQs, we can deduce the following:

1. The number of papers reviewed had a larger number of use cases for non-clinical applications than clinical applications.
2. This indicates that CEP is effective and efficient in pattern matching for non-clinical applications but has limited capability of reacting in real-time to opportunities and risks detected that are related to clinical applications and patient's treatment processes.
3. The most used scenarios where CEP has been demonstrated is for Hygiene Compliances-prevention of infections – HyReminder example and for Remote Healthcare-Telecare, Telemedicine.
4. The use of sensor technology (Personal and Environmental sensors, RFID, Wearable sensors) has been widely implemented.
5. It is evident from this research that sensor technologies have given rise to a rapid growth in healthcare data and this can make a significant impact to healthcare delivery. However, it should be noted that it also introduces a data overload problem, for both systems and stakeholders that need to utilise this data. This confirms the need to apply efficient and effective event processing techniques to transform the large volumes of data into meaningful intelligence.
6. All use cases considered implemented some form of rule based processing. There is ample evidence that there is no single Event Processing Language (EPL) which is best suited for all use cases, but that different representation approaches are needed such as rule-based EPLs for describing

higher-level conditional event patterns and pattern-matching, SQL like EPLs for defining patterns of low-level aggregation views according to event types defined as nested queries.

7. All CEP techniques relied on some form of ontology, either the use of semantics, knowledge based repository or both.

8. In the example of Emergency Medical Assistance (EMA) system, the availability of information in the control centre served as an important basis for reactions and decisions. The EMA co-ordination centre uses reliable and concise interpretations of emergency situation derived from incoming sensor readings that are captured without having to consider all events that actually occurred. Thus, ontologies formally model knowledge about a domain and allow reasoning over this knowledge.

From the analysis of papers reviewed, it can be deduced that the application of CEP techniques is thought of as transforming of raw event(s) produced by a variety of data sources into an aggregated or correlated form followed by the knowledge application phase where formalised rules are applied to make inferences in order to detect or trigger a range of action(s).

CONCLUSION

Based on the analysis provided in this work, healthcare organisations need to accept that Big Data is more than a buzzword and that with the widespread adaptation of the "Internet of Things" technologies, there is potential for envisaging a unified central healthcare system.

Healthcare is being looked at as a continuum expanding outside of traditional clinical settings with goals to make it more proactive to reduce stress on medical institutions. Providing healthcare support outside of clinical environments with smart monitoring devices and e-health technology has been the focus of much research recently, especially in the ubiquitous computing research community. (Aggarwal, 2014)

Currently, studies of healthcare systems focus on a variety of systems including large-scale in-hospital systems such as Electronic Medical Records (EMR), computerised communication tools for medics and systems that are designed for use outside clinical settings such as those for the management of chronic conditions and personal health information. These systems serve different purposes, and they all have the potential to benefit patient care through improving clinical practices conducted in hospitals and clinics, or facilitating various self-care activities in patient's homes and other non-clinical settings.

There has been a growing interest in studying and designing health technologies to meet the mounting healthcare needs of the aging population. Technologies are thus designed to help shift the burden of care from the clinical setting to home or other non-clinical settings. In all these cases, technologies can offer a seamless transition by bridging the health practices between clinical and non-clinical settings.

Developing systems that bridge clinical and non-clinical settings is no trivial task, as health practices, knowledge, stakeholders, environment, constraints, expectations, and liabilities are all distinctly different in these two environments. Therefore it is necessary to bring together researchers, designers, medical practitioners, and other stakeholders to design interactive systems that can bridge the trajectory work across the two settings. It is also important to consider the implications and impacts of the systems designed for one setting (e.g., clinical setting) on the other setting (e.g., non-clinical setting).

Many issues remain open when designing healthcare systems for bridging health practices in clinical and non-clinical settings. For examples, to design a patient monitoring system for home use, we need to consider how to capture critical information that is meaningful for healthcare professionals to use, and how to visualise the home-monitored data so physicians can effectively engage and utilise the information during their busy schedules.

When using the EMR system to share patient records with patients, how can we maximize the likelihood that the patients correctly interpret the medical information? Other questions include: what consequences may result when designing systems for supporting healthcare practices in non-traditional settings such as care homes? These questions are important when designing technologies to bridge between clinical and non-clinical practices.

From the literature reviewed, it is clear that big data analytics can help hospitals in efficient resources management by reducing emergency waiting times, track patient movements, prevent infections by complying with hygiene processes etc.

Operational data sources together with big data sources create an on-demand analytical view across key areas in the health sector in order to gain powerful insights into patient's medical details, treatments, clinical processes and services. Thus, the fusion of diverse data sources, both big data and traditional data sources will provide a full holistic view to most aspects of healthcare related data.

Big Data Analytics, Complex Event Processing and IoT together have extreme potential in solving existing and future problem of healthcare industry. Application of these technologies is still in infancy in the healthcare domain. With renewed focus on better healthcare, growth in population and increasing costs, healthcare industry has to embrace such technologies for effective and efficient functioning (Nagishbandi, Sheriff & Qazi, 2015).

REFERENCES

Aggarwal, C. (2014). *Managing and Mining Sensor Data*. Retrieved 16 May 2015, from http://charuaggarwal.net/sensortoc.pdf

Badreddin, O., & Peyton, L. (2013). Real time patient flow management using business process management, location tags, and complex events processing. In *Proceedings of the 2013 Conference of the Center for Advanced Studies on Collaborative Research* (CASCON '13). Retrieved March 4th, 2015 from https://www.researchgate.net/publication/262172837

Binnewies, S., & Stantic, B. (2012). OECEP: enriching complex event processing with domain knowledge from ontologies. In *Proceedings of the Fifth Balkan Conference in informatics (BCI '12)*. Retrieved March 4, 2015, from doi:10.1145/2371316.2371322

Eckert, M., Bry, F., Brodt, S., Poppe, O., & Hausmann, S. (2011). A CEP Babelfish: Languages for Complex Event Processing and Querying Surveyed. *Reasoning in Event-Based Distributed Systems*, 47–70. http://doi.org/<ALIGNMENT.qj></ALIGNMENT>10.1007/978-3-642-19724-6_3

Luckham, D., & Schulte, W. R. (2012). *Complex event processing and the future of business decisions*. Retrieved March 29, 2015 from http://www.complexevents.com/2012/07/12/complex-event-processing-and-the-future-of-business-decisions

Magid, Y., Adi, A., Barnea, M., Botzer, D., & Rabinovich, E. (2008). Application generation framework for real-time Complex Event Processing. *32nd Annual IEEE International Computer Software and Applications Conference (COMPSAC '08)* (pp.1162-1167). Retrieved March 29, 2015 from doi:10.1109/COMPSAC.2008.146

Naqishbandi, T., Sheriff, C. I., & Qazi, S. (2015). Big Data, CEP and IoT: Redefining holistic healthcare information systems and analytics. *International Journal of Engineering Research & Technology*, *4*(1). Retrieved from http://www.ijert.org

Paschke, A., & Kozlenkov, A. (2009). Rule-Based Event Processing and Reaction Rules. *Rule Interchange and Applications*, 53–66. http://doi.org/<ALIGNMENT.qj></ALIGNMENT>10.1007/978-3-642-04985-9_8

Wang, D., Rundensteiner, E., Ellison, R. T., & Wang, H. (2010). Active Complex Event Processing: Applications in real-time health care. *Proceedings of the VLDB Endowment*, *3*(1-2), 1545–1548. RetrievedMarch42015. doi:10.14778/1920841.1921034

Yao, W., Chu, C.-H., & Li, Z. (2011). Leveraging complex event processing for smart hospitals using RFID. *Journal of Network and Computer Applications*, *34*(3), 799–810. doi:10.1016/j.jnca.2010.04.020

ADDITIONAL READING

Adi, A., & Opher, E. (2004). Amit - the situation manager. *The VLDB Journal*, *13*(2), 177–203. RetrievedApril282015. doi:10.1007/s00778-003-0108-y

Baarah, A., & Peyton, L. (2012). Engineering a state monitoring service for real-time patient flow management. In *Proceedings of the 9th Middleware Doctoral Symposium of the 13th ACM/IFIP/USENIX International Middleware Conference (MIDDLEWARE '12)*. Retrieved March 4, 2015, from doi:10.1145/2405688.2405696

Badreddin, O., & Peyton, L. (2013). Real time patient flow management using business process management, location tags, and complex events processing. In *Proceedings of the 2013 Conference of the Center for Advanced Studies on Collaborative* Research *(CASCON '13)*. Retrieved March 4th, 2015 from https://www.researchgate.net/publication/262172837_Real_time_patient_flow_management_using_business_process_management_location_tags_and_complex_events_processing

Baffoe, S. A., Baarah, A., & Peyton, L. (2013). Inferring state for real-time monitoring of care processes. In *Proceedings of the 5th International Workshop on Software Engineering in Health Care (SEHC '13)*. Retrieved March 4, 2015, from http://dl.acm.org/citation.cfm?id=2663575.2663590&coll=DL&dl=ACM&CFID=674387497&CFTOKEN=19858697

Berry, A., & Milosevic, Z. (2013). Real-time analytics for legacy data streams in health: monitoring health data quality. *17th IEEE International Enterprise Distributed Object Computing Conference (EDOC)*. Retrieved March 4th, 2015 from doi:10.1109/EDOC.2013.19

Billhardt, H., Lujak, M., Ossowski, S., Bruns, R., & Dunkel, J. (2014). Intelligent event processing for emergency medical assistance. In *Proceedings of the 29th Annual ACM Symposium on Applied Computing (SAC '14)*. Retrieved March 4, 2015, from doi:10.1145/2554850.2554975

Binnewies, S., & Stantic, B. (2011) Introducing knowledge-enrichment techniques for Complex Event Processing. In *Proceedings of Informatics Engineering and Information Science (ICIEIS 2011)*. Retrieved March 4, 2015, from http://www98.griffith.edu.au/dspace/bitstream/handle/10072/43576/76486_1. pdf?sequence=1

Carminati, B., Ferrari, E., & Guglielmi, M. (2011). Secure information sharing on support of emergency management. *3rd IEEE International Conference on Privacy, Security, Risk and Trust (PASSAT) and 3rd IEEE International Conference on Social Computing (SocialCom*. Retrieved March 4th, 2015 from doi:10.1109/PASSAT/SocialCom.2011.69

Liu, M., Ray, M., Zhang, D., Rundensteiner, E., Dougherty, D., & Gupta, C., … Ari, I. (2012). Realtime healthcare services via nested complex event processing technology. In *Proceedings of the 15th International Conference on Extending Database Technology (EDBT '12)*. Retrieved March 4, 2015, from doi:10.1145/2247596.2247681

Liu, M., Rundensteiner, E., Dougherty, D., Gupta, C., Wang, S., Ari, I., & Mehta, A. (2011a) High-performance nested CEP query processing over event streams. *27th IEEE International Conference on Data Engineering (ICDE)*. Retrieved March 4, 2015, from doi:10.1109/ICDE.2011.5767839

Liu, M., Rundensteiner, E., Dougherty, D., Gupta, C., Wang, S., Ari, I., & Mehta, A. (2011b). NEEL: The nested complex event language for real-time event analytics. In Enabling Real-Time Business Intelligence. Retrieved March 4, 2015, from doi:10.1007/978-3-642-22970-1_9

Meister, S., Schafer, S., & Stahlmann, V. (2013). TiEE – The Telemedical ILOG event engine: optimization of information supply in telemedicine. Retrieved March 4, 2015, from http://ceur-ws.org/Vol-1028/paper-03.pdf

Nogueira, M., & Greis, N. P. (2011). Rule-Based Complex Event Processing for Food Safety and Public Health. In Rule-Based Reasoning, Programming, and Applications. Retrieved March 4, 2015, from doi:10.1007/978-3-642-22546-8_31

Ottenwälder, B., Koldehofe, B., Rothermel, K., Hong, K., Lillethun, D., & Ramachandran, U. (2014). MCEP: A Mobility-Aware Complex Event Processing System. *ACM Transactions on Internet Technology*, *14*(1), 1–24. RetrievedMarch42015. doi:10.1145/2633688

Skałkowski, K., & Zieliński, K. (2013). Applying formalized rules for treatment procedures to data delivered by personal medical devices. *Journal of Biomedical Informatics*, *46*(3), 530–540. RetrievedMarch42015. doi:10.1016/j.jbi.2013.04.005 PMID:23618997

Vaidehi, V., Bhargavi, R., Ganapathy, K., & Sweetlin Hemalatha, C. (2012). Multi-sensor based in-home health monitoring using Complex Event Processing. *International Conference on Recent Trends In Information Technology (ICRTIT)*. Retrieved March 4, 2015, from doi:10.1109/ICRTIT.2012.6206847

Viceconti, M., & Clapworthy, G. (n.d.). *Physio-environmental sensing and live modelling and the role of U-CEP*. Retrieved March 4, 2015, from http://www.citt-online.de/downloads/4-Castiglione-Diaz-Gaggioli-RvA-et-al.pdf

Wang, D., Rundensteiner, E., Ellison, R. T., & Wang, H. (2010). Active Complex Event Processing: Applications in real-time health care. *Proceedings of the VLDB Endowment*, *3*(1-2), 1545–1548. RetrievedMarch42015. doi:10.14778/1920841.1921034

Wang, D., Rundensteiner, E., Ellison, R. T., & Wang, H. (2011). Active Complex Event Processing infrastructure: monitoring and reacting to event streams. *27th IEEE International Conference on Data Engineering Workshops (ICDEW)*. Retrieved March 4th, 2015 from doi:10.1109/ICDEW.2011.5767635

Wienhofen, L. W. M., & Landmark, A. D. (2011). Representing events in a clinical environment a case study. In *Proceedings of the 5th ACM international conference on Distributed event-based system (DEBS '11)*. Retrieved March 4, 2015, from doi:10.1145/2002259.2002326

KEY TERMS AND DEFINITIONS

CEP: Complex Event Processing.
CO: Composition Operators.
CQL: Continuous Query Language.
EMA: Emergency Medical Assistance.
EMR: Electronic Medical Records.
EPL: Event Processing Language.
ESP: Event Stream Processing.
GPS: Global Positioning System.
IOT: Internet of Things.
RBL: Rule Based Language.
RDMS: Relational Database Management System.
RFID: Radio Frequency Identification.
RTLS: Real Time Location system.
SQL: Sequential Query Language.

Chapter 13
Using Big Data in Collaborative Learning

Liz Sokolowski
University of West London, UK

Samia Oussena
University of West London, UK

ABSTRACT

Big data emerged as a dominant trend for predictive analytics in many areas of industry and commerce. The study aimed to explore whether similar trends and benefits have been observed in the area of collaborative learning. The study looked at the domains in which the collaborative learning was undertaken. The results of the review found that the majority of the studies were undertaken in the Computing and Engineering or Social Science domains, primarily at undergraduate level. The results indicate that the data collection focus is on interaction data to describe the process of the collaboration itself, rather than on the end product of the collaboration. The student interaction data came from various sources, but with a notable concentration on data obtained from discussion forums and virtual learning environment logs. The review highlighted some challenges; the noisy nature of this data and the need for manual pre-processing of textual data currently renders much of it unsuitable for automated 'big data' analytical approaches.

INTRODUCTION

With the rise of pervasive computing and the internet of things (IoT), data of a quantity inconceivable just a decade ago is being generated and logged daily by machines and sensors, without the need for human intervention. With it has come the requirement for new methods to process and understand this data. Big data has emerged as a dominant trend for predictive analytics in many areas of industry and commerce, fuelling applications that have automated decision making and allowing timely interventions to be made based on patterns discovered through techniques such as data mining. From systems that calculate insurance premiums based on claims history, to fraud detection systems that automatically block transactions that are outside the limits of what a system considers to be a customer's normal purchas-

DOI: 10.4018/978-1-5225-0293-7.ch013

ing behaviour, examples of the practical use of big data analytics abound: "Although largely unseen, it drives millions of decisions, determining who to call, mail, investigate, incarcerate, set up on a date, or medicate" (Ryu, 2013, p64).

This study aimed to explore whether similar trends, benefits and practical uses have been observed in Big Data generated in the course of collaborative working, by carrying out a systematic literature review of case studies. Employers are increasingly requiring graduates to enter the job market with a raft of soft skills that allow them to slip seamlessly and productively into the working environment. One of these is the ability to engage in team working (Robles, 2012) and to be able to collaborate effectively on any team projects set by the employer. As a result, team working and collaborative learning are increasingly being incorporated into student assessments. From an educational point of view, collaborative learning is also a desired educational goal, enabling students to generate a richer pool of ideas than if they were to work on their own, and to learn from each other through social interaction, promoting deeper understanding and constructivist learning (Jonassen, 1999). However it is often difficult to ensure a group operates effectively and productively, with all members experiencing high levels of satisfaction in the process, and this applies equally to teams in the workplace as well as to teams of students. This has prompted research into ways that data from group work processes and outcomes can be captured and analysed to predict a team's performance and ultimately allow timely interventions to be made to help dysfunctional groups. Given that a lot of group interaction is now conducted electronically, this raises possibilities for mining Big Data generated from these interactions. In the field of education, research into mining learning data to predict an individual student's success is now in its maturity. However, much less appears to exist on mining data to predict group work success, whether in the field of education or in the workplace.

BIG DATA

The term 'Big Data' is often described in terms of volume, variety and velocity: Volume: Big Data implies enormous volumes of data being generated primarily by websites, sensors, social media, and so on; Variety refers to the many sources and types of data, both structured and unstructured. Structured data is well defined and can easily be represented as numbers or categories, whereas unstructured can encompass textual information, videos, photos, which creates problems for storing and analysing such data. Velocity refers to the speed with which Big Data is generated - most is produced by machines, rather than by humans and the flow of data is often continuous and massive. Accelerating digitization taking place in all areas of industry and society has meant that Big Data is appearing at an increasing rate in every domain and is available for analysis in ever more creative ways.

This is also true in the context of collaborative learning, where large data sets are potentially available for analysis from students' interactions with online learning and learning support systems. Learning Management Systems (LMS) such as Moodle and Blackboard record every action a student makes while using the platform, generating a digital footprint of their activity. As well as providing scope for a range of quantitative measures of student activity, these data logs can reveal associations between learners and the structure of networks to which they belong.

In addition, large volumes of textual data can be collected from emails, discussion boards, wikis, phone transcripts, and so forth. As this is primarily unstructured data it needs to be pre-processed and coded in some way prior to analysis.

COLLABORATIVE LEARNING

The overall objective of the systematic review was to investigate the extent to which Big Data analytical approaches are being used in evidencing collaboration and predicting its success. The study aimed to provide insights into what technologies are currently being used to support collaborative learning, what data is being generated by those technologies in order to evidence levels of engagement and success factors of collaboration, and what methods are being used to analyse that data.

The importance of group work is reflected in the huge body of research into collaborative learning. A number of reviews targeting specific aspects of collaborative learning have been undertaken in recent years, many of these focusing on computer assisted collaborative learning (CSCL), reflecting the fact that the bulk of collaborative learning is conducted, at least in part, online. Longchamp (2012) carried out a review of research topics covered in the International Journal of Computer-Supported Collaborative Learning from 2006 to 2012; a more extensive study covering research topics found in nine leading journals between 2003 and 2012 was undertaken by Zheng et al (2014) which showed evidence of an increasing trend in quantitative approaches to studies. Jeong & Hmelo-Silver (2010) conducted a meta-content analysis of technology use in CSCL empirical case studies and Noroozi et al (2012) analyzed the research foci on argumentation-based CSCL. Song (2014) conducted a systematic review of methodologies used in mCSCL, reflecting the growing use of mobile devices to support collaborative learning.

Collaborative learning, its broadest sense, can be defined as "a situation in which two or more people learn or attempt to learn something together" (Dillenbourg, 1999) and for the purposes of this study, has been limited to collaboration by small groups of students who are required to work together to produce some specific artefact/outcome as a group. This excludes situations where a whole cohort or class is participating in a general discussion forum which may simply be for the exchange of ideas, without any learning outcome attached to the activity.

ANALYTICS

The rise in Big Data has prompted the development of new ways of analysing it, focusing on predictive analytics. Analytics has been defined as "use of data, statistical analysis, and explanatory and predictive models to gain insights and act on complex issues" (Bichsel, 2012). In the domain of education, Learning Analytics is 'the measurement, collection, analysis and reporting of data about learners and their contexts' (Ferguson, 2012) and is increasingly being used to make sense of the stream of trace data that students generate while using LMS and other support tools. Research in this area has grown, however, a number of issues are still outstanding or problematical. An on-going area for research is how to determine the most useful indicators of successful collaboration, from the wealth of Big Data that is now available. Another is how to capture and merge all the heterogeneous data that is produced from an ever widening range of sources available to support collaborative learning, and furthermore to distil and present findings in an understandable form to allow educators to improve their awareness and management of their students' learning.

The availability of logs of student-computer interaction and emergence of data-intensive approaches in education has fuelled the rise of Educational Data Mining (EDM), defined by Baker & Jacef (2009) as "concerned with developing methods for exploring the unique types of data that come from educational settings, and using those methods to better understand students, and the settings which they learn in." Table 1 shows a classification of educational data mining methods.

Table 1. Classification of educational data mining methods

• Prediction:
o Classification
o Regression
o Density estimation
• Clustering
• Relationship mining
o Association rule mining
o Correlation mining
o Sequential pattern mining
o Causal data mining
• Distillation of data for human judgment
• Discovery with models

Baker & Yacef, 2009 .

As well as EDM, a Learning Analytics and Knowledge (LAK) community has developed separately to address the need to investigate educational data. Here, the focus has been on a more holistic approach, with a stronger emphasis on attempting to understand the full complexity of systems as wholes. The techniques and methods typically employed within LAK have tended to reflect this, as can be seen in Table 2.

The rest of this paper aims to examine the extent to which these approaches are prevalent in the empirical studies conducted into collaborative learning between 2012 and 2015.

SYSTEMATIC REVIEW OF CASE STUDIES

The writers undertook a systematic review following established guidelines (Kitchenham & Charters, 2007), of empirical case studies of collaborative learning. As explained above, the focus was on groups of students who were working collaboratively to achieve a given task, rather than on whole cohorts of students who were using collaborative technology, such as discussion boards, as part of a general strategy to share information. In this respect, the groups chosen mirrored the general organisation of groups within a work environment, where members would be expected to collaborate and work toward a common goal, generating heterogeneous interaction data for analysis.

The research process comprised the following stages:

1. Formulation of appropriate research questions.
2. Formulation of search strategy for identification of case studies in relevant literature.
3. Selection of case studies based on the established criteria.

Table 2. Techniques and methods used in LAK

• Social Network Analysis
• Sentiment Analysis
• Influence analysis
• Discourse analysis
• Learner success prediction
• Concept analysis
• Sensemaking models

Siemens & Baker, 2010.

4. Design of coding systems for elements.
5. Extraction of relevant data.
6. Synthesis of evidence and interpretation of findings.

Formation of Research Questions

The main purpose of the review was to investigate empirical studies of collaborative learning between 2012 and 2015 to establish the primary types of data being collected to evidence collaboration and the methods employed for analysing this data. The study ultimately sought to establish the degree to which 'Big Data' analytical approaches are being used in the field of collaborative learning, and the environments in which this is being conducted.

The research questions that the review aimed to answer were:

RQ1: What are the primary domains in which the case studies are undertaken?
RQ2: What mode of collaborative learning is being conducted and what technologies are being used to support this collaboration?
RQ3: What types of data are used to evidence collaborative learning?
RQ4: What data analysis techniques are undertaken on this data?

Selection of Search Terms for Identification of Relevant Papers

As explained, the review was limited to papers published between 2012 and 2015 with the focus on research which analysed empirical data obtained from case studies. The aim was to exclude papers which were largely theoretical or were based on simulations, or which only considered secondary data.

After some initial experimentation and evaluation of a number of search terms and their combinations ('collaborative learning', 'collaboration', 'team working', 'analysis', 'analytics', 'Big Data') the final search terms chosen were 'collaborative learning' + 'analytics'. These appeared to present papers of the right content and calibre.

Search Criteria and Literature Sources

The following sources were selected due to their availability and ability to provide high impact journals and conference proceedings. The number of papers obtained from each is shown in Table 3.

The title, authors, abstract, and keywords of the retrieved papers were inserted into a spreadsheet, grouped by source, for further evaluation.

Table 3. Number of papers retrieved from each source

Source	No. of Papers
ACM	204
IEEE	194
ScienceDirect	79

Extraction of Primary Studies

In order to extract papers for study from those initially identified, the abstract of each paper was examined and, if necessary, parts of the paper were skim-read, to establish whether it should be included in the study.

The initial studies were filtered according to the following criteria:

- **Inclusion Criteria:**
  - Publication between 2012 and 2015.
  - Publication type: journals, proceedings and transactions.
  - Studies were empirical studies of collaborative learning research.
  - Case studies related to small group collaboration, rather than MOOCs, etc.
- **Exclusion Criteria:**
  - Duplicated papers.
  - Editorials or papers from workshops.

At the end of this stage 36 papers, as shown in Table 4, were considered for detailed assessment and were inserted into a new spreadsheet.

Data to answer the research questions was extracted from each of the articles and was recorded in the spreadsheet using a coding system adapted from Zheng et al (2014). Two academics independently checked a range of papers to ensure the coding was consistent and a close level of correlation was established.

ANALYSIS OF RESULTS

The results for each research question are given below.

RQ1: What are the primary educational domains into which the case studies fall?

The majority of the studies were carried out in the Computing and Engineering domain, followed by Social Sciences (dominated by studies in the field of Education), with only one study taking place in the area of medical science (see Table 5). These results are broadly consistent with Zhen et al's (2014) findings and are perhaps unsurprising: as CSCL and learning analytics fall primarily within the computing/education fields, the convenience factor for researchers of carrying out empirical research on students in the same discipline would be a major influence on these high numbers.

The same reason of convenience could account for most of the studies being conducted at undergraduate level (see Table 6). However, this could also reflect the renewed demand being placed on Higher

Table 4. Number of papers selected for detailed study

Source	No. of Papers
ACM	18
IEEE	5
ScienceDirect	13

Table 5. Number and percentage of studies in each domain

Domain	No. of Studies	%
Computing or Engineering	17	47.2
Social Science	11	30.6
Natural Science	7	19.4
Medical Science	1	2.7

Table 6. Number and percentage of studies for each educational level

Educational Level	No. of Studies	%
Primary/Secondary school	6	16.7
Undergraduate	24	66.7
Postgraduate	3	8.3
Teachers	2	5.6
Unspecified	1	2.7

Education (HE) establishments to produce graduates with 'soft skills' such as effective team-working, which has fuelled research in this area.

RQ2: What mode of collaborative learning is being conducted and what technologies are being used to support this collaboration?

The research studies were coded as 1) online collaboration, 2) face-to-face or 3) both online and face-to-face. The number of studies in each mode is shown in Table 7.

Collaborative learning can be undertaken in a number of modes, using a range of different support mechanisms, not all of them computer based. Face-to-face social interactions have been shown to be crucial in achieving desired learning and collaborative skills (Zurita et al, 2003). Learners are able to ask questions in order to get a better understanding of a problem and get an immediate response. They are also able to read face-to face nuances, body language and emotion to build up a rapport with their group members. The review found that 26 (72%) of the empirical studies included face to face collaboration, though only 8 studies (22%) used it exclusively. Studies of pure face-to-face interaction analysis in group work are relatively rare. The literature in this area seems to focus on examining tools that might be useful to support face to face collaboration. Traditionally, support has centred on the production of manual records of meeting minutes, diaries, log books and so forth, but an increasing range of digital

Table 7. Number of studies for each mode of collaboration

Mode of Collaboration	No. of Studies
Online	10
Face-to-face	8
Both online and face-to-face	18

tools, such as videoconferencing and audio recording, are now being utilised for this purpose. Some relative newcomers to this area include interactive tabletops, providing a large horizontal interaction area for face to face, multi-touch shared interaction, as used in the studies by Martinez-Maldonado et al (2015) and Bordin et al (2013) and digital pens (Oviatt & Cohen, 2014), both of which are able to record users' digital footprints and make this available for analysis.

Increasingly, the bulk of collaborative learning is virtual and online. The results of the systematic review showed that 28 studies (approx. 78%) included online collaboration, 10 (28%) of them exclusively online. Online collaboration is underpinned by a number of enabling technologies. LMSs are now ubiquitous in education and come packaged with a range of tools – email, wiki, discussions boards, chat rooms - which allow for synchronous and asynchronous communication. Through LMS logs, the complete digital footprint of a group can be extracted for analysis. An increasing number of specialist collaborative learning environments are also being utilised, specifically tailored to particular learning tasks, and each providing a rich source of log data.

The results of the systematic review show that the dominant technologies for supporting collaboration were LMS and CSCL environments, which together accounted for half of the total studies. The next significant entry was the category of multi-touch/tangible technologies for supporting face to face collaboration. Groupware was used in four of the studies and social media in three (see Table 8).

The popularity of social media has resulted in studies using Facebook and other social media for collaboration. Where it is controlled by a researcher, metrics on group pages can be downloaded for analysis. For many learners, however, social media can be a preferred but private route for communicating with colleagues, rendering this aspect of collaboration inaccessible to researchers.

As costs associated with equipment have reduced and computational power has increased, growing interest has been shown in the use of multi-touch, 'tangible' technology, and also in 3-D virtual world and 'Second Life' platforms for supporting collaborative learning. Three-dimensionality, temporal support and interactivity are the most important features that distinguish 3-D learning environments from other types of virtual learning environments. A number of studies have suggested that 3D immersive platforms have significant potential for increased levels of collaboration (Dickey, 2005; Dalgarno & Lee, 2010). The analysis of these studies has been largely based on qualitative methods, however huge potential exists for mining the complex, multi-channel log data from 3D environments.

RQ3: What types of data are used to evidence collaborative learning?

Table 8. Technology used to support collaborative learning

Technology Used	Number of Studies	% of Studies
LMS	9	25.0
CSCL Environment	9	25.0
Multi-touch/Tangible Technology/ Tabletop	6	16.7
Groupware	4	11.1
Social Media	3	8.3
Games	1	2.7
Videoconferencing	1	2.7
Voice recorder	1	2.7
Multiple technologies	2	5.5

Type of data obtained was coded as (1) Process data, which included discussions and email transcripts, video records, audio records and log data, (2) Outcome data, including tests, artifacts (such as products, solutions, assignments, reports, presentations), maps (such as trace diagrams, concept maps, mind maps), and (3) Miscellaneous data, which included questionnaires, interview data, notes (such as written field notes, reflection, observation records).

As can be seen from Table 9, 32 studies (approximately 90% of the total sample) collected process data to evidence collaboration. 16 of these collected process data exclusively, the remainder combining process data with outcome or miscellaneous data in equal measures. Three studies collected all three types of interaction data. These findings are broadly in line with those obtained by Zheng et al (2014), who noted in their study of CSCL research conducted from 2003 to 2012 that 'process data' was utilized the most. This reflects that fact that the main focus of research is increasingly on analysis of the process of collaboration itself, rather than on the end product of the collaborative effort, in order to throw more light on the mechanics of the learning processes and successful collaboration.

Further examination of the process data revealed a wide variety of sources, but with a notable concentration on data obtained from discussion forums, followed by LMS log data (Table 10).

Table 9. Data collected to evidence collaborative learning

Type of Data	No. of Studies	% of Studies
Process	16	44.4
Outcome	2	5.5
Miscellaneous	2	5.5
Process & Outcome	7	19.4
Process and Miscellaneous	6	16.6
Process, Outcome & Miscellaneous	3	8.3

Table 10. Sources of process data used in studies

Type of Process Data	No of Studies
Asynchronous discussion forums	11
LMS logs	6
Online chat	3
Wiki data	4
Audio logs	3
Table top system interaction logs	3
Email	1
Mobile phone logs	1
Discourse tracking	2
Observation data	1
Digital pen log	1
Eye tracking data	1
Electronic whiteboard log	1
Video	1

RQ4: What data analysis methods are undertaken on this data?

Data analysis techniques were coded into two main groups, 1) Qualitative analysis, which included discourse analysis and interaction analysis, and 2) Quantitative methods, which included content analysis, statistical methods, social network analysis, modelling analytical methods (eg Markov model, hierarchical linear model), eye-tracking analysis, participation graph analysis and cluster analysis, as shown in Table 11.

Qualitative Methods

Qualitative methods were employed primarily on data obtained from face-to-face collaboration. Interaction analysis, used in 4 of the studies, has a long history, with pioneering work undertaken by as early as 1950 into dynamically capturing and classifying direct face-to-face interactions (Bales, 1950). Today, interaction can also be recorded by video for more detailed analysis after the learning has taken place. An underlying assumption in interaction analysis is that knowledge is an on-going social process and any analysis of it should identify the interaction of human beings with each other through speech, non-verbal actions and with artefacts in their environment. Analysis will typically use a pre-arranged coding system which identifies regularities in the way participants interact, use resources and acknowledge that learning has taken place.

Three studies used discourse analysis, two of them in conjunction with other methods. Broadly speaking, discourse analysis can be divided up into three domains: "the study of social interaction, the study of minds and sense-making, and the study of culture/social relations" (Wetherell, et al, 2001, p5). Lubold & Pon-Barry (2014) analyzed the intensity, pitch, voice quality, and speaking rate in collaborative learning dialogues to establish the extent to which they could indicate entrainment, and whether entrainment could in turn facilitate detection of rapport, a social quality of interaction. In Molenaar & Chiu (2015) students' face-to-face conversations were audio-taped with voice-recorders and their learning activities were then analysed using discourse analysis and content analysis, in a study that investigated the application of sequences of regulated learning to group performance.

Table 11. Data analysis methods used

Data Analysis Method	Single	Used with Other Analysis Methods	Total No. of Studies
Qualitative Methods			
Discourse Analysis	1	2	3
Interaction Analysis	2	2	4
Quantitative Methods			
Statistical Analysis	10	8	18
Content Analysis	4	7	11
Social Network Analysis	1	4	5
Modelling Analytical Methods	2	0	2
Eye-tracking Analysis	0	1	1
Participation Graphs Analysis	0	1	1
Cluster Analysis	3	2	5

However, discourse analysis does not lend itself to analysis of large volumes of data; as has been pointed out by Dascalu et al (2015), the time required for a thorough analysis of a chat session greatly exceeds the actual duration of that conversation, making the manual evaluation process virtually impossible for large volumes of conversations. This has resulted in the search for content analysis methods that can be automated. In Dascalu, et al (2015) the authors use Readerbench, a system capable of automatically evaluating collaboration between participants based on 'textual cohesion' in their wiki and discussion board messages.

Quantitative Methods

The data analysis category with the highest number of entries was the broad category of 'statistical analysis' which covered basic statistical analysis of data largely generated by virtual learning environments, for example the total number of logs of students creating posts on forums or discussion boards, amending posts, accessing learning resources, responding to posts, and similar events. As time is automatically recorded by the VLE, a temporal dimension can also be obtained. Results can then be correlated to reveal various aspects of the learning experience, or can be compared against an 'optimum' measure to spot any deviations from the norm. In Haythornthwaite & Gruzd (2012), the authors compared the density of postings on bulletin boards in order to provide insights on patterns that suggested successful collaboration.

Content analysis was the second largest analysis category, used mainly in conjunction with other methods. In the majority of cases content emanated from posts on discussion boards or Wikis and analysis focused on different features of the posts, depending on the study. Content analysis typically involves the human coding of messages, or other units of analysis, according to a pre-arranged scheme, with statistical analysis then being carried out on the resulting coded units. For example, in Joksimovic et al (2014), online discussions within an asynchronous forum were first manually coded according to phases of cognitive presence, and automated analysis was then conducted on the coded messages. Tarmazdi et al (2015) used natural language processing and sentiment analysis to analyse students' online teamwork discussion data to visualise team mood, role distribution and emotional climate. Natural language processing typically uses text analysis to extract information from a document or discussion post and to distil it into a format that can then be used for analytical purposes. Content is usually pre-processed, or 'normalized' by first removing 'stop words' that appear frequently but add little to the overall meaning (such as 'a','the','is'). Next, 'stemming' takes place to remove the inflection from words and replace them with their root (so that words such as 'finished', 'finishes' and 'finishing' would all be replaced by 'finish'). Finally the text is standardised to remove synonyms and infrequent words. The resulting text is then much more amenable to analysis. Text analytics can then scan documents to extract predictor variables. These can be of two types: the first, document predictors which indicate that the document contains certain features that provide information about the topic under discussion, or that highlight the frequency of explicit words or phrases; and the second, across document predictors which provide measures of correlation or similarity with other documents, allowing documents or posts to be grouped together based on the subjects to which they refer.

Sentiment analysis is a development on basic text analysis which attempts to extract learners' thoughts and feelings about events from their written interactions. A common approach is to construct a lexicon of words or phrases associated with positive and negative sentiments and then to count up the number of occurrences of each word within the text. The lexicon will assign a positive or negative rating to each word, so that, for example "detest" would get a rating of -10 while, at the other end of the scale, "adore" would get a rating of +10 to indicate very strong positive association. To create an overall rating for a document or a single chat message, the individual ratings for all the words in the lexicon that appear in the text are added together. Sentiment analysis may in addition require identification of the subject of the sentiment, i.e what is being 'despised' or 'adored'? Often this may not be apparent, or may be something totally unrelated to a discussion topic. In such cases entity extraction methods will be applied, typically using software that can determine fairly accurately which words in a text describe subjects and which do not.

Social network analysis (SNA) places pre-eminence on the premise that individuals are interdependent and is a popular method for analysing interaction networks formed in the course of collaborative learning. It is effective in identifying the structure of relationships, for example showing that learner A talked to learner B, or learner C collaborated with learner D, and provides various indices for analysing these relationships. The interactions between different learners can be modelled as a graph of nodes connected by ties, with numeric values on the ties defining the intensity of the links. The ties may be undirected, or directed, with arrows showing the direction of the relationship (see Figure 1). From this, various measures can be obtained for analysis, such as activity levels of members of the network, the prominence of particular members, the identification of cliques of learners, and so on.

Although a number of tools exist for automating SNA, substantial preparatory work still needs to be carried out to structure data in the formats required by these tools. Another drawback is that it does not convey the dynamic evolution of the collaborative networks being studied, a limitation that is starting to be addressed in experiments into using 3-D network visualisations, with time represented on a z-axis. Nevertheless it remains a useful approach to analysing collaborative interaction and was employed in four of the studies in the review, in three cases in conjunction with other methods. In Tobarra et al (2014) researchers analysed the interest propagation of their group of students using SNA. In Iglesias-Paradas et al (2015), postings by groups to a bulletin board were used to construct social network visualisations and produce basic statistics on bulletin use by each group, allowing comparisons to be made. While this

Figure 1.

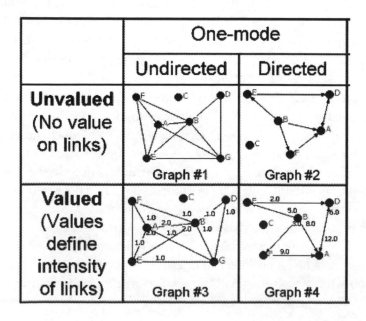

can show collaborative interaction levels, it does so without any consideration of the subject of the postings. However, Smith (2001) has pointed out that the act of engaging with another – whatever the subject matter – is significant in itself, so the sequence of conversational interaction, even without examination of the content or user perceptions can be useful in providing a window into students' interaction patterns and social engagement. Other studies concentrated on identifying various roles in collaborative learning through computing SNA indexes. For example Marcos-García et al (2015) used SNA to identify emergent roles in collaborative learning, while Xie, Yu & Bradshaw (2014) looked at the influence of moderator role assignment on social networks of online groups.

Clustering is a popular data mining technique which groups cases with similar attributes together. There are two types commonly employed, the first K-means which groups things that are most like each other (without reference to their actual behaviour, on the assumption that the same type of things will behave in the same way); the second, employed for predictive behaviour is K-nearest neighbour. Four studies used cluster analysis for analysing their data, one of them in conjunction with other methods. In Xing et al (2014) clustering was used to generate a predictive model of student performance: cluster analysis was applied to students' attained learning outcomes (which were assessed by human evaluators) to generate granular categories for student groups, from 'excellent' to 'at risk'. In a study of collaboration on maths problems, Xing, Wadholm & Goggins (2014) assessed student activities holistically and used K-means cluster analysis to evaluate strengths and weaknesses in individual students' participation in collaborative activities.

DISCUSSION

Summarising the findings from the systematic review, there is a wealth of data available for analysis of collaborative learning, primarily from virtual learning environments where student interactions with the LMS and CSCL platforms provide easily accessible logs of activity. Similarly, the almost ubiquitous use of discussion boards/forums and chat systems provide a rich pool of textual data that can be used for analysis. The increasing appearance of studies using 'multi-touch' platforms suggests that this may be an important source of multi-faceted data in the future. In a sense, this data could be considered 'big data', as it is varied – structured, semi-structured and unstructured - and generated, in part, automatically and continually by VLEs. However, the review revealed low levels of large scale data mining in the empirical case studies. Most of the analyses were based on standard statistical analysis of log data or discussion posts – for example, total number, length, frequency, and distribution of posts. While some generalisations can be made from such studies, such approaches do not take account of the content of posts which may, or may not be contributing to a learning task. Where textual analysis was undertaken this involved time consuming coding of messages or more fine grained units of discourse, before progressing to clustering or other statistical techniques.

The survey highlights some of the challenges raised by data associated with collaborative learning: much of it is noisy, temporal and incomplete and may lack enough samples for some tasks. Few of the case studies considered in the review could be categorised as being 'Big Data' from a 'volume' perspective. Educational datasets are usually relatively small, typically using population samples of less than 100 students. Student collaborative assignments are unlikely to run over more than a 10 week semester, usually far less, so data gathered in a typical study is modest, by 'Big Data' standards. Many studies produce mixed results with respect to prediction models, and this scarcity of data has been put forward as an explanation for this. Xing et al (2014) remarked that, 'Decision tree based models and rule based models typically require thousands of rows of data to properly train the algorithms. Even if some modelling algorithms have a good prediction rate in other disciplines, those algorithms do not necessarily perform equally well when addressing educational problems. The potential gap is due to limitations in the availability of training data' (Xing et al, 2014,p170).

The need to manually code interaction data makes the whole process of applying data analytics to collaborative learning a laborious, human work-intensive task and not readily scalable to large classes of hundreds of students. Typically, before it can be categorised, data needs to be filtered to eliminate 'noise' – for example to remove discussion posts that are not related to learning, or that relate to other learning not covered by the study. Data generated by a collaborating group will emanate from a number of individual group members, as well as from a number of different sources, which requires combination and synchronisation of data, including a consideration of its temporal aspects. All this makes for time-consuming analysis. A number of studies highlight the importance of analysing the conversations between group members (Hmelo-Silver, 2010) but given that the ultimate aim of research into collaborative learning is to provide some kind of student performance predictive models to allow for real time interventions to be made by instructors, the lengthy cleaning and coding renders this difficult. According to Martinez-Maldonaldo (2015) studies have shown that even quite modest indicators of speech can be effective in aiding understanding of several aspects of collaboration. However, current methods of analysis cannot be applied in classrooms to deliver information to help teachers or students in real-time.

Another observation from the review is that it is difficult to make overall generalisations from the body of empirical case studies, as each group work investigation is treated, in a sense, as a unique experiment. Suthers & Medina (2007) remark that researchers have neither a shared representation of data, nor a common vocabulary to discuss collaborative data, making it difficult to build on each other's work or reuse analysis tools that have been developed in different studies. This sentiment is echoed more recently by Song (2015) who points out that "There is a lack of replication of practices across different contexts and collaborative models, and a lack of instruments for examining the collaborative processes", suggesting that, in this respect, little has changed over the last decade or so.

CONCLUSION

This review has examined research into collaborative learning in the period from 2012 to 2015, covering a range of domains and supporting technologies, in order to assess the significance of Big Data for this area. The study looked at the domains in which the collaborative learning was undertaken and the mode of the collaboration used, namely whether face-to-face, online or a combination of both. It then considered the supporting technologies being used in the case studies and the data that was collected through these technologies. An examination was undertaken of the method of analysis carried out on that data. The results of the review found that the majority of the studies were undertaken in the Computing and Engineering or Social Science domains, primarily at undergraduate level. Half of the empirical studies included both face-to-face and online collaboration, with approximately 28 per cent being conducted purely online. The results indicate that the focus of the data collection is on interaction data to describe the process of the collaboration itself, rather than on the end product of the collaborative effort, with only 5 per cent of case studies collecting end product data exclusively. A number of studies attempted to combine data emanating from a number of different sources in order to establish indicators of successful collaboration. The dominant technologies for supporting collaboration were Learning Management Systems and Computer Supported Collaborative Learning (CSCL) environments, which together accounted for half of the total studies, however a broad range of other supporting technologies were used, including multi-touch, tangible computing such as digital pens and table-top displays. The various studies have made a contribution to the understanding of group work processes and student interactions, but the holy grail of providing a reliable predictive tool to allow educators to make timely, corrective interventions into collaborative learning remains elusive. Although data mining has become more sophisticated, bringing in new methods of analysis, data from collaborative learning remains a challenge to mine. The overall findings were that the noisy nature of this data and the need for manual pre-processing of textual data currently renders much of it unsuitable for automated 'big data' analytical approaches.

REFERENCES

Baker, R. S., & Yacef, K. (2009). The State of Educational Data Mining in 2009: A Review and Future Visions. *Journal of Educational Data Mining*, *1*(1), 3–17.

Bales, R. (1950). *Interaction process analysis; a method for the study of small groups*. Oxford, UK: Addison-Wesley.

Bichsel, J. (2012). *Analytics in higher education: Benefits, barriers, progress, and recommendations. EDUCAUSE*. Center for Applied Research.

Bordin, S., Zancanaro, M., & De Angeli, A. (2013). Touching dante: a proximity-based paradigm for tabletop browsing. In *Proceedings of the Biannual Conference of the Italian Chapter of SIGCHI*.

Dalgarno, B., & Lee, M. J. W. (2010). 7 Lee, M (2010) What are the learning affordances of 3-D virtual environments? *British Journal of Educational Technology*, *41*(1), 10–32. doi:10.1111/j.1467-8535.2009.01038.x

Dascalu, M., Bodea, C., Moldoveanu, A., Mohora, A., Lytras, M., & Ordoriez de Pablos, P. (2015). A recommender agent based on learning styles for better virtual collaborative learning experiences. *Computers in Human Behavior*, *45*, 43–53. doi:10.1016/j.chb.2014.12.027

Dickey, M. D. (2005). Three-dimensional virtual worlds and distance learning: Two case studies of Active Worlds as a medium for distance education. *British Journal of Educational Technology*, *36*(3), 439–451. doi:10.1111/j.1467-8535.2005.00477.x

Dillenbourg, P. (1999) What do you mean by collaborative learning? *Collaborative-learning: Cognitive and Computational Approaches*, 1-19.

Ferguson, R. (2012). Learning analytics: Drivers, developments and challenges. *International Journal of Technology Enhanced Learning*, *4*(5-6), 304–317. doi:10.1504/IJTEL.2012.051816

Haythornthwaite, C., & Grusz, A. (2012). Exploring patterns and configurations in networked learning texts. In *Proceedings from the 45th Hawaii International Conference on System Sciences*. IEEE Computer Society. doi:10.1109/HICSS.2012.268

Joksimovic, S., Gasevic, D., Kovanovic, V., Adesope, O., & Hatala, M. (2014). Psychological characteristics in cognitive presence of communities of inquiry: A linguistic analysis of online discussions, 2014. *The Internet and Higher Education*, *22*, 1–10. doi:10.1016/j.iheduc.2014.03.001

Jonassen, D. H. (1999). Designing constructivist learning environments. In C. M. Reigeluth (Ed.), Instructional design theories and models: A new paradigm of instructional theory, (vol. 2, pp. 371–396). Academic Press.

Jeong, H., & Hmelo-Silver, C. (2011). A portrait of CSCL methodologies. In H. Spada, G. Stahl, N. Miyake & N. Law (Eds.), *Connecting Research to Policy and Practice. InProceedings of CSCL 2011*, (vol. 1, pp. 550–557).

Kitchenham, B., & Charters, S. (2007). *Guidelines for Performing Systematic Literature Reviews In Software Engineering*. Keele University and Durham University Joint Report.

Iglesias-Paradas, S., Ruiz-de-Azcarate, C., & Agudo-Peregrina, A. (2015). Assessing the suitability of student interactions from Moodle data logs as predictors of cross curricular competencies. *Computers in Human Behavior*, *47*(June), 81–89. doi:10.1016/j.chb.2014.09.065

Lonchamp, J. (2012). Computational analysis and mapping of ijCSCL content. *International Journal of Computer-Supported Collaborative Learning*, *7*(4), 475–497. doi:10.1007/s11412-012-9154-z

Lubold, N., & Pon-Barry, H. (2014). Acoustic-prosodic entrainment and rapport in collaborative learning dialogues. In *Proceedings of the 2014 ACM workshop on Multimodal Learning Analytics Workshop and Grand Challenge*, (pp. 5–12). doi:10.1145/2666633.2666635

Marcos-García, J., Martinex-Mones, A., & Dimitriadis, Y. (2015). DESPRO: A method based on roles to provide collaboration analysis support adapted to the participants in CSCL situations, 2015. *Computers & Education*, *82*, 335–353. doi:10.1016/j.compedu.2014.10.027

Martinez-Maldonado, R., Yacef, K., & Kay, J. (2015). TSCL: A conceptual model to inform understanding of collaborative learning processes at interactive tabletops. *International Journal of Human-Computer Studies*, *83*, 62–82. doi:10.1016/j.ijhcs.2015.05.001

Molenaar, I., & Chiu, M. (2015). Effects of sequences of socially regulated learning on group performance. In *Proceedings of the 5th International Conference of Learning Analytics and Knowledge*, (pp. 236-240). doi:10.1145/2723576.2723586

Noroozi, O., Weinberger, A., Biemans, H. J. A., Mulder, M., & Chizari, M. (2012). Argumentation-based computer supported collaborative learning (ABCSCL): A synthesis of 15 years of research. *Educational Research Review*, *7*(2), 79–106.

Oviatt, S., & Cohen, A. (2014). Written Activity, Representations and Fluency as Predictors of Domain Expertise in Mathematics. In *Proceedings of the 16th International Conference on Multimodal Interaction* (pp. 10-17). ACM.

Reffay, C., & Martinez-Mones, A. (2013). Basic Concepts and Techniques in Social Network Analysis. In R. Luckin, S. Puntambekar, P. Goodyear, B. Grabowski, J. Underwood, & N. Winters (Eds.), *Handbook of Design in Educational Technology* (pp. 448–456). Routledge.

Robles, M. M. (2012). Executive perceptions of the top 10 soft skills needed in today's workplace. *Business Communication Quarterly*, *75*(4), 453–465. doi:10.1177/1080569912460400

Ryu, S. (2013). 2013, Predictive Analytics: The Power to Predict Who Will Click, Buy, Lie or Die. *Healthcare Information Research*, *19*(1), 63–65. doi:10.4258/hir.2013.19.1.63

Song, Y. (2014). Methodological Issues in Mobile Computer-Supported Collaborative Learning (mC-SCL): What Methods, What to Measure and When to Measure? *Journal of Educational Technology & Society*, *17*(4), 33–48.

Tarmazdi, H., Vivian, R., Szabo, C., Falkner, K., & Falkner, N. (2015). Using Learning Analytics to Visualise Computer Science Teamwork. In *Proceedings of the 2015 ACM Conference on Innovation and Technology in Computer Science Education*, (pp. 165-170). doi:10.1145/2729094.2742613

Tobarra, L., Ros, S., Hernandez, R., Robles-Gómez, A., Caminero, A. C., & Pastor, R. (2014). Integrated Analytic dashboard for virtual evaluation laboratories and collaborative forums. In Tecnologias Aplicadas a la Ensenanza de la Electronica (Technologies Applied to Electronics Teaching)(TAEE), 2014 XI (pp. 1-6). IEEE. doi:10.1109/TAEE.2014.6900177

Xie, K., Yu, C., & Bradshaw, A. (2014). Impacts of role assignment and participation in asynchronous discussions in college-level online classes, 2014. *The Internet and Higher Education*, *20*, 10–19. doi:10.1016/j.iheduc.2013.09.003

Xing, W., Gui, R., Petakovic, E., & Goggins, S. (2014). Participation-based student final performance prediction model through interpretable Genetic Programming: Integrating learning analytics, educational data mining and theory. *Computers in Human Behavior*, *47*, 168–181. doi:10.1016/j.chb.2014.09.034

Xing, W., Wadholm, B., & Goggins, S. (2014). Learning analytics in CSCL with a focus on assessment: an exploratory study of activity theory-informed cluster analysis. In *Proceedings of the Fourth International Conference on Learning Analytics and Knowledge Conference*, (pp. 59-67). ACM. doi:10.1145/2567574.2567587

Zheng, L., Huang, R., & Yu, J. (2014). Identifying Computer-Supported Collaborative Learning (CSCL) Research in Selected Journals Published from 2003 to 2012: A Content Analysis of Research Topics and Issues. *Journal of Educational Technology & Society*, *17*(4), 335–351.

Compilation of References

Abuobieda, A., Salim, N., Binwahlan, M. S., & Osman, A. H. (2013). Differential evolution cluster-based text summarization methods. *Computing, Electrical and Electronics Engineering (ICCEEE), 2013 International Conference on,*. doi:10.1109/ICCEEE.2013.6633941

Abuobieda, N., Salim, A., Albaham, A., Osman, Y., & Kumar. (2012). Text summarization features selection method using pseudo genetic-based model. In *International Conference on Information Retrieval Knowledge Management (CAMP)*. doi:10.1109/InfRKM.2012.6204980

Adedoyin-Olowe, M., Gaber, M. M., & Stahl, F. (2013). TRCM: A methodology for temporal analysis of evolving concepts in Twitter. In Artificial Intelligence and Soft Computing (LNAI), (Vol. 7895, pp. 135–145). Springer. doi:10.1007/978-3-642-38610-7_13

Adi, A., Botzer, D., Nechushtai, G., & Sharon, G. (2006). Complex Event Processing for Financial Services. In 2006 IEEE Services Computing Workshops (pp. 7–12). IEEE. doi:10.1109/SCW.2006.7

Aggarwal, C. (2014). *Managing and Mining Sensor Data*. Retrieved 16 May 2015, from http://charuaggarwal.net/sensortoc.pdf

Aggarwal, C. C. (2014). A Survey of Stream Clustering Algorithms. In Data Clustering: Algorithms and Applications (pp. 231–255). CRC Press.

Aggarwal, C. C., Han, J., Wang, J., & Yu, P. S. (2003). A Framework for Clustering Evolving Data Streams.*Proceedings of the 29th International Conference on Very Large Data Bases*, *29*, 81–92. doi:10.1016/B978-012722442-8/50016-1

Agrawal, D., Das, S., & El Abbadi, A. (2011). *Big Data and Cloud Computing: Current State and Future Opportunities in*. EDBT. doi:10.1145/1951365.1951432

Agrawal, R., Imieliński, T., & Swami, A. (1993). Mining association rules between sets of items in large databases. *SIGMOD Record*, *22*(2), 207–216. doi:10.1145/170036.170072

Agrawal, R., & Srikant, R. (1994). *Quest synthetic data generator*. IBM Almaden Research Center.

Albrechtsen, H. (1993). Subject analysis and indexing: From automated indexing to domain analysis. *The Indexer*, *18*, 219–219.

Aliguliyev, R. M. (2009). A new sentence similarity measure and sentence based extractive technique for automatic text summarization. *Expert Systems with Applications*, *36*(4), 7764–7772. doi:10.1016/j.eswa.2008.11.022

Ambler, H., Nichols, A., Slavens, B., Benitez, L., Schimmer, R., & Livingston, S. (2014). *IBM Connections 5.0 Reviewer's Guide*. Retrieved April 27, 2015, from http://public.dhe.ibm.com/software/dw/lotus/connections/connections5/connections5reviewersguide.pdf

Andrzejewski, D., & Zhu, X. (2009). Latent Dirichlet Allocation with topic-in-set knowledge. *Proceedings of the NAACL HLT 2009 Workshop on Semi-Supervised Learning for Natural Language Processing*, (pp. 43-48). doi:10.3115/1621829.1621835

Antoniou, G., & van Harmelen, F. (2008). A Semantic Web Primer (2nd ed.). Cambridge, MA: MIT Press.

Arasu, A., Babcock, B., Babu, S., Cieslewicz, J., Mayur, D., Ito, K., ... Widom, J. (2004). *STREAM. The Stanford Data Stream Management System*. Academic Press.

Arasu, A., Babu, S., & Widom, J. (2006). The CQL continuous query language: Semantic foundations and query execution. *The VLDB Journal*, *15*(2), 121–142. doi:10.1007/s00778-004-0147-z

Atzmueller, M. (2014). Data Mining on Social Interaction Networks. *Journal of Data Mining & Digital Humanities*.

Atzmueller, M., & Puppe, F. (2006). SD-Map – A Fast Algorithm for Exhaustive Subgroup Discovery. In *Proc. PKDD 2006* (LNAI), (vol. 4213, pp. 6–17). Springer.

Atzmueller, M., & Puppe, F. (2006). SD-Map – A Fast Algorithm for Exhaustive Subgroup Discovery. In *Proc. PKDD 2006*. Springer.

Atzmueller, M., Kibanov, M., Hayat, N., Trojahn, M., & Kroll, D. (2015c) Adaptive Class Association Rule Mining for Human Activity Recognition. In *Proceedings of the International Workshop on Mining Ubiquitous and Social Environments* (MUSE2015).

Atzmueller, M. (2007). *Knowledge-Intensive Subgroup Mining -- Techniques for Automatic and Interactive Discovery. Dissertations in Artificial Intelligence-Infix (Diski), (307)*. IOS Press.

Atzmueller, M. (2012). Mining social media: Key players, sentiments, and communities. *Wiley Interdisciplinary Reviews: Data Mining and Knowledge Discovery*, *2*(5), 411–419.

Atzmueller, M. (2015). *Subgroup Discovery – Advanced Review*. WIREs. *Data Mining and Knowledge Discovery*, *5*(1), 35–49. doi:10.1002/widm.1144

Atzmueller, M., Baumeister, J., & Puppe, F. (2005a). Quality Measures and Semi-Automatic Mining of Diagnostic Rule Bases. *Proc. 15th International Conference on Applications of Declarative Programming and Knowledge Management*. Springer. doi:10.1007/11415763_5

Atzmueller, M., Doerfel, S., Hotho, A., Mitzlaff, F., & Stumme, G. (2012). *Face-to-Face Contacts at a Conference: Dynamics of Communities and Roles. Modeling and Mining Ubiquitous Social Media, LNCS 7472*. Heidelberg, Germany: Springer Verlag.

Atzmueller, M., Doerfel, S., & Mitzlaff, F. (2015a). Description-Oriented Community Detection using Exhaustive Subgroup Discovery. *Information Sciences*, *329*, 965–984. doi:10.1016/j.ins.2015.05.008

Atzmueller, M., Kluegl, P., & Puppe, F. (2008). Rule-Based Information Extraction for Structured Data Acquisition using TextMarker. In *Proc. LWA 2008*. University of Wuerzburg.

Atzmueller, M., & Lemmerich, F. (2009) Fast Subgroup Discovery for Continuous Target Concepts. *Proc. 18th International Symposium on Methodologies for Intelligent Systems (ISMIS 2009)*. Springer Verlag. doi:10.1007/978-3-642-04125-9_7

Atzmueller, M., & Lemmerich, F. (2012). VIKAMINE - Open-Source Subgroup Discovery, Pattern Mining, and Analytics. In *Proc. ECML/PKDD 2012: European Conference on Machine Learning and Principles and Practice of Knowledge Discovery in Databases*. Springer. doi:10.1007/978-3-642-33486-3_60

Atzmueller, M., & Lemmerich, F. (2013). Exploratory Pattern Mining on Social Media using Geo-References and Social Tagging Information. *International Journal of Web Science*, *1/2*(2), 2013.

Atzmueller, M., Mueller, J., & Becker, M. (2015b). *Exploratory Subgroup Analytics on Ubiquitous Data. Mining, Modeling and Recommending 'Things' in Social Media, LNCS 8940*. Heidelberg, Germany: Springer Verlag.

Atzmueller, M., & Nalepa, G. J. (2009). A Textual Subgroup Mining Approach for Rapid ARD+ Model Capture.*Proc. 22nd International Florida Artificial Intelligence Research Society Conference (FLAIRS)*. AAAI Press.

Atzmueller, M., & Puppe, F. (2005). Semi-Automatic Visual Subgroup Mining using VIKAMINE. *Journal of Universal Computer Science*, *11*(11), 1752–1765.

Atzmueller, M., & Puppe, F. (2008). A Case-Based Approach for Characterization and Analysis of Subgroup Patterns. *Journal of Applied Intelligence*, *3*(28), 210–221. doi:10.1007/s10489-007-0057-z

Atzmueller, M., Puppe, F., & Buscher, H.-P. (2005b). Profiling Examiners using Intelligent Subgroup Mining.*Proc. 10th International Workshop on Intelligent Data Analysis in Medicine and Pharmacology (IDAMAP-2005)*.

Atzmueller, M., & Roth-Berghofer, T. (2010). The Mining and Analysis Continuum of Explaining Uncovered.*Proc. 30th SGAI International Conference on Artificial Intelligence (AI-2010)*.

Auschitzky, E., Hammer, M., & Rajagopaul, A. (2014). *How big data can improve manufacturing*. McKinsey.

Austin, P., & Brunner, L. (2004). Inflation of the Type I Error Rate When a Continuous Confounding Variable Is Categorized in Logistic Regression Analyses. *Statistics in Medicine*, *23*(7), 1159–1178. doi:10.1002/sim.1687 PMID:15057884

Axelsson, S. (2000). Intrusion Detection Systems: A Survey and Taxonomy. *Computer Engineering*, 1–27.

Babcock, B., Babu, S., Datar, M., Motwani, R., & Widom, J. (2002). Models and Issues in Data Stream Systems. In *Proceedings of the twenty-first ACM SIGMOD-SIGACT-SIGART symposium on Principles of database systems* (pp. 1–16). ACM. doi:10.1145/543613.543615

Babu, S., Srivastava, U., & Widom, J. (2004). Exploiting K-Constraints To Reduce Memory Overhead in Continuous Queries Over Data Streams. *ACM Transactions on Database Systems*, *29*(3), 545–580. doi:10.1145/1016028.1016032

Badreddin, O., & Peyton, L. (2013). Real time patient flow management using business process management, location tags, and complex events processing. In *Proceedings of the 2013 Conference of the Center for Advanced Studies on Collaborative Research* (CASCON '13). Retrieved March 4th, 2015 from https://www.researchgate.net/publication/262172837

Baker, R. S., & Yacef, K. (2009). The State of Educational Data Mining in 2009: A Review and Future Visions. *Journal of Educational Data Mining*, *1*(1), 3–17.

Bakshi, K. (2013). Technologies for Big Data. In *Big Data Management, Technologies, and Applications*. IGI Global.

Baldwin, B., & Morton, T. S. (1998). Dynamic co reference based summarization. In *Proceedings of the Third Conference on Empirical Methods in Natural Language Processing (EMNLP-3)*.

Bales, R. (1950). *Interaction process analysis; a method for the study of small groups*. Oxford, UK: Addison-Wesley.

Barzilay, R., & Elhadad, M. (1997). Using Lexical Chains for Text Summarization. In *Proceedings of the ACL/EACL'97 Workshop on Intelligent Scalable Text Summarization* (pp. 10–17).

Bastian, M., Heymann, S., & Jacomy, M. (2009). Gephi: an open source software for exploring and manipulating networks. In *Proceedings of the Third International Conference on Weblogs and Social Media (ICWSM 2009)*. San Jose, CA: The AAAI Press.

Baxendale, P. B. (1958). Machine-made index for technical literature: An experiment. *IBM Journal of Research and Development*, *2*(4), 354–361. doi:10.1147/rd.24.0354

Beath, C., Becerra-Fernandez, I., Ross, J., & Short, J. (2012). Finding value in the information explosion. *MIT Sloan Management Review, 53*(4).

Beckett, D., Berners-Lee, T., & Prud'hommeaux, E. (2014, February 25). *Turtle - Terse RDF Triple Language*. Retrieved May 15, 2015, from http://www.w3.org/TR/turtle/

Behrendt, S., Richter, A., & Trier, M. (2014). Mixed methods analysis of enterprise social networks. *Computer Networks, 75*(Part B), 560–577.

Behrendt, S., Richter, A., & Riemer, K. (2014). Conceptualisation of Digital Traces for the Identification of Informal Networks in Enterprise Social Networks. In *ACIS 2014 Proceedings*. Auckland: AIS.

Berger, K., Klier, J., Klier, M., & Richter, A. (2014). "who is Key...?" - Characterizing Value Adding Users in Enterprise Social Networks. In M. Avital, J. M. Leimeister, & U. Schultze (Eds.), *22st European Conference on Information Systems*. Tel Aviv: AIS.

Bertin-Mahieux, T., Ellis, D. P., Whitman, B., & Lamere, P. (2011). The million song dataset. In *ISMIR 2011: Proceedings of the 12th International Society for Music Information Retrieval Conference* (pp. 591-596). University of Miami.

Bichsel, J. (2012). *Analytics in higher education: Benefits, barriers, progress, and recommendations. EDUCAUSE*. Center for Applied Research.

Bifet, A. (2013). Mining Big Data in Real Time. *Informatica*, (37), 15–20.

Bifet, A., & Frank, E. (2010). *Sentiment Knowledge Discovery in Twitter Streaming Data. Discovery Science*. Berlin: Springer.

Binnewies, S., & Stantic, B. (2012). OECEP: enriching complex event processing with domain knowledge from ontologies. In *Proceedings of the Fifth Balkan Conference in informatics (BCI '12)*. Retrieved March 4, 2015, from doi:10.1145/2371316.2371322

Binwahlan, M. S., Salim, N., & Suanmali, L. (2009). Swarm Based Text Summarization. In *Proceedings of the International Association of Computer Science and Information Technology - Spring Conference. IACSITSC '09* (pp. 145-150). doi:10.1109/IACSIT-SC.2009.61

Binwahlan, M. S., Salim, N., & Suanmali, L. (2010). Fuzzy swarm diversity hybrid model for text summarization. *Information Processing & Management, 46*(5), 571–588. doi:10.1016/j.ipm.2010.03.004

BITKOM. (2013). *Einsatz und Potenziale von Social Business für ITK-Unternehmen*. Retrieved April 29, 2015, from http://www.bitkom.org/files/documents/Studie_SocialBusiness_Potenziale.pdf

Blei, D. M., Ng, A. Y., & Jordan, M. I. (2003). Latent Dirichlet Allocation. *Journal of Machine Learning Research, 3*, 993–1022.

Bordin, S., Zancanaro, M., & De Angeli, A. (2013). Touching dante: a proximity-based paradigm for tabletop browsing. In *Proceedings of the Biannual Conference of the Italian Chapter of SIGCHI*.

Borgatti, S. P., Everett, M. G., & Freeman, L. C. (2002). *UCINET 6 for Windows: Software for Social Network Analysis*. Analytic Technologies.

Borkar, V. R., Deshmukh, K., & Sarawagi, S. (2001). Automatic Segmentation of Text into Structured Records. In S. Mehrotra, & T. K. Sellis (Ed.), *SIGMOD Conference* (pp. 175-186). ACM. doi:10.1145/376284.375682

Box, G., & Cox, D. (1964). An Analysis of Transformations. *Journal of the Royal Statistical Society. Series B. Methodological*, 211–252.

Boyd, d. m., & Ellison, N. (2007). Social Network Sites: Definition, History, and Scholarship. *Journal of Computer-Mediated Communication, 13*(1), 210–230.

Bradley, A. (1997). The use of the area under the ROC curve in the evaluation of machine learning algorithms. *Pattern Recognition, 30*(7), 1145–1159. doi:10.1016/S0031-3203(96)00142-2

Bramer, M. A. (2013). *Principles of Data Mining* (2nd ed.). London: Springer. doi:10.1007/978-1-4471-4884-5

Brandow, R., Mitze, K., & Rau, L. F. (1995). Automatic condensation of electronic publications by sentence selection. *Information Processing & Management, 31*(5), 675–685. doi:10.1016/0306-4573(95)00052-I

Brickley, D., & Guha, R. (2014, February 14). *RDF Schema 1.1*. Retrieved May 15, 2015, from http://www.w3.org/TR/rdf-schema/

Brutti, P., Santis, F. D., & Gubbiotti, S. (2009). Mixtures of prior distributions for predictive Bayesian sample size calculations in clinical trials. *Statistics in Medicine, 28*(17), 2185–2201. doi:10.1002/sim.3609 PMID:19462415

Bucklin, R. E., & Sismeiro, C. (2015). A Model of Web Site Browsing Behavior Estimated on Clickstream Data. *JMR, Journal of Marketing Research, 40*(3), 249–267. doi:10.1509/jmkr.40.3.249.19241

Buitelaar, P., & Cimiano, P. (2008). *Ontology learning and population: bridging the gap between text and knowledge* (Vol. 167). IOS Press.

Cameron, M. a., Power, R., Robinson, B., & Yin, J. (2012). Emergency situation awareness from twitter for crisis management.*Proceedings of the 21st International Conference Companion on World Wide Web - WWW '12 Companion*, 695. doi:10.1145/2187980.2188183

Cao, F., Ester, M., Qian, W., & Zhou, A. (2006). Density-based Clustering over an Evolving Data Stream with Noise. *SDM, 6*, 328–339.

Carlberg, C. (2013). *Predictive analytics: Microsoft excel*. Pearson Education, Inc.

Carpineto, C., Osinski, S., Romano, G., & Weiss, D. (2009). A survey of Web clustering engines. *ACM Computing Surveys, 41*(3), 1–38. doi:10.1145/1541880.1541884

Celjuska, D., & Vargas-Vera, M. (2004). Ontosophie: A semi-automatic system for ontology population from text.*Proceedings of the 3rd International Conference on Natural Language Processing (ICON)*.

Cendrowska, J. (1987). PRISM: An algorithm for inducing modular rules. *International Journal of Man-Machine Studies, 27*(4), 349–370. doi:10.1016/S0020-7373(87)80003-2

Chakraborthy, G., Pagolu, M., & Garla, S. (2013). *Text mining and analysis Practical methods, Examples and case studies using SAS*. SAS Publishing.

Chakravarthy, S., Krishnaprasad, V., Anwar, E., & Kim, S.-K. (1994). Composite Events for Active Databases: Semantics, Contexts and Detection. In VLDB (pp. 606–617).

Chapman, P., Clinton, J., Kerber, R., Khabaza, T., Reinartz, T., Shearer, C., & Wirth, R. (2000). *CRISP-DM 1.0: Step-by-step data mining guide*. Retrieved April 28, 2015, from http://www.crisp-dm.org/CRISPWP-0800.pdf´

Chatterjee, P., Hoffman, D. L., & Novak, T. P. (2003). Modeling the clickstream: Implications for web-based advertising e⌐orts. *Marketing Science, 22*(4), 520–541. doi:10.1287/mksc.22.4.520.24906

Chaudhry, N., Shaw, K., & Abdelguerfi, M. (2006). *Stream Data Management*. Springer.

Cheatham, M., & Hitzler, P. (2013). String similarity metrics for ontology alignment. In The Semantic Web - ISWC 2013 (pp. 294-309). Springer. doi:10.1007/978-3-642-41338-4_19

Chemudugunta, C., Holloway, A., Smyth, P., & Steyvers, M. (2008). *Modeling documents by combining semantic concepts with unsupervised statistical learning.* Springer. doi:10.1007/978-3-540-88564-1_15

Chen, M., Mao, S., & Liu, Y. (2014). Big data: A survey. *Mobile Networks and Applications*, *19*(2), 171–209. doi:10.1007/s11036-013-0489-0

Chiticariu, L., Li, Y., & Reiss, F. R. (2013). *Rule-Based Information Extraction is Dead! Long Live Rule-Based Information Extraction Systems!.* EMNLP.

Choi, F. Y. (2000). *Advances in domain independent linear text segmentation.* ANLP.

Church, K., & Gale, W. A. (1995). Inverse document frequency (idf): A measure of deviations from poisson. In *Proceedings of the Third Workshop on Very Large Corpora.*

Cloud Security Alliance. (2013). *Big Data Analytics for Security Intelligence.* Retrieved from www.cloudsecurityalliance.org/research/big-data

Cohen, W., Ravikumar, P., & Fienberg, S. (2003). A comparison of string metrics for matching names and records. In Kdd workshop on data cleaning and object consolidation, (vol. 3, pp. 73–78).

Conroy, J., & O'leary, D. (2001). Text summarization via hidden Markov models. In *Proceedings of the 24th annual international ACM SIGIR conference on Research and development in information retrieval* (pp. 406-407). New Orleans, LA: ACM.

Cowie, J., & Lehnert, W. (1996). Information extraction. *Communications of the ACM*, *39*(1), 80–91. doi:10.1145/234173.234209

Creighton, M. P. (2015). *School Library infographics - How To Create Them Why To Use Them.* Libraries Unlimited Publishers.

Crosman. (2010). 3 of Banking's Most Unusual Analytics Deployments. *InformationWeek.* Retrieved 19 November 2010 from http://www.banktech.com/data-and-analytics/3-of-bankings-most-unusual-analytics-deployments/d/d-id/1294335?

Crowe, C. M. (1996). Data reconciliation—progress and challenges. *Journal of Process Control*, *6*(2), 89–98. doi:10.1016/0959-1524(96)00012-1

Csardi, G., & Nepusz, T. (2006). The igraph software package for complex network research, InterJournal. *Complex Systems*, 1695.

Cugola, G., & Margara, A. (2012). Processing Flows of Information: From Data Stream to Complex Event Processing. *ACM Comput. Surv.*, *44*(1), 15:1–15:62.

Dalgarno, B., & Lee, M. J. W. (2010). 7 Lee, M (2010) What are the learning affordances of 3-D virtual environments? *British Journal of Educational Technology*, *41*(1), 10–32. doi:10.1111/j.1467-8535.2009.01038.x

Dascalu, M., Bodea, C., Moldoveanu, A., Mohora, A., Lytras, M., & Ordoriez de Pablos, P. (2015). A recommender agent based on learning styles for better virtual collaborative learning experiences. *Computers in Human Behavior*, *15*, 43–53. doi:10.1016/j.chb.2014.12.027

Dasu, T., & Johnson, T. (2003). *Exploratory data mining and data cleaning.* New York, NY: John Wiley & Sons.

Dean, J., & Ghemawat, S. (2008). MapReduce: Simplified Data Processing on Large Clusters. *Communications of the ACM, 51*(1), 107–113. doi:10.1145/1327452.1327492

Debar, H., Becker, M., & Siboni, D. (1992). A neural network component for an intrusion detection system. In *Proceedings 1992 IEEE Computer Society Symposium on Research in Security and Privacy* (pp. 240–250). IEEE. doi:10.1109/RISP.1992.213257

Deerwester, S. C., Dumais, S. T., Landauer, T. K., Furnas, G. W., & Harshman, R. A. (1990). Indexing by latent semantic analysis. *JAsIs, 41*(6), 391–407. doi:10.1002/(SICI)1097-4571(199009)41:6<391::AID-ASI1>3.0.CO;2-9

Dehkordi, P.-K., Kumarci, F., & Khosravi, H. (2009). Text Summarization Based on Genetic Programming. *Proceedings of the International Journal of Computing and ICT Research, 3*, 57–64.

Demers, A., Gehrke, J., Hong, M., Panda, B., Riedewald, M., Sharma, V., & White, W. (2007). Cayuga: A General Purpose Event Monitoring System. *CIDR 2007, Third Biennial Conference on Innovative Data Systems Research.*

Desouza, K. C., & Smith, K. L. (2014). *Big Data for Social Innovation | Stanford Social Innovation Review.* Retrieved February 9, 2015, from http://www.ssireview.org/articles/entry/big_data_for_social_innovation

Dickey, M. D. (2005). Three-dimensional virtual worlds and distance learning: Two case studies of Active Worlds as a medium for distance education. *British Journal of Educational Technology, 36*(3), 439–451. doi:10.1111/j.1467-8535.2005.00477.x

Dillenbourg, P. (1999) What do you mean by collaborative learning? *Collaborative-learning: Cognitive and Computational Approaches*, 1-19.

DiMicco, J. M., Geyer, W., Millen, D. R., Dugan, C., & Brownholtz, B. (2009). People Sensemaking and Relationship Building on an Enterprise Social Network Site. In *2009 42nd Hawaii International Conference on System Sciences* (pp. 1–10). IEEE.

DiMicco, J. M., Millen, D. R., Geyer, W., Dugan, C., Brownholtz, B., & Muller, M. (2008). Motivations for Social Networking at Work. In *Proceedings of the 2008 ACM Conference on Computer Supported Cooperative Work* (pp. 711–720). New York: ACM.

DIN 192271. (n.d.). *Control technology; graphical symbols letters for process control engineering; symbolic representation functions.* Deutsche Institut für Normung e. V. Std.

Dittrich, K. R., Gatziu, S., & Geppert, A. (1995). The Active Database Management System Manifesto: A Rulebase of ADBMS Features.*2nd Workshop on Rules in Databases.* doi:10.1007/3-540-60365-4_116

Domingos, P., & Hulten, G. (2000). Mining high-speed data streams.*Proceedings of the Sixth ACM SIGKDD International Conference on Knowledge Discovery and Data Mining - KDD '00.* doi:10.1145/347090.347107

Drakos, N., Mann, J., & Gotta, M. (2014). *Magic quadrant for social software in the workplace.* Retrieved April 28, 2015, from https://www.jivesoftware.com/discover-jive/analyst-reports/gartner-magic-quadrant/

Duggal, P. S., & Paul, S. (2013), Big Data Analysis:Challenges and Solutions. *Proceedings of International conference on cloud, Big data and trust.*

Duivesteijn, W., Feelders, A., & Knobbe, A. (2016). Exceptional Model Mining. *Data Mining and Knowledge Discovery, 30*(1), 47–98. doi:10.1007/s10618-015-0403-4

Ebbers, M., Abdel-Gayed, A., Budhi, V., & Dolot, F. (2013). *Addressing Data Volume, Velocity, and Variety with IBM InfoSphere Streams V3.0.* Academic Press.

Eckert, M., Bry, F., Brodt, S., Poppe, O., & Hausmann, S. (2011). A CEP Babelfish: Languages for Complex Event Processing and Querying Surveyed. *Reasoning in Event-Based Distributed Systems*, 47–70. http://doi.org/<ALIGNMENT.qj></ALIGNMENT>10.1007/978-3-642-19724-6_3

Eckert, M., Bry, F., Brodt, S., Poppe, O., & Hausmann, S. (2011). A CEP babelfish: Languages for complex event processing and querying surveyed. *Studies in Computational Intelligence*, *347*(242438), 47–70. doi:10.1007/978-3-642-19724-6_3

Eckert, M., Oriented, S., Soa, A., & Eda, E. A. (2009). Complex Event Processing (CEP) Types of Complex Event Processing Event Queries. *Informatik-Spektrum*, *32*(2), 1–8. doi:10.1007/s00287-009-0329-6

Ediger, D., Jiang, K., Jason, E., & Bader, D. (2012). GraphCT: Multithreaded Algorithms for Massive Graph Analysis. In Proceedings of IEEE Transactions On Parallel And Distributed Systems.

Edmundson, H. P. (1969). New methods in automatic extracting. *Journal of the ACM*, *16*(2), 264–285. doi:10.1145/321510.321519

Edwards, J. (2013). *Twitter's "Dark Pool": IPO doesn't mention 651 million users who abandoned twitter.* Retrieved April 20, 2015, from http://www.businessinsider.com/twitter-total-registered-users-v-monthly-active-users-2013-11

Elmagarmid, A. K. (2005). Stream Data Management. New York: Springer.

Elmagarmid, A. K., Ipeirotis, P. G., & Verykios, V. S. (2007). Duplicate record detection: A survey. *Knowledge and Data Engineering. IEEE Transactions*, *19*(1), 1–16.

EMC Education Services. (2015). *Data Science and Big Data analytics: Discovering, analyzing, visualizing and presenting Data.* Indianapolis, IN: John Wiley & Sons.

Ester, M., Kriegel, H.-P., Sander, J., & Xiaowei, X. (1996). A Density-Based Algorithm for Discovering Clusters in Large Spatial Databases with Noise. *KDD*, *96*(34), 226–231.

Etzion, O. (1995). *Reasoning about the behavior of active databases applications. Rules in Database Systems.* Springer.

Etzion, O., & Niblett, P. (2010). *Event Processing in Action. Online.* Stamford, CT: Manning Publications Co.

Eugster, P. T., Felber, P., Guerraoui, R., & Kermarrec, A.-M. (2003). The many faces of publish/subscribe. *ACM Computing Surveys*, *35*(2), 114–131. doi:10.1145/857076.857078

Euzenat, J., & Shvaiko, P. (2007). *Ontology Matching.* Heidelberg, Germany: Springer.

Evans, J. R., & Lindner, C. H. (2012). Business Analytics: The Next Frontier for Decision Sciences. *Decision Line*, *43*(2).

Fan, W., & Bifet, A. (2013). Mining Big Data: Current Status and Forecast to the Future. *SIGKDD Explorations*, *14*(2), 1–5. doi:10.1145/2481244.2481246

Fan, W., & Geerts, F. (2012). Foundations of data quality management. *Synthesis Lectures on Data Management*, *4*(5), 1–217. doi:10.2200/S00439ED1V01Y201207DTM030

Farrell, S., Lau, T., Nusser, S., Wilcox, E., & Muller, M. (2007). Socially augmenting employee profiles with people-tagging. In *Proceedings of the 20th annual ACM symposium on User interface software and technology - UIST '07* (p. 91). New York: ACM Press.

Fattah, M. A., & Ren, F. (2009). Ga, mr, ann, pnn and gmm based models for automatic text summarization. *Computer Speech & Language*, *23*(1), 126–144. doi:10.1016/j.csl.2008.04.002

Felicio, J. A., Couto, E., & Caiado, J. (2014). Human capital, social capital and organizational performance. *Management Decision*, *52*(2), 350–364. doi:10.1108/MD-04-2013-0260

Fellbaum, C. (Ed.). (1998). *WordNet: An Electronic Lexical Database*. Cambridge, MA: MIT Press.

Ferguson, R. (2012). Learning analytics: Drivers, developments and challenges. *International Journal of Technology Enhanced Learning*, *4*(5-6), 304–317. doi:10.1504/IJTEL.2012.051816

Field, A. (2009). *Discovering statistics using SPSS* (3rd ed.). Thousand Oaks, CA: Sage Publications.

Fischbach, K., Schoder, D., & Gloor, P. a. (2008). Analyse informeller Kommunikationsnetzwerke am Beispiel einer Fallstudie. *Wirtschaftsinformatik*, *51*(2), 164–174.

Fowler, A. (2015). *10 Advantages of NoSQL over RDBMS. NoSQL For Dummies*. Wiley.

Frantzi, K., Ananiadou, S., & Mima, H. (2000). Automatic recognition of multi-word terms. the C-value/NC-value method. *International Journal on Digital Libraries*, *3*(2), 115–130. doi:10.1007/s007999900023

Freeman, L. C. (1978). Centrality in social networks conceptual clarification. *Social Networks*, *1*(3), 215–239.

Friedman, J., Hastie, T., & Tibshirani, R. (2010). Regularization Paths for Generalized Linear Models via Coordinate Descent. *Journal of Statistical Software*, *33*(1), 1–22. doi:10.18637/jss.v033.i01 PMID:20808728

Fry, B. (2007). *Visualizing data: exploring and explaining data with the Processing environment*. O'Reilly Media, Inc.

Fülöp, L. J., Tóth, G., Rácz, R., Pánczél, J., Gergely, T., Beszédes, Á., & Farkas, L. (2010). Survey on Complex Event Processing and Predictive Analytics. In *Proceedings of the Fifth Balkan Conference in Informatics* (pp. 26–31). Citeseer.

Fülöp, L. J., Beszédes, Á., Tóth, G., Demeter, H., Vidács, L., & Farkas, L. (2012). Predictive Complex Event Processing : A Conceptual Framework for Combining Complex Event Processing and Predictive Analytics.*Proceedings of the Fifth Balkan Conference in Informatics, September*, (pp. 26–31). doi:10.1145/2371316.2371323

Gabrilovich, E., & Markovitch, S. (2007). Computing semantic relatedness using Wikipedia-based explicit semantic analysis.*Proceedings of the 20th international joint conference on artificial intelligence*.

Gaikwad, P. (2014). *List of 23 Mobile Analytics Tools useful for your Inbound Marketing*, Retrieved on January 7, 2014 from http://www.inboundio.com/blog/list-of-23-mobile-analytics-tools-useful-for-your-inbound-marketing/

Gandomi, A., & Haider, M. (2015). Beyond the hype: Big data concepts, methods, and analytics. *International Journal of Information Management*, *35*(2), 137–144.

Garcia, H. R., & Ledeneva, Y. (2013). Single Extractive Text Summarization Based on a Genetic Algorithm. In J. Carrasco-Ochoa, J. Martínez-Trinidad, J. Rodríguez, & G. Baja (Eds.), *Pattern Recognition* (Vol. 7914, pp. 374–383). Springer Berlin Heidelberg. doi:10.1007/978-3-642-38989-4_38

Garlasu, D., Sandulescu, V., Halcu, I., & Neculoiu, G. (2013). A Big Data implementation based on Grid Computing. In *Proceeding ofRoedunet International Conference (RoEduNet)*.

Gartner Group. (n.d.). *Major myths about Big Data's impact on information infrastructure*. Retrieved from https://www.gartner.com/doc/2846217/major-myths-big-datas-impact

Gartner. (2013). *Magic Quadrant for Social Software in the Workplace*. Retrieved April 28, 2015, https://www.jivesoftware.com/discover-jive/analyst-reports/gartner-magic-quadrant/

George, D., & Mallery, P. (2014). *IBM SPSS statistics 21 step by step: A simple guide and reference* (13th ed.). Boston, MA: Allyn and Bacon.

Geyer, W., Dugan, C., DiMicco, J. M., Millen, D. R., Brownholtz, B., & Muller, M. (2008). Use and reuse of shared lists as a social content type. In *Proceeding of the twenty-sixth annual CHI conference on Human factors in computing systems - CHI '08* (p. 1545). New York: ACM Press.

Ginsberg, J., Mohebbi, M. H., Patel, R. S., Brammer, L., Smolinski, M. S., & Brilliant, L. (2009). Detecting influenza epidemics using search engine query data. *Nature, 457*(7232), 1012–1014. doi:10.1038/nature07634 PMID:19020500

Gohil, A. (2015). *R data Visualization cookbook*. Mumbai: PACKT publishers.

Golab, L., & Özsu, M. T. (2010). *Data Stream Management. Synthesis Lectures on Data Management* (Vol. 2). Morgan & Claypool Publishers.

GoodData Corporation. (2015). *GoodData Yammer Analytics Dashboard*. Retrieved April 28, 2015, from http://www.gooddata.com/bi-solutions/enterprise-analytics/yammer-analytics

Gotta, M., Drakos, N., & Mann, J. (2015). *Magic Quadrant for Social Software in the Workplace*. Retrieved December 3, 2015, from https://www.ibm.com/services/forms/signup.do?source=gts-LITS-WebOrganic-NA&S_PKG=ov35194

Granovetter, M. S. (1973). The strength of weak ties. *American Journal of Sociology, 78*(6), 1360–1380.

Grishman, R. (1997). Information extraction: Techniques and challenges. In *Information Extraction: A Multidisciplinary Approach to an Emerging Information Technology*. Springer. doi:10.1007/3-540-63438-X_2

Grosskreutz, H., Rüping, S., & Wrobel, S. (2008) Tight Optimistic Estimates for Fast Subgroup Discovery. In *Proceedings of the ECML/PKDD*. Springer Verlag. doi:10.1007/978-3-540-87479-9_47

Grubbs, F. E. (1969). Procedures for Detecting Outlying Observations in Samples. *Technometrics, 11*(1), 1–21. doi:10.1080/00401706.1969.10490657

Gu, B., Hu, F., & Liu, H. (2001). 'Modelling Classification Performance for Large Data Sets', Advances in The authorsb-Age. *Information & Management*, 317–328.

Guha, R., McCool, R., & Miller, E. (2003). Semantic search.*Proceedings of the 12th international conference on World Wide Web*, (pp. 700-709).

Gupta, V., & Lehal, G. S. (2010). A survey of text summarization extractive techniques. *Journal of Emerging Technologies in Web Intelligence, 2*(3), 258-268.

Hadoop. (2015). *Apache Software Foundation (ASF)*. Retrieved on 18 December 2015 from http://hadoop.apache.org

Hair, J. F. Jr. (2007). Knowledge creation in marketing: The role of predictive analytics. *European Business Review, 19*(4), 303–315. doi:10.1108/09555340710760134

Hammond, M. (2013). Video Analytics: How it Works, It's Benefits and it's Limitations. *Socialnomics*. Retrieved on October 1 2013 from http://www.socialnomics.net/2013/10/01/video-analytics-how-it-works-it%E2%80%99s-benefits-and-it%E2%80%99s-limitations/

Han, J., Kamber, M., & Pei, J. (2012). *Data mining: concepts and techniques* (3rd ed.). Waltham: Morgan Kaufmann/Elsevier.

Han, J., Pei, J., & Yin, Y. (2000) Mining Frequent Patterns without Candidate Generation. In *ACM SIGMOD International Conference on Management of Data*. ACM Press.

Hansen, D. L., Shneiderman, B., & Smith, M. A. (2010). Visualizing Threaded Conversation Networks: Mining Message Boards and Email Lists for Actionable Insights. In A. An, P. Lingras, S. Petty, & R. Huang (Eds.), *Active Media Technology SE - 7* (Vol. 6335, pp. 47–62). Berlin: Springer.

Harris, S., & Seaborne, A. (2013, March 21). *Webpage*. Retrieved May 15, 2015, from SPARQL 1.1 Query Language: http://www.w3.org/TR/sparql11-query/

Harrison, G. (2010). 10 things you should know about NoSQL databases. *Data Management*. Retrieved on August 2010, from http://www.techrepublic.com/resource-library/downloads/10-things-you-should-know-about-nosql-databases/?docid=2006531

Haythornthwaite, C., & Grusz, A. (2012). Exploring patterns and configurations in networked learning texts. In *Proceedings from the 45th Hawaii International Conference on System Sciences*. IEEE Computer Society. doi:10.1109/HICSS.2012.268

Hearst, M. A. (1997). TextTiling: Segmenting text into multi-paragraph subtopic passages. *Computational Linguistics*, *23*(1), 33–64.

Heger, D. A. (2014). Big Data Analytics - Where to go from Here. *International Journal of Developments in Big Data and Analytics,* (1), 42 - 58.

Hinze, A., Sachs, K., & Buchmann, A. (2009). Event-based Applications and Enabling Technologies. In *Proceedings of the Third ACM International Conference on Distributed Event-Based Systems* (pp. 1:1–1:15). New York: ACM Press. doi:10.1145/1619258.1619260

Hirao, T., Sasaki, Y., Isozaki, H., & Maeda, E. (2002). NTT's Text Summarization system for DUC-2002. In *Workshop on Text Summarization(In conjunction with the ACL 2002 and including the DARPA/NIST sponsored DUC 2002 Meeting on Text Summarization)*.

Hitzler, P., Krötzsch, M., Parsia, B., Patel-Schneider, P. F., & Rudolph, S. (2012, December 11). *OWL 2 Web Ontology Language: Primer*. Retrieved May 15, 2015, from http://www.w3.org/TR/owl2-primer/

Hoeffding, W. (1963). Probability inequalities for sums of bounded random variables. *Journal of the American Statistical Association*, *58*(301), 13–30. doi:10.1080/01621459.1963.10500830

Hollender, M. (2010). *Collaborative Process Automation Systems*. ISA.

Horrocks, I., Parsia, B., Patel-Schneider, P., & Hendler, J. (2005). Semantic Web Architecture: Stack or Two Towers? In F. Fages & S. Soliman (Eds.), *Principles and Practice of Semantic Web Reasoning (PPSWR)* (pp. 37–41). Springer. doi:10.1007/11552222_4

Hota, J. (2013). Adoption of in-memory analytics. *CSI Communications*, 20-22.

Hotelling, H. (1933). Analysis of a complex of statistical variables into principal components. *Journal of Educational Psychology*, *24*(6), 417–441. doi:10.1037/h0071325

Hovy, E., & Lin, C.-Y. (1998). Automated text summarization and the summarist system. In *Proceedings of a Workshop onAssociation for Computational Linguistics*.

Huffman, D. A. (1952). A Method for the Construction of Minimum-Redundancy Codes.*Proc. IRE*, *40*, 1098–1101. doi:10.1109/JRPROC.1952.273898

Huiskes, M. J., & Lew, M. S. (2008, October). The MIR Flickr retrieval evaluation. In *Proceedings of the 1st ACM international conference on Multimedia information retrieval* (pp. 39-43). ACM. doi:10.1145/1460096.1460104

Hutchins, W. J. (1978). The concept of aboutness in subject indexing. *Aslib Proceedings*, *30*(5), 172–181. doi:10.1108/eb050629

Hutchison, D., & Mitchell, J. C. (2011). *Transactions on Large-Scale Data- and Knowledge-Centered Systems III* (A. Hameurlain, J. Küng, & R. Wagner, Eds.). Heidelberg, Germany: Springer-Verlag Berlin Heidelberg.

Hwang, J. H., Balazinska, M., Rasin, A., Çetintemel, U., Stonebraker, M., & Zdonik, S. (2005). High-availability algorithms for distributed stream processing. *Proceedings - International Conference on Data Engineering*, (pp. 779–790).

Hyvönen, E., & Mäkelä, E. (2006). Semantic autocompletion. In The Semantic Web - ASWC 2006 (pp. 739-751). Springer. doi:10.1007/11836025_72

IBM. (2014). *IBM Named Worldwide Market Share Leader in Enterprise Social Software for Fifth Consecutive Year.* Retrieved April 27, 2015, from http://www-03.ibm.com/press/us/en/pressrelease/43703.wss

Iglesias-Paradas, S., Ruiz-de-Azcarate, C., & Agudo-Peregrina, A. (2015). Assessing the suitability of student interactions from Moodle data logs as predictors of cross curricular competencies. *Computers in Human Behavior*, *47*(June), 81–89. doi:10.1016/j.chb.2014.09.065

Imran, R., Majeed, M., & Ayub, A. (2015). Impact of organizational justice, job security and job satisfaction on organizational productivity. *Journal of Economics. Business and Management*, *3*(9), 840–845. doi:10.7763/JOEBM.2015.V3.295

Intel IT Center. (2013a). *Big Data Visualization: Turning Big Data Into Big Insights.* Retrieved on 1 March 2013 from http://www.intel.com/content/dam/www/public/us/en/documents/white-papers/big-data-visualization-turning-big-data-into-big-insights.pdf

Intel IT center. (2013b). Predictive Analytics 101: Next-Generation Big Data Intelligence. *Intel IT center.* Retrieved on 1 March 2013 from http://www.intel.in/content/dam/www/public/us/en/documents/best-practices/big-data-predictive-analytics-overview.pdf

Jaseena, K. U., & David, J. M. (2014). *Issues, Challenges, And Solutions: Big Data Mining* (pp. 131–140). CS & IT-CSCP.

Jeong, H., & Hmelo-Silver, C. (2011). A portrait of CSCL methodologies. In H. Spada, G. Stahl, N. Miyake & N. Law (Eds.), *Connecting Research to Policy and Practice. InProceedings of CSCL 2011*, (vol. 1, pp. 550–557).

Jezek, K., & Steinberger, J. (2008). Automatic Text Summarization (The state of the art 2007 and new challenges). In Znalosti 2008 (pp. 1-12).

Jiang, J. J., & Conrath, D. W. (1997). Semantic similarity based on corpus statistics and lexical taxonomy.*Proceedings of ROCLING X.* Taiwan.

Jive Software. (2015a). *Jive 7.0 Community User Help: Using Impact Metrics.* Retrieved December 4, 2015, from https://docs.jivesoftware.com/jive/7.0/community_user/index.jsp?topic=/com.jivesoftware.help.sbs.online/user/WhatareImpactMetrics.html

Jive Software. (2015b). *Jive Analytics: Community Manager Reports.* Retrieved December 4, 2015, from https://docs.jivesoftware.com/cloud_int/comm_mgr/jive.help.analytics/#user/AboutReportsv3.html

Jive Software. (2015c). *Jive features.* Retrieved April 28, 2015, from https://www.jivesoftware.com/products-solutions/jive-n/#tab-features

Johnson, T., Muthukrishnan, S., & Rozenbaum, I. (2005). Sampling Algorithms in a Stream Operator.*SIGMOD '05: Proceedings of the 2005 ACM SIGMOD International Conference on Management of Data*, (pp. 1–12). doi:10.1145/1066157.1066159

Joksimovic, S., Gasevic, D., Kovanovic, V., Adesope, O., & Hatala, M. (2014). Psychological characteristics in cognitive presence of communities of inquiry: A linguistic analysis of online discussions, 2014. *The Internet and Higher Education, 22*, 1–10. doi:10.1016/j.iheduc.2014.03.001

Jonassen, D. H. (1999). Designing constructivist learning environments. In C. M. Reigeluth (Ed.), Instructional design theories and models: A new paradigm of instructional theory, (vol. 2, pp. 371–396). Academic Press.

Jones, K. S. (1998). Automatic summarising: Factors and directions. In *Advances in Automatic Text Summarization* (pp. 1–12). MIT Press.

Kageura, K., & Umino, B. (1996). Methods of automatic term recognition: A review. *Terminology, 3*(2), 259–289. doi:10.1075/term.3.2.03kag

Kalaian, S. A., & Kasim, R. M. (2015). Predictive analytics. In M. Tavana, S. B. Zhou, & S. K. Puranam (Eds.), *Handbook of research on organizational transformations through big data analytics* (pp. 12–29). Hershey, PA: IGI Global.

Kan, M.-Y., Klavans, J. L., & McKeown, K. (1998). Linear Segmentation and Segment Significance. *CoRR.*

Khan, M., & Khan, S. S. (2011). Data and Information Visualization Methods and Interactive Mechanisms: A Survey. *International Journal of Computers and Applications, 34*(1), 1–14.

Kitchenham, B., & Charters, S. (2007). *Guidelines for Performing Systematic Literature Reviews In Software Engineering*. Keele University and Durham University Joint Report.

Kloepper, B., Dix, M., Siddapura, D., & Taverne, L. (2015). *Integrated Search for Hetereogenous Data in Process Industry Applications - A Proof of Concept.32nd IEEE International Conference on Data Engineering*, Helsinki, Finland.

Klösgen, W. (1996). Explora: A multipattern and multistrategy discovery assistant. In Advances in Knowledge Discovery and Data Mining, (pp. 249–271). AAAI.

Klösgen, W. (1996). Explora: A Multipattern and Multistrategy Discovery Assistant. In Advances in Knowledge Discovery and Data Mining. Palo Alto, CA: AAAI Press.

Kluegl, P., Atzmueller, M., & Puppe, F. (2009) Meta-Level Information Extraction. *The 32nd Annual Conference on Artificial Intelligence*. Springer. doi:10.1007/978-3-642-04617-9_30

Kluegl, P., Atzmueller, M., & Puppe, F. (2009). Textmarker: A tool for rule-based information extraction.*Proceedings of the Biennial GSCL Conference*, (pp. 233-240).

Koch, M., & Richter, A. (2009). *Enterprise 2.0: Planung, Einführung und erfolgreicher Einsatz von Social-Software in Unternehmen*. München: Oldenbourg.

Koch, M., Richter, A., & Schlosser, A. (2007). Produkte zum IT-gestützten Social Networking in Unternehmen. *Wirtschaftsinformatik, 49*(6), 448–455.

Kogilavani, A., & Balasubramanie, P. (2010). Clustering and Feature Specific Sentence Extraction Based Summarization of Multiple Documents. *International Journal of Computer Science and Information Technology, 2*(4), 99–111. doi:10.5121/ijcsit.2010.2409

Koplowitz, R. (2014). *The Forrester Wave: Enterprise Social Platforms, Q2 2014*. Retrieved April 28, 2015, from https://www.jivesoftware.com/discover-jive/analyst-reports/forrester-wave-social/

Kuang, H., & Zhi Gang, L. (2012). *Using the Metrics application in IBM Connections 4.0. IBM Connections wiki*. Retrieved April 27, 2015, from http://www-10.lotus.com/ldd/lcwiki.nsf/dx/Using_the_Metrics_application_in_IBM_Connections_4.0

Kuhns, M., & Johnson, K. (2013). *Applied predictive modeling*. New York: Springer. doi:10.1007/978-1-4614-6849-3

Kupiec, J., Pedersen, J., & Chen, F. (1995). A trainable document summarizer. In *Proceedings of the 18th annual international ACM SIGIR conference on Research and development in information retrieval*. Seattle, WA: ACM.

Kurzlechner, W, (2011). Social Software: IBM, Microsoft und Jive im Vergleich. *CIO Magazin*. Retrieved April 28, 2015, from http://www.cio.de/a/ibm-microsoft-und-jive-im-vergleich,2298192

Kwon, Y., Lee, W. Y., Balazinska, M., & Xu, G. (2008). Clustering events on streams using complex context information. In *Proceedings - IEEE International Conference on Data Mining Workshops, ICDM Workshops 2008* (pp. 238–247). Washington, DC: IEEE. doi:10.1109/ICDMW.2008.138

Larg George. (2014). *Getting Started with Big Data Architecture*. Retrieved on 10 September 2014 from http://blog.cloudera.com/blog/2014/09/getting-started-with-big-data-architecture/

Laurie, B., & Roberts, S. A. (2008). The convergence of information systems and information management: Environmental changes and pedagogical challenges. *Aslib Proceedings*, *60*(6), 661–671. doi:10.1108/00012530810924320

Lavrac, N., Kavsek, B., Flach, P., & Todorovski, L. (2004). Subgroup Discovery with CN2-SD. *Journal of Machine Learning Research*, *5*, 153–188.

Leavitt, N. (2010). Will NoSql live to Their Promise? *Computer*, *43*(2), 12–14. doi:10.1109/MC.2010.58

Lee, O., You, E., Hong, M., & Jung, J. J. (2015). Adaptive Complex Event Processing Based on Collaborative Rule Mining Engine. In Intelligent Information and Database Systems (Vol. 9011, pp. 430–439). Springer International Publishing. doi:10.1007/978-3-319-15702-3_42

Lee, M. (2015). Business intelligence, knowledge management, customer relations, and technological support in enterprise competitive competence. In M. Tavana, S. B. Zhou, & S. K. Puranam (Eds.), *Handbook of research on organizational transformations through big data analytics* (pp. 243–262). Hershey, PA: IGI Global.

Leman, D., Feelders, A., & Knobbe, A. (2008) Exceptional Model Mining. In *Proceedings of ECML/PKDD*. Springer Verlag. doi:10.1007/978-3-540-87481-2_1

Lemmerich, F., Becker, M., & Atzmueller, M. (2012). Generic Pattern Trees for Exhaustive Exceptional Model Mining. In *Proceedings of ECML/PKDD*. Springer Verlag. doi:10.1007/978-3-642-33486-3_18

Le, T., Stahl, F., Gomes, J. B., Gaber, M. M., & Di Fatta, G. (2008). Computationally Efficient Rule-Based Classification for Continuous Streaming Data. In *Research and Development in Intelligent Systems XXIV* (p. 2014). Springer International Publishing.

Levenshtein, V. (1966). Binary Codes Capable of Correcting Deletions, Insertions, and Reversals. *Soviet Physics, Doklady*, *10*(8), 707–710.

Lewandowski, D. (2005). Web searching, search engines and Information Retrieval. *Inf. Serv. Use, 25*(3-4), 137-147.

Lidwell, W., Holden, K., & Butler, J. (2003). *Universal Principles of Design*. Rockport Publishers.

Li, H., Wang, Y., Zhang, D., Zhang, M., & Chang, E. (2008). PFP: Parallel FP-Growth for Query Recommendation. *Proc. 2008 ACM conference on Recommender systems*. ACM. doi:10.1145/1454008.1454027

Li, M. (2010). Robust Complex Event Pattern Detection over Streams. *Evaluation*, 176.

Li, M., Liu, M., Ding, L., Rundensteiner, E. A., & Mani, M. (2007). Event Stream Processing with Out-of-Order Data Arrival. In *27th International Conference on Distributed Computing Systems Workshops*. IEEE. doi:10.1109/ICDCSW.2007.35

Lin, C.-Y. (2004). Rouge: a package for automatic evaluation of summaries. In *Proceedings of the ACL-04 Workshop on Text Summarization Branches Out* (pp. 74-81).

Lin, C.-Y., & Hovy, E. (1997). Identifying topics by position. In *Proceedings of the fifth conference on Applied natural language processing (ANLC '97)*. Association for Computational Linguistics. doi:10.3115/974557.974599

Lin, D. (1998). An information-theoretic definition of similarity. *ICML*, *98*, 296–304.

Litvak, M., Last, M., & Friedman, M. (2010). A new approach to improving multilingual summarization using a genetic algorithm. In *Proceedings of the 48th Annual Meeting of the Association for Computational Linguistics* (pp. 927-936). Uppsala, Sweden: Association for Computational Linguistics.

Liu, M., Li, M., Golovnya, D., Rundensteiner, E. A., & Claypool, K. (2009). Sequence pattern query processing over out-of-order event streams. In *IEEE 25th International Conference on Data Engineering* (pp. 784–795). IEEE. doi:10.1109/ICDE.2009.95

Liu, X., Webster, & Kit, C. (2009). An Extractive Text Summarizer Based on Significant Words. In *Proceedings of the 22nd International Conference on Computer Processing of Oriental Languages. Language Technology for the Knowledge-based Economy* (ICCPOL '09). Springer-Verlag.

Liu, H., Shah, S., & Jiang, W. (2004). On-line outlier detection and data cleaning. *Computers & Chemical Engineering*, *28*(9), 1635–1647. doi:10.1016/j.compchemeng.2004.01.009

Lloret, E., & Palomar, M. (2012, January). Text summarization in progress: A literature review. *Artificial Intelligence Review*, *37*(1), 1–41. doi:10.1007/s10462-011-9216-z

Lonchamp, J. (2012). Computational analysis and mapping of ijCSCL content. *International Journal of Computer-Supported Collaborative Learning*, *7*(4), 475–497. doi:10.1007/s11412-012-9154-z

Loshin, D. (2013). *Big data analytics: From strategic planning to enterprise integration with tools, techniques, NoSQL, and Graph*. Waltham, MA: Elsevier.

Lubold, N., & Pon-Barry, H. (2014). Acoustic-prosodic entrainment and rapport in collaborative learning dialogues. In *Proceedings of the 2014 ACM workshop on Multimodal Learning Analytics Workshop and Grand Challenge*, (pp. 5–12). doi:10.1145/2666633.2666635

Luckham, D. (2006). *What's the difference between ESP and CEP?* Retrieved April 20, 2015, from http://www.complexevents.com/2006/08/01/what's-the-difference-between-esp-and-cep/

Luckham, D., & Schulte, R. (2011). *Event Processing Technical Society - Event Processing Glossary - Version 2*. Retrieved April 15, 2015, from http://www.complexevents.com/wp-content/uploads/2011/08/EPTS_Event_Processing_Glossary_v2.pdf

Luckham, D., & Schulte, W. R. (2012). *Complex event processing and the future of business decisions*. Retrieved March 29, 2015 from http://www.complexevents.com/2012/07/12/complex-event-processing-and-the-future-of-business-decisions

Luhn, H. P. (1957). A statistical approach to mechanized encoding and searching of literary information. *IBM Journal of Research and Development*, *1*(4), 309–317. doi:10.1147/rd.14.0309

Luhn, H. P. (1958). The automatic creation of literature abstracts. *IBM Journal of Research and Development*, *2*(2), 159–165. doi:10.1147/rd.22.0159

Machlis, S. (2011). 22 free tools for data visualization and analysis. *Computer World.* Retrieved on 20 April 2011 from http://www.computerworld.com/article/2507728/enterprise-applications/enterprise-applications-22-free-tools-for-data-visualization-and-analysis.html

Magid, Y., Adi, A., Barnea, M., Botzer, D., & Rabinovich, E. (2008). Application generation framework for real-time Complex Event Processing. *32ⁿᵈ Annual IEEE International Computer Software and Applications Conference (COMPSAC '08)* (pp.1162-1167). Retrieved March 29, 2015 from doi:10.1109/COMPSAC.2008.146

Mahmood, M. A., & Mann, G. J. (2005). Information technology investments and organizational productivity and performance: An empirical investigation. *Journal of Organizational Computing and Electronic Commerce, 15*(3), 185–202. doi:10.1207/s15327744joce1503_1

Maisel, L. S., & Cokins, G. (2014). *Predictive business analytics: Forward looking capabilities to improve business performance.* Hoboken, NJ: John Wiley & Sons, Inc.

Maletic, J. I., & Marcus, A. (2010). Data Cleansing Data Mining and Knowledge Discovery Handbook. In O. Mainmon & L. Rokach (Eds.), Data Mining and Knowledge Discovery Handbook (pp. 19–32). New York: Springer.

Mani, I., & Maybury, M. T. (1999). Advances in Automatic Text Summarization. MIT Press.

Mansouri-Samani, M., & Sloman, M. (1999). GEM: A generalized event monitoring language for distributed systems. *Distributed Systems Engineering, 4*(2), 96–108. doi:10.1088/0967-1846/4/2/004

Marchand, D. (n.d.). *Competing with information: a manager's guide to creating business value with information content.* Academic Press.

Marcos-García, J., Martinex-Mones, A., & Dimitriadis, Y. (2015). DESPRO: A method based on roles to provide collaboration analysis support adapted to the participants in CSCL situations, 2015. *Computers & Education, 82*, 335–353. doi:10.1016/j.compedu.2014.10.027

Marcu, D. (1998). Improving summarization through rhetorical parsing tuning. In *Proceedings of The Sixth Workshop on Very Large Corpora* (pp. 206-215).

Marcus, A., Bernstein, M. S., Badar, O., Karger, D. R., Madden, S., & Miller, R. C. (2011). Tweets as data: Demonstration of TweeQL and Twitinfo. In *Proceedings of the 2011 international conference on Management of data - SIGMOD '11* (p. 1259). New York: ACM. doi:10.1145/1989323.1989470

Martinez-Maldonado, R., Yacef, K., & Kay, J. (2015). TSCL: A conceptual model to inform understanding of collaborative learning processes at interactive tabletops. *International Journal of Human-Computer Studies, 83*, 62–82. doi:10.1016/j.ijhcs.2015.05.001

Marz, N., & Warren, J. (2015). Big Data Principles and best practices of scalable realtime data systems. Manning Publications.

Marz, N., & Warren, J. (2015). *Big Data: Principles and best practices of scalable realtime data systems.* Shelter Island, NY: Manning Publications Co.

Mathioudakis, M., & Koudas, N. (2010). Twittermonitor: trend detection over the twitter stream. *Proceedings of the 2010 ACM SIGMOD International Conference on Management of Data*, (pp. 1155–1158). doi:10.1145/1807167.1807306

McAfee, A. P. (2006a). *Enterprise 2.0, version 2.0. Andrew McAfee's Blog.* Retrieved April 28, 2015, from http://andrewmcafee.org/2006/05/enterprise_20_version_20/

McAfee, A. P. (2006b). Enterprise 2.0: The Dawn of Emergent Collaboration. *MIT Sloan Management Review, 47*(3), 21–28.

McAfee, A., Brynjolfsson, E., Davenport, T. H., Patil, D. J., & Barton, D. (2012). Big data. *The management revolution. Harvard Business Review, 90*(10), 61–67. PMID:23074865

McCallum, A., Freitag, D., & Pereira, F. (2000). *Maximum Entropy Markov Models for Information Extraction and Segmentation. In Proceeding 17th International Conforence on Machine Learning* (pp. 591–598). San Francisco, CA: Morgan Kaufmann.

McCallum, A., Freitag, D., & Pereira, F. C. (2000, June). *Maximum Entropy Markov Models for Information Extraction and Segmentation* (Vol. 17). ICML.

McIntyre, S. (2014). *IBM Connections: Components.* Retrieved April 28, 2015, from http://ibmconnections.com/features/components/

Meek, C., Thiesson, B., & Heckerman, D. (2002). The Learning-Curve Sampling Method Applied to Model-Based Clustering. *Journal of Machine Learning Research, 2,* 397–418.

Meena, Y. K., & Gopalani, D. (2014). Analysis of Sentence Scoring Methods for Extractive Automatic Text Summarization. *International Conference on Information and Communication Technology for Competitive Strategies (ICTCS-2014).* ACM. doi:10.1145/2677855.2677908

Melton, G., & Hripcsak, G. (2005). Automated detection of adverse events using natural language processing of discharge summaries. *Journal of the American Medical Informatics Association, 12*(4), 448–457. doi:10.1197/jamia.M1794 PMID:15802475

Mendoza, M., Bonilla, S., Noguera, C., Cobos, C., & Leon, E. (2014). Extractive single-document summarization based on genetic operators and guided local search. *Expert Systems with Applications, 41*(9), 4158–4169. doi:10.1016/j.eswa.2013.12.042

Mertler, C. A., & Vannatta, R. A. (2013). *Advanced and multivariate statistical methods* (5th ed.). Glendale, CA: Pyrczak Publishing.

Microsoft. (2015). *Monitoring your Yammer data.* Retrieved April 27, 2015, from https://support.office.com/en-au/article/Monitoring-your-Yammer-data-Yammer-admin-guide-8c4651fa-12c2-4ced-b4ea-2200c0a630ed?ui=en-US&rs=en-AU&ad=AU

Mihalcea, R., & Tarau, P. (2004). Textrank: Bringing order in to texts. In Proceedinngs of EMNLP 2004. Barcelona, Spain: Association for Computational Linguistics.

Misr, A. (2009). *Tapestrea: Techniques And Paradigms For Expressive Synthesis, Transformation, And Re-Composition Of Environmental Audio.* (Thesis). Princeton University.

Mitchell, R. L. (2014). 8 big trends in big data analytics. *Computerworld.* Retrieved on 23 October 2014 from http://www.computerworld.com/article/2690856/8-big-trends-in-big-data-analytics.html

Molenaar, I., & Chiu, M. (2015). Effects of sequences of socially regulated learning on group performance. In *Proceedings of the 5th International Conference of Learning Analytics and Knowledge,* (pp. 236-240). doi:10.1145/2723576.2723586

Mont, O. K. (2001). *Clarifying the concept of product–service system.* The International. *Journal of Cleaner Production, 10*(3), 237–245. doi:10.1016/S0959-6526(01)00039-7

Moreau, E., Yvon, F., & Cappé, O. (2008). Robust similarity measures for named entities matching. In *Proceedings of the 22nd International Conference on Computational Linguistics*. Association for Computational Linguistics. doi:10.3115/1599081.1599156

Mori, T. (2002). Information gain ratio as term weight: the case of summarization of ir results. In *Proceedings of the 19th International Conference on Computational Linguistics*. Association for Computational Linguistics. doi:10.3115/1072228.1072246

Morik, K. (2002). Detecting Interesting Instances. In Pattern Detection and Discovery (LNCS), (vol. 2447, pp. 13-23). Springer. doi:10.1007/3-540-45728-3_2

Muller, M. J., Freyne, J., Dugan, C., Millen, D. R., & Thom-Santelli, J. (2009). Return On Contribution (ROC): A Metric for Enterprise Social Software. In I. Wagner, H. Tellioğlu, E. Balka, C. Simone, & L. Ciolfi (Eds.), *ECSCW'09: Proceedings of the 11th European Conference on Computer Supported Cooperative Work* (pp. 143–150). London: Springer London.

Nadeau, D., & Sekine, S. (2007). A survey of named entity recognition and classification. *Lingvisticae Investigationes*, *30*(1), 3–26. doi:10.1075/li.30.1.03nad

Naqishbandi, T., Sheriff, C. I., & Qazi, S. (2015). Big Data, CEP and IoT: Redefining holistic healthcare information systems and analytics. *International Journal of Engineering Research & Technology*, *4*(1). Retrieved from http://www.ijert.org

Nathans, L. L., Oswald, F. L., & Nimon, K. (2012). Interpreting multiple linear regression: A guidebook of variable importance. *Practical Assessment, Research & Evaluation*, *17*(9). Available online http://pareonline.net/getvn.asp?v=17&n=9

Naumann, F. (2014). Data profiling revisited. *SIGMOD Record*, *42*(4), 40–49. doi:10.1145/2590989.2590995

Needleman, S. B., & Wunsch, C. D. (1970). A general method applicable to the search for similarities in the amino acid sequence of two proteins. *Journal of Molecular Biology*, *48*(3), 443–453. doi:10.1016/0022-2836(70)90057-4 PMID:5420325

Nenkova, A., & McKeown, K. (2012). A Survey of Text Summarization Techniques. In C. C. Aggarwal & C. Zhai (Eds.), *Mining Text Data* (pp. 43–76). Springer, US. doi:10.1007/978-1-4614-3223-4_3

Nesreen, K. A., & Ryan, A. R. (2015). Interactive visual graphics analytics on web. In *Proceedings of the Ninth International AAAI Conference on Web and Social Media* (pp 566- 569). Association for the Advancement of Artificial Intelligence

Neto, J. L., Freitas, A. A., & Kaestner, C. A. A. (2002). Automatic text summarization using a machine learning approach. In Advances in Artificial Intelligence (LNCS), (vol. 2507, pp. 205-215). Springer Berlin Heidelberg. doi:10.1007/3-540-36127-8_20

Newman, M. E. J. (2006). Modularity and Community Structure in Networks. *Proceedings of the National Academy of Sciences of the United States of America*, *103*(23), 8577–8582. doi:10.1073/pnas.0601602103 PMID:16723398

Nobata, C., Sekine, S., Isahara, H., & Grishman, R. (2002). Summarization System Integrated with Named Entity Tagging and IE pattern Discovery. *Proceedings of Third International Conference on Language Resources and Evaluation (LREC 2002)*.

Nobata, C., Sekine, S., Murata, M., Uchimoto, K., Utiyama, M., & Isahara, H. (2001). Sentence extraction system assembling multiple evidence. In *Proceedings of the Second NTCIR Workshop Meeting*.

Noroozi, O., Weinberger, A., Biemans, H. J. A., Mulder, M., & Chizari, M. (2012). Argumentation-based computer supported collaborative learning (ABCSCL): A synthesis of 15 years of research. *Educational Research Review*, *7*(2), 79–106.

Nottorf, F., & Funk, B. (2013). A cross-industry analysis of the spillover effect in paid search advertising. *Electronic Markets, 23*(3), 205–216. doi:10.1007/s12525-012-0117-z

Okoye, P. V. C., & Ezejiofor, R. A. (2013). The effect of human resources development on organizational productivity. *International Journal of Academic Research in Business and Social Sciences, 3*(10), 250–268. doi:10.6007/IJARBSS/v3-i10/295

Olmezogullari, E., & Ari, I. (2013). Online Association Rule Mining over Fast Data. In *IEEE International Congress on Big Data* (pp. 110–117). IEEE. doi:10.1109/BigData.Congress.2013.77

Ono, K., Sumita, K., & Miike, S. (1994). Abstract generation based on rhetorical structure extraction. In *Proceedings of the 15th conference on Computational linguistics* (Vol. 1, pp. 344-348). Kyoto, Japan: Association for Computational Linguistics. doi:10.3115/991886.991946

Osimo, D., Szkuta, K., Foley, P., Biagi, F., Thompson, M., Bryant, L., . . . Ritzek, J. (2010). *Enterprise 2.0 study D4 Final report*. Retrieved from http://enterprise20eu.files.wordpress.com/2010/09/e20d3.pdf

Oussous, A., Benjelloun, F. Z., Lahcen, A. A., & Belfkih, S. (2015). Comparison and Classification of NoSQL Databases for Big Data. In *Proceedings of International conference on Big Data, Cloud and Applications.*

Oviatt, S., & Cohen, A. (2014). Written Activity, Representations and Fluency as Predictors of Domain Expertise in Mathematics. In *Proceedings of the 16th International Conference on Multimodal Interaction* (pp. 10-17). ACM.

Owens, T. J. (2007). *Survey of Event Processing*. New York.

Park, Y., Byrd, R. J., & Boguraev, B. K. (2002). Automatic glossary extraction: beyond terminology identification. *Proceedings of the 19th international conference on Computational linguistics-Volume 1*, (pp. 1-7). doi:10.3115/1072228.1072370

Paschke, A., & Kozlenkov, A. (2009). Rule-Based Event Processing and Reaction Rules. *Rule Interchange and Applications*, 53–66. http://doi.org/<ALIGNMENT.qj></ALIGNMENT>10.1007/978-3-642-04985-9_8

Patel, A. B., Birla, M., & Nair, U. (2012). Addressing Big Data Problem Using Hadoop and Map Reduce. In *Proceedings of NUiCONE -Nirma University International Conference on Engineering.*

Paton, N. W., & Díaz, O. (1999). Active database systems. *ACM Computing Surveys, 31*(1), 63–103. doi:10.1145/311531.311623

Patterson, M. G., Michael, A., West, M. A., Shackleton, V. J., Dawson, J. F., Lathom, R., & Wallace, A. M. et al. (2005). Validating the organizational climate measure: Links to managerial practices, productivity and innovation. *Journal of Organizational Behavior, 26*(4), 379–408. doi:10.1002/job.312

Pazienza, M., Pennacchiotti, M., & Zanzotto, F. (2005). Terminology Extraction: An Analysis of Linguistic and Statistical Approaches. In S. Sirmakessis (Ed.), *Knowledge Mining Series: Studies in Fuzziness and Soft Computing*. Springer Verlag. doi:10.1007/3-540-32394-5_20

Perer, A., Guy, I., Uziel, E., Ronen, I., & Jacovi, M. (2011). Visual social network analytics for relationship discovery in the enterprise. In *2011 IEEE Conference on Visual Analytics Science and Technology (VAST)* (pp. 71–79). IEEE.

Perlich, C., Dalessandro, B., & Hook, R. (2012). Bid optimizing and inventory scoring in targeted online advertising. *Proceedings of the 18th ACM SIGKDD international conference on Knowledge discovery and data mining* (pp. 804–812). doi:10.1145/2339530.2339655

Pezzini, M. (2011). *In - Memory Computing, Thinking the Unthinkable Applications*. Retrieved on 9 July 2012 from: http://agendabuilder.gartner.com/ESC23/webpages/SessionDetail.aspx?EventSessionId=1066

Pingali, J. J., & Varma, V. (2005). Sentence extraction based on single document summarization. In *Workshop on Document Summarization*.

Pollock, J. J., & Zamora, A. (1975). Automatic Abstracting Research at Chemical Abstracts Service. *Chemical Information and Computer Sciences, 15*(4), 226–232.

Porselvi, A., & Gunasundari, S. (2013). Survey on web page visual summarization. *International Journal of Emerging Technology and Advanced Engineering, 3*, 26–32.

Porter, M. F. (1980). An algorithm for suffix stripping. *Program, 14*(3), 130–137. doi:10.1108/eb046814

Prassad, R., Shardanand, & Kulkarni, U. (2010). Implementation and evaluation of evolutionary connectionist approaches to automated text summarization. Journal of Computer Science, 1366-1376.

Provost, F., & Fawcett, T. (2013). *Data Science for Business*. Sebastopol, CA: O'Reilly Media, Inc.

Quinlan, J. R. (1993). *C4.5: Programs for Machine Learning*. San Francisco: Morgan Kaufmann.

Raab, J. (2010). Netzwerke und Netzwerkanalyse in der Organisationsforschung. In C. Stegbauer & R. Häußling (Eds.), *Handbuch Netzwerkforschung*. Wiesbaden: VS Verlag für Sozialwissenschaften.

Radev, D., Blair-Goldensohn, S., & Zhang, Z. (2001). Experiments in single and multi-document summarization using MEAD. In *First Document Understanding Conference*.

Rafael, F., Freitas, F., De Souza, C. L., Dueire, L. R., Lima, R., Franca, G., … Favaro, L. (2014). A Context Based Text Summarization System. *2014 11th IAPR International Workshop on Document Analysis Systems (DAS)*.

Ramage, D., Hall, D., Nallapati, R., & Manning, C. D. (2009). Labeled LDA: A supervised topic model for credit attribution in multi-labeled corpora.*Proceedings of the 2009 Conference on Empirical Methods in Natural Language Processing* (pp. 248-256). doi:10.3115/1699510.1699543

RapidMiner Inc. (2015). *RapidMiner Studio*. Retrieved April 28, 2015, from https://rapidminer.com/

Reffay, C., & Martinez-Mones, A. (2013). Basic Concepts and Techniques in Social Network Analysis. In R. Luckin, S. Puntambekar, P. Goodyear, B. Grabowski, J. Underwood, & N. Winters (Eds.), *Handbook of Design in Educational Technology* (pp. 448–456). Routledge.

Reynar, J. C. (1999). Statistical Models for Topic Segmentation. In R. Dale & K. W. Church (Eds.), *ACL. Association of Computer Linguistics*. doi:10.3115/1034678.1034735

Richard, P. J., Devinney, T. M., Yip, G. S., & Johnson, G. (2009). Measuring organizational performance: Towards methodological best practice. *Journal of Management, 35*(3), 718–804. doi:10.1177/0149206308330560

Richter, A., & Riemer, K. (2009). Corporate Social Networking Sites – Modes of Use and Appropriation through Co-Evolution. In ACIS 2009 Proceedings.

Richter, A., & Riemer, K. (2013). The Contextual Nature Of Enterprise Social Networking: A Multi Case Study Comparison. In *ECIS 2013 Completed Research*. Retrieved from http://aisel.aisnet.org/ecis2013_cr/94

Richter, A., & Stocker, A. (2011). Exploration & Promotion: Einführungsstrategien von Corporate Social Software. In Wirtschaftinformatik Proceedings 2011.

Richter, A., Behrendt, S., & Koch, M. (2012). APERTO: A Framework for Selection, Introduction, and Optimization of Corporate Social Software. *All Sprouts Content*, Paper 488.

Richter, A., Heidemann, J., Klier, M., & Behrendt, S. (2013). Success Measurement of Enterprise Social Networks. In Wirtschaftsinformatik Proceedings 2013.

Richter, A., Stocker, A., Müller, S., & Avram, G. (2011). Knowledge Management Goals Revisited–A Cross-Sectional Analysis of Social Software Adoption in Corporate Environments. In ACIS 2011 Proceedings.

Richter, A. (2010). *Der Einsatz von Social Networking Services in Unternehmen. Der Einsatz von Social Networking Services in Unternehmen.* Wiesbaden: Gabler.

Riemer, K., & Johnston, R. B. (2012). Place-making: A Phenomenological Theory of Technology Appropriation. In ICIS 2012 Proceedings.

Riemer, K., & Richter, A. (2012). *SOCIAL-Emergent Enterprise Social Networking Use Cases: A Multi Case Study Comparison.* Retrieved April 27, 2015, from http://ses.library.usyd.edu.au/handle/2123/8845

Riemer, K., & Scifleet, P. (2012). Enterprise social networking in knowledge-intensive work practices: a case study in a professional service firm. In ACIS 2012 Proceedings.

Riemer, K., Diederich, S., Richter, A., & Scifleet, P. (2011). Short Message Discussions: On The Conversational Nature Of Microblogging In A Large Consultancy Organisation. In PACIS 2011 Proceedings.

Riemer, K., Overfeld, P., Scifleet, P., & Richter, A. (2012). Eliciting the Anatomy of Technology Appropriation Processes: A Case Study in Enterprise Social Media. In ECIS 2012 Proceedings.

Rijsbergen, C. V. (1979). *Information Retrieval.* Butterworth-Heinemann Newton.

Robles, M. M. (2012). Executive perceptions of the top 10 soft skills needed in today's workplace. *Business Communication Quarterly, 75*(4), 453–465. doi:10.1177/1080569912460400

Ross, R. (2014). *Yammer Analytics – Basic Reports.* Retrieved April 28, 2015, from http://blogs.perficient.com/microsoft/2014/03/yammer-analytics-basic-reports/

Roth-Berghofer, T. R. (2004). Explanations and case-based reasoning: Foundational issues. In *Advances in case-based reasoning* (pp. 389–403). Springer Berlin Heidelberg. doi:10.1007/978-3-540-28631-8_29

Roth-Berghofer, T., Cassens, J., & Sørmo, F. (2005). *Goals and Kinds of Explanations in Case-Based Reasoning.* Wissensmanagement.

Rubner, Y., Tomasi, C., & Guibas, L. J. (2000). The Earth Mover's Distance as a Metric for Image Retrieval. *International Journal of Computer Vision, 40*(2), 99–121. doi:10.1023/A:1026543900054

Rush, J. E., Salvador, R., & Zamora, A. (1971). Automatic abstracting and indexing. ii. production of indicative abstracts by application of contextual inference and syntactic coherence criteria. *Journal of the American Society for Information Science, 22*(4), 260–274. doi:10.1002/asi.4630220405

Ryu, S. (2013). 2013, Predictive Analytics: The Power to Predict Who Will Click, Buy, Lie or Die. *Healthcare Information Research, 19*(1), 63–65. doi:10.4258/hir.2013.19.1.63

Sagiroglu, S., & Sinanc, D. (2013). Big data: A review. Institute of Electrical and Electronics Engineers, 42 -47.

Sahu, S., & Smith, T. (2006). A Bayesian method of sample size determination with practical applications. *Journal of the Royal Statistical Society. Series A, (Statistics in Society), 169*(2), 235–253. doi:10.1111/j.1467-985X.2006.00408.x

Salton, G., & Buckley, C. (1988). Term-Weighting Approaches in Automatic Text Retrieval. *Information Processing & Management, 24*(5), 513–523. doi:10.1016/0306-4573(88)90021-0

Salton, G., Fox, E. A., & Wu, H. (1983). Extended Boolean information retrieval. *Communications of the ACM*, *26*(11), 1022–1036. doi:10.1145/182.358466

Salton, G., Singhal, A., Mitra, M., & Buckley, C. (1997, March). Automatic text structuring and summarization. *Information Processing & Management*, *33*(2), 193–207. doi:10.1016/S0306-4573(96)00062-3

Salton, G., Wong, A., & Yang, C. S. (1975). A Vector Space Model for Automatic Indexing. *Communications of the ACM*, *18*(11), 613–620. doi:10.1145/361219.361220

Sampson, M. (2014). *Use and Adoption of IBM Connections: State of the Market 4Q2014*. Retrieved from April 28, 2015, https://michaelcollabguy.files.wordpress.com/2014/11/use-and-adoption-of-ibm-connections-by-michael-sampson.pdf

Santis, F. (2007). Alternative Bayes factors: Sample size determination and discriminatory power assessment. *Test*, *16*(3), 504–522. doi:10.1007/s11749-006-0017-7

Sauermann, L., Grimnes, G. A., Kiesel, M., Fluit, C., Maus, H., & Heim, D. et al.. (2006). Semantic Desktop 2.0: The Gnowsis Experience.*Proceedings of the 5th International Semantic Web Conference, LNCS 4273*, (pp. 887-900). doi:10.1007/11926078_64

Savas, O., Sagduyu, Y., Deng, J., & Tactical, L. J. (2013). *Big Data Analytics: Challenges, Use Cases and Solutions*. Big Data Analytics Workshop in Conjunction with ACM Sigmetrics.

Schmarzo, B. (2014). How Can Graph Analytics Uncover Valuable Insights About Data? *EMC² Infocus*. Retrieved from https://infocus.emc.com/william_schmarzo/how-can-graph-analytics-uncover-valuable-insights-about-data/

Schneckenberg, D. (2009). Web 2.0 and the empowerment of the knowledge worker. *Journal of Knowledge Management*, *13*(6), 509–520.

Schultz-Møller, N. P., Migliavacca, M., & Pietzuch, P. (2009). Distributed complex event processing with query rewriting.*Proceedings of the Third ACM International Conference on Distributed EventBased Systems DEBS 09*, 1. doi:10.1145/1619258.1619264

Schultz-Moller, P. N. (2008). *Distributed Detection of Event Patterns*. Imperial College of Science, Technology and Medicine.

Sclano, F., & Velardi, P. (2007). Termextractor: a web application to learn the shared terminology of emergent web communities. In Enterprise Interoperability II (pp. 287-290). Springer. doi:10.1007/978-1-84628-858-6_32

Sebastian, L. R., Babu, S., & Kizhakkethottam, J. K. (2015). Challenges with big Data Mining – A Review.*International Conference on Soft computing and Network Security*.

Serneels, S., Nolf, E., & Espen, P. (2006). Spatial Sign Pre-processing: A Simple Way to Impart Moderate Robustness to Multivariate Estimators. *Journal of Chemical Information and Modeling*, *46*(3), 1402–1409. doi:10.1021/ci050498u PMID:16711760

Sharma, P. P., & Navdeti, C. P. (2014). Securing Big Data Hadoop: A Review of Security Issues, Threats and Solution. *International Journal of Computer Science and Information Technologies*, *5*(2), 2126–2131.

Shearer, C. (2000). The CRISP-DM Model: The New Blueprint for Data Mining. *Journal of Data Warehousing*, *5*(4), 13–22.

Shen, D., Sun, J.-T., Li, H., Yang, Q., & Chen, Z. (2007). Document summarization using conditional random fields. In *Proceedings of the 20th international joint conference on Artifical intelligence* (pp. 2862-2867). Hyderabad, India: Morgan Kaufmann Publishers Inc.

Siegel, E. (2014). *Predictive Analysis: The power to predict who will click, buy, lie, or die*. Indianapolis, IN: John Wiley & Sons, Inc.

Singh, D., & Reddy, C. K. (2014). A survey on platforms for big data analytics. *Journal of Big Data*, *1*(8). PMID:26191487

Skinner, M. (2015). *The big deal about big data*. Retrieved from http://www.lba.org/files/MikeSkinner%20-%20Big%20 Data.pdf

Smith, T., & Waterman, M. (1981). Identification of Common Molecular Subsequences. *Journal of Molecular Biology*, *147*(1), 195–197. doi:10.1016/0022-2836(81)90087-5 PMID:7265238

Song, Y. (2014). Methodological Issues in Mobile Computer-Supported Collaborative Learning (mCSCL): What Methods, What to Measure and When to Measure? *Journal of Educational Technology & Society*, *17*(4), 33–48.

Sparck Jones, K. (1972). A statistical interpretation of term specificity and its application in retrieval. *The Journal of Documentation*, *28*(1), 11–21. doi:10.1108/eb026526

Sprinthall, R. C. (2011). *Basic statistical analysis* (9th ed.). Boston, MA: Allyn & Bacon.

Stahl, F., Gaber, M. M., & Salvador, M. M. (2012). eRules: A modular adaptive classification rule learning algorithm for data streams. *Res. and Dev. in Intelligent Syst. XXIX: Incorporating Applications and Innovations in Intel. Sys. XX - AI 2012, 32nd SGAI Int. Conf. on Innovative Techniques and Applications of Artificial Intel.*, (pp. 65–78).

Stange, M., & Funk, B. (2014). Real-Time-Advertising. *Business & Information Systems Engineering*, *56*(5), 305–308. doi:10.1007/s12599-014-0346-0

Stange, M., & Funk, B. (2015). How Much Tracking Is Necessary - The Learning Curve in Bayesian User Journey Analysis. *23rd European Conference of Information Systems*.

Steinfield, C. W., DiMicco, J. M., Ellison, N. B., & Lampe, C. (2009). Bowling online. In *Proceedings of the fourth international conference on Communities and technologies - C&T '09* (p. 245). ACM.

Stonebraker, M., Çetintemel, U., & Zdonik, S. (2005). The 8 requirements of real-time stream processing. *SIGMOD Record*, *34*(4), 42–47. doi:10.1145/1107499.1107504

Stuempflen, V. (2015). CEO, Clueda AG. *Real-Time Text Analytics for Event Detection in the Financial World*. Retrieved on 1 April 2015 from http://www.textanalyticsworld.com/pdf/SF/2015/Day1_1015_Stuempflen.pdf

Svore, K., Vanderwende, L., & Burges, C. (2007). Enhancing single-document summarization by combining RankNet and third-party sources. In *Proceedings of the EMNLP-CoNLL* (pp. 448-457).

Tabachnick, B. G., & Fidell, L. S. (2012). *Using multivariate statistics* (6th ed.). Pearson Education.

Tarmazdi, H., Vivian, R., Szabo, C., Falkner, K., & Falkner, N. (2015). Using Learning Analytics to Visualise Computer Science Teamwork. In *Proceedings of the 2015 ACM Conference on Innovation and Technology in Computer Science Education*, (pp. 165-170). doi:10.1145/2729094.2742613

Tennant, M., Stahl, F., & Gomes, J. B. (2015). Fast Adaptive Real-Time Classification for Data Streams with Concept Drift. In *Internet and Distributed Computing Systems* (pp. 265–272). Springer. doi:10.1007/978-3-319-23237-9_23

Thornhill, N. F., Choudhury, M. S., & Shah, S. L. (2004). The impact of compression on data-driven process analyses. *Journal of Process Control*, *14*(4), 389–398. doi:10.1016/j.jprocont.2003.06.003

Tobarra, L., Ros, S., Hernandez, R., Robles-Gómez, A., Caminero, A. C., & Pastor, R. (2014). Integrated Analytic dashboard for virtual evaluation laboratories and collaborative forums. In Tecnologias Aplicadas a la Ensenanza de la Electronica (Technologies Applied to Electronics Teaching)(TAEE), 2014 XI (pp. 1-6). IEEE. doi:10.1109/TAEE.2014.6900177

Torres, M., Juan-Manuel, P. M., & Meunier, J.-G. (2002). Condenses de textes par des methodes numeriques. In *JADT* (Vol. 2, pp. 723–734). JADT.

Trabold, D., & Grosskreutz, H. (2013). Parallel Subgroup Discovery on Computing Clusters—First results. In *2013 IEEE International Conference on Big Data* (pp. 575-579). IEEE doi:10.1109/BigData.2013.6691625

Trier, M., & Richter, A. (2015). The deep structure of organizational online networking - an actor-oriented case study. *Information Systems Journal, 25*(5), 465–488.

Tsymbal, A., Pechenizkiy, M., Cunningham, P., & Puuronen, S. (2008). Dynamic integration of classifiers for handling concept drift. *Information Fusion, 9*(1), 56–68. doi:10.1016/j.inffus.2006.11.002

Tucker, P., Maier, D., Sheard, T., & Fegaras, L. (2003). Exploiting punctuation semantics in continuous data streams. *IEEE Transactions on Knowledge and Data Engineering, 15*(3), 555–568. doi:10.1109/TKDE.2003.1198390

Twitter. (2015). *The Twitter Firehose API.* Retrieved March 24, 2015, from https://dev.twitter.com/streaming/firehose

Vilalta, R., Ma, S., & Hellerstein, J. (2001). *Rule Induction of Computer Events.* Academic Press.

Vilalta, R., & Ma, S. M. S. (2002). Predicting rare events in temporal domains. In *IEEE International Conference on Data Mining* (pp. 474–481). IEEE.

Viol, J., & Hess, J. (2016). Information Systems Research on Enterprise Social Networks – A State-of-the-Art Analysis. In MKWI 2016 Proceedings.

Vitter, J. S. (1985). Random Sampling with a Reservoir. *ACM Transactions on Mathematical Software, 11*(1), 37–57. doi:10.1145/3147.3165

Wald, A. (2010). Netzwerkansätze in der Managementforschung. In C. Stegbauer & R. Häußling (Eds.), *Handbuch Netzwerkforschung.* Wiesbaden: VS Verlag für Sozialwissenschaften.

Waller, M., & Fawcett, S. E. (2013). Data Science, Predictive Analytics, and Big Data: A Revolution That Will Transform Supply Chain Design and Management. *Journal of Business Logistics, 34*(2), 77–84. doi:10.1111/jbl.12010

Wang, D., Rundensteiner, E., Ellison, R. T., & Wang, H. (2010). Active Complex Event Processing: Applications in real-time health care. *Proceedings of the VLDB Endowment, 3*(1-2), 1545–1548. RetrievedMarch42015. doi:10.14778/1920841.1921034

Wang, F., Liu, S., Liu, P., & Bai, Y. (2006). Bridging physical and virtual worlds: Complex event processing for RFID data streams. *Advances in Database Technology-EDBT, 2006*, 588–607.

Wang, F., Zhou, C., & Nie, Y. (2013). Event Processing in Sensor Streams. In C. C. Aggarwal (Ed.), *Managing and Mining Sensor Data* (pp. 77–102). Springer Science & Business Media. doi:10.1007/978-1-4614-6309-2_4

Wang, L., Wang, G., & Alexander, C. A. (2015). Big Data and Visualization: Methods, Challenges and Technology Progress. *Digital Technologies, 1*(1), 33–38.

Wang, R. Y., & Strong, D. M. (1996). Beyond accuracy: What data quality means to data consumers. *Journal of Management Information Systems, 12*(4), 5–33. doi:10.1080/07421222.1996.11518099

Wang, W. (2014). Big Data, Big Challenges In *Proceedings of IEEE International conference on Semantic computing.*

Wasserkrug, S., Gal, A., Etzion, O., & Turchin, Y. (2008). Complex event processing over uncertain data. In *Proceedings of the second international conference on Distributed event-based systems* (Vol. 332, pp. 253–264). ACM. doi:10.1145/1385989.1386022

Wasserman, S., & Faust, K. (1994). *Social network analysis: methods and applications*. Cambridge, UK: Cambridge University Press.

Wei, M., Liu, M., Li, M., Golovnya, D., Rundensteiner, E. A., & Claypool, K. T. (2009). Supporting a spectrum of out-of-order event processing technologies: from aggressive to conservative methodologies.*Proc. ACM SIGMOD Int. Conf. on Management of Data*, (pp. 1031–1034). doi:10.1145/1559845.1559973

Widder, A., von Ammon, R., Schaeffer, P., & Wolff, C. (2007). Identification of suspicious, unknown event patterns in an event cloud. In *Proceedings of the inaugural international conference on Distributed eventbased systems* (pp. 164–170). Toronto: ACM. doi:10.1145/1266894.1266926

Widder, A., von Ammon, R., Schaeffer, P., & Wolff, C. (2008). Combining Discriminant Analysis and Neural Networks for Fraud Detection on the Base of Complex Event Processing. In *Proceedings of the 2nd international conference on Distributed event-based systems*. ACM.

Widmer, G., & Kubat, M. (1996). Learning in the presence of concept drift and hidden contexts. *Machine Learning*, *23*(3), 69–101. doi:10.1007/BF00116900

Widom, J., & Ceri, S. (1996). *Active database systems: Triggers and rules for advanced database processing*. Morgan Kaufmann.

Witten, I. H., Moffat, A., & Bell, T. C. (1999). *Managing gigabytes: compressing and indexing documents and images*. Morgan Kaufmann.

Wong, K.-F., Wu, M., & Li, W. (2008). Extractive summarization using supervised and semi-supervised learning. In *Proceedings of the 22nd International Conference on Computational Linguistics* (Vol. 1, pp. 985-992). Manchester, UK: Association for Computational Linguistics. doi:10.3115/1599081.1599205

Wrobel, S. (1997) An Algorithm for Multi-Relational Discovery of Subgroups. In *Proceedings of the 1st European Symposium on Principles of Data Mining and Knowledge Discovery*. Heidelberg, Germany: Springer Verlag. doi:10.1007/3-540-63223-9_108

Wu, X., Zhu, X., Wu, G. Q., & Ding, W. (2014). Data Mining with Big Data. *IEEE Transactions on Knowledge and Data Engineering*, *26*(1).

Xiaoyan, C., Wenjie, L., You, O., & Hong, Y. (2010). Simultaneous ranking and clustering of sentences: a reinforcement approach to multi-document summarization. In *Proceedings of the 23rd International Conference on Computational Linguistics* (COLING '10). Association for Computational Linguistics.

Xie, K., Yu, C., & Bradshaw, A. (2014). Impacts of role assignment and participation in asynchronous discussions in college-level online classes, 2014. *The Internet and Higher Education*, *20*, 10–19. doi:10.1016/j.iheduc.2013.09.003

Xing, W., Gui, R., Petakovic, E., & Goggins, S. (2014). Participation-based student final performance prediction model through interpretable Genetic Programming: Integrating learning analytics, educational data mining and theory. *Computers in Human Behavior*, *47*, 168–181. doi:10.1016/j.chb.2014.09.034

Xing, W., Wadholm, B., & Goggins, S. (2014). Learning analytics in CSCL with a focus on assessment: an exploratory study of activity theory-informed cluster analysis. In *Proceedings of the Fourth International Conference on Learning Analytics and Knowledge Conference*, (pp. 59-67). ACM. doi:10.1145/2567574.2567587

Yammer. (2015). *Yammer Full Feature List*. Retrieved April 27, 2015, from https://about.yammer.com/product/feature-list/

Yao, W., Chu, C.-H., & Li, Z. (2011). Leveraging complex event processing for smart hospitals using RFID. *Journal of Network and Computer Applications*, *34*(3), 799–810. doi:10.1016/j.jnca.2010.04.020

Yeo, I., & Johnson, R. (2000). A new family of power transformations to improve normality or symmetry. *Biometrika*, *87*(4), 954–959. doi:10.1093/biomet/87.4.954

Yu, G., Li, C. W., Gu, Y., & Hong, B. (2011). Aggressive complex event processing with confidence over out-of-order streams. *Journal of Computer Science and Technology*, *26*(July), 685–696.

Zhang, Z., Iria, J., Brewster, C. A., & Ciravegna, F. (2008). A comparative evaluation of term recognition algorithms. *Proceedings of The sixth international conference on Language Resources and Evaluation*.

Zheng, L., Huang, R., & Yu, J. (2014). Identifying Computer-Supported Collaborative Learning (CSCL) Research in Selected Journals Published from 2003 to 2012: A Content Analysis of Research Topics and Issues. *Journal of Educational Technology & Society*, *17*(4), 335–351.

Zikopoulos, C., Eaton, C., deRoos, D., Deutsch, T., & Lapis, G. (2012). *Understanding Big data Analytics for Enterprise class Hadoop and Streaming data*. New York: McGraw Hill.

Ziman, J. M. (1968). *Public knowledge: the social dimension of science*. Cambridge, UK: Cambridge University Press.

About the Contributors

Martin Atzmueller is adjunct professor (Privatdozent) at the University of Kassel and heads the Ubiquitous Data Mining Team at the Research Center for Information System Design (ITeG), Hertie Chair for Knowledge and Data Engineering. His research areas include data mining, ubiquitous social computing, web and network science, machine learning, and Big Data. He earned his habilitation (Dr. habil.) in 2013 at the University of Kassel, and received his Ph.D. in Computer Science from the University of Wuerzburg in 2006. He studied Computer Science at the University of Texas at Austin (USA) and at the University of Wuerzburg where he completed his MSc in Computer Science.

Samia Oussena is a reader at University of West London and has a research background in methodologies and software application development. Prior to academia, she gained an extensive industrial experience in software development. She has led and been involved in a number of application development projects for the Insurance and oil and gas sector. More recently, her research interests are in developing software methods to support the development of enterprise applications/systems. Of particular interest is the use of model driven practice to the development of smart enterprise systems.

* * *

David Arnu studied 'data analysis and management' and computer science at the TU Dortmund University (Germany). He holds a Master of Science degree in computer science from the same university. At RapidMiner, he worked as software engineer and project engineer in the R&D team. Now, he is a data scientist at RapidMiner working on research projects and innovative predictive analytics use cases.

Joachim Baumeister did his PhD in Applied Artificial Intelligence in 2004 in Wurzburg, Germany, and habilitated on Knowledge Engineering techniques in 2010. He gives lectures on Knowledge-Based Systems and Semantic Web Technologies. He authored and co-authored more than 100 reviewed publications in the field of Knowledge-based Systems and the Semantic Web. Since 2010, he is fully working at the company denkbares GmbH, where semantic information systems and knowledge systems are designed and implemented in industrial settings.

Freimut Bodendorf is the director of the Institute of Information Systems at the University of Erlangen-Nuremberg. He graduated with a degree in Computer Science (School of Engineering) and obtained his doctoral degree (Ph.D.) in Information Systems (School of Management). Subsequently he was head of an Information Systems department at the University of Freiburg/Germany (School of

Medicine), full professor at the Postgraduate School of Engineering in Nuremberg/Germany, and full professor at the Department of Computer Science and Information Systems at the University of Fribourg/Switzerland. His main areas of research are Service Management & Engineering, Business Process Management, and Business Intelligence.

Sivamathi Chokkalingam is pursuing Ph.D. in the Department of Computer Science, Bharathiar University, Coimbatore, India. She has Completed Master of Science in Computer Science and Information Technology by 2006. Then she completed Master of Philosophy in Computer Science. Her research areas include data mining, utility mining, data streams and big data. She has five years of teaching experience in the Department of Computer Science, Subbalakshmi Lakshmipathy College of Science, Madurai, India.

Giuseppe Di Fatta is an Associate Professor of Computer Science and the Director of the MSc in Advanced Computer Science at the University of Reading, UK. In 1999, he was a research fellow at the International Computer Science Institute (ICSI), Berkeley, CA, USA. From 2000 to 2004, he was with the High-Performance Computing and Networking Institute of the National Research Council, Italy. From 2004 to 2006, he was with the University of Konstanz, Germany. His research interests include data mining algorithms, distributed and parallel computing, and multidisciplinary applications. He has published over 80 articles in peer-reviewed conferences and journals. He serves in the editorial board of the Elsevier Journal of Network and Computer Applications. He has chaired international conferences and workshops, such as the IEEE ICDM Workshop on Data Mining in Networks and the International Conference on Internet and Distributed Computing Systems.

Marcel Dix is scientist at ABB Corporate Research Center, Germany, with research focus on industrial analytics. and He holds a computer science degree from Hochschule Mannheim, University of Applied Sciences, and a degree in general managment from Europäische Fernhochschule Hamburg, University of Applied Sciences.

Burkhardt Funk is a full professor for information systems at Leuphana University Lüneburg and as the CIO a member of the presidential board. His research interests include building decision models and support systems, based on methods from machine learning, in a variety of application areas such as e-Mental-Health and e-Business. When building statistical models Burkhardt often uses methods from Bayesian Statistics. He has co-authored more than 60 scientific articles and 3 books. He has a wealth of practical experience and is a regular advisor to leading companies.

Sebastian Furth is Software Engineer and Consultant at denkbares GmbH in Würzburg, Germany. His research focuses on practical natural language processing techniques in the context of semantic information systems. In various industrial projects Sebastian Furth gained hands-on experience in coordinating, designing, implementing and applying semantification approaches on large technical data sets.

Dinesh Gopalani received his PhD in Computer Science & Engineering from Malaviya National Institute of Technology, Jaipur, India. He is Assistant Professor at the Department of Computer Science & Engineering Malaviya National Institute of Technology, Jaipur, India from past 15 years. His research interests include issues related to Aspect Oriented Programming, Compiler Design, Natural Language

Processing and Knowledge Management. He has published research papers at national and international journals, conference proceedings as well as chapters of books.

Martin Hollender graduated from the University of Kassel in 1995 with a PhD degree. He is a principal scientist for ABB Corporate Research. He is a member of the IEC TC65A WG 15 standards group for Alarm Management and has edited the ISA textbook on Collaborative Process Automation Systems.

Sema A. Kalaian (Professor of Statistics and Research Methods) in the College of Technology at Eastern Michigan University. Professor Kalaian was a recipient of the (1) "Best Paper" award from the American Educational Research Association (AERA), and (2) "Distinguished Paper Award" from the Society for the Advancement of Information Systems (SAIS). Over the years, Dr. Kalaian taught introductory and advanced statistical courses such as Research Methods, Research Design, Multivariate Statistics, Survey Research, Multilevel Modeling, Structural Equation Modeling, Meta-Analysis, and Program Evaluation. Professor Kalaian's research interests focus on the development of new statistical methods and its applications. Much of her methodological developments and applications have focused on the (a) development of the multivariate meta-analytic techniques for combining evidence from multiple primary studies; (b) applications of the meta-analysis methods to various projects in different fields of study such as STEM education and Medical and Health Education; and (c) developments of statistical methods for analyzing Delphi survey data. She has authored and co-authored more than 50+ scientific articles and 10 book chapters in various fields of study such as Statistics, Big Data Analytics, Meta-Analysis, STEM Education, Medical Education, and Online Learning.

Vidhyalakshmi Karthikeyan is a Senior Researcher at BT and specialises in the application of data analytics and machine learning to network management. She completed an MSc in Telecommunications from UCL and currently also pursues a PhD in VoD delivery using adaptive multicast stream merging. She is an inventor on 16 patent applications in autonomous network management.

Nabeel Kasim is a Master's degree candidate at the College of Engineering in the Industrial and Operations Engineering department at the University of Michigan in USA. He holds a Bachelor's of Science degree also in Industrial and Operations Engineering from the University of Michigan in USA. His academic interests are aimed at operations research and engineering management.

Rafa M. Kasim, Professor of Statistics and Research Methods at Indiana Institute of Technology. Professor Kasim was a recipient of the "Best Paper" award from the American Educational Research Association (AERA). Professor Kasim is a senior research consultant; his research focuses on the application of multilevel analysis to study the effects of educational and social contexts on educational outcomes and human development for large-scale longitudinal data sets. Some of Dr. Kasim work also addresses the issues of selection and attrition bias in multi-site large studies. He has collaborated on numerous studies in fields such as adult literacy, education, and substance abuse treatments. Some of his work appears in Application of Multilevel Models (book chapter), Journal of Educational and Behavioral Statistics, Harvard Educational Review and Advances in Health Science Education.

Benjamin Klöpper is a senior scientist in the group analytics and software applications in the ABB corporate research center Germany. He is leading a joint research project funded by the German government working on Big Data support for plant operators and is involved in several other research projects in the areas of IoTSP and Big Data.

Bruce Laurie teaches on the masters courses in information systems especially in IT / IS Project Management and Consultancy and Technology Innovation in the School of Computing and Engineering at the University of West London. He has very extensive industrial experience working for British Gas and other UK companies and has served as the Board Chair: Great Western Hospital NHS Foundation Trust at Swindon.

Pascal Lorenz received his M.Sc. (1990) and Ph.D. (1994) from the University of Nancy, France. Between 1990 and 1995 he was a research engineer at WorldFIP Europe and at Alcatel-Alsthom. He is a professor at the University of Haute-Alsace, France, since 1995. His research interests include QoS, wireless networks and high-speed networks. He is the author/co-author of 3 books, 3 patents and 200 international publications in refereed journals and conferences. He was Technical Editor of the IEEE Communications Magazine Editorial Board (2000-2006), Chair of Vertical Issues in Communication Systems Technical Committee Cluster (2008-2009), Chair of the Communications Systems Integration and Modeling Technical Committee (2003-2009) and Chair of the Communications Software Technical Committee (2008-2010). He has served as Co-Program Chair of IEEE WCNC'2012, ICC'2004 and ICC'2017, tutorial chair of VTC'2013 Spring and WCNC'2010, track chair of PIMRC'2012, symposium Co-Chair at Globecom 2007-2011, ICC 2008-2010, ICC'2014 and '2016. He has served as Co-Guest Editor for special issues of IEEE Communications Magazine, Networks Magazine, Wireless Communications Magazine, Telecommunications Systems and LNCS. He is associate Editor for International Journal of Communication Systems (IJCS-Wiley), Journal on Security and Communication Networks (SCN-Wiley) and International Journal of Business Data Communications and Networking, Journal of Network and Computer Applications (JNCA-Elsevier). He is senior member of the IEEE, IARIA fellow and member of many international program committees. He has organized many conferences, chaired several technical sessions and gave tutorials at major international conferences. He was IEEE ComSoc Distinguished Lecturer Tour during 2013-2014.

Y. K. Meena is Assistant Professor in Department of Computer Science & Engineering in Malaviya National Institute of Technology (MNIT) Jaipur. He was graduated in Information Technology from MNIT, Jaipur in the year 2005. He obtained Master's degree in Computer Applications from IIT Delhi and Ph.D. from MNIT Jaipur. His research interests include issues related to Data Mining, Natural Language Processing, Pattern Recognition and Knowledge Management. He has published 15 research papers in various International Conferences. He has 08 years of Teaching and Industrial experience.

Fehmida Mohamedali is a Senior Lecturer in Information Technology for the School of Computing and Engineering. Have been working for the University of West London in this capacity since 2008. Currently, pursuing PhD studies (part-time) within the research area of Complex Event Processing.

Detlef Nauck is Chief Research Scientist for Data Science with BT's Research and Innovation Division located at Adastral Park, Ipswich, UK. He is leading a group of international scientists working on Intelligent Data Analysis and Autonomic Systems. Detlef has been working on data analytics projects across a number of areas like customer service analytics, real time business intelligence, business process analytics and network analytics. His current work focusses on introducing autonomic principles like self-learning, self-healing and self-optimisation into business processes and network management. Detlef is a Visiting Professor at Bournemouth University and a Private Docent at the Otto-von-Guericke University of Magdeburg, Germany. Detlef holds an MSc (1990) and a PhD (1994) in Computer Science both from the University of Braunschweig, Germany. He also holds a Habilitation (post-doctoral degree) in Computer Science from the Otto-von-Guericke University of Magdeburg, Germany (2000).

Stephen A. Roberts, Associate Professor (Information Management), teaches on master's courses in information management, information systems, and project management in the School of Computing and Engineering at the University of West London. In his career he has worked in research teams in social science information, library and information services and information management and taught in these areas for some thirty years. His main research interests are in • Transnational Knowledge Networks (TKNs) • Information management and knowledge management • Organizational information strategy and policy (including corporate and business communication) • Library and information services • Education and learning (including information and computer literacy). He has supervised a doctoral students in his main research areas. He has been external examiner for doctoral students at University of Sheffield, City University, UCL and Aberystwyth and at universities in Kenya, Pakistan, South Africa and Australia.

Andreas Schmidt is research assistant at the Hertie Chair on Knowledge and Data Engineering at the University of Kassel. His research interests include data mining, information retrieval and machine learning in the context of Big Data. He holds a M.Sc. degree in Computer Science from the University of Kassel. Before starting his Ph.D., he acquired experience working in business intelligence.

Dikshith Siddapura has studied computer science at the Georg-August University Göttingen, Germany. He has written his master thesis at ABB Corporate Research Center, Germany. He holds a master degree from the University of Göttingen.

Liz Sokolowski is a Senior Lecturer in the School of Computing & Engineering at the University of West London, where her specialist subjects are database management systems, systems analysis and e-commerce. Her research focuses on the use of Big Data and learning analytics for the improvement of collaborative processes in education and the workplace.

Frederic Stahl is a Lecturer at the University of Reading. His research interests are in the area of Big Data Analytics, in particular in parallel and distributed data mining; data stream mining; and data mining in resource constraint environments. Before joining the University of Reading, Dr Stahl was working at Bournemouth University as a lecturer until 2012 and as Senior Research Associate at the University of Portsmouth from 2010-2012. He also obtained his PhD from the University of Portsmouth titled 'Parallel Rule Induction' in 2010. Frederic has published over 40 peer reviewed articles. Since December 2013 he is serving as committee member of the BCS Specialist Group on Artificial Intelligence (SGAI). More details about Frederic's research can be found at: https://fredericstahl.wordpress.com/.

Martin Stange is a doctoral student at the Leuphana University in Lueneburg, Germany. His research focuses on modeling user decisions on the Internet, in particular in e-commerce contexts. Based on large data sets, he uses machine learning techniques (in particular Bayesian methods) to predict consumer behavior and to better understand user decisions. Martin Stange has a Master's degree in physics and Information Systems.

G. Vijayarani, is an Assistant Professor of Department of Computer Science at Bharathiar University, Coimbatore, India. She has obtained M.C.A., M.Phil., and Ph.D., in Computer Science. She has 8 years of teaching/research and 10 years of technical experience. Her research interests include data mining, privacy issues in data mining, text mining, web mining, data streams and information retrieval. She has published more than 60 research articles in national/international journals. She also presented research papers in international/national conferences. She has authored a book and guided more than 25 research scholars.

Janine Viol Hacker has been a research associate and Ph.D. candidate at the Institute of Information Systems at the University of Erlangen-Nuremberg since 2011. Her research interests lie in the field of Enterprise Social Networks, knowledge management, and social network analysis. Her work has been published in the Communications of the Association of Information Systems, in conference proceedings, such as the proceedings of the Australasian Conference on Information Systems, as well as in several edited books. Within her doctoral thesis, Janine Viol Hacker focuses on the discovery of user roles in Enterprise Social Networks.

Chris Wrench was awarded a BA from the University of Winchester in 2009 and most recently a BSc in Cybernetics and Artificial Intelligence from the University of Reading in 2014. He is currently a PhD researcher in the field of Data Stream Mining at the University of Reading.

Index

A

Abstractive Summarization 143
Active Databases 24, 34, 41-43
Analytics 1, 2, 10-15, 24-74, 81-90, 97-108, 123, 146-176, 195, 217-237
Annotation 154, 172-199
Anonymization 164, 169
Artificial Neural Networks (ANN) 39, 40, 47, 141
Association Rule Mining (ARM) 38-40, 47
Audio Analytics 52, 58-60
Automatic Text Summarization 126-132, 140-142

B

Batch Layer 52, 150-156
Big Data 1, 2, 10-53, 59-85, 101, 102, 108, 110, 122-126, 146-166, 172, 201-225, 233-235
Big Data Analytics 24-37, 48, 52, 59-67, 81, 82, 108, 146-159, 217, 222
Business Strategy 13, 19, 20

C

Clickstream Data 1, 2, 42
Collaborative Learning 221-237
Comma Separated Values (CSV) 98, 148, 155, 165
Community Detection 56, 113, 121, 122
Complex Event Processing 24, 35-47, 201-209, 217-220
Complex Event Processing (CEP) 24, 25, 34-47, 201-220
Composition Operators (CO) 43, 140, 155, 168, 197, 213, 220
Computational Costs 3, 160
Computer Supported Collaborative Learning (CSCL) 221-237
Continuous Query Language (CQL) 27, 34, 41, 204, 220
Critical Discriminant Function (CDF) 39, 47

Cross Industry Standard Process for Data Mining (CRISP-DM) 85, 93, 94, 103, 158, 159, 167, 169

D

Data Analysis 3, 5, 49-53, 62, 82-108, 123, 150, 168, 225-231
Data Analysis Process 85, 93, 101-106
Data Mining 1, 2, 11, 15, 24-30, 36-49, 55-64, 84, 85, 93-109, 122-125, 146-149, 155-159, 167-169, 223, 224, 233-237
Data Mining Process 84, 93, 96, 102, 159
Data Preprocessing 157-166
Data Stream Management Systems 24, 34, 47
Data Stream Management Systems (DSMS) 25, 34, 41, 47
Data Streams 24-46, 204, 205, 218
Data Visualization 48-53, 60-68, 81
Data Visualization Analytics 48-53, 60
Descriptive Analytics 66-72
Document Corpus 176, 194, 200
Domain Terminology 173, 177, 186, 191, 200
Dummy Variable 160, 169

E

Educational Data Mining 221-224, 235, 237
Emergency Medical Assistance (EMA) 216, 220
Emergency Medical Records (EMR) 216-220
Enrichment 173, 186, 196, 200, 214
Enterprise 2.0 84-86, 102-106
Enterprise Social Network 84, 103, 106
Entity Integration 172
Event Clouds 24, 35, 40
Event-Condition-Action (ECA) Rules 34-40, 47
Event Processing Agents (EPA) 35, 47
Event Processing Language (EPL) 34, 36, 215, 220
Event Stream Processing (ESP) 24-29, 37-47, 220
Exceptional Model Mining 108-124, 167, 168